THE WEALTH ARCHITECT

BUILDING YOUR BUSINESS AND PERSONAL FINANCES

M.L. RUSCSAK

Copyright © 2024 Trient Press

All rights reserved. No portion of this publication may be reproduced, distributed, or transmitted in any form or by any means, including photocopying, recording, or other electronic or mechanical methods, without the prior written permission of the publisher. This restriction excludes brief quotations utilized in critical reviews and certain other noncommercial usages as permitted by copyright law. For permission inquiries, direct correspondence to the publisher, marked "Attention: Permissions Coordinator," at the following address:
Trient Press
3375 S Rainbow Blvd
#81710, SMB 13135
Las Vegas, NV 89180

Criminal copyright infringement, including instances without financial gain, is subject to investigation by the FBI and incurs penalties of up to five years in federal imprisonment and a fine of $250,000.

Excepting the original narrative material authored by M.L. Ruscsak, all songs, song titles, and lyrics cited within The Wealth Architect: Building Your Business and Personal Finances remain the exclusive property of their respective artists, songwriters, and copyright holders.

Ordering Information:
For quantity sales, Trient Press offers special discounts to corporations, associations, and other organizations. For detailed information, contact the publisher at the address provided above.
For orders by U.S. trade bookstores and wholesalers, please reach out to Trient Press at Tel: (775) 996-3844, or visit www.trientpress.com.

Printed in the United States of America
Publisher's Cataloging-in-Publication Data
Ruscsak, M.L.
The Wealth Architect: Building Your Business and Personal Finances
Hardcover: 979-8-88990-194-5
Paperback: ISBN 979-8-88990-195-2
E-Book: 979-8-88990-196-9

The Wealth Architect: Building Your Business and Personal Finances

Chapter 1: Foundations of Financial Mastery
Chapter 2: Advanced Budgeting Techniques
Chapter 3: Debt Consolidation and Management
Chapter 4: Credit Partnership and Investment Strategies
Chapter 5: Scaling to $1,000,000 a Month
Chapter 6: Personal Financial Empowerment
Chapter 7: Manifesting a Million: The Subconscious Blueprint for Action

Chapter 1: Foundations of Financial Mastery

1. Introduction to Financial Mastery

Welcome to a journey unlike any other—a journey where the destination is as rewarding as the path you'll take to get there. This is the journey to financial mastery, a quest not just for wealth, but for the freedom and peace that come with it. Financial mastery is more than numbers on a bank statement; it's the profound understanding and control over one's financial destiny, impacting every facet of personal and professional life.

You might wonder, "What exactly is financial mastery?" At its core, financial mastery is the ability to make your money work for you, rather than the other way around. It's the skill to manage, grow, and protect your finances, ensuring that you can achieve your dreams, whether that's owning a home, securing a comfortable retirement, or living debt-free. For too long, the path to financial prosperity has seemed obscured by myths and misunderstandings, particularly for hardworking individuals from blue-collar backgrounds. The misconception that wealth is reserved for the lucky few, or that financial success is beyond reach, is not just misleading—it's fundamentally untrue.

This book is designed to dismantle those barriers. Through personal anecdotes, historical examples, and fictional parables, we will explore the essence of financial mastery. From the Abundance Mindset to the Law of Attraction, and the transformative principles of positive psychology and neuro-linguistic programming, we'll delve into philosophies that can rewire our approach to wealth and prosperity.

Our narrative will embrace you like a conversation with an old friend, using the first person to create intimacy and a motivational tone to lift your spirits. Imagine, for a moment, achieving your financial goals effortlessly. See yourself living a life of abundance, making smart financial decisions with confidence, and witnessing your wealth grow as you wisely invest. This is not just a dream; it's a preview of what's to come.

As we move through this journey, we will employ subliminal messaging techniques to reinforce your belief in your ability to create wealth and take control of your financial future today. Our discussion will be non-linear, mirroring the flow of life itself—unpredictable yet full of opportunity. We will engage in self-reflection, visualization, and practical exercises designed to integrate wealth-building habits into your everyday life seamlessly.

This book is grounded in proven psychological theories and economic principles, and it's differentiated by its approach: speaking directly to you, the hardworking individual who might have thought true financial mastery was out of reach. Let's embark on this journey together, transforming not just our finances, but our lives, as we uncover the secrets to financial mastery.

2. The Psychology of Money

The Psychological Landscape of Money Management

At the core of financial mastery lies an intricate dance between the mind and money—a relationship governed by the principles of behavioral finance. This field of study goes beyond the traditional assumptions of economics, probing deeper into why we often make irrational financial decisions that contradict our best interests.

Why do we splurge on items we don't need the moment our paycheck arrives, despite our long-term goals of saving for a home? Or why do we hold onto investments plummeting in value, driven by an irrational hope they'll rebound? These are not mere lapses of judgment but manifestations of our psychological wiring.

The Influence of Cognitive Biases

Our financial behaviors are heavily influenced by cognitive biases—systematic patterns of deviation from rationality in judgment and decision-making. For instance, the **loss aversion bias** makes the pain of losing money feel more intense than the joy of gaining an equal amount, often leading us to avoid risks that could benefit us financially in the long run. Similarly, the **status quo bias** nudges us towards maintaining our current financial situation, even when change is necessary for growth.

Emotional Finance: The Heart's Role in Financial Decisions

Emotions play a pivotal role in our financial decisions. The fear of missing out (FOMO) can drive us to make hasty investments without due diligence, while the warmth of instant gratification lures us away from the disciplined path of saving. Recognizing these emotional triggers is the first step toward mastering them.

Reprogramming Our Financial Mindset

The journey to financial mastery involves reprogramming our mindset to align with our financial goals. Techniques drawn from positive psychology and neuro-linguistic programming offer powerful tools for this transformation. By embedding positive affirmations in our daily lives, such as "I am a wise steward of my finances," we begin to rewrite the subconscious scripts that dictate our financial behaviors.

Visualization exercises also play a crucial role. Imagine yourself achieving your financial goals with ease—feel the security of a robust savings account, the pride of debt freedom, and the joy of financial independence. These mental rehearsals not only motivate but also prepare our psyche for the realities of wealth and prosperity.

Towards Behavioral Change

Understanding the psychological aspects of money management is the foundation upon which we can build lasting behavioral change. It's about recognizing our biases, understanding our emotional triggers, and then consciously choosing a path that aligns with our aspirations for financial mastery. This journey is not just about acquiring wealth; it's about cultivating a mindset that values growth, resilience, and the abundant possibilities that financial mastery brings into our lives.

In the chapters that follow, we will delve deeper into practical strategies and exercises designed to fortify this mindset, ensuring that you, the reader, are equipped not just with the knowledge, but also with the psychological tools necessary to navigate the complex landscape of personal finance.

Building upon our exploration of the psychological aspects of money management, it becomes imperative to identify and overcome the common psychological barriers that impede financial success. These barriers, often deep-rooted within our psyche, can derail even the most disciplined financial plans. Understanding these obstacles and employing strategies to navigate them is crucial for anyone on the path to financial mastery.

Identifying Psychological Barriers to Financial Success

1. Fear of Failure

Fear of failure looms large in financial decision-making, paralyzing individuals from taking necessary risks or making significant changes to their financial strategies. This fear often stems from past mistakes or societal pressures, leading to a risk-averse mentality that shuns investment opportunities and innovative income streams.

Strategies for Overcoming Fear of Failure:

- **Embrace a Growth Mindset:** View financial setbacks not as failures but as learning opportunities. This shift in perspective encourages resilience and a willingness to take calculated risks.
- **Small Steps Approach:** Start with small, manageable financial risks to build confidence over time.

The fear of failure is a formidable adversary in the realm of financial decision-making. It's a shadow that darkens our judgment, making the prospect of taking even the smallest financial risks seem daunting. This fear can be deeply ingrained, often rooted in previous financial blunders or the daunting narratives of fiscal downfall that pervade our culture. Yet, it is essential to confront and overcome this fear to foster a prosperous financial future.

When we talk about the fear of failure, we're delving into not just the anxiety of losing money but also the dread of what that loss represents—perhaps a blow to our self-esteem, a perceived loss of security, or the fear of judgment from our peers. This fear can immobilize us, creating a barrier that prevents the exploration of new financial avenues and the embrace of potentially lucrative opportunities.

Embracing a Growth Mindset

One of the most transformative approaches to mitigating the fear of failure is adopting a growth mindset. This perspective doesn't trivialize the pain of loss but reframes setbacks as essential stepping stones in the learning process. With a growth mindset, every financial misstep is not a dead-end but a detour on the road to wisdom.

Imagine perceiving each financial setback not as a testament to your inadequacy but as a valuable lesson that hones your decision-making prowess. This shift in viewpoint liberates you from the shackles of fear, enabling you to approach financial risks with a learner's curiosity rather than a pessimist's dread.

Taking Small Steps

Another effective strategy to overcome the fear of financial failure is the incremental approach. Begin with minor, less intimidating financial decisions that carry a lower risk. This could mean investing a small sum in a new venture, experimenting with a low-risk investment, or even attending a financial workshop to enhance your understanding and skills.

Each small step taken is a victory over fear, a building block in constructing a more robust financial foundation. With every minor risk that pays off or provides a lesson, your confidence grows, gradually dismantling the towering fear of failure.

In essence, overcoming the fear of failure in finance is about shifting perspectives and taking measured, conscious steps forward. It's about recognizing that the path to financial abundance is paved with lessons learned from risks taken, not avoided. By nurturing a growth mindset and embracing the philosophy of small, progressive steps, you can transform the fear of failure into a catalyst for growth and financial empowerment.

2. Procrastination

Procrastination in managing finances, such as delaying investment decisions or failing to budget, can significantly hinder wealth accumulation. This often results from a lack of urgency or overwhelming feelings associated with financial planning.

Strategies for Overcoming Procrastination:

- **Set Clear, Achievable Goals:** Break down financial goals into smaller, actionable steps to reduce overwhelm and create momentum.
- **Use Positive Reinforcement:** Reward yourself for completing financial tasks, reinforcing positive behavior.

Procrastination can be a significant barrier to achieving financial well-being. It often results from feeling overwhelmed by the complexity of financial planning or the discomfort associated with dealing with money matters. However, by implementing strategies that focus on setting clear, achievable goals and utilizing positive reinforcement, individuals can effectively combat procrastination and take proactive steps towards their financial objectives.

Setting Clear, Achievable Goals

The first step in overcoming procrastination is to articulate your financial goals with clarity and precision. Ambiguous or lofty goals can be daunting and are more likely to be deferred. Instead, by breaking down your financial ambitions into smaller, manageable objectives, the task at hand becomes less intimidating and more attainable.

Consider a goal like saving for retirement. Rather than setting a vague intention like "save more money," specify how much you want to save each month and identify the actions you need to take to achieve this. For example, you might decide to contribute a certain percentage of your monthly income to a retirement account. By delineating your goal into tangible steps, you transform the abstract concept of "saving more" into a series of actionable items, thereby reducing the urge to procrastinate.

Using Positive Reinforcement

Positive reinforcement is a powerful tool in modifying behavior, including financial habits. By rewarding yourself for accomplishing financial tasks, you create a positive association with these activities, making you more inclined to undertake them in the future.

The rewards can be simple and need not undermine your financial goals. For instance, after adhering to your savings plan for a month, you might treat yourself to a small luxury or a favorite activity. The key is to select rewards that are meaningful to you and that do not counteract your financial objectives.

This strategy taps into the pleasure principle, where your brain begins to associate financial diligence with immediate positive outcomes, thereby increasing your motivation to engage in these activities. Over time, this positive reinforcement loop encourages a more proactive and less procrastinatory approach to financial management.

In conclusion, by setting clear, achievable goals and integrating positive reinforcement into your financial routine, you can overcome the inertia of procrastination. These strategies help to demystify financial tasks, making them more approachable and less likely to be deferred, thereby fostering a more active and empowered approach to personal finance.

3. Lifestyle Inflation

Lifestyle inflation, where spending increases as income rises, often without corresponding growth in savings or investments, can trap individuals in a cycle of living paycheck to paycheck, regardless of their earnings.

Strategies for Overcoming Lifestyle Inflation:

- **Conscious Spending:** Implement a budget that includes savings and investment goals as non-negotiable items, ensuring these priorities are funded before discretionary spending.
- **Value-Based Spending:** Align spending with personal values and long-term goals, rather than societal expectations or immediate gratification.

Navigating the Temptations of Lifestyle Inflation

Imagine this: you've just received a significant raise or a lucrative job offer. Naturally, joy and excitement wash over you. It's a testament to your hard work and dedication. However, as your income grows, so does the temptation to elevate your spending, indulging in finer things, perhaps a bigger home, a luxury car, or exotic vacations. This is the essence of lifestyle inflation, a subtle yet potent force that can derail your financial well-being if left unchecked.

Now, let's delve into strategies that can help you maintain financial equilibrium, ensuring that your growing income also boosts your financial wealth, not just your lifestyle expenses.

Embracing Conscious Spending

Conscious spending isn't about frugality or denying yourself the joys of hard-earned success. It's about making informed, deliberate choices. When you receive that paycheck boost, before you plan that lavish holiday or upgrade your car, pause. Reflect on your financial foundation. Is your emergency fund robust? Are your retirement savings on track?

Envision your budget as a blueprint for your financial house. Just as the foundations and structure are crucial before you adorn the house with decor, ensuring you allocate funds to savings and investments is essential before indulging in discretionary spending. This approach doesn't just safeguard your financial future; it also instills a sense of empowerment and peace, knowing you're building a sturdy financial edifice.

Cultivating Value-Based Spending

Now, consider the concept of value-based spending. It's a powerful perspective that encourages you to align your expenditures with your deepest values and aspirations. Ask yourself, what truly brings you joy and fulfillment? Is it the fleeting thrill of a new gadget or the enduring satisfaction of a family vacation that creates lifelong memories?

By anchoring your spending decisions to your values and long-term objectives, you resist the societal pressures to 'keep up with the Joneses.' It's about crafting a lifestyle that reflects who you are and what you cherish, not what billboards or social media influencers dictate.

In essence, overcoming lifestyle inflation is not merely about budgeting or saving; it's about crafting a financial identity that resonates with your core values and life goals. It's about embracing the joy and freedom that comes from financial security and independence. As you navigate your financial journey, remember that each spending decision is a building block in the life you're constructing. Choose those blocks wisely, ensuring they contribute to a future brimming with prosperity, joy, and peace.

4. Confirmation Bias

Confirmation bias, the tendency to search for, interpret, and recall information in a way that confirms one's preexisting beliefs about money, can lead to missed opportunities and entrenched financial habits that are hard to break.

Strategies for Overcoming Confirmation Bias:

- **Seek Diverse Perspectives**: Actively seek out information and advice that challenge your financial beliefs and assumptions.
- **Reflective Journaling**: Regularly reflect on financial decisions to identify patterns of thought and behavior that may be influenced by confirmation bias

.Addressing Confirmation Bias in Financial Decisions

Picture yourself cozily ensconced in your financial comfort zone, surrounded by ideas and decisions that feel as familiar and reassuring as a well-worn sweater. This comfort zone is where confirmation bias thrives, subtly steering you toward information that aligns with your existing financial beliefs and away from insights that could challenge or broaden your perspective. While it's human nature to seek validation for our beliefs, in the realm of finance, this bias can be a formidable barrier to growth and opportunity.

Let's explore how you can dismantle these barriers and foster a more open-minded approach to your financial life.

Embracing Diverse Perspectives

Imagine walking into a room filled with people from all walks of life, each with a unique financial story and perspective. One person advocates for the transformative power of real estate investment, another shares success in the stock market, and yet another recounts their journey with cryptocurrencies. Instead of tuning out the unfamiliar or uncomfortable, you listen, inquire, and absorb.

By actively seeking diverse financial viewpoints and engaging with a variety of investment philosophies, you expose yourself to a broader spectrum of knowledge and experience. This doesn't mean you should act on every piece of advice or jump on every trend. Rather, it's about opening your mind to possibilities beyond your financial echo chamber, allowing you to make more informed and rounded decisions.

Engaging in Reflective Journaling

Now, imagine sitting down with a journal at the end of each week, reflecting on your financial decisions, large and small. You contemplate why you made those choices, what influenced them, and how they align with your broader financial goals. This practice isn't about self-criticism or second-guessing but about uncovering and understanding your financial thought patterns.

Reflective journaling offers a mirror to your financial psyche, revealing how confirmation bias might color your decisions. Did you ignore a piece of financial advice because it contradicted your beliefs? Did you choose a comfortable investment route over a potentially more lucrative one because it felt safer and more familiar?

By regularly examining your financial choices and the motivations behind them, you cultivate an awareness that can illuminate and gradually erode ingrained biases. This self-awareness is a powerful ally in your journey toward financial wisdom and independence.

In essence, overcoming confirmation bias in finance is about broadening your horizons and deepening your self-awareness. It's a journey that requires curiosity, openness, and introspection, transforming your financial decision-making into a more balanced, informed, and dynamic process. As you venture beyond the familiar territory of your preconceptions, you unlock new avenues for growth, learning, and financial empowerment.

Empowering Strategies for Psychological Growth

Visualization and Affirmation: Employ visualization techniques to imagine achieving financial goals, paired with affirmations that reinforce a positive financial identity. This practice can reshape your internal narrative, fostering a mindset aligned with prosperity and success.

Educational Empowerment: Knowledge is a powerful tool against fear and uncertainty. Commit to continuous learning about personal finance, investment strategies, and economic principles. This not only demystifies the financial world but also empowers you to make informed decisions.

Community and Support: Surround yourself with a community that supports your financial goals. This could be a formal financial advisor, a mentor, or a peer group focused on financial literacy. Sharing experiences and strategies can provide motivation and accountability, helping you navigate through psychological barriers.

Mindfulness and Emotional Regulation: Practicing mindfulness can enhance emotional regulation, helping you make financial decisions from a place of calm and clarity rather than impulsive emotional reactions. Techniques such as deep breathing, meditation, or yoga can be beneficial.

By confronting these psychological barriers head-on and implementing targeted strategies to overcome them, individuals can pave the way for financial success. This journey is not devoid of challenges, but with perseverance, a willingness to adapt, and a deep understanding of one's psychological makeup, achieving financial mastery is within reach. Each barrier overcome is a step closer to the ultimate goal of financial independence and prosperity.

3. Principles of Financial Health

- Key principles underpinning financial health, including budgeting, saving, investing, and debt management.

Transitioning from the discussion on psychological barriers and strategies for overcoming them, we now focus on the concrete pillars of financial health. These key principles—budgeting, saving, investing, and debt management—form the bedrock of sound financial management. Mastering these areas is crucial for anyone aiming to achieve financial stability and growth.

As we shift our gaze from the intricacies of psychological barriers to the foundational aspects of financial health, it becomes apparent that mastering certain core principles is vital for anyone aspiring to financial stability and growth. These principles—budgeting, saving, investing, and debt management—aren't just strategies; they're the cornerstones upon which we build our financial future.

Budgeting: The Blueprint of Financial Health

Think of budgeting as crafting the blueprint for your financial house. It's about understanding where your money is coming from and where it's going, ensuring that every dollar serves a purpose. A well-structured budget isn't about restriction but about empowerment, providing clarity and control over your financial choices.

Engaging in regular budgeting allows you to prioritize your spending, distinguishing between needs and wants, and aligning your financial resources with your most cherished goals and values. It's the first step in transforming your financial dreams into achievable plans.

Saving: The Art of Financial Preservation

Now, let's talk about saving, the very essence of financial preservation. Saving is about setting aside a portion of your income for future use, whether for unexpected emergencies, planned expenditures, or long-term objectives. It's the safety net that catches you when life throws curveballs and the seed money for future financial endeavors.

Developing a robust saving habit requires discipline and foresight. It means looking beyond the immediate gratification of spending to the broader canvas of your financial future, recognizing that each saved dollar is a step toward financial resilience and independence.

Investing: The Engine of Financial Growth

While saving is about preservation, investing is about growth. It's the process of deploying your resources in avenues that offer potential returns, allowing your wealth to expand over time. Investing can take various forms, from stocks and bonds to real estate and beyond, each with its own risk and reward profile.

The key to successful investing is understanding your risk tolerance, investment horizon, and the fundamental principles of diversification and asset allocation. It's about making your money work for you, harnessing the power of compound interest, and building a portfolio that grows and evolves with your financial journey.

Debt Management: The Art of Financial Balance

Lastly, effective debt management is crucial for maintaining financial health. It's about understanding the cost of borrowing, prioritizing high-interest debt, and ensuring that your debt levels remain sustainable. Proper debt management prevents the accumulation of burdensome liabilities that can stifle your financial growth and stability.

It involves making informed decisions about when and how to use debt, distinguishing between productive debt that can enhance your financial position and destructive debt that undermines it. It's about balance, discernment, and strategic planning, ensuring that debt serves as a tool for advancement, not a barrier to success.

In essence, these principles of budgeting, saving, investing, and debt management are not just strategies but the very fabric of a healthy financial life. They interweave to form a comprehensive approach to money management, each element reinforcing the others. By mastering these principles, you lay the groundwork for a financial future characterized by stability, growth, and freedom, turning your financial aspirations from mere possibilities into realities.

Budgeting: The Blueprint for Financial Success

Budgeting is foundational in managing your finances effectively. It involves tracking income and expenses, setting spending limits, and planning for both short-term needs and long-term goals. A well-structured budget provides a clear overview of where your money is going, helping to identify areas for cost reduction and savings enhancement.

Strategies for Effective Budgeting:

- **Zero-Based Budgeting:** Allocate every dollar of income to specific expenses, savings, and investments until you have zero unallocated funds.
- **50/30/20 Rule:** A guideline where 50% of your income goes to needs, 30% to wants, and 20% to savings and debt repayment.

Budgeting stands as the cornerstone of prudent financial management, akin to creating a roadmap for your fiscal journey. It's about harnessing the power of your income, guiding it purposefully towards various facets of your life, ensuring that each dollar serves your broader financial narrative, be it securing daily necessities, fulfilling desires, or forging a brighter future through savings and investments.

Embracing Zero-Based Budgeting

Imagine starting each month with every dollar assigned a role, be it covering living expenses, padding your savings, or paying down debt. This is the essence of zero-based budgeting. It's a proactive approach that requires you to account for every dollar, ensuring there's no financial leakage on non-essential or unnoticed expenditures. By giving each dollar a purpose, you cultivate a mindset of intentionality with your finances, fostering a deeper connection between your daily spending choices and your overarching financial goals.

This method doesn't just illuminate your financial picture; it empowers you to make informed adjustments. For instance, if you find a category consistently underspent, you can reallocate those funds towards areas that might need a boost, like an emergency fund or retirement savings, thereby optimizing your financial resources.

Leveraging the 50/30/20 Rule

Now, imagine structuring your budget with a simple, yet effective guideline: the 50/30/20 rule. It's a strategy that balances pragmatism with aspiration, ensuring that your financial essentials are met while still allowing room for life's pleasures and the vital act of building your financial future.

50% to Needs: Half of your income is dedicated to absolute necessities—the roof over your head, the food on your table, and the utilities that keep your home running. This focus ensures that your foundational needs are securely met without compromising your financial stability.

30% to Wants: This portion allows you to enjoy the fruits of your labor, allocating funds to hobbies, dining out, or entertainment. It acknowledges that enjoying life's pleasures is a crucial aspect of a balanced financial life, preventing the sense of deprivation that can often derail more stringent budgeting efforts.

20% to Savings and Debts: The final segment underscores the importance of future-focused financial planning. Allocating this slice of your income to savings and debt repayment not only fortifies your financial resilience but also propels you towards your long-term wealth aspirations.

Effective budgeting is not about restriction but empowerment, providing a structured yet flexible framework to navigate your financial landscape. Whether you're drawn to the meticulousness of zero-based budgeting or the balanced approach of the 50/30/20 rule, the key is to find a strategy that resonates with your lifestyle and goals, turning the act of budgeting from a chore into a powerful ally on your journey to financial well-being.

Saving: Building Your Financial Safety Net

Saving is crucial for creating a financial safety net and preparing for future financial goals. Whether it's an emergency fund to cover unexpected expenses or saving for a down payment on a home, cultivating a habit of saving is essential for financial health.

Strategies for Boosting Savings:

- **Automate Your Savings:** Set up automatic transfers to your savings account to ensure you save a consistent portion of your income before you have a chance to spend it.
- **High-Yield Savings Accounts:** Utilize high-yield savings accounts to earn more interest on your savings over time.

Imagine your savings as the sturdy keel of a ship, a fundamental component that keeps your financial vessel stable and upright, even when the economic seas get rough. It's this foundational element that not only provides immediate security but also propels you toward those bright horizons of future financial goals. Whether it's weathering an unexpected storm or charting a course toward a significant milestone like homeownership, the act of saving is undeniably central to your financial well-being.

Embracing the Power of Automation

Consider the idea of automating your savings. In a world brimming with distractions and temptations, it's all too easy for our hard-earned money to slip through our fingers on non-essentials. But what if, before those temptations even arise, a portion of your income discreetly and automatically nestles itself into your savings account? This is the beauty of automation.

By setting up automatic transfers, you prioritize your future needs and desires over immediate whims. It's like having a diligent financial assistant who ensures that a slice of every paycheck is reserved for your future self, fortifying your financial foundation with each passing month.

Leveraging High-Yield Savings Accounts

Now, let's elevate your savings strategy by placing your funds in a high-yield savings account. Unlike the more traditional savings accounts, which offer minimal interest, high-yield accounts allow your money to grow faster, harnessing the power of higher interest rates.

Imagine your savings not just sitting idly but actively growing, day and night, like a tree reaching steadily toward the sky. By choosing a high-yield account, you're essentially planting your savings in fertile soil, giving it the best possible conditions to thrive and expand.

In both these strategies—automation and high-yield savings—the key is consistency and foresight. It's about making strategic choices that align with your financial goals, ensuring that each decision propels you one step closer to financial security and freedom. By cultivating a robust saving habit, underscored by these effective strategies, you're not just safeguarding your present but also nurturing your future, enabling a journey toward financial health that is both rewarding and empowering.

Investing: The Path to Wealth Accumulation

Investing is the key to building wealth over the long term. By investing in stocks, bonds, real estate, or other assets, you can grow your wealth through the power of compound interest and market appreciation.

Principles of Smart Investing:

- Diversification: Spread your investments across different asset classes to reduce risk.
- Risk Management: Understand your risk tolerance and invest accordingly, balancing the potential for higher returns against the risk of loss.
- Long-Term Perspective: Focus on long-term investment strategies rather than short-term market fluctuations.

Embarking on the journey of investing is akin to setting sail toward uncharted territories, each with its own promise of treasure but also its perils. The allure of building substantial wealth over time, leveraging the dual forces of compound interest and market appreciation, is compelling and achievable with the right strategies and mindset.

Embracing Diversification

Picture diversification as the art of not putting all your eggs in one basket. It's about creating a vibrant mosaic of investments, each with its unique pattern of risks and returns, coming together to form a resilient and dynamic portfolio. By spreading your investments across various asset classes—be it stocks, bonds, real estate, or others—you're not just mitigating risk; you're also positioning yourself to capture growth from multiple sources.

Imagine your investment portfolio as a garden, where you cultivate a diverse array of plants, each responding differently to the same environment. Just as a garden benefits from the variety, bringing resilience and beauty, your diversified portfolio can weather market volatility and provide steady growth over time.

Understanding and Managing Risk

Investing invariably involves risk, but smart investing is about understanding and managing this risk, not avoiding it altogether. Recognize your risk tolerance, which is essentially your financial and emotional capacity to endure market downturns. It's about finding that sweet spot where you're taking enough risk to achieve meaningful growth but not so much that you lose sleep at night.

Consider risk management as the compass that guides you through your investing journey, informing decisions and helping you navigate through turbulent markets. By aligning your investments with your risk tolerance, you create a portfolio that you can commit to over the long haul, avoiding panic-driven decisions during market downturns.

Adopting a Long-Term Perspective

The true power of investing unfolds over time, harnessing the magic of compound interest and market appreciation. It requires a long-term perspective, focusing on the horizon rather than the waves at your feet. Short-term market fluctuations can be dramatic and captivating, but they are merely distractions in the grand narrative of long-term investing.

Think of your investment journey as a marathon, not a sprint. It's about consistent, disciplined progress toward your financial goals, not rapid gains or speculative bets. By committing to a long-term strategy, you allow your investments the time they need to grow, to overcome the inevitable valleys, and to reach new peaks.

In conclusion, the principles of smart investing—diversification, risk management, and a long-term perspective—are your navigational stars in the vast universe of wealth building. By adhering to these principles, you can steer your investment ship with confidence and purpose, navigating through market storms and sunny days alike, toward the ultimate destination of financial prosperity and security.

Debt Management: Controlling Your Liabilities

Debt Management involves strategies to manage and reduce debt. High-interest debt, such as credit card debt, can significantly hinder financial progress, making effective debt management a critical component of financial health.

Strategies for Managing Debt:

- **Debt Snowball Method:** Pay off debts from smallest to largest, gaining momentum as each debt is cleared.
- **Debt Avalanche Method:** Focus on paying off debts with the highest interest rates first, reducing the amount of interest paid over time.

Embarking on the journey of debt management is akin to navigating a ship through stormy seas. The weight of high-interest debt, especially from credit cards, can feel like a heavy anchor, dragging down your financial progress and peace of mind. But with the right strategies and a bit of perseverance, you can lift that anchor and sail towards calmer, more prosperous financial waters.

Navigating Debt with the Snowball Method

Imagine starting with your smallest debt, much like tackling the gentlest wave first. As you pay off each debt, you gain momentum and confidence, just as a ship gains speed when the wind fills its sails. This method, known as the debt snowball, creates a series of victories, each one empowering you to tackle the next, larger debt with increased vigor and determination.

The beauty of the debt snowball method lies in its psychological rewards. Every debt you clear gives you a boost, a tangible sign that you're taking control and making real progress. It transforms the daunting task of debt repayment into a manageable, even exhilarating journey, turning what once felt overwhelming into a series of achievable steps.

Scaling the Avalanche of High-Interest Debt

Now, envision confronting the most formidable wave head-on, targeting the debts with the highest interest rates first. This approach, known as the debt avalanche method, is a strategic assault on the most costly debts, those that grow fastest and can capsize your financial stability if left unchecked.

By prioritizing these high-interest debts, you're not just chipping away at what you owe; you're also reducing the total interest you'll pay over the life of your debts. It's a method that requires discipline and patience, as the initial progress can feel slow. But just as an avalanche gains power and speed, so too does your debt repayment momentum, accelerating as you eliminate each high-interest debt and reducing your overall financial burden more efficiently.

Charting Your Course to Debt Freedom

Whether you choose the debt snowball's motivational path or the debt avalanche's strategic approach, the key is to start, to commit to a course of action. Debt management is not just about numbers; it's about setting a direction, taking the helm, and steering with purpose and resolve.

Remember, the journey to debt freedom is a marathon, not a sprint. There will be challenges and setbacks, but with a solid strategy and unwavering commitment, you can navigate through the tempest of debt and emerge into the clear, calm waters of financial health and independence. As you reduce and eventually eliminate your debts, you reclaim your freedom, your choices, and your future, setting a course for a brighter, more secure financial horizon.

Integrating the Principles into Daily Life

Achieving financial health requires a holistic approach, integrating these key principles into your daily life. It's not just about making a plan but living it, adjusting as your financial situation and goals evolve. Regularly review your budget, savings progress, investment portfolio, and debt levels to ensure you remain on track toward your financial objectives.

Empowerment Through Education:

Educate yourself continuously on financial matters. Stay informed about economic trends, investment strategies, and new financial tools and products. Knowledge empowers you to make informed decisions, adapt to changes, and seize opportunities for financial growth.

The Role of Technology:

Leverage financial technology tools to streamline budgeting, saving, investing, and debt management. Apps and online platforms can provide real-time insights into your financial health, making it easier to track progress and make adjustments.

By embracing these principles and incorporating them into your financial strategy, you lay the groundwork for lasting financial health and prosperity. The journey to financial mastery is a continuous process of learning, adapting, and growing—a journey well worth embarking on.

- The concept of financial freedom and its components.

Financial freedom is often misconceived as merely accumulating a vast wealth that allows one to live without working for the rest of their lives. While this can be one aspect, at its core, financial freedom is about achieving a state of financial security and independence where your living expenses are comfortably covered by passive income or investments, freeing you from the necessity to work for survival. It's about gaining the liberty to make life decisions without being overly stressed about the financial impact.

Components of Financial Freedom

1. Passive Income Streams

Creating sources of income that do not require your active involvement is crucial. Whether through investments, rental properties, or side businesses, these streams ensure money flows into your life, even when you're not working.

2. Savings and Emergency Funds

A robust savings account and an emergency fund act as a safety net, providing peace of mind and stability. They ensure that unexpected expenses or financial downturns do not derail your journey toward freedom.

3. Debt Freedom

Eliminating high-interest debt and managing manageable debt levels are fundamental to financial freedom. Debt often acts as a shackle, limiting your financial growth and choices.

4. Investment Portfolio

A diversified investment portfolio tailored to your risk tolerance and financial goals can grow your wealth over time, contributing significantly to your financial independence.

5. Financial Literacy

Understanding the principles of personal finance, investment strategies, and economic trends empowers you to make informed decisions that align with your freedom goals.

Achieving Financial Freedom: A Journey of Mind and Action

Embrace the Abundance Mindset

Shifting from scarcity to abundance changes how you perceive opportunities and challenges. Believe in the limitless possibilities for creating wealth and the abundance that surrounds you.

Visualize Your Financially Free Life

Imagine the life you wish to lead once financial freedom is achieved. This vivid imagery serves as a powerful motivator, guiding your decisions and actions towards making that vision a reality.

Set Clear, Actionable Goals

Define what financial freedom means to you, whether it's retiring early, owning your dream home, or having the flexibility to pursue your passions. Break down these goals into achievable steps and pursue them with determination.

Educate Yourself Continuously

Invest in your financial education. Read books, attend workshops, and seek mentorship to understand the complexities of finance and investment. Knowledge is a tool that empowers you to navigate the path to freedom with confidence.

Cultivate Multiple Income Streams

Explore avenues to diversify your income. This could mean investing in stocks, starting a side hustle, or acquiring rental property. The key is to build assets that work for you, generating income even as you sleep.

Practice Gratitude and Generosity

Financial freedom is also about the ability to give back and share your abundance with others. Generosity and gratitude enrich your journey, bringing joy and fulfillment beyond material wealth.

In this narrative of financial freedom, remember that the journey is uniquely yours. It's a path paved with personal victories, lessons, and discoveries. As we delve deeper into the components of financial freedom, let this chapter serve as a guide and an inspiration, reminding you that financial freedom is not only about the wealth you accumulate but the freedom it brings to live your life on your terms.

Budgeting: The Foundation of Financial Planning

- Steps to creating a realistic and effective budget.

Embarking on the journey toward financial mastery, the creation of a realistic and effective budget stands as a cornerstone practice. A budget, far from being a mere numerical constraint, is a reflection of your values and a roadmap towards achieving your financial aspirations, such as homeownership, debt freedom, or early retirement. The process of budgeting, when approached with the right mindset, can be empowering, offering clarity and control over your financial landscape. Herein, we shall outline the steps to crafting a budget that not only aligns with your financial goals but also integrates seamlessly with your lifestyle, ensuring both practicality and effectiveness.

1. Gather Your Financial Statements

Begin by compiling all your financial information—bank statements, bills, investment accounts, and any sources of income. This comprehensive overview is crucial for understanding your starting point.

2. Record Your Income

Identify all sources of income after taxes, including salaries, bonuses, investments, and any side hustles. The sum of these amounts forms the foundation upon which your budget is built, representing the total funds available for allocation.

3. Categorize Expenses

Segment your expenses into fixed and variable categories. Fixed expenses remain constant each month, such as rent or mortgage, insurance premiums, and loan payments. Variable expenses, such as groceries, entertainment, and personal spending, can fluctuate. Listing these expenses provides insight into where your money is currently going.

4. Set Realistic Goals

Reflect on your financial aspirations and set goals that resonate with your vision of financial freedom. Whether saving for a down payment, building an emergency fund, or investing in your future, these goals should be specific, measurable, achievable, relevant, and time-bound (SMART).

5. Create Your Budget Plan

Utilizing the information gathered, draft a budget that supports your goals while covering your essential expenses. Employ budgeting methods that align with your financial behavior and preferences, such as the zero-based budget, the 50/30/20 rule, or the envelope system. This plan should be flexible, allowing for adjustments as your financial situation evolves.

6. Monitor and Adjust Your Budget

A budget is not set in stone; it's a living document that requires regular review and adjustment. Track your spending, compare it against your budget, and adjust as necessary. Life changes, and so will your financial needs and goals. Embrace this flexibility as a tool for sustained financial health.

7. Prioritize Savings and Debt Repayment

Incorporate savings and debt repayment into your budget as non-negotiable items. Even a modest allocation toward these categories can compound over time, contributing significantly to your financial well-being and freedom.

8. Leverage Technology

Consider using budgeting apps or financial software to streamline the budgeting process. These tools can automate much of the tracking and categorization work, providing insights and alerts to keep you on track.

9. Cultivate a Budgeting Mindset

Adopt a positive perspective on budgeting. View it as a tool for empowerment, not restriction. Celebrate the freedom and peace of mind that comes from knowing your financial affairs are in order, aligning with the abundance mindset and principles of financial mastery.

10. Seek Continuous Improvement

Regularly assess your budgeting process for opportunities to refine and improve. Stay informed about financial management practices and remain open to adjusting your approach as you discover what works best for your unique circumstances.

Creating a realistic and effective budget is a dynamic process that mirrors your journey towards financial mastery. It requires honesty, commitment, and a willingness to adapt. By following these steps, you lay a solid foundation for financial health, bringing your dreams of financial freedom within reach.

Category	Budgeted Amount	Actual Amount	Difference

Income
Fixed Expenses: Rent/Mortgage
Fixed Expenses: Utilities
Fixed Expenses: Insurance
Fixed Expenses: Loan Payments
Variable Expenses: Groceries
Variable Expenses: Dining Out
Variable Expenses: Entertainment
Variable Expenses: Personal Spending
Variable Expenses: Transportation
Savings: Emergency Fund
Savings: Investment
Savings: Other Goals
Total

- Tools and techniques for tracking expenses and income.

In the quest for financial mastery, the diligent tracking of expenses and income is indispensable. It not only provides clarity on where your money is going but also empowers you to make informed decisions to optimize your financial health. Here, we explore various tools and techniques designed to facilitate effective monitoring of your financial flows, enabling you to stay aligned with your budgeting goals and financial aspirations.

Traditional Tools

1. **Pen and Paper**

- **Technique:** The simplest method, involving recording your daily expenses and income by hand in a notebook.
- **Benefits:** Helps inculcate discipline and mindfulness about spending. It's highly customizable and requires no technical knowledge.

Limitations: Time-consuming and prone to human error. Lacks the convenience of automated calculations and analysis.

In the realm of personal finance management, there's something almost ritualistic about the pen and paper method. It's akin to planting a garden with your own hands, feeling the soil between your fingers—it connects you to the process in a profoundly personal way. Let's delve deeper into this time-honored technique, exploring how it serves not just as a method of record-keeping but as a tool for financial mindfulness and discipline.

When you take up a pen and commit the details of your financial life to paper, you're engaging in an act of mindfulness. Each stroke, each number, each note you write serves as a moment of reflection on your spending habits and financial decisions. This method, in its simplicity and tactility, demands a level of engagement that digital methods often gloss over. You're not just observing your financial flow; you're actively participating in its documentation, creating a tangible, living record of your financial journey.

The Art of Manual Tracking

Visualize opening your notebook at the end of the day, the pages filled with the story of your financial interactions. There's a narrative quality to this method, where each entry tells a part of your day, your choices, your priorities, and even your indulgences. By categorizing these transactions, you start to see patterns emerge, like themes in a novel—where you're thrifty, where you tend to splurge, and how your financial decisions align with your personal values and goals.

Customization and Creativity

One of the joys of the pen and paper method is its inherent flexibility. You're not constrained by preset categories or software limitations. You can create your own categories, design your layout, and even add personal touches like color-coding or illustrations. This notebook can become a financial journal that not only serves practical purposes but also reflects your personality and creativity.

Acknowledging the Limitations

Despite its benefits, it's important to acknowledge the limitations of this method. It can be time-consuming, a daily ritual that requires consistency and dedication. There's also the risk of human error—misplaced receipts, miscalculations, or forgotten entries. And unlike digital tools, it doesn't offer instant analytics or the ability to crunch numbers with a click.

However, for some, these limitations are outweighed by the benefits. The very act of writing by hand can reinforce memory and understanding, embedding financial awareness deep into your consciousness. And while it may not offer the convenience of automated calculations, it provides something arguably more valuable: a deep, personal engagement with your financial reality.

In essence, the pen and paper method is more than just a technique for tracking finances; it's a practice in financial mindfulness, a way to cultivate a deliberate and thoughtful approach to money management. Whether you're a seasoned financier or just beginning to navigate your financial path, this method offers a foundation for building a relationship with your finances that is attentive, intentional, and informed.

Technique:

The pen and paper method is a foundational approach to financial tracking, harking back to the earliest days of bookkeeping. This technique entails manually jotting down every transaction—both expenses and income—on a daily basis. Individuals typically use a dedicated notebook or ledger for this purpose, categorizing each entry to facilitate easier tracking and review. The process might involve outlining columns for dates, descriptions, amounts, and additional notes to provide context for each entry.

Benefits:

Mindfulness and Intentionality: Engaging physically with pen and paper to note down transactions encourages a deeper connection with one's financial habits, fostering a greater awareness of where money is going and coming from.

Customization and Flexibility: This method allows for complete personalization of how financial information is recorded and organized. Users can tailor their tracking systems to their specific needs, preferences, and financial goals without being constrained by the structure of digital tools.

Accessibility and Reliability: Pen and paper do not require access to technology, making this method universally accessible and free from technical glitches or data breaches. It offers a tangible, always-available means to record and access financial information.

Educational Value: For those new to budgeting, the manual process of recording and calculating can provide invaluable insights into personal finance management, teaching the fundamental principles of accounting and financial discipline.

Limitations:

Efficiency and Time: Manual entry is inherently time-consuming, especially as the volume of transactions increases. It demands a daily commitment and can become burdensome over time, particularly for busy individuals or those with complex financial portfolios.

Error Susceptibility: Human error in calculations or omissions can lead to inaccuracies in financial tracking, potentially skewing the understanding of one's financial situation. Unlike digital tools, there is no automated error-checking or balance tallying.

Analysis and Reporting: The pen and paper method offers limited capabilities for analyzing financial data. Generating reports or insights requires additional manual effort to collate and interpret the data, and there is no straightforward way to visualize trends or generate predictive insights.

Scalability and Backup: As financial transactions become more complex or voluminous, the pen and paper method can become unwieldy and harder to maintain. Moreover, physical records are vulnerable to loss, damage, or degradation over time, and duplicating these records for backup purposes is labor-intensive.

In conclusion, while the pen and paper method is imbued with the virtues of simplicity and tactile engagement, its effectiveness is bounded by the demands of manual data management and analysis. It suits individuals who prefer a tangible, straightforward approach to budgeting and those who are just beginning to cultivate financial discipline. However, for more intricate financial tracking and analysis, more sophisticated tools may be warranted.

2. Spreadsheets

- **Technique:** Utilizing software like Microsoft Excel or Google Sheets to create detailed budgets and track finances.
- **Benefits:** Offers flexibility in designing your tracking system. Formulas can automate calculations, and charts can visualize financial trends.
- **Limitations:** Requires a basic understanding of spreadsheet software. Initial setup and regular updates can be time-intensive.

Diving into the digital realm, spreadsheets stand as a powerful ally in the quest for financial clarity and control. These dynamic tools, exemplified by stalwarts like Microsoft Excel or Google Sheets, provide a canvas where your financial data can be meticulously organized, analyzed, and transformed into actionable insights. Let's explore this digital technique, understanding how it blends precision with adaptability to enhance your financial management practices.

Crafting Your Financial Dashboard

Imagine opening your spreadsheet to see a comprehensive dashboard of your financial life: income streams, expenses, savings, and investments, all neatly organized and updated. With spreadsheets, you're the architect of your financial tracking system, designing it to reflect your unique circumstances and goals. You can create categories that resonate with your spending habits, set up formulas to track your progress towards savings goals, or visualize cash flows to spot trends and patterns.

The Power of Automation and Visualization

One of the standout features of using spreadsheets is the ability to automate repetitive calculations, freeing you from the drudgery of manual computation. Formulas can instantly update your financial status, calculate percentages of income saved or spent, or forecast future trends based on historical data. Moreover, the integration of charts and graphs transforms your data into visual narratives, making it easier to grasp your financial standing and progress at a glance.

Navigating the Learning Curve

While the benefits are compelling, it's essential to acknowledge the learning curve associated with spreadsheet software. Mastery of these tools requires time and practice, and the initial setup of your financial tracking system can be particularly labor-intensive. However, once established, the spreadsheet becomes a highly efficient tool, streamlining your financial tracking and analysis processes.

For those willing to invest the time to learn and tailor their spreadsheet system, the rewards can be significant. Not only do you gain a detailed understanding of your financial landscape, but you also equip yourself with the knowledge and skills to adapt and fine-tune your financial strategy as your life and goals evolve.

In conclusion, spreadsheets offer a potent blend of flexibility, precision, and depth, making them an invaluable resource for those committed to taking an active, informed role in managing their finances. By leveraging these tools to their full potential, you can transform raw numbers into meaningful insights, guiding your financial decisions and strategies with clarity and confidence.

Technique:

Spreadsheets, facilitated by software applications such as Microsoft Excel or Google Sheets, represent a significant advancement in financial tracking and budgeting methodologies. Users can design and implement detailed, customized budgeting templates or financial models that align with their specific financial tracking requirements. This technique involves entering financial data into cells, organizing it into columns and rows to delineate categories like dates, descriptions, amounts, and categories. Users can leverage formulas to perform automatic calculations, such as summing monthly expenses, calculating averages, or comparing income against outlays.

Benefits:

Automated Calculations: One of the most compelling advantages of spreadsheets is their ability to automate complex calculations, reducing manual computation errors and saving time. Functions and formulas can instantly update financial totals or averages as new data is entered.

Customization and Scalability: Spreadsheets offer vast customization options, allowing users to tailor their financial tracking systems to their precise needs. Users can create various tabs for different financial aspects, such as daily expenses, monthly budgets, or annual summaries, and easily scale these as their financial data grows.

Data Visualization: With built-in tools for creating graphs and charts, spreadsheets enable users to visualize their financial data, highlighting trends, patterns, and anomalies that might not be evident from raw numbers alone. This can aid in better understanding financial habits and making informed decisions.

Accessibility and Portability: Many spreadsheet programs offer cloud-based options, enabling users to access their financial data from any device with internet connectivity. This also facilitates easy sharing and collaboration on financial planning or review.

Limitations:

Learning Curve: While basic spreadsheet functions are accessible to many, utilizing advanced features for more sophisticated financial tracking requires a certain level of proficiency with the software. Users unfamiliar with spreadsheet functionalities may need to invest time in learning to use them effectively.

Initial Setup Time: Designing a personalized financial tracking system in a spreadsheet can be time-consuming, particularly if the user aims for a detailed and comprehensive setup. This initial time investment is necessary to ensure the system's effectiveness and user-friendliness.

Manual Data Entry: Despite automation in calculations, spreadsheets still require manual entry of financial data. This process can be tedious and time-consuming, especially for users with extensive or complex financial transactions.

Error Risk: While spreadsheets reduce calculation errors, they are still susceptible to input errors or formula mistakes. An incorrect formula or data entry can propagate errors throughout the document, potentially leading to misinformed financial decisions.

In summary, spreadsheets are a powerful tool for financial tracking and budgeting, offering a blend of flexibility, automation, and visualization capabilities. They are well-suited for individuals and businesses seeking an adaptable and detailed approach to managing their finances. However, maximizing the benefits of spreadsheets requires a foundational understanding of the software and a commitment to meticulous data management.

Digital Tools

1. Budgeting Apps

- **Examples:** Mint, You Need A Budget (YNAB), and PocketGuard.
- **Benefits:** These apps automate the process of tracking expenses and income by linking directly to your bank accounts and credit cards. They categorize transactions, offer insights into spending habits, and provide alerts for budget limits or unusual activity.
- **Limitations:** Privacy and security concerns with linking financial accounts. Some apps require a subscription fee.

In the digital age, budgeting apps have emerged as indispensable allies for those seeking to demystify and master their financial landscapes. Envision having a personal financial advisor in your pocket, one that diligently monitors your finances, offering real-time insights and guidance. This is the essence of what apps like Mint, You Need A Budget (YNAB), and PocketGuard offer. Let's delve deeper into how these digital tools can transform your approach to budgeting and financial management.

Seamless Financial Tracking at Your Fingertips

Imagine every transaction you make—be it your morning coffee or a monthly utility bill—being automatically logged, categorized, and analyzed. Budgeting apps offer this seamless tracking, pulling data directly from your bank accounts and credit cards to provide a comprehensive view of your financial activity. No more sifting through bank statements or manually inputting data; these apps do the heavy lifting for you.

Beyond mere tracking, these tools dissect your spending patterns, highlighting areas where your dollars flow most freely and identifying opportunities for savings. They empower you to set budgetary limits for different categories, nudging you when you're nearing these thresholds and fostering a more disciplined approach to spending.

Insights and Alerts to Keep You on Track

The true power of these apps lies in their ability to offer tailored insights and alerts. They learn from your spending behaviors, offering personalized recommendations to optimize your financial health. Whether it's suggesting a tighter budget for dining out or alerting you to a subscription you rarely use, these apps are proactive partners in your financial well-being.

Moreover, the visual representations of your financial data—through graphs and charts—offer a clear, intuitive understanding of where your money is going, making it easier to identify trends and adjust your spending habits accordingly.

Navigating Privacy and Security Considerations

While the benefits are compelling, it's crucial to approach these tools with an awareness of privacy and security implications. Linking your financial accounts to a third-party app inherently involves a degree of risk. It's essential to conduct thorough research, choosing apps with robust security measures and transparent privacy policies to safeguard your financial information.

Additionally, while many budgeting apps offer free versions, some of the more advanced features might require a subscription. It's important to weigh the cost against the potential benefits, ensuring that the app provides value commensurate with its price.

In essence, budgeting apps represent a confluence of convenience and technology, offering a dynamic and interactive approach to financial management. By harnessing these tools, you can gain a deeper understanding of your financial habits, make informed decisions, and navigate your financial journey with greater confidence and control. Whether you're looking to tighten your spending, save for a future goal, or simply gain clearer visibility into your finances, these apps offer a pathway to enhanced financial literacy and empowerment.

Examples:

Budgeting applications such as Mint, You Need A Budget (YNAB), and PocketGuard represent the forefront of personal finance technology, offering users a comprehensive and user-friendly platform for managing their finances. These apps integrate advanced features and algorithms to provide a holistic view of the user's financial landscape.

Benefits:

Automated Financial Tracking: By connecting directly to your bank accounts and credit cards, these apps automatically import and categorize transactions, significantly reducing the manual effort required in tracking spending and income. This automation ensures that all transactions are accounted for without the need for manual entry.

Real-Time Insights and Notifications: Budgeting apps analyze your financial data to offer insights into your spending habits, helping you identify areas where you can cut back. They also provide real-time alerts for when you approach or exceed budget limits, as well as notifications for unusual account activity, which can be crucial for fraud detection.

Goal Setting and Progress Tracking: Many budgeting apps allow users to set financial goals, such as saving for a vacation or paying off debt, and track their progress over time. This feature can be incredibly motivating and can help users stay committed to their financial objectives.

Accessible and User-Friendly: With intuitive interfaces and mobile access, budgeting apps offer the convenience of managing your finances on the go. Users can check their budgets, track their spending, or review their financial goals anytime, anywhere.

Limitations:

Privacy and Security Concerns: Linking personal financial accounts with these apps raises valid concerns regarding data privacy and security. While most reputable apps employ robust security measures, the risk of data breaches cannot be entirely eliminated, making some users hesitant to use these services.

Subscription Fees: Some budgeting apps require a monthly or annual subscription fee, which can be a deterrent for users looking for free financial tools. While many apps offer basic features for free, premium features that provide more detailed analyses or personalized advice typically come at a cost.

Accuracy of Transaction Categorization: While these apps are designed to automatically categorize transactions, they may not always do so accurately. Users may need to periodically review and correct categorizations to ensure their budget reflects their actual spending habits accurately.

Dependence on Technology: Relying solely on a budgeting app can create a dependency on technology, potentially leaving users at a disadvantage if the service is disrupted or if they lose access to their device. Additionally, over-reliance on automated tools may hinder the development of personal financial literacy and discipline.

In conclusion, budgeting apps offer a powerful and convenient solution for personal finance management, especially for those looking to streamline their budgeting process and gain deeper insights into their financial habits. However, users should carefully consider the privacy, security, and cost implications before choosing an app and remain actively involved in the budgeting process to ensure the most accurate and beneficial outcomes.

2. Personal Finance Software

- **Examples:** Quicken and Personal Capital.
- **Benefits:** More comprehensive than most apps, offering features for investment tracking, retirement planning, and wealth management, in addition to budgeting and expense tracking.
- **Limitations:** Often comes with a higher cost. May offer more features than a typical user needs, leading to complexity.

Examples:

Quicken and Personal Capital are exemplary of advanced personal finance software, providing a robust suite of tools for comprehensive financial management. These platforms cater to a wide range of financial needs, extending well beyond basic budgeting to include investment analysis, retirement planning, and wealth management.

Benefits:

All-in-One Financial Management: This software consolidates various financial tasks into a single platform, offering users a holistic view of their finances. Users can track their spending, manage investments, plan for retirement, and even assess their overall net worth, all within the same ecosystem.

Investment Tracking and Analysis: Unlike simpler budgeting apps, personal finance software often includes sophisticated tools for tracking and analyzing investments. Users can monitor their portfolios, assess asset allocations, and evaluate the performance of individual investments against market benchmarks.

Retirement and Wealth Management: These platforms provide features to help users plan for long-term financial goals, such as retirement. Tools may include retirement calculators, wealth forecasting, and scenarios to test different saving and investment strategies, giving users insights into how their choices today affect their future financial health.

Detailed Reporting and Insights: Personal finance software typically offers comprehensive reporting capabilities, allowing users to generate detailed analyses of their spending habits, investment performance, and financial progress over time. These insights can inform more strategic financial decisions.

Limitations:

Cost: Advanced personal finance software like Quicken and Personal Capital often comes with subscription fees or charges for premium features. While the investment can be worthwhile for the functionality provided, the cost may be prohibitive for users seeking only basic budgeting tools.

Complexity: With an extensive array of features, personal finance software can be overwhelming, particularly for users who are new to financial management or only interested in basic budgeting and tracking. The learning curve can be steep, and users may find themselves navigating through an array of options they seldom use.

Over-Reliance on Software: There's a risk that users may become overly reliant on the software to manage their finances, potentially neglecting to develop their own understanding and intuition about their financial health and decision-making.

Data Privacy and Security: As with any digital financial tool, there is a risk associated with entrusting sensitive financial information to a software platform. Users must weigh the benefits of comprehensive financial management against the potential risks of data breaches or unauthorized access.

In conclusion, personal finance software like Quicken and Personal Capital offers an extensive suite of tools for those looking to take a deep dive into their financial management. While the benefits of detailed analysis, comprehensive tracking, and strategic planning features are significant, users should consider the cost, complexity, and privacy implications before integrating such software into their financial routine.

Innovative Techniques

1. The Envelope System

- **Technique:** Allocating cash for various spending categories into physical envelopes each month. Once an envelope is empty, spending in that category stops.
- **Benefits:** Provides a tangible way to manage spending and stick to a budget. Helps prevent overspending.
- **Limitations:** Not suitable for all expenses, especially online purchases or bills. Carrying large amounts of cash can be risky.

The Envelope System harks back to a simpler era, evoking a sense of nostalgia and tactile interaction with one's finances. This method, rooted in the physical allocation of cash into designated envelopes, transforms the abstract concept of budgeting into a vivid, hands-on experience. Let's explore how this venerable technique can serve as a cornerstone for disciplined spending and financial mindfulness in our increasingly digital world.

Embracing the Tangibility of Money

Imagine sitting down at the beginning of each month, a stack of cash before you, ready to be distributed into a series of labeled envelopes—groceries, entertainment, utilities, and so forth. Each envelope represents a finite resource, a boundary not to be crossed. This ritualistic act of dividing your money instills a deep awareness of your financial limits and priorities.

The beauty of the Envelope System lies in its simplicity and immediacy. There's no need to log into an account or swipe a card to understand your financial status. A quick glance into an envelope reveals the truth of your remaining budget, fostering a mindful relationship with your spending.

Cultivating Financial Discipline

The Envelope System excels in its ability to curb impulsive spending. When the envelope for dining out is empty, the message is clear: no more restaurant meals until the next cycle. This clear-cut rule eliminates the gray areas and mental gymnastics often associated with budgeting, reinforcing discipline and helping to build enduring financial habits.

Moreover, the act of parting with physical cash can evoke a stronger emotional response than swiping a card, enhancing your awareness of spending decisions and their impact on your financial well-being.

Navigating the System's Limitations

While the Envelope System offers distinct advantages, it's important to recognize its limitations in our modern financial landscape. In an age where online transactions and electronic payments are ubiquitous, relying solely on cash can be impractical or even impossible for certain expenses.

Additionally, the security concern of carrying or storing substantial sums of cash cannot be overlooked. It introduces risks of loss or theft, alongside the practical inconveniences associated with managing physical currency.

Integrating the Envelope System in Today's World

For those drawn to the tactile and straightforward nature of the Envelope System but wary of its limitations, a hybrid approach might offer a solution. Consider using the system for variable, discretionary categories like groceries and entertainment, while maintaining digital payments for fixed expenses like rent and utilities.

By adapting the Envelope System to fit within the context of modern financial practices, you can harness its benefits—tangible budgeting and enhanced spending awareness—without forgoing the convenience and security of digital transactions. In this way, the system can serve as a valuable tool in your financial toolkit, offering a grounding, hands-on complement to the array of digital resources at your disposal.

2. Zero-Based Budgeting

- **Technique:** Allocating every dollar of income to specific expenses, savings, and investments, so your income minus your expenditures equals zero.
- **Benefits:** Ensures every dollar is purposefully spent or saved. Can lead to more intentional financial decisions.
- **Limitations:** Requires meticulous planning and can be time-consuming. May be challenging to predict every expense.

The technique you're referring to is known as zero-based budgeting, a method that empowers you to give every dollar a specific job, ensuring that your income is fully accounted for across your expenses, savings, and investments. This approach fosters a proactive stance toward financial management, encouraging you to engage deeply with your spending habits and financial priorities. Let's delve into how this method can transform your relationship with money and highlight the steps to navigate its challenges effectively.

Crafting a Purpose for Every Dollar

Visualize your monthly income as a team of employees, each with a specific role to contribute to your financial well-being. Some are tasked with handling the essentials like rent and groceries, while others are assigned to future projects like savings or investments. This methodical allocation ensures that each dollar is working towards your broader financial objectives, leaving no room for aimless spending.

The beauty of zero-based budgeting lies in its emphasis on intentionality. It prompts you to scrutinize every financial commitment, asking whether it aligns with your goals and values. This level of engagement can lead to more mindful spending, greater savings rates, and a clearer path to achieving your financial aspirations.

Navigating the Challenges of Zero-Based Budgeting

Despite its merits, zero-based budgeting demands diligence and adaptability. The process of categorizing every expense and income source can be intricate, especially when unexpected costs arise. However, with a few strategic practices, you can harness the full potential of this budgeting method:

Regular Review and Adjustment: Your financial landscape is dynamic, so your budget should be too. Regularly revisiting your budget to adjust for unforeseen expenses or changes in income ensures that your allocations remain accurate and purposeful.

Buffer Categories: While aiming for zero at the end of each month is the goal, creating buffer categories within your budget can provide flexibility and peace of mind. Allocating funds for unexpected expenses ensures that you're prepared for life's surprises without derailing your financial plan.

Leveraging Technology: While zero-based budgeting can be executed manually, numerous digital tools and apps are designed to streamline the process. These platforms can automate much of the legwork involved in tracking and categorizing transactions, allowing you to focus on the strategic aspects of your financial planning.

In essence, zero-based budgeting is not just a method but a mindset—one that champions deliberate and informed financial choices. By embracing this approach, you can elevate your financial awareness, optimize your resource allocation, and progress confidently toward your economic goals. While it may require a commitment to meticulous planning and ongoing adjustment, the clarity and control it offers can significantly enhance your financial health and peace of mind.

Best Practices for Effective Tracking

- **Consistency**: Regularly update your tracking system, ideally daily or weekly, to maintain an accurate picture of your finances.
- **Review and Reflect**: Periodically review your recorded expenses and income to identify trends, adjust your budget, and set financial goals.
- **Simplify Where Possible**: Streamline the tracking process by consolidating accounts, automating payments, and minimizing unnecessary expenses.
- **Educate and Adapt**: Stay informed about new tools, techniques, and financial management practices. Be willing to adapt your approach as your financial situation and technology evolve.

By employing these tools and techniques, you can achieve greater control over your financial life, making informed decisions that pave the way to financial freedom and stability. Remember, the best system is the one that works for you, fitting seamlessly into your lifestyle while helping you reach your financial goals.

- Case studies illustrating successful budgeting strategies.

To illuminate the path toward financial mastery through effective budgeting, let's explore several case studies that exemplify successful budgeting strategies. These real-life examples highlight the transformative power of disciplined financial planning and adaptability, providing valuable insights and inspiration for anyone looking to enhance their financial well-being.

Case Study 1: The Zero-Based Budget Journey

Sarah, a dedicated teacher, found her financial situation paradoxical—despite receiving a regular income, she felt trapped in a cycle of living paycheck to paycheck, her dreams of homeownership and a secure retirement seemingly out of reach. The realization that her financial habits were not aligning with her long-term goals sparked a determination for change. The challenge was not only to break free from the immediate constraints of her financial circumstances but to lay a sustainable foundation for her future aspirations.

Detailed Strategy Implementation

Sarah's choice of the zero-based budgeting system was deliberate. This methodology required her to account for every dollar earned, assigning it a specific purpose—be it expenses, savings, or debt repayment. This approach necessitated a meticulous review of her financial inflows and outflows, compelling her to differentiate between wants and needs.

The first step involved a thorough analysis of her monthly income versus her expenditures. Sarah categorized her expenses, identifying fixed costs (such as rent and utilities) and variable costs (including groceries, entertainment, and personal spending). She then scrutinized her spending patterns, seeking areas where adjustments could yield savings without significantly impacting her quality of life.

In-Depth Results

Debt Reduction: The zero-based budgeting strategy illuminated the stark reality of how interest from her $10,000 credit card debt was compounding her financial strain. By reallocating funds from less critical spending categories to debt repayment, Sarah was able to systematically eliminate this burden within a year. This achievement not only freed up additional resources for savings and investment but also lifted a significant emotional weight, enhancing her financial and personal well-being.

Savings Increase: The establishment of a $5,000 emergency fund marked a pivotal moment in Sarah's financial journey, providing her with a buffer against unexpected expenses and reducing her reliance on credit. Additionally, her increased contributions towards her retirement account reflected a forward-looking approach, securing her vision of a comfortable and dignified retirement.

Financial Awareness: The process of zero-based budgeting fostered a heightened awareness of her spending habits. Sarah became adept at distinguishing between immediate gratifications and investments in her future happiness and security. This mindfulness translated into more deliberate and fulfilling spending decisions, aligning her daily actions with her long-term aspirations.

Expanded Key Takeaways

Zero-based budgeting emerged as more than a mere financial management tool for Sarah; it became a catalyst for profound personal growth and empowerment. This journey underscored several critical insights:

- **Intentionality in Spending:** The practice of assigning every dollar a purpose facilitated a shift from passive to intentional spending, ensuring that Sarah's financial resources were being utilized in ways that directly contributed to her life goals.
- **Adaptability and Resilience:** The discipline required to adhere to a zero-based budget cultivated adaptability and resilience, qualities that extended beyond financial management to inform Sarah's personal and professional life decisions.
- **Empowerment through Financial Literacy:** Engaging deeply with her finances elevated Sarah's financial literacy, empowering her to make informed decisions and advocate for her financial interests.
- **The Psychological Benefits of Financial Control:** Achieving control over her financial situation had a liberating effect, reducing stress, enhancing her sense of security, and increasing her overall life satisfaction.

Sarah's story illustrates that the journey to financial freedom is as much about personal transformation as it is about financial acumen. Through zero-based budgeting, she not only navigated her way out of financial precarity but also charted a course towards a future rich with possibility and promise.

Case Study 2: Embracing Technology for Financial Clarity

Mark, despite his tech-savvy background as a software developer, found himself ensnared in a cycle of impulsive purchases that led to considerable financial stress. This paradoxical situation, where his proficiency in technology did not extend to his personal financial management, underscored the need for a change. His aspirations for financial stability and achieving personal goals, such as vacations and investment in a diversified portfolio, seemed distant amidst his current financial practices.

Detailed Strategy Implementation

Mark's decision to embrace technology as a solution to his financial management challenges marked a turning point. After researching various budgeting tools, he selected a budgeting app known for its intuitive interface, robust security measures, and comprehensive financial management features. This app's ability to sync with his bank accounts and credit cards was pivotal, automating the tracking and categorization of his transactions, which provided him with real-time insights into his spending patterns.

In-Depth Results

Budget Compliance: The transition to using a budgeting app brought immediate benefits. The real-time notifications and alerts for approaching budget limits played a crucial role in curbing his discretionary spending. By reducing such spending by 30%, Mark was not only able to adhere to his budget more effectively but also redirect funds towards more meaningful financial goals.

Savings Goals Met: The clarity and control gained through the app enabled Mark to systematically save for a vacation, a goal that previously seemed unattainable due to his impulsive spending habits. Furthermore, the app's insights into his financial habits allowed him to identify opportunities to invest, leading to the creation of a diversified investment portfolio. This proactive approach to savings and investment marked a significant shift towards long-term financial planning and wealth building.

Financial Confidence: Perhaps the most transformative outcome for Mark was the increase in his financial confidence. The visibility into his financial health provided by the app, coupled with the empowerment of making informed decisions, significantly reduced his financial stress. This newfound confidence was not just about managing his finances more effectively but also about envisioning and working towards a future where his financial goals were within reach.

Expanded Key Takeaways

Mark's experience underscores the profound impact technology can have on personal finance management. Key insights from his journey include:

- **Empowerment Through Automation:** The automation of tracking and categorizing transactions can significantly reduce the manual effort required for budgeting, making it easier to maintain financial discipline.
- **Real-Time Insights for Proactive Management:** Access to real-time financial data enables individuals to make proactive adjustments to their spending and saving habits, fostering a more dynamic and responsive approach to financial management.
- **Behavioral Change Through Visibility:** The increased visibility into financial habits can lead to significant behavioral changes, shifting from impulsive spending to intentional financial planning.
- **Enhanced Financial Planning and Goal Achievement:** Technology facilitates more than just budget compliance; it enables individuals to plan for the future with greater precision, setting and achieving goals that were previously hindered by financial mismanagement.

Mark's story vividly illustrates that with the right technological tools, individuals can transform their financial management practices, turning aspirations into achievements. The integration of technology into personal finance management not only simplifies the process but also opens up new possibilities for achieving financial clarity, stability, and growth.

Case Study 3: The Power of the Envelope System

Emily and Alex, both in their early 40s, faced a common predicament that plagues many families: their expenses were steadily rising, outpacing their income growth. This financial imbalance threatened their ability to save for crucial long-term goals, notably their children's education. Despite having a stable household income, the couple found it increasingly difficult to manage their spending, particularly in categories such as groceries, entertainment, and personal expenditures. The realization that their financial habits were jeopardizing their children's future educational opportunities served as a wake-up call.

Detailed Strategy Implementation

In search of a practical solution, Emily and Alex turned to the envelope system, a budgeting technique renowned for its simplicity and effectiveness in controlling variable expenses. They began by identifying major discretionary spending categories and allocated a fixed amount of cash for each, placing the money in labeled envelopes.

- Groceries
- Entertainment
- Personal Spending
- Miscellaneous

Each month, they withdrew a predetermined amount of cash to fill these envelopes, committing to spend only the cash allocated for each category.

In-Depth Results

Spending Discipline: The tactile nature of handling physical cash and the finite amount available in each envelope made Emily and Alex acutely aware of their spending. This awareness led to a significant 25% reduction in their grocery and entertainment expenses as they became more judicious in their purchasing decisions, prioritizing needs over wants.

Education Savings: The savings generated from their disciplined spending were directly channeled into a dedicated college savings plan for their children. This strategic reallocation of funds not only put their children's education fund on a solid footing but also imparted a sense of accomplishment and peace of mind to Emily and Alex, knowing they were securing their children's future.

Family Engagement: Perhaps one of the most unexpected and rewarding outcomes of adopting the envelope system was its impact on family engagement. The process of dividing money into envelopes became a monthly family activity, involving their children in discussions about budgeting and financial priorities. This inclusion helped cultivate a sense of financial literacy and responsibility among their children, reinforcing the value of money and the importance of budgeting.

Expanded Key Takeaways

The journey of Emily and Alex with the envelope system highlights several critical insights into the nature of financial management within a family context:

- **Tangible Interaction with Money:** The physical act of handling cash provides a concrete sense of spending and limits, which can be more effective in controlling expenditures compared to the abstract nature of digital transactions.
- **Prioritization and Sacrifice:** The envelope system forces individuals to confront their spending habits directly, necessitating prioritization and, at times, sacrifice, which are essential skills for sound financial management.
- **Family Involvement in Financial Planning:** Engaging the whole family in the budgeting process promotes a culture of financial responsibility and collective goal-setting, enriching the family's financial health and cohesion.
- **Adaptability of Traditional Methods:** Despite the rise of digital budgeting tools, traditional methods like the envelope system remain highly effective for many families, demonstrating the adaptability of budgeting strategies to diverse needs and preferences.

Emily and Alex's experience underscores the power of the envelope system to not only curb overspending but also to foster a deeper understanding and engagement with personal finance. Their story is a testament to the fact that sometimes, returning to basics can provide the most profound solutions to modern-day financial challenges.

5. Savings and Emergency Funds

- The importance of saving and how to calculate an adequate emergency fund.

The importance of saving, particularly for an emergency fund, cannot be overstated in the realm of personal finance. An emergency fund acts as a financial buffer, safeguarding against unexpected events such as medical emergencies, sudden job loss, or urgent home repairs. This fund is the cornerstone of financial stability, providing peace of mind and preventing the need to incur debt in times of crisis. Here, we explore the significance of savings and offer guidance on calculating an adequate emergency fund.

The Importance of Saving

1. **Financial Security:** Savings offer a safety net that can help you navigate through life's uncertainties without jeopardizing your financial stability.

2. **Stress Reduction:** Knowing you have financial reserves in the event of an emergency can significantly reduce stress and anxiety associated with unforeseen financial demands.

3. **Debt Avoidance:** With an emergency fund in place, you're less likely to rely on credit cards or loans during a financial crunch, thereby avoiding high-interest debt.

4. **Financial Freedom:** Savings contribute to your overall financial freedom, providing the flexibility to make choices that align with your long-term goals and values, such as career changes, travel, or early retirement.

Imagine you're on a serene boat journey, navigating through the calm waters of your financial life. Everything seems smooth, with the sun shining brightly overhead. However, as with any voyage, there's always the possibility of a sudden storm or an unexpected obstacle lurking beneath the surface. This is where your emergency fund comes into play, serving as your lifeboat, ready to keep you afloat during turbulent financial times.

Now, let's talk about how you can calculate this essential financial safety net, ensuring it's robust enough to weather any storm. Picture sitting down at your favorite spot in your home, a place where you feel at ease and inspired. You start to reflect on your monthly expenses, the non-negotiables that you need to live your life—shelter, food, utilities, and the like. This contemplation gives you a clear understanding of what it truly costs to maintain your lifestyle each month.

Next, consider the nature of your income. Is it steady and predictable, or does it ebb and flow like the tide? If you're in a field where the waves of income are less consistent, your emergency fund might need to be a bit more substantial, like a sturdier boat built to withstand rougher seas.

Then, think about those who are sailing with you—your family. If you're responsible for others, your lifeboat needs to be larger, ensuring it can keep everyone safe and secure, not just yourself.

Now, it's about finding your own comfort level. Some sailors are content with a smaller vessel, confident in their ability to navigate back to calm waters swiftly. Others may prefer a larger, more robust craft, offering additional security and peace of mind. Whether it's three months' worth of expenses or six, the key is to choose a size that allows you to sleep soundly at night, knowing you're well-prepared for any unexpected events.

Begin building your lifeboat piece by piece, plank by plank. You don't need to construct it all at once. Regular, consistent contributions can gradually build up your emergency fund, turning it into a sturdy vessel that's ready when you need it.

And just like any seasoned sailor who knows the importance of maintaining their boat, revisit your emergency fund regularly. Life changes—perhaps your expenses grow, or your family expands—and your lifeboat needs to adapt accordingly.

By considering your emergency fund in this personalized, narrative-driven way, you're not just crunching numbers; you're crafting a story of preparedness and resilience. It's about setting the stage for a future where financial surprises, while they may still be unwelcome, don't have the power to capsize your boat. With each dollar saved, you're reinforcing your lifeboat, ensuring that when the seas of life get choppy, you're ready to weather the storm and emerge even stronger on the other side.

Calculating an Adequate Emergency Fund

The size of an adequate emergency fund can vary based on individual circumstances, including job stability, the presence of dependents, and lifestyle. However, a general guideline is to save enough to cover 3 to 6 months' worth of living expenses. Here's how to calculate it:

1. List Monthly Expenses: Start by listing your essential monthly expenses, including housing (rent or mortgage), utilities, groceries, insurance premiums, transportation, and any other non-negotiable costs.

2. Determine Your Monthly Expense Total: Add up these essential expenses to find your total monthly expenditure. This figure represents the minimum amount you need to get by each month without additional spending on non-essentials.

3. **Calculate Your Emergency Fund Target**: Multiply your total monthly expenses by the number of months you aim to cover. For many, this will be between 3 and 6 months. If you're in a dual-income household with stable jobs, you might lean towards the lower end. However, if you're self-employed or in a single-income household, aiming for the higher end or even beyond may be prudent.

Picture yourself in a cozy, quiet space, with all the necessary tools at hand—a notepad, a calculator, perhaps a warm cup of tea. You're about to embark on a thoughtful journey, one that will lead you to a place of financial security and peace of mind. This journey involves calculating your emergency fund, a crucial step in fortifying your financial well-being.

Embarking on the Calculation Voyage

First, we dive into the realm of your monthly expenses. Imagine sifting through your bank statements, bills, and receipts, not with anxiety but with the calm focus of a cartographer charting a map. You're delineating the contours of your financial landscape. Itemize those expenses that are your lifelines—housing, food, utilities, and transportation. These are your essentials, the costs you must meet to maintain your daily life.

Now, with your essentials listed, it's time to tally them up, translating your monthly needs into a clear, definitive number. This total is your beacon, guiding you toward how much you'll need to navigate through each month without additional income.

Setting Your Sights on the Target

With your monthly expenditure in hand, you're ready to calculate your emergency fund target. If your financial seas are relatively calm—a stable job and a predictable lifestyle—a three-month buffer might suffice. However, if you're sailing solo with a single income, or if the tides of your industry are more turbulent, setting your sights on a six-month reserve—or even more—would be wise.

Imagine this fund as your financial anchor, offering stability no matter how the economic winds may shift. If you're navigating with a partner, consider how your combined resources and obligations impact your emergency fund needs. And if your voyage includes dependents, your fund must be robust enough to safeguard their well-being too.

Reaching Your Destination

As you piece together this financial puzzle, remember that your emergency fund is a living entity—it grows, adapts, and evolves with you. Periodically revisit your calculations, adjusting for life's inevitable changes, be they new family members, shifts in living costs, or transitions in income.

In crafting this emergency fund, you're not merely crunching numbers; you're laying the foundation for a resilient financial future. Each step in this calculation is a stride toward security, equipping you to face life's uncertainties with confidence and calm. And when you've reached your target, you'll find not just financial stability but also a profound sense of achievement and peace, knowing you're prepared for whatever lies ahead.

Example Calculation:

- Monthly Essential Expenses: $3,000
- Target Duration: 6 months
- Emergency Fund Target: $3,000 x 6 = $18,000

Strategies for Building Your Emergency Fund

1. Start Small: Begin by setting aside a small, manageable amount each month. Even a modest savings contribution can grow over time.

2. Automate Your Savings: Set up automatic transfers from your checking account to your savings account to ensure consistent contributions to your emergency fund.

3. Cut Unnecessary Expenses: Review your spending habits to identify areas where you can cut back and redirect those funds to your emergency fund.

4. Increase Your Income: Consider side hustles, freelance work, or selling unused items to boost your savings rate.

5. Keep It Accessible: Your emergency fund should be easily accessible without incurring penalties or significant losses. High-yield savings accounts are a good option, offering higher interest rates while keeping your funds liquid.

Remember, the goal of an emergency fund is not just to save a specific amount of money but to build a buffer that can help you navigate through life's uncertainties with confidence and stability. Start where you are, and gradually build your fund to achieve the level of security you need to protect yourself and your loved ones.

- Different savings strategies for short-term and long-term goals.

Saving for financial goals requires a tailored approach depending on the timeline and nature of the goals themselves. Differentiating between short-term and long-term saving strategies is crucial for effective financial planning. Here, we explore various techniques tailored to meet both types of financial objectives, ensuring a well-rounded approach to achieving your financial aspirations.

Short-Term Saving Strategies

Short-term financial goals typically span a period of less than five years. These can include saving for a vacation, establishing an emergency fund, or accumulating a down payment for a car.

1. **High-Yield Savings Accounts:** Ideal for short-term goals due to their higher interest rates compared to regular savings accounts, while still offering liquidity and security.

2. **Money Market Accounts:** These accounts often offer higher interest rates than traditional savings accounts and come with check-writing privileges, making them suitable for short-term savings that may need to be accessed quickly.

3. **Certificates of Deposit (CDs):** For goals with a slightly longer horizon, CDs can offer higher interest rates for locking in funds for a predetermined period, such as six months to a few years. Choose a CD term that aligns with your goal timeline to avoid early withdrawal penalties.

4. **Automated Savings Plans:** Automating transfers to a dedicated savings account can help ensure consistent savings contributions without the need to manually set aside money each month.

Long-Term Saving Strategies

Long-term financial goals might include saving for retirement, a child's college education, or purchasing a home. These goals often require more substantial funds and a longer time horizon to achieve.

1. **Retirement Accounts (401(k)s, IRAs):** Taking advantage of retirement accounts can be highly effective for long-term savings, especially with employer matching programs, tax advantages, and the power of compound interest.

2. **Investment Accounts:** Investing in stocks, bonds, mutual funds, or exchange-traded funds (ETFs) can offer higher potential returns than traditional savings methods. A diversified investment portfolio tailored to your risk tolerance can help grow your savings over the long term.

3. **Education Savings Accounts:** Accounts like 529 plans or Coverdell Education Savings Accounts (ESAs) offer tax-advantaged ways to save for education expenses, making them ideal for long-term goals like saving for a child's college tuition.

4. **Real Estate:** For some, investing in real estate can be a viable long-term saving strategy, whether through purchasing property directly or investing in real estate investment trusts (REITs).

Key Considerations for Saving Strategies

Risk Tolerance: Understanding your risk tolerance is crucial, especially for long-term saving strategies that involve investments. Higher-risk options may offer higher returns but can also lead to greater volatility.

Time Horizon: Align your saving strategy with your goal's timeline. Short-term goals require more liquid and less volatile saving methods, while long-term goals can benefit from the higher growth potential of investments.

Diversification: Especially relevant for long-term savings, diversifying your investment portfolio can help manage risk and increase the potential for returns.

Regular Reviews: Regularly review and adjust your saving strategies to ensure they remain aligned with your financial goals and life changes.

By employing specific saving strategies tailored to the nature and timeline of your financial goals, you can effectively navigate the path to achieving both your short-term and long-term aspirations. Remember, the most effective strategy is one that reflects your unique financial situation, goals, and risk tolerance, adapting as your circumstances evolve.

- Overview of savings accounts, money market accounts, and other savings instruments.

To navigate the landscape of personal finance effectively, understanding the various savings instruments available is paramount. Savings accounts, money market accounts, and other investment vehicles each offer unique benefits and limitations. This overview will provide clarity on these options, helping you make informed decisions aligned with your financial goals.

Savings Accounts

Description: A savings account is a deposit account held at a bank or other financial institution that provides a modest interest rate.

Benefits:

- **Liquidity:** Funds are relatively easy to access, though transfers may sometimes be limited.
- **Security:** Savings accounts are insured up to $250,000 per depositor, per insured bank, by the Federal Deposit Insurance Corporation (FDIC) in the US or by similar insurance schemes in other countries.
- **Low Risk:** There is minimal risk of losing the money deposited in these accounts.

Limitations:

- **Lower Interest Rates:** Compared to other savings or investment options, traditional savings accounts often offer lower interest rates.
- **Minimum Balance Requirements:** Some accounts may require a minimum balance to maintain the account or to earn the advertised interest rate.

Imagine walking into a serene, secure financial sanctuary, where your hard-earned money isn't just stored—it's nurtured. This is the essence of what a savings account offers. As you consider the path of your financial journey, understanding the pivotal role of a savings account can illuminate its value in your financial landscape.

The Haven of Liquidity and Security

Think of a savings account as a tranquil pool of water, readily accessible and reassuringly stable. The liquidity it offers means you can draw from this pool whenever necessary, whether for unexpected expenses or planned purchases. While there might be a few ripples—like transfer limits—the core principle is that your funds remain within easy reach, offering a blend of convenience and flexibility.

Now, let's consider the security aspect. In a world rife with uncertainties, a savings account provides a reassuring embrace of safety. In the US, for example, the FDIC insures your deposits up to $250,000, serving as a robust financial life vest that ensures your funds stay afloat even if the bank faces turbulence. This insurance acts as a powerful shield, guarding your financial well-being and offering peace of mind.

Navigating the Calm Waters of Low Risk

In the realm of financial instruments, a savings account is akin to a gentle stream, offering a steady, if modest, flow. The risk associated with these accounts is minimal, making them an ideal reservoir for your funds. You won't encounter the volatile currents found in higher-risk investments, ensuring that your principal amount remains intact and secure.

Contemplating the Trade-Offs

However, every sanctuary has its constraints. The tranquility of a savings account comes with the trade-off of relatively lower interest rates compared to other vehicles like stocks or bonds. It's the price of peace and security, a consideration to weigh as you allocate your financial resources.

Moreover, some savings accounts come with minimum balance requirements, a threshold you must maintain to either keep the account active or qualify for the interest earnings. It's akin to ensuring your pool has enough water to serve its purpose, a factor that requires attention and planning.

Crafting Your Financial Mosaic

Incorporating a savings account into your financial portfolio is like adding a serene blue to your mosaic, offering balance and harmony amidst more vibrant hues. It's a fundamental component that complements your riskier investments, providing a stable foundation upon which to build your financial dreams.

In conclusion, while a savings account may not offer the thrill of high returns, its value lies in its reliability and security. It's a testament to the power of steady growth and the peace of mind that comes from knowing your funds are safe and accessible.

As you chart your financial course, consider how this tranquil financial haven can play a role in achieving your broader monetary goals, ensuring that your journey is both prosperous and serene.

Money Market Accounts (MMAs)

Description: Money market accounts are interest-bearing accounts that typically offer higher interest rates than traditional savings accounts, along with check-writing privileges.

Benefits:

- **Higher Interest Rates:** MMAs often offer higher yields compared to regular savings accounts.
- **Check-Writing and Debit Card Access:** These accounts may provide more flexibility in accessing funds.
- **Safety:** Like savings accounts, MMAs are FDIC-insured up to the legal limit.

Limitations:

- **Minimum Balance Requirements:** Higher minimum balances might be required to open an account or to qualify for the best interest rates.
- **Limited Transactions:** Federal regulations may limit the number of certain types of transactions.

Venture with me into the realm of Money Market Accounts (MMAs), a financial instrument that blends the benefits of savings and checking accounts, offering an attractive middle ground for those seeking both growth and accessibility in their financial assets. As we unpack the characteristics of MMAs, envision a financial vessel that not only harbors your funds safely but also nurtures them with favorable winds of higher interest rates.

Sailing Towards Higher Yields

MMAs are like favorable trade winds in the world of finance, propelling your savings forward with higher interest rates compared to traditional savings accounts. This enhanced growth potential means your money doesn't just sit idly; it actively works for you, accumulating wealth over time. It's akin to finding a more fruitful terrain, where every dollar planted has the potential to sprout with greater vigor.

Navigating with Flexibility

Now, imagine you're at the helm of your financial ship with an MMA, equipped not just with a robust sail (the interest-bearing feature) but also with versatile tools at your disposal—check-writing privileges and debit card access. This flexibility allows you to navigate your daily financial waters with ease, whether it's handling an unexpected expense or managing regular transactions, all the while your funds continue to grow in this fertile account.

Anchoring in Safety

The safety of MMAs is paramount, akin to a sturdy anchor that secures your financial vessel in turbulent seas. These accounts are protected by the FDIC up to the legal limit, offering you a haven of security where your capital is shielded from the storms of economic uncertainty. It's a reassurance that, regardless of the financial weather, your resources remain safeguarded, providing a stable base for your financial endeavors.

Heeding the Navigational Charts

However, every seasoned navigator knows the importance of understanding the seascape's limitations. MMAs come with their own set of navigational charts that outline certain constraints:

Minimum Balance Requirements: To set sail with an MMA, you might need to load a substantial initial cargo—higher minimum balance requirements. This threshold ensures your journey is profitable, aligning with the account's promise of higher yields but necessitating careful financial planning.

Regulated Transactions: Just as there are rules of the sea, federal regulations guide the use of MMAs, limiting the number of certain types of transactions. This ensures the account maintains its intended purpose—balancing growth with liquidity, without veering into the territory of transactional accounts like checking accounts.

Incorporating an MMA into your financial fleet allows you to sail a course that is both growth-oriented and flexible. It offers a strategic waypoint between the high seas of investments and the calm harbors of traditional savings, providing a versatile tool in your financial navigation arsenal.

As you chart your course through the financial waters, consider how an MMA can complement your journey, offering a blend of growth, access, and security that can help you reach your desired financial destinations, all while navigating with confidence and foresight.

Certificates of Deposit (CDs)

Description: A CD is a time deposit with a fixed interest rate and maturity date. Early withdrawal penalties may apply.

Benefits:

- **Guaranteed Rate of Return:** Interest rates are fixed for the term of the CD, providing a predictable return.
- **Safety:** CDs are FDIC-insured up to the legal limit, making them a low-risk investment.

Limitations:

- **Limited Access to Funds:** Money invested in a CD is not easily accessible before the maturity date without incurring penalties.
- **Interest Rate Risk:** The fixed interest rate may be a disadvantage if interest rates rise significantly.

Imagine embarking on a financial journey with a clear destination and a guaranteed reward upon arrival. This is the essence of investing in Certificates of Deposit (CDs), a time-honored financial vehicle that promises a defined return in exchange for your commitment to save. Let's navigate through the attributes of CDs, understanding how they serve as both a beacon of stability and a testament to the virtues of patience and foresight in the realm of personal finance.

The Beacon of Predictability

CDs stand as lighthouses in the often turbulent seas of investment, offering a guaranteed rate of return. When you purchase a CD, you agree to deposit a sum of money for a fixed period, during which your funds grow at a predetermined interest rate. This fixed rate is your guiding star, illuminating your financial path with predictability and reassurance. It allows you to calculate your exact financial gain at the CD's maturity, enabling precise planning for future financial needs or goals.

Anchoring in Safety

The safety of CDs is akin to a secure harbor, sheltering your capital from the storms of market volatility. Being FDIC-insured up to the legal limit, CDs provide a sanctuary for your savings, ensuring that your principal amount is protected against the tides of economic change. This level of security makes CDs an ideal choice for conservative investors or those seeking a stable component within a diversified portfolio.

Navigating Limited Access

While CDs offer many advantages, they also require you to chart your financial course with care. The funds you allocate to a CD are like provisions stored in the hold of a ship, meant to be untouched until your journey's end. Accessing these funds prematurely—before the CD matures—can incur penalties, akin to losing part of your cargo. This characteristic of CDs necessitates thoughtful consideration of your liquidity needs, ensuring you can commit to the term without needing to tap into these reserved funds.

Assessing Interest Rate Risk

In a landscape where interest rates can rise and fall like the tide, the fixed rate of a CD can be a double-edged sword. While it provides certainty, there's a risk that if interest rates increase significantly, your CD's rate may lag behind, akin to watching ships pass by with more favorable winds. This interest rate risk is an essential factor to consider, particularly in environments where rates are expected to climb.

Incorporating CDs into your financial voyage offers a blend of security, predictability, and discipline, encouraging a long-term perspective on wealth accumulation. They remind us that sometimes, the most reliable path to financial growth is not the fastest or the most thrilling but one marked by patience and steadfast commitment. As you chart your personal finance journey, consider how CDs might fit into your broader financial strategy, serving as a steady and secure complement to more dynamic investment choices, guiding you steadily toward your financial goals.

High-Yield Savings Accounts

Description: These accounts offer higher interest rates than traditional savings accounts and are available through both online and brick-and-mortar institutions

Benefits:

- **Competitive Interest Rates:** Often significantly higher than those of traditional savings accounts.
- **Liquidity and Security:** Provide easy access to funds while still being FDIC-insured.

Limitations:

- **Variable Interest Rates:** Rates can fluctuate over time based on the economic environment.
- **Online Account Management:** While this is a benefit to some, others may prefer the in-person services offered by traditional banks.

Imagine discovering a financial stream that flows faster and richer than your average brook, offering nourishment and growth to your savings. This is the essence of High-Yield Savings Accounts (HYSAs), modern financial reservoirs designed to maximize your savings potential while maintaining the accessibility and security you cherish. Let's wade into the waters of HYSAs, appreciating their benefits and understanding their limitations.

The Wellspring of Competitive Interest Rates

HYSAs stand out in the financial landscape like wells brimming with clearer, fresher water. They offer interest rates that are often significantly higher than those of traditional savings accounts, making them an attractive choice for savers looking to accelerate their financial growth. This enhanced yield means that your savings don't just sit idly; they actively burgeon, working harder for you and amplifying your financial reserves over time.

The Confluence of Liquidity and Security

Despite their higher yields, HYSAs maintain the fluidity and safety that are hallmarks of traditional savings accounts. The liquidity they offer ensures that you can access your funds when you need them, whether for an emergency, a significant purchase, or a sudden investment opportunity. Coupled with FDIC insurance, this liquidity doesn't come at the expense of security, providing a safe harbor for your savings up to the legal limit.

Navigating the Ebb and Flow of Interest Rates

While HYSAs offer verdant pastures for your savings, it's important to recognize that the landscape can change. The interest rates of HYSAs are not fixed; they can rise and fall with the economic tides. This variability means that while you might enjoy lush growth rates today, the future could bring leaner times, necessitating vigilance and adaptability in your savings strategy.

The Digital Terrain of Account Management

In the digital age, HYSAs often thrive in the online realm, offering streamlined, efficient account management from the comfort of your device. However, this digital focus may not resonate with everyone. Some individuals draw reassurance from the tangible world of brick-and-mortar institutions, where financial conversations occur face to face, and decisions are made across desks, not screens.

Incorporating an HYSA into your financial strategy is akin to tapping into a more bountiful aquifer, enriching your savings and offering a blend of growth, liquidity, and security. As you navigate your financial journey, weigh these attributes against the backdrop of your preferences and needs, determining how an HYSA can best complement your broader financial landscape. Whether you embrace its digital nature or seek a balance with traditional banking, an HYSA can serve as a potent tool in your quest for financial well-being, helping you cultivate a more prosperous and secure financial future.

Investment Accounts

Beyond traditional savings instruments, investment accounts offer the potential for higher returns by investing in the stock market, bonds, mutual funds, or other securities. While these accounts can provide significant growth opportunities, they also come with higher risk and should be considered as part of a diversified financial strategy.

Benefits:

- **Potential for Higher Returns:** Investments can yield higher returns compared to savings accounts or CDs.
- **Diversification:** A wide range of investment options can help spread risk.

Limitations:

- **Risk of Loss:** The value of investments can fluctuate, potentially leading to loss of principal.
- **Complexity:** Requires more knowledge and active management compared to traditional savings options.

In choosing the right savings or investment vehicle, consider your financial goals, risk tolerance, and the time horizon for your savings. Whether you prioritize accessibility, safety, or the potential for higher returns, there's a financial instrument suited to your needs. Always conduct thorough research or consult with a financial advisor to make the most informed decision for your personal financial situation.

Venture with me now beyond the calm waters of traditional savings, out into the broader and more dynamic ocean of investment accounts. Here, the horizons expand, and the potential for growth stretches out before us, vast and varied. While the allure of higher returns beckons, these waters are deeper and less predictable, necessitating a keen eye and a steady hand at the helm.

The Horizon of Higher Returns

Investment accounts are like sails hoisted to catch the wind, harnessing the market's inherent energies to propel your wealth forward. By venturing into the realms of stocks, bonds, mutual funds, or other securities, you open yourself to the potential for significant growth, far surpassing the gentle currents of savings accounts or CDs. This is the realm where fortunes can be made, where your financial dreams can gain the momentum they need to become reality.

Charting a Course Through Diversification

In this vast sea of opportunity, diversification is your compass. Just as a wise captain sails with the winds from many quarters, so too should your investments span a variety of sectors, asset classes, and geographies. This strategy helps spread risk, ensuring that a squall in one market doesn't capsize your entire financial journey. By spreading your investments, you create a resilient financial fleet, capable of weathering market volatility and capitalizing on opportunities from diverse sources.

Navigating the Risks

Yet, with the promise of greater returns comes the specter of greater risk. The value of your investments can rise and fall with the market's tides, and there is always the potential that you could lose your principal. This inherent uncertainty is a fundamental aspect of investing, a reminder that with great potential comes the need for caution and respect for the forces at play.

Mastering the Complexities

Investment accounts also demand a more sophisticated approach than their savings counterparts. They require you to engage, to learn, and to make decisions with an informed mind. Whether it's understanding the nuances of stock market trends, the implications of bond yields, or the strategies behind mutual fund selections, this realm demands both your attention and your intellect.

Choosing Your Vessel

As you contemplate the vast array of financial vehicles at your disposal, consider what you seek from your journey. Are you in pursuit of rapid growth, or is steady progress more your pace? How much risk are you willing to accept, and how actively do you wish to manage your financial course? Your answers to these questions will guide your choice, helping you select the vessel that best suits your journey toward financial prosperity.

In this expansive financial seascape, whether you choose the solid ground of savings or the expansive potential of investments, remember that knowledge is your chart and prudence your compass. Conduct thorough research, seek guidance when needed, and always remain attuned to the shifting winds and tides of the economic world. With a thoughtful approach and a clear vision, you can navigate these waters to find your path to financial success and security.

6. Introduction to Investing

- Basic concepts of investing, including the risk-reward spectrum.

In the realm of personal finance, the journey toward investing stands as a pivotal chapter in the narrative of financial empowerment. For many, particularly those hailing from blue-collar backgrounds, the venture into investing is often shrouded in a veil of complexity and perceived risk. Yet, it is through understanding and embracing these concepts that the doors to wealth creation and financial freedom are unlocked. Let us embark on an exploration of the basic concepts of investing, illuminated by the principles of the Abundance Mindset, the Law of Attraction, and the Theory of Sufficient Capital, weaving a tapestry of knowledge that demystifies the risk-reward spectrum.

The Essence of Investing

At its core, investing is the act of allocating resources, typically money, with the expectation of generating an income or profit. Unlike the instant gratification of spending, investing is the art of delayed gratification—sowing seeds today to harvest financial abundance tomorrow. It is a testament to the belief in future prosperity, an embodiment of the Abundance Mindset.

The Risk-Reward Spectrum

The risk-reward spectrum is a fundamental concept in investing that posits a direct correlation between the level of risk undertaken and the potential for reward. It is a continuum that ranges from low-risk, low-reward options like savings accounts to high-risk, high-reward ventures such as stocks or real estate investments.

- **Low-Risk Investments:** These are characterized by a lower potential for loss but also offer lower potential returns. Examples include savings accounts and government bonds. They are akin to the steady, reliable streams that slowly sculpt the landscape, offering security and peace of mind.
- **High-Risk Investments:** At the other end of the spectrum, these investments offer the potential for higher returns but come with a greater risk of loss. Stocks, commodities, and cryptocurrency represent this category, each a testament to the belief in one's ability to navigate the tumultuous waters of the market and emerge prosperous.

Imagine you're setting out on a vast and varied financial landscape, where the terrain ranges from the gentle undulations of low-risk investments to the rugged peaks of high-risk opportunities. This landscape is shaped by the fundamental principle of the risk-reward spectrum, a concept that guides travelers in their quest for financial growth and security.

Traversing the Low-Risk Terrain

Envision yourself following a serene and well-trodden path, the realm of low-risk investments. Here, the ground is steady underfoot, the progress is gradual, and the scenery changes subtly. Savings accounts and government bonds are the gentle brooks and streams in this landscape, flowing with reliability and offering a soothing rhythm of predictable, albeit modest, returns. They represent the financial equivalent of a peaceful hike through familiar woods, where the risk of losing one's way is minimal, and the journey is marked by tranquility rather than thrill.

Choosing these investments is akin to selecting a safe and steady course, one that prioritizes preservation of capital over the allure of rapid gain. It's a path favored by those who seek to maintain a calm and steady progression toward their financial goals, valuing security and peace of mind above the prospects of greater, albeit uncertain, rewards.

Scaling the High-Risk Heights

Now, imagine the opposite end of the spectrum, where the terrain becomes steep and the paths less defined. This is the domain of high-risk investments, the financial equivalents of towering mountains and rushing rivers. Stocks, commodities, and cryptocurrencies dwell here, each offering the allure of significant returns but also posing the risk of abrupt and severe declines.

Embarking on this route is like choosing a mountainous trail, where the potential for breathtaking vistas and exhilarating heights comes with the inherent risk of sudden storms or treacherous paths. Investors drawn to these ventures are often those with a keen sense of adventure, a tolerance for uncertainty, and a belief in their capacity to weather the market's vicissitudes and capitalize on its opportunities.

Choosing Your Path

As you stand at the crossroads of this vast financial landscape, consider your position on the risk-reward spectrum. Your choice will depend on your financial goals, your tolerance for risk, and the time frame within which you hope to achieve your objectives. Just as a seasoned hiker selects a trail that aligns with their experience, fitness level, and the thrill they seek, you must choose investments that resonate with your financial aspirations, risk tolerance, and the peace of mind you desire.

In the journey of investing, understanding the risk-reward spectrum is like possessing a map of the terrain ahead. It empowers you to navigate the financial landscape with awareness and confidence, making informed decisions that harmonize with your personal vision of financial success. Whether you opt for the steady, gentle paths of low-risk investments or the challenging, lofty climbs of high-risk opportunities, your journey will be uniquely yours, a personal expedition in the pursuit of financial growth and security.

Navigating the Spectrum

1. Understanding Your Risk Tolerance: This is a deeply personal journey, requiring introspection and honesty. Reflect on your financial goals, your capacity to absorb loss, and the timeline for your investments. Are you a cautious navigator, preferring the calm waters of low-risk investments, or are you an intrepid explorer, willing to brave the high seas for the promise of greater treasures?

2. Diversification: The ancient wisdom of not putting all your eggs in one basket holds true in investing. Diversification involves spreading your investments across different asset classes to reduce risk. Imagine a mosaic, each piece representing a different investment, collectively creating a resilient and beautiful picture of your financial future.

3. Education and Empowerment: Arm yourself with knowledge. Understand the markets, the instruments, and the strategies. Knowledge is the compass that will guide you through the investing journey, enabling you to make informed decisions that align with your vision of financial freedom.

4. The Long-Term Perspective: Investing is not a sprint; it is a marathon. It requires patience, persistence, and faith in the process. Visualize your goals, be they retirement, homeownership, or financial independence. See yourself achieving these goals, not through luck, but through strategic, informed investing.

In weaving these threads together—embracing risk and reward, understanding one's risk tolerance, diversifying, seeking knowledge, and maintaining a long-term perspective—we craft a narrative of investing that demystifies its complexities. This narrative is not just about financial transactions; it is about transforming one's financial destiny through the deliberate, informed, and empowered allocation of resources. Let this exploration serve not only as a guide but as an inspiration to take control of your financial future, armed with the confidence that comes from understanding the fundamental principles of investing.

- An overview of different types of investments: stocks, bonds, mutual funds, ETFs, and real estate.

In the realm of personal finance, diversifying one's investment portfolio is akin to navigating a vast ocean, with each type of investment representing a unique vessel designed for specific conditions. From the robust ships of stocks and bonds to the versatile crafts of mutual funds, exchange-traded funds (ETFs), and the steadfast vessels of real estate, understanding the characteristics and benefits of each investment type is crucial for charting a course toward financial prosperity. Let us embark on an exploration of these investment vehicles, guided by principles of financial wisdom and empowerment.

Stocks

Essence: Stocks represent ownership shares in a company. Investors who purchase stocks become shareholders, essentially owning a piece of the company's earnings and assets.

Benefits: Stocks offer significant growth potential. Over time, the value of stocks can increase, offering investors capital appreciation. Additionally, some stocks pay dividends, providing a steady income stream.

Considerations: The stock market is known for its volatility. Stock prices can fluctuate widely in the short term, making them a higher-risk investment. The reward of substantial returns is often balanced by the risk of potential loss.

Let's delve into the world of stocks, a vibrant and bustling marketplace where ownership in corporations is bought, sold, and traded. When you invest in stocks, you're not merely purchasing a piece of paper or a digital number in an account; you're acquiring a share of a company's story, its future, and its potential for prosperity.

Embarking on the Journey of Stock Ownership

Imagine walking into a marketplace where pieces of various enterprises are up for grabs. When you choose to buy a stock, you're essentially saying, "I believe in the future of this company." You become a part-owner, however small, of its narrative, its successes, and its challenges. As the company grows and prospers, so do your investments, reflecting the intrinsic link between your financial destiny and the fortunes of the businesses you've chosen to embrace.

Navigating the Waves of Growth Potential

Stocks stand out in the investment landscape for their remarkable growth potential. Over the long arc of time, they have the capacity to not just grow but to multiply an initial investment, offering a pathway to significant wealth accumulation that is difficult to replicate through more conservative avenues. Moreover, dividends can add a delightful rhythm to this journey, providing regular payouts that can be reinvested or used as a steady income stream, enhancing the compounding effect and the overall return on investment.

Steering Through Volatility

Yet, the voyage through the stock market is not without its storms. Prices ebb and flow with the tides of market sentiment, economic indicators, and a myriad of other factors, both predictable and unforeseen. This inherent volatility requires a steadfast heart and a clear-eyed view of the horizon. It's a realm where patience is not just a virtue but a necessity, where the tempests of today's market fluctuations must be weathered with an eye on the long-term potential of your investments.

Balancing Risk with Vision

The allure of stocks, with their potential for substantial returns, is invariably intertwined with the specter of risk. It's a financial ecosystem where fortunes can be both made and lost, often swayed by forces beyond any individual investor's control.

Yet, it's this very interplay of risk and reward that makes stocks a compelling choice for those looking to grow their wealth.

As you consider incorporating stocks into your financial portfolio, think of yourself as a navigator charting a course through both calm and turbulent waters. Your success in this realm will hinge not just on the stocks you choose but on your approach to investing—your ability to stay the course through market ups and downs, your diligence in researching and understanding your investments, and your capacity to align your stock choices with your broader financial goals and risk tolerance.

In the grand narrative of your financial journey, stocks offer a chapter brimming with potential, a chance to partake in the economic growth and innovation that drive our world forward. With a thoughtful approach and a steadfast commitment to your financial goals, you can harness the power of stocks to carve a path toward prosperity and financial freedom.

Bonds

Essence: Bonds are essentially loans made by investors to issuers, which can be corporations, municipalities, or governments. In return, the issuer agrees to pay back the principal amount on a specified maturity date, along with periodic interest payments.

Benefits: Bonds are generally considered safer than stocks. They provide a predictable income through interest payments and return the principal at maturity, making them appealing for conservative investors seeking stability.

Considerations: While safer, bonds typically offer lower returns compared to stocks. Additionally, they are subject to interest rate risk; as interest rates rise, bond prices usually fall.

Picture yourself as a lender, not in the traditional sense to a friend or family member, but on a much grander scale—to corporations, cities, or even entire nations. This is the fundamental role you assume when you invest in bonds. You're providing these entities with the capital they need to grow, develop, and serve, and in return, they commit to repaying you, with interest, over a set period.

The Steady Companion of Bonds

When you hold a bond, you hold a promise—an issuer's vow to pay you back your initial investment plus regular interest payments. These payments are like the steady pulse of a lighthouse, providing consistent, predictable returns in the often turbulent sea of investment options. This reliability makes bonds a cornerstone for those who seek to anchor their portfolio in stability, especially appealing to conservative investors who prioritize the preservation of capital.

Sailing on the Current of Returns

While bonds are generally associated with lower risk, they are not without their own currents and undercurrents. The returns on bonds, typically more modest compared to the potential highs of stock investments, reflect their safer nature. Yet, these returns offer a vital stream of income, particularly appealing in the later stages of an investor's journey or for those who seek a buffer against the volatility of the stock market.

Navigating the Waters of Risk

Even the calm waters where bonds sail are not without their risks. Interest rate fluctuations can affect bond prices inversely; when interest rates climb, bond prices tend to dip. This interest rate risk is a crucial consideration, especially in an environment where rates are on the rise. However, by holding a bond to maturity, you can mitigate this risk, as you'll typically receive the full principal amount back, barring the issuer defaulting.

Moreover, not all bonds are created equal. The issuer's creditworthiness, the bond's duration, and the economic context all play roles in defining a bond's risk and return profile. It's akin to choosing a ship for your sea voyage; just as you would select a vessel based on its sturdiness, destination, and the conditions it will face, so too must you assess each bond to ensure it aligns with your financial goals and risk tolerance.

Charting Your Course

In the grand expedition of investing, bonds offer a path of measured progress and relative calm. They provide a mechanism to earn income, diversify your investment portfolio, and reduce overall risk. As you chart your financial course, consider how bonds can complement your investment strategy, providing balance and stability amidst the more turbulent waters of higher-risk investments.

By understanding the essence and dynamics of bonds, you equip yourself with the knowledge to make informed decisions, to select bonds that resonate with your investment philosophy, and to integrate them thoughtfully into your broader financial plan. In doing so, you can harness the steady, reliable benefits of bonds to navigate toward your financial objectives with confidence and poise.

Mutual Funds

Essence: Mutual funds are pooled investment vehicles managed by professionals. They collect money from multiple investors to buy a diversified portfolio of stocks, bonds, or other securities, offering investors exposure to a broad array of assets.

Benefits: Mutual funds offer diversification, reducing the risk of investing in individual securities. They are managed by professional fund managers, providing expertise and convenience for investors.

Considerations: Mutual funds charge management fees, which can impact overall returns. Performance is reliant on fund management, and there's no guarantee of returns.

Imagine you and a group of friends decide to combine your resources to invest in a variety of ventures, from restaurants and tech startups to real estate and green energy projects. Each of you brings a certain amount of money to the table, and you hire an expert to choose the investments and manage them on your behalf. This collective investment endeavor is akin to a mutual fund, where you, along with numerous other investors, pool your capital to invest in a diversified portfolio managed by professionals.

The Symphony of Diversification

In the world of investing, diversification is akin to a symphony orchestra. Just as an orchestra blends the sounds of strings, winds, brass, and percussion to create harmonious music, a mutual fund combines various types of investments to create a balanced financial portfolio. This diversification helps mitigate the risk of loss if any one investment underperforms, much like how a missed note by one musician can be absorbed by the ensemble's collective performance, minimizing its impact.

Guided by the Maestro

The fund manager, much like a maestro, conducts the mutual fund's investment strategy, making decisions on buying and selling securities based on research and expertise. For investors who may lack the time or expertise to manage their investments directly, this professional management is invaluable. It provides the convenience of having an expert steward your investments, making tactical decisions to navigate the ever-changing market dynamics.

Tuning into the Fees

However, this expert management comes with a cost—management fees. These fees, along with other expenses associated with mutual funds, can vary widely and have a tangible impact on your investment returns. It's crucial, therefore, to be mindful of these costs and weigh them against the potential benefits of professional management.

Harmonizing Expectations with Reality

While mutual funds provide an accessible avenue to a diversified and professionally managed portfolio, they are not without their limitations. The performance of a mutual fund is intrinsically tied to the acumen of the fund manager and the fund's underlying assets. Despite the expertise of professional management, there are no guarantees in the investment world; mutual funds, like all investments, carry the inherent risk of fluctuating markets.

Crafting Your Investment Ensemble

As you contemplate adding mutual funds to your investment repertoire, consider them as part of your broader financial symphony. They can play a crucial role, offering a blend of diversification, professional management, and accessibility that might be challenging to replicate on your own. Yet, like any investment, they should be chosen with care, attuned to your financial goals, risk tolerance, and the investment landscape's nuances.

In embracing mutual funds, you entrust your capital to the collective expertise and shared fortunes of a broader investment community, guided by the strategic baton of professional management. With informed selection and mindful consideration of fees and management, mutual funds can offer a harmonious addition to your investment portfolio, contributing to your journey toward financial crescendo.

Exchange-Traded Funds (ETFs)

Essence: ETFs are similar to mutual funds in that they offer diversified exposure to a portfolio of assets. However, ETFs are traded on stock exchanges, similar to individual stocks, offering greater flexibility and liquidity.

Benefits: ETFs provide the diversification benefits of mutual funds with the added advantage of lower expense ratios and the ability to buy and sell shares throughout the trading day at market prices.

Considerations: While ETFs offer lower fees than mutual funds, trading ETFs incurs brokerage commissions, which can add up. Market fluctuations can affect pricing, requiring more active management.

Embark on a journey into the dynamic world of Exchange-Traded Funds (ETFs), where the collective power of diversified investing meets the agility and accessibility of the stock market. Imagine a vessel that combines the strength of a cargo ship—carrying a varied and substantial load—with the speed and maneuverability of a sailboat. This is the essence of ETFs, offering you a unique way to navigate the financial waters.

Sailing with Diversification and Flexibility

ETFs, like mutual funds, are composed of a multitude of assets, providing you a balanced and diversified portfolio in a single transaction. Yet, unlike mutual funds, ETFs offer the added flexibility of being traded on stock exchanges, much like individual stocks. This means you can buy or sell ETF shares throughout the trading day at current market prices, responding swiftly to changes in the market or your investment strategy, just as a sailor adjusts the sails to the shifting winds.

Charting a Course with Lower Costs

One of the most compelling advantages of ETFs is their cost efficiency. Generally, ETFs boast lower expense ratios compared to mutual funds, primarily because they are often passively managed, tracking a specific index rather than relying on active management. This can result in significant cost savings over time, enhancing your investment returns like a favorable wind propelling your ship forward.

Navigating the Waters of Trading and Market Fluctuations

However, the journey with ETFs is not without its navigational challenges. While the ability to trade ETFs throughout the day adds a layer of flexibility, it also introduces the potential for market fluctuations to impact pricing. Moreover, each trade may incur brokerage commissions, which, if not carefully considered, can accumulate like small leaks in a boat, potentially offsetting the benefits of lower expense ratios.

Moreover, while ETFs provide an efficient way to achieve a diversified investment portfolio, they require a degree of vigilance and engagement from you, the investor. Keeping a steady hand on the tiller involves monitoring market conditions, understanding the factors that influence ETF pricing, and making informed decisions about when to buy or sell.

Embarking on Your ETF Voyage

As you consider incorporating ETFs into your investment strategy, view them as versatile vessels in your financial fleet, offering a blend of diversification, cost-efficiency, and liquidity. Whether you're charting a long-term investment course or navigating the short-term currents of the market, ETFs can be a valuable tool in your investment arsenal.

Remember, the key to a successful voyage with ETFs lies in understanding their characteristics, recognizing the costs associated with trading, and aligning their use with your overall financial goals and risk tolerance. With thoughtful navigation and strategic use, ETFs can help you explore new investment horizons, harnessing the power of the market to propel you toward your financial destinations.

Real Estate

Essence: Real estate investing involves purchasing property to generate rental income or capital appreciation. This can include residential properties, commercial real estate, or real estate investment trusts (REITs).

Benefits: Real estate can offer steady income through rent, potential tax advantages, and diversification outside of traditional stock and bond markets. It's often seen as a hedge against inflation.

Considerations: Real estate requires significant capital and management effort, especially for direct property investments. It's also subject to market and regulatory risks, and liquidity can be an issue compared to more liquid assets like stocks and ETFs.

Each investment type offers a unique blend of risk and reward, serving different roles within a diversified portfolio. By understanding the characteristics of stocks, bonds, mutual funds, ETFs, and real estate, investors can make informed decisions that align with their financial goals, risk tolerance, and investment horizon. The journey to financial prosperity is a deliberate one, paved with knowledge, diversification, and strategic planning.

- Principles of diversification and asset allocation.

Embarking on a journey through the financial landscape, one discovers the profound wisdom embedded within the principles of diversification and asset allocation. These principles, akin to the ancient art of navigation, guide us through the tumultuous seas of market volatility, safeguarding our treasures from the whims of economic storms. Let us delve into these principles, not merely as concepts to be understood but as intuitive actions to be embraced and woven into the very fabric of our financial decisions.

The Symphony of Diversification

Imagine a symphony, each instrument contributing its unique sound to create a harmonious ensemble. Diversification in investing mirrors this symphony, where each investment plays its part, ensuring that the performance is resilient, even if one instrument falls silent. By spreading investments across different asset classes—stocks, bonds, real estate, and more—we not only mitigate risk but also open ourselves to the melody of potential opportunities. The beauty of this approach lies not in avoiding risk altogether but in creating a balance that can withstand the ebb and flow of economic tides.

Subliminal Insight: As you ponder the diversity of the world around you, let your mind gently acknowledge the strength found in variety. Each financial decision you make, infused with the principle of diversification, becomes a note in the symphony of your prosperity.

The Art of Asset Allocation

Asset allocation is the deliberate positioning of one's investments across various asset categories. This strategic distribution is based on an intimate understanding of one's goals, time horizon, and risk tolerance. It's akin to planting a garden, where the mix of flowers, herbs, and vegetables is carefully selected to ensure growth throughout the seasons, despite the unpredictable weather.

Subliminal Insight: Envision your financial garden thriving, each asset a carefully chosen plant that brings beauty, sustenance, and balance to your life. With every investment choice, imagine tending to this garden, nurturing it with thoughtful asset allocation, allowing it to flourish and adapt over time.

The Journey of Adaptation and Growth

The path of diversification and asset allocation is not static; it is a journey of constant adaptation and growth. As seasons change in life, so too should your financial strategies. Rebalancing your portfolio becomes a practice as natural as the changing tides, ensuring that your investments remain aligned with your evolving aspirations and circumstances.

Subliminal Insight: Feel the rhythm of the seasons within you, a reminder of the natural cycle of growth and renewal. Let this rhythm inspire a dynamic approach to your financial journey, where adaptability and mindfulness pave the way to abundance.

The Beacon of Financial Empowerment

Embracing the principles of diversification and asset allocation illuminates the path to financial empowerment. It's a path that leads not only to wealth but to a deeper understanding of the interplay between risk and opportunity.

Subliminal Insight: As you gaze upon the stars, guiding lights for ancient mariners, allow the principles of diversification and asset allocation to be your celestial guides. With each step forward, feel the empowerment that comes from navigating your financial voyage with wisdom and confidence.

In the quiet moments of reflection, as you contemplate your journey towards financial mastery, let the principles of diversification and asset allocation resonate within you, not merely as strategies but as intuitive guides. They beckon you towards a future where financial stability and growth are not just possible but inevitable, a future you navigate with the ease and grace of a seasoned voyager.

Case Studies

Integrating the principles of financial management into daily life requires more than just theoretical understanding; it necessitates practical application through exercises and real-world case studies. Below are thoughtfully crafted exercises and illustrative case studies designed to embed the core financial concepts deeply into your subconscious, encouraging not just comprehension but action.

Practical Exercises

Exercise 1: Financial Reflection Journal

- **Objective:** Cultivate awareness of your financial habits and beliefs.
- **Action:** For one month, maintain a daily journal. Each day, write down your thoughts on money, noting any expenses that day, how they made you feel, and whether they align with your financial goals.

Objective:

The primary aim of this exercise is to foster a heightened consciousness of your financial behaviors and convictions. By engaging in this introspective practice, you will gain invaluable insights into your relationship with money, which is essential for cultivating a healthy financial mindset and making informed decisions that align with your long-term objectives.

Action:

You are tasked with maintaining a daily journal over the course of one month. This journal will serve as a reflective tool, enabling you to scrutinize your daily financial interactions and their underlying emotions and beliefs. Below are the detailed steps and guiding questions to assist you in this endeavor:

Daily Entries: Each day, dedicate a moment to reflect on your financial activities. Record all monetary transactions, no matter how insignificant they may seem. This includes purchases, savings, investments, and even contemplative thoughts about finances that did not lead to actual expenditure.

Emotional Responses: After noting each financial transaction, delve into the emotions that accompanied it. Did the expense evoke feelings of guilt, satisfaction, regret, or empowerment? Understanding your emotional responses can provide profound insights into your financial decision-making processes.

Alignment with Goals: Evaluate whether each expense or financial thought aligns with your broader financial objectives. Are you spending in a manner that propels you toward your goals, or are there discrepancies between your actions and aspirations? This analysis will help you identify patterns and areas for improvement.

Insightful Reflections: At the end of each week, allocate time for a more comprehensive reflection. Review your entries to discern overarching themes, unexpected discoveries, and progress toward aligning your financial habits with your goals. This weekly synthesis can reveal deeper insights and guide your future financial behaviors.

Concluding Synthesis: Upon completing the month-long journaling exercise, synthesize your observations to construct a coherent narrative of your financial mindset and behaviors. Identify key lessons learned, areas for growth, and strategies to enhance your financial well-being.

Expected Outcomes:

Engaging diligently in this exercise is expected to yield the following benefits:

- Enhanced self-awareness regarding financial habits and beliefs.
- Identification of spending patterns that either support or hinder your financial goals.
- Improved financial decision-making skills through reflective practice.
- Development of a proactive and purposeful approach to managing finances.

This exercise is not merely about tracking expenses; it is an opportunity to engage in a profound dialogue with oneself about values, goals, and the role of money in achieving personal fulfillment and security. By the end of this reflective journey, you should possess a clearer understanding of your financial identity and be better equipped to navigate your financial future with intention and wisdom.

Exercise 2: The Diversification Experiment

Objective:

The core objective of this exercise is to impart the fundamental concept and benefits of investment diversification through a practical, hands-on approach. By engaging in this exercise, participants will gain firsthand experience of how diversification can mitigate risk and enhance the stability of an investment portfolio, particularly in the context of fluctuating market conditions.

Action:

Participants are required to construct a hypothetical investment portfolio, utilizing a designated virtual budget. This portfolio should encapsulate a variety of asset classes to illustrate the principle of diversification. Here is a step-by-step guide to facilitate this process:

Portfolio Allocation:

- Allocate the virtual funds among different asset classes, including stocks, bonds, and real estate. Consider incorporating additional categories, such as commodities or mutual funds, to broaden the diversification scope.
- Determine the proportion of investment in each asset class based on risk tolerance and investment objectives. For instance, a more risk-averse individual might favor bonds, while a risk-tolerant investor may allocate more to stocks or real estate.

Investment Simulation Tool:

- Utilize a reputable investment simulation platform that allows you to monitor the performance of your mock portfolio over a specified period. These tools simulate real market conditions, offering a realistic experience of how various asset classes respond to market dynamics.
- Engage with the simulation tool regularly to track the performance of each asset class within your portfolio, noting any significant fluctuations or trends.

Observation and Analysis:

- Observe how different asset classes perform under varying market conditions. Pay particular attention to how diversification helps in stabilizing the portfolio against market volatility.
- Analyze the correlation between asset classes. In ideal diversification, when one asset class underperforms, another should outperform or remain stable, thereby offsetting potential losses.

Reflection and Learning:

- At the conclusion of the simulation period, reflect on the performance of your diversified portfolio. Identify which asset classes provided stability and which were more volatile.
- Consider how diversification impacted the overall performance of your portfolio, especially in comparison to a hypothetical non-diversified portfolio.

Report and Application:

- Compile a report summarizing your experiences, observations, and the lessons learned about the significance of diversification in investment strategy.
- Articulate how the insights gained from this exercise can be applied to real-world investing scenarios, emphasizing the practical value of diversification in managing investment risks and pursuing financial goals.

Expected Outcomes:

Through active participation in this exercise, individuals are expected to:

- Develop a nuanced understanding of diversification and its pivotal role in investment risk management.
- Acquire practical skills in constructing and managing a diversified investment portfolio.
- Gain insights into how different asset classes behave and interact within a portfolio context, especially under varying economic conditions.
- Enhance their strategic thinking and analytical skills in the realm of investment management.

This exercise aims not only to educate but also to empower individuals with the knowledge and skills necessary to make informed, strategic investment decisions, thereby fostering financial acumen and confidence.

Exercise 3: The Budgeting Challenge

- Objective: Sharpen your budgeting skills.

- **Action:** For the next two months, use a budgeting app or spreadsheet to plan your monthly budget. Aim to reduce one variable expense category by 10-15%. Track your progress and reflect on the strategies that helped you achieve this reduction.

Objective:

The principal aim of this exercise is to refine your budgeting acumen through a structured, practical approach. By meticulously planning and monitoring your monthly budget, with a specific focus on reducing expenditure in one variable expense category, you will cultivate disciplined financial habits and develop more nuanced insights into effective budget management.

Action:

You are to adopt a methodical approach to budgeting over the ensuing two months, utilizing either a sophisticated budgeting application or a meticulously structured spreadsheet. Herein is a detailed guideline to navigate this exercise:

Budget Planning:

- Commence with an in-depth review of your current financial status, cataloging all sources of income and enumerating your expenses, categorizing them into fixed and variable costs.
- Select one variable expense category for targeted reduction, such as dining out, entertainment, or discretionary shopping. Set an explicit goal to curtail spending in this category by 10-15%.

Budgeting Tool Utilization:

- Employ a budgeting app or create a detailed spreadsheet to delineate your monthly budget. Ensure that it allows for real-time tracking of income and expenditures, categorization of expenses, and visualization of your financial data.
- Document every financial transaction meticulously, ensuring that your tracking is as accurate and comprehensive as possible.

Monitoring and Adjustment:

- Regularly review your budgeting tool to monitor your adherence to the set budget, paying particular attention to the selected variable expense category.
- Should you observe deviations exceeding your targeted reductions, reassess and adjust your spending behavior accordingly. Implement strategic measures to curb unnecessary expenses, such as opting for more economical alternatives or eliminating non-essential purchases.

Reflection and Strategy Analysis:

- At the end of each month, conduct a thorough analysis of your budgeting performance, focusing on the reduction achieved in the specified variable expense category.

- Reflect on the strategies and behaviors that facilitated this financial discipline. Were certain approaches particularly effective in curtailing expenditure? Did specific challenges arise, and how were they addressed?

Synthesis and Application:

- Synthesize your observations and insights into a comprehensive reflection, articulating the key lessons learned about budget management and expense reduction.
- Consider how these budgeting skills and strategies can be applied to broader financial contexts or future fiscal planning, underscoring the practical implications of your learning experience.

Expected Outcomes:

Engagement in this exercise is anticipated to yield the following benefits:

- Enhanced proficiency in budget planning and execution, fostering more informed and strategic financial decision-making.
- Practical experience in identifying and implementing effective cost-reduction strategies, contributing to more sustainable financial habits.
- Improved financial awareness and discipline, facilitating a proactive approach to expense management and budget optimization.

Ultimately, this exercise is designed not merely as a task in financial reduction but as a holistic learning experience, aiming to instill robust budgeting skills that will serve as invaluable tools in your financial literacy and acumen repertoire.

Case Studies

Case Study 1: Emily's Emergency Fund

Emily, a talented graphic designer, found herself in a precarious financial situation when her car broke down unexpectedly. The repair costs were substantial, and without an emergency fund, Emily had no choice but to charge the expense to her high-interest credit card. This event was a wake-up call, highlighting the precariousness of her financial health and the need for a proactive approach to avoid similar situations in the future.

Detailed Solution

1. **Financial Audit:** Emily began her journey by conducting a thorough audit of her monthly expenses. She meticulously reviewed bank statements and receipts, identifying non-essential expenses that could be reduced or eliminated. Dining out, subscription services, and impulse purchases were identified as areas where significant savings could be achieved.

2. **Lifestyle Adjustments:** Recognizing the importance of her goal, Emily made conscious lifestyle adjustments. She started preparing meals at home, canceled underused subscription services, and curtailed her online shopping habits. These changes, though initially challenging, became more manageable over time, reflecting a growing commitment to her financial well-being.

3. Generating Additional Income: Emily leveraged her skills as a graphic designer, taking on freelance projects outside her regular job. She marketed her services through social media and professional networks, gradually building a clientele that provided her with a supplemental income stream.

4. Setting Savings Goals: Emily set a clear, achievable goal of building a $1,000 emergency fund. She calculated how much she needed to save each month to meet this goal within four months and tracked her progress diligently.

Expanded Outcome

1. Establishment of Emergency Fund: Within four months, Emily achieved her initial goal of saving $1,000. This milestone was more than just a financial achievement; it was a testament to her discipline, adaptability, and resilience.

2. Development of Saving Habits: The process of establishing her emergency fund instilled in Emily a habit of regular saving. What began as a response to a financial crisis evolved into a systematic approach to managing her finances, prioritizing savings as a non-negotiable part of her monthly budget.

3. Enhanced Financial Security: The creation of the emergency fund provided Emily with a tangible sense of security. Knowing she had funds set aside for unexpected expenses significantly reduced her stress and anxiety, allowing her to focus more on her career and personal growth.

4. Continued Financial Education: Motivated by her success, Emily became more engaged in learning about personal finance. She sought out resources on budgeting, investing, and financial planning, committed to building a solid foundation for her future financial decisions.

5. Expansion of Emergency Fund: Encouraged by her initial success, Emily didn't stop at $1,000. She continued to save, setting new goals for her emergency fund, aiming to cover three to six months of living expenses. This forward-thinking approach underscored her commitment to a financially secure future.

Emily's journey from financial vulnerability to stability and resilience underscores the power of proactive financial management. Her story illustrates that with determination, discipline, and strategic planning, anyone can overcome financial challenges and lay the groundwork for a secure and prosperous future.

Case Study 2: The Rodriguez Family's Debt-Free Journey

The Rodriguez family found themselves in a common yet daunting predicament: $15,000 deep in credit card debt. This financial burden was not just a numerical figure—it was a source of constant stress, affecting their daily lives and casting a shadow over their future aspirations. The realization that they needed a systematic approach to tackle this challenge was the first step on their path to financial recovery.

Detailed Solution

1. Embracing the Debt Snowball Method: The family chose the debt snowball method for its psychological benefits, focusing on paying off their smallest debts first while maintaining minimum payments on larger debts. This approach provided them with quick wins, essential for maintaining motivation.

2. Crafting a Strict Budget: To support their debt repayment strategy, they meticulously reviewed their monthly spending. Every expense was scrutinized, leading to significant lifestyle adjustments. Luxuries and non-essential expenses were curtailed, and the family focused on maximizing the value of every dollar spent.

3. Increasing Income: Recognizing the need to accelerate their debt repayment, members of the Rodriguez family sought opportunities to increase their income. This included taking on extra shifts at work, freelancing, and even selling items they no longer needed.

4. Regular Family Financial Meetings: The journey to debt freedom became a united family mission. Regular financial meetings were held to review progress, adjust the budget, and keep everyone aligned with the family's financial goals.

Expanded Outcome

1. Debt Freedom Achieved: Eighteen months later, the Rodriguez family's diligent efforts culminated in complete freedom from credit card debt. This achievement was not just a financial victory but a profound emotional relief.

2. Financial Discipline and Literacy: The process instilled in them a deep sense of financial discipline and literacy. Budgeting became second nature, and they became adept at distinguishing between wants and needs, making informed spending decisions.

3. Psychological Empowerment: The psychological impact of paying off each debt piece by piece was immense. Each "debt cleared" milestone was celebrated, reinforcing their commitment and motivation. The sense of progress was palpable, transforming their outlook on money and debt.

4. Strengthened Family Bonds: The journey brought the Rodriguez family closer together. Shared goals and collective efforts towards debt repayment strengthened their bonds, with each member playing a pivotal role in the family's financial turnaround.

5. Long-Term Financial Planning: Freed from the immediate pressure of debt, the family shifted their focus to long-term financial planning. They began building an emergency fund, contributing to retirement accounts, and saving for their children's education, laying the groundwork for a secure financial future.

6. Community Inspiration: The Rodriguez family's story became a source of inspiration within their community. By sharing their journey, they motivated friends and neighbors to take control of their finances, spreading the ripple effects of their success.

The Rodriguez family's narrative illustrates the transformative power of disciplined financial management and the importance of a supportive family dynamic in overcoming debt. Their journey from debt to financial freedom is a testament to the fact that, with the right strategy, dedication, and collective effort, overcoming even the most daunting financial challenges is possible.

Case Study 3: Anita's Investment Exploration

Anita, like many in their late 20s, recognized the importance of investing for her future but was met with a barrage of complex information and a fear of potential loss. The array of choices—stocks, bonds, ETFs, mutual funds—coupled with the jargon of the financial world, left her feeling paralyzed. Anita's challenge was not just about where to invest her money but overcoming the psychological barriers that made the investment landscape seem insurmountable.

Detailed Solution

1. **Starting Small with ETFs:** Anita's decision to start her investment journey with a diversified Exchange-Traded Fund (ETF) was strategic. ETFs offered her exposure to a wide range of assets within a single investment, reducing the risk associated with picking individual stocks. This initial step was manageable, both financially and psychologically, providing a gentle entry point into the world of investing.

2. **Engaging with a Community:** Joining an investment club proved to be a pivotal move for Anita. Surrounded by peers with varying levels of experience, she found a supportive environment where questions were encouraged, and knowledge was shared freely. This community became a crucial resource, offering both moral support and practical advice.

3. **Prioritizing Financial Education:** Anita actively sought out learning opportunities, attending workshops, and seminars on investing. She dedicated time to reading books and online resources, gradually demystifying the complex concepts that had once overwhelmed her. This self-directed education was instrumental in building her financial literacy.

Expanded Outcome

1. **Growth in Confidence:** As Anita's understanding of the investment landscape deepened, so did her confidence. Knowledge replaced fear, and she became more comfortable making informed decisions. This newfound confidence extended beyond investing, influencing her approach to financial planning and personal goal setting.

2. **Successful Initial Investment:** Anita's cautious yet strategic entry into investing through a diversified ETF paid off. The positive performance of her initial investment served as a tangible affirmation of her learning and decision-making process, reinforcing her confidence in her ability to navigate the investment world.

3. **Diversification of Portfolio:** Encouraged by her initial success, Anita expanded her investment horizon. She began to diversify her portfolio further, including individual stocks and bonds, always guided by the principles of risk management and long-term growth. This step marked her transition from a novice investor to an engaged, proactive participant in her financial well-being.

4. Integration of Investing into Financial Strategy: Investing became a core component of Anita's overall financial strategy. She set clear goals, aligned her investment choices with her risk tolerance and time horizon, and committed to ongoing education to refine her investment approach.

5. Empowerment and Advocacy: Anita's journey inspired her to become an advocate for financial literacy among her peers. She shared her experiences and learnings, encouraging others to embark on their own paths to financial empowerment.

Anita's story is a powerful testament to the transformative impact of education, community, and strategic action in the realm of investing. By starting small, seeking knowledge, and engaging with a supportive community, she overcame her initial apprehensions, turning investing from a source of overwhelm into a pillar of her financial strategy and personal empowerment.

Integrating Learning into Life

These exercises and case studies are designed not just to be read but to be lived. By engaging with these practical applications, you move beyond passive learning to active financial empowerment. Reflect on these experiences, journal your insights, and discuss your journey with peers or mentors. Each step you take, no matter how small, is a stride towards mastery of your financial destiny.

- Questions for reflection and discussion to facilitate deeper understanding and engagement with the material.

To foster a deeper understanding and engagement with the principles of financial management and investment, reflective questioning can be a powerful tool. Here are thought-provoking questions designed to stimulate discussion and reflection, whether in a classroom setting, within investment clubs, or even in personal contemplation. These questions aim to challenge conventional thinking, encourage exploration of personal financial beliefs, and catalyze actionable insights.

Reflective Questions on Financial Management

What are your initial feelings towards budgeting and financial planning? How do these feelings influence your approach to managing your finances?

This question encourages individuals to explore their emotional relationship with money and how it affects their financial behaviors and decisions.

Reflect on a time when you faced a financial challenge. What strategies did you employ to overcome it, and what lessons did you learn?

Sharing personal financial challenges and resolutions can offer valuable insights and foster a sense of community and shared experience.

How does the concept of the 'Abundance Mindset' versus the 'Scarcity Mindset' resonate with your personal financial philosophy? Can you identify instances where one mindset has overtaken the other in your financial decision-making?

This encourages individuals to analyze their underlying beliefs about money and how these beliefs shape their financial actions and goals.

Questions on Investing and Wealth Building

Considering the different types of investment vehicles (stocks, bonds, ETFs, mutual funds, real estate), which do you feel most drawn to and why?

This question helps individuals explore their comfort levels, interests, and perceptions regarding various investment options.

How does the principle of diversification alter your view of risk in investing? Can you think of ways to apply this principle in your current or future investment strategy?

Discussing diversification allows individuals to conceptualize risk management and strategic investment planning in a practical context.

Reflect on the 'Risk-Reward Spectrum'. Where do you currently place yourself on this spectrum, and where would you like to be? What steps are you willing to take to move towards your desired position?

This question challenges individuals to assess their risk tolerance and to consider concrete steps to align their investment actions with their risk appetite and financial goals.

Questions for Personal Growth and Financial Empowerment

How do you perceive the relationship between financial literacy and personal empowerment? Share a situation where increased financial knowledge impacted your life positively.

This prompts reflection on the transformative power of financial education and its role in fostering independence and confidence in financial matters.

What are your long-term financial goals, and how do they reflect your values and aspirations? How are you planning to achieve these goals?

Encouraging individuals to articulate their financial goals fosters clarity and intentionality, linking financial planning to personal values and life aspirations.

Discuss the role of patience and long-term thinking in achieving financial success. Can you identify habits or beliefs you need to change to adopt a more long-term perspective?

This question invites individuals to consider the importance of patience and persistence in financial growth, encouraging a mindset shift towards long-term planning and delayed gratification.

By engaging with these questions, individuals are invited to delve into their financial psyche, challenge their preconceptions, and emerge with a deeper, more nuanced understanding of personal finance and investment. These discussions can illuminate paths to financial resilience, informed decision-making, and ultimately, a more empowered and financially secure life.

Chapter 2: Advanced Budgeting Techniques

- Brief overview of the transition from basic to advanced budgeting techniques, emphasizing the importance of evolving budgeting practices for financial growth and stability.

In the journey toward wealth creation and financial stability, the evolution from basic to advanced budgeting techniques is not merely a step; it is a transformative leap. This progression is akin to shifting from the foundational strokes of a painter to the masterful techniques that bring depth, texture, and nuance to a canvas. Basic budgeting lays the groundwork, teaching us the importance of tracking income and expenses, setting aside savings, and avoiding debt. However, as our financial landscape grows in complexity and our goals ascend in ambition, these foundational practices must evolve into something more sophisticated, dynamic, and tailored.

Advanced budgeting techniques go beyond mere arithmetic; they involve a deep understanding of one's financial flow, the strategic allocation of resources, and the anticipation of future needs and opportunities. This advanced stage introduces methods such as cash flow analysis, forecasting, scenario planning, and the integration of behavioral finance principles. These methods are not just about managing money; they are about optimizing it to serve our greater goals of wealth accumulation and financial freedom.

Embracing advanced budgeting techniques signifies a commitment to financial growth and stability. It requires a mindset that views budgeting not as a restrictive tool, but as a liberating force. This mindset, cultivated through practice and persistence, enables us to navigate the complexities of our financial realities with confidence and foresight. It empowers us to make informed decisions that align with our long-term objectives, turning aspirations of wealth and stability into tangible realities.

Moreover, the transition to advanced budgeting reflects an understanding that wealth creation is not a product of chance but of choice. It is a deliberate process shaped by our decisions, habits, and the sophistication with which we manage our financial resources. By programming our minds to adopt and apply advanced budgeting techniques, we unlock the potential to transform our financial future, laying a foundation for lasting prosperity that transcends generations.

In essence, the journey from basic to advanced budgeting is a pivotal chapter in our financial narrative. It marks the moment we take full control of our financial destiny, leveraging our knowledge and skills to create a future rich with possibility, stability, and wealth. This evolution in budgeting practices is not just a recommendation; it is a necessity for anyone determined to achieve financial excellence and secure a legacy of abundance.

Section 1: Mastery of Cash Flow Analysis

- **Understanding Cash Flow:** Deep dive into the significance of cash flow in personal and business finances, and how it differs from simple income and expense tracking.

Understanding cash flow—both in personal and business finances—is akin to charting the lifeblood of financial health and vitality. Unlike the straightforward tracking of income and expenses, which provides a snapshot of financial status at a given moment, cash flow analysis offers a dynamic, comprehensive view of financial activity over time. This deeper insight is crucial for sustaining and nurturing the growth of wealth, as well as ensuring stability through the ebbs and flows of economic cycles.

The Essence of Cash Flow

Cash flow, in its essence, is the movement of money into and out of your financial sphere. It encompasses not only the income you receive and the expenses you incur but also the timing of these transactions. In personal finance, positive cash flow occurs when the money coming in from sources like salaries, investments, and other incomes exceeds the money going out for bills, discretionary spending, and savings. For businesses, cash flow measures the net amount of cash being transferred into and out of a company, reflecting its ability to operate effectively, pay obligations, and invest in growth.

Significance in Personal Finance

In personal finance, mastering cash flow is key to achieving financial freedom and wealth accumulation. It's not enough to simply spend less than you earn; understanding when you receive income and when expenses are due is vital for maintaining financial balance. Effective cash flow management allows individuals to plan for future expenses, avoid unnecessary debt, and allocate surplus funds towards investments, thereby programming the mind and financial habits towards wealth creation.

Importance in Business Finance

For businesses, cash flow is the cornerstone of financial health. A company can be profitable on paper but still face challenges if its outgoing cash exceeds the incoming cash at critical times. This can lead to difficulties in covering operational costs, paying employees, or investing in opportunities for growth. Positive cash flow, conversely, provides a buffer against market volatility, supports expansion, and signals to investors and creditors the business's financial robustness.

Cash Flow vs. Income and Expense Tracking

While income and expense tracking provides a valuable baseline for budgeting, it falls short of capturing the full financial picture. This method is static, offering no insight into the timing of cash movements. Cash flow analysis, by contrast, is dynamic, illustrating not just how much money is made or spent, but when these transactions occur. This timing is crucial for:

- Avoiding cash shortages that can lead to debt.
- Planning investments more strategically.
- Ensuring liquidity and financial flexibility.

Programming the Mind for Wealth Creation

Understanding and managing cash flow is integral to programming the mind for wealth creation. It encourages a forward-thinking approach, where financial decisions are made not just based on current status but anticipated future conditions. This mindset shift—from reactive to proactive financial management—is essential for navigating the complexities of wealth accumulation and achieving long-term financial stability.

By prioritizing cash flow analysis in both personal and business finances, individuals and entrepreneurs can unlock deeper insights into their financial health, enabling them to make informed decisions that drive growth, enhance stability, and pave the way for a prosperous financial future. This advanced understanding transcends basic budgeting, offering a more nuanced, powerful tool for financial empowerment and success.

- **Tools and Methods for Cash Flow Analysis:** Introduction to advanced tools and methodologies for analyzing cash flow, including software solutions and analytical frameworks.

In the intricate dance of managing finances, understanding and analyzing cash flow is pivotal. Advanced tools and methodologies offer both individuals and businesses the precision and insight needed to choreograph their financial moves with grace and foresight. This section delves into the sophisticated instruments and analytical approaches that can transform raw financial data into a clear, actionable strategy for wealth creation and stability.

Software Solutions for Cash Flow Analysis

1. **Personal Finance Management Software:**

Embrace a journey through the innovative realm of personal finance management software, where tools like Quicken, Mint, and You Need A Budget (YNAB) serve not merely as applications but as catalysts for profound financial transformation.

Embark on a Holistic Financial Voyage: Discover the power of viewing your finances as a cohesive whole. By integrating all your financial data—encompassing income, expenses, investments, and debts—these platforms offer you not just numbers, but a narrative of your financial life. As you witness the interconnectedness of your financial activities, allow yourself to adopt a holistic perspective, seeing beyond isolated transactions to the broader canvas of your financial well-being.

Cultivate Financial Mindfulness Through Categorization: As your transactions are neatly categorized, a pattern emerges—a direct reflection of your spending habits and priorities. This clarity invites you to introspect, encouraging a shift from sporadic spending to intentional financial choices. Embrace this opportunity to align your spending with your values and goals, fostering a lifestyle of financial mindfulness and purpose.

Visualize Your Financial Journey: Through vivid charts and graphs, your cash flow is rendered into a visual story, illustrating the ebb and flow of your financial life. This visualization is not just data; it's a mirror reflecting your financial habits over time. Engage with these visuals to glean insights into how your choices shape your financial landscape, inspiring a proactive stance towards nurturing positive cash flow patterns.

Anticipate Your Financial Future: Leverage the power of projection tools to cast your financial gaze forward. Experiment with different scenarios to see potential future outcomes of today's choices. This foresight equips you with the wisdom to make decisions that not only serve your present needs but also honor your future aspirations, instilling a forward-thinking ethos in your financial philosophy.

Embrace Proactivity with Actionable Insights: Transform passive observation into active financial stewardship. Armed with tailored insights and alerts, you're prompted to engage with your finances dynamically, taking informed actions that foster healthier financial habits. Whether it's optimizing savings, reducing unnecessary spending, or planning for future investments, these nudges guide you towards a path of continuous financial improvement.

By integrating these powerful tools and perspectives into your daily life, you're not just managing finances; you're cultivating a philosophy of financial empowerment. Let this journey with personal finance management software be the catalyst that propels you from mere financial existence to proactive, informed financial flourishing, setting the stage for a future of financial stability and fulfillment.

2. Business Cash Flow Analysis Tools:

Embark on a transformative journey with business cash flow analysis tools like QuickBooks, Xero, and FreshBooks, which are more than mere software solutions; they are your partners in fostering a financially astute and forward-looking business culture.

Embrace Comprehensive Financial Insight: Dive into the depths of your business's financial dynamics with tools designed to offer you a panoramic view of your cash flow. These platforms amalgamate data from various streams—sales, expenses, receivables, and payables—crafting a coherent narrative of your business's financial health. Engage deeply with this integrated perspective to foster a strategic mindset, viewing each financial decision as a thread in the larger tapestry of your business's success.

Master the Art of Proactive Financial Management: Transform the way you interact with your business finances by leveraging the meticulous tracking and forecasting capabilities of these tools. As you monitor invoices, track expenses, and navigate through your financial data, allow yourself to cultivate a proactive approach to financial management. Recognize patterns, identify trends, and anticipate future needs, empowering your business to stay one step ahead.

Visualize Financial Trajectories: With advanced visualization features, witness your cash flow scenarios come to life, offering vivid insights into the financial future of your business. These visual tools are not mere representations but a lens through which you can perceive and interpret the financial narrative of your enterprise. Let these visuals guide you to discern the impacts of today's decisions on tomorrow's outcomes, inspiring informed and visionary financial planning.

Strategize with Confidence: Leverage the scenario planning features to explore various financial futures and prepare for them with confidence. Whether it's planning for growth, adapting to market changes, or navigating potential hurdles, these tools empower you with the knowledge to strategize effectively. By understanding potential cash flow fluctuations, your business can make decisions that are not just reactive but are rooted in strategic foresight.

Cultivate a Culture of Financial Excellence: As you integrate these powerful tools into your business operations, champion a culture that values financial intelligence and strategic planning. Encourage your team to engage with the data, insights, and forecasts, fostering a collective commitment to financial prudence and proactive management. Through this shared journey, your business doesn't just grow financially but also evolves in its financial acumen and strategic sophistication.

By adopting business cash flow analysis tools like QuickBooks, Xero, and FreshBooks, you're not merely adopting software; you're embracing a philosophy of financial excellence and strategic foresight. Let these tools be the catalysts that propel your business toward a future marked by financial stability, strategic agility, and sustained growth, ensuring that every financial decision is a step toward realizing your business vision.

3. Spreadsheet Software:

Engage in a journey of financial empowerment and strategic insight through spreadsheet software like Microsoft Excel and Google Sheets, which serve as potent tools in the art of financial analysis and foresight.

Harness the Power of Customization: With spreadsheet software at your fingertips, you embark on a path of unparalleled financial clarity and customization. These platforms enable you to craft cash flow analyses that resonate with the unique rhythm and structure of your business. By inputting, organizing, and analyzing your data, you transform raw numbers into a coherent financial story, tailored precisely to your business needs and objectives.

Elevate Analysis with Advanced Functions: Dive into the depths of your financial data using sophisticated functions like pivot tables, financial formulas, and what-if analyses. These powerful features allow you to dissect and examine your cash flow from multiple angles, offering insights that go beyond surface-level observations. Embrace the opportunity to delve into detailed tracking and forecasting, where each financial variable is a piece of a larger puzzle, waiting to be understood and optimized.

Visualize Your Financial Narrative: With spreadsheet software, you're not just analyzing numbers, you're painting a picture of your business's financial trajectory. Utilize charts and graphs to bring your cash flow analysis to life, providing a visual representation that speaks volumes. These visuals serve as a bridge, connecting abstract financial concepts to tangible insights, enabling you and your stakeholders to engage with the data more intuitively and meaningfully.

Empower Decision-Making with Scenario Planning: Leverage the flexibility of spreadsheets to explore various financial scenarios and their potential impacts on your cash flow. This capability allows you to prepare for a range of possibilities, ensuring that your business remains resilient and responsive to changing financial landscapes. By simulating different financial futures, you equip your business with the foresight and agility to navigate uncertainties and capitalize on opportunities.

Foster a Culture of Financial Literacy and Innovation: As you integrate spreadsheet software into your financial analysis practices, you also cultivate a culture of financial literacy and innovation within your organization. Encourage your team to engage with the software, explore its functionalities, and contribute to the financial dialogue. This collaborative approach not only enhances individual and collective financial acumen but also fosters an environment where financial insights are valued and leveraged for strategic advantage.

In embracing spreadsheet software like Microsoft Excel and Google Sheets for your cash flow analysis, you're not merely adopting a tool; you're championing a mindset of financial sophistication and strategic empowerment. Allow these platforms to illuminate the financial path of your business, guiding you toward informed decisions, strategic growth, and sustained financial health.

Analytical Frameworks for Cash Flow

1. Direct vs. Indirect Cash Flow Analysis:

In the realm of financial strategy, understanding the nuances between direct and indirect cash flow analysis can significantly empower business leaders and financial enthusiasts to make informed decisions. Each method offers distinct insights and implications for your financial narrative, enabling a deeper comprehension and strategic foresight in financial planning.

Direct Method:

The direct method of cash flow analysis is akin to walking through your business's financial transactions with a magnifying glass, examining each cash inflow and outflow in its purest form. This method illuminates the actual cash movements, providing a granular view of where your money originates and where it is expended.

Strategic Empowerment:

- **Operational Insight:** By tracking actual cash transactions, the direct method offers clear visibility into the operational efficiency of your business, allowing you to pinpoint areas of strength and opportunities for improvement.
- **Enhanced Transparency:** This approach demystifies cash flow, enabling stakeholders to grasp the company's financial health without needing to decode complex accounting adjustments.
- **Immediate Relevance:** For businesses where cash transactions are pivotal to operational performance, the direct method offers immediate and actionable insights, enabling swift responses to emerging financial challenges or opportunities.

Embark on a journey into the heart of your business's financial narrative with the direct method of cash flow analysis. Picture yourself delving into the intricate tapestry of your company's cash transactions, tracing each thread from its source to its destination. This method doesn't just skim the surface; it dives deep, offering a vivid, detailed account of your financial flows, akin to exploring a vibrant coral reef, observing each creature and current to understand the ecosystem's dynamics.

Illuminating the Depths of Operational Insight

Imagine each cash transaction as a beacon, shedding light on the operational gears of your enterprise. With the direct method, you can observe these beacons closely, understanding precisely how each dollar enters and exits your business. This clarity transforms abstract numbers into tangible insights, revealing the pulse of your company's financial health and operational vigor.

Through this meticulous examination, strengths shine brightly, and weaknesses reveal themselves, offering you the roadmap to fortify and streamline your business operations. Like a captain who knows every nook and cranny of their ship, you gain the knowledge to navigate your enterprise toward greater efficiency and profitability.

Enhancing Transparency for Stakeholders

Transparency is the bedrock of trust in any relationship, including that between a business and its stakeholders. By adopting the direct method, you invite your investors, employees, and partners to view your financial landscape with clarity and confidence. They need not wade through obscure accounting adjustments or decipher indirect indicators; the cash flow story is laid bare, fostering understanding and confidence across all levels of your business community.

Harnessing Immediate Relevance for Operational Agility

In the dynamic world of business, where opportunities and challenges emerge with swift unpredictability, the direct method serves as your financial radar, detecting shifts in your cash flow with precision and timeliness. This immediate relevance empowers you to react swiftly, whether it's capitalizing on a sudden opportunity or mitigating an unforeseen expense. Your business becomes not just a vessel floating on financial tides but a nimble craft, adept at riding the waves and navigating through storms.

In essence, the direct method of cash flow analysis is not merely a financial tool; it's a lens through which the very heartbeat of your business becomes visible and comprehensible. It equips you with the insights to make informed decisions, the transparency to build trust, and the agility to adapt and thrive in the ever-evolving landscape of commerce. Embrace this method, and steer your enterprise toward a future marked by clarity, confidence, and sustained financial health.

Indirect Method:

Conversely, the indirect method serves as a comprehensive lens, broadening your financial view beyond mere cash transactions to encompass the broader implications of your company's activities. By adjusting net income for non-cash transactions and working capital changes, this method reveals the undercurrents that influence your operating cash flow.

Strategic Empowerment:

The indirect method of cash flow analysis stands as a beacon for those seeking to understand the intricate dance between a company's operational activities and its financial vitality. By delving into this nuanced approach, you engage with a level of financial intellect that transforms raw data into strategic wisdom, empowering you to steer your business with foresight and precision.

Comprehensive Overview

- **Strategic Integration:** The indirect method does not merely report numbers; it weaves a narrative that integrates various facets of your business operations, from revenue generation to capital investment and expense management. By viewing your cash flow through this integrative lens, you gain a comprehensive understanding of how different business activities interlock and influence your financial health.
- **Operational Synergy:** Recognize how strategic decisions in one area of your business, like adjustments in inventory management or credit terms, ripple through your financial ecosystem, impacting cash flow. This holistic view encourages cross-functional alignment and synergy, fostering decisions that consider the company's broader financial interdependencies.

Embark on a journey into the strategic depths of your business's financial narrative with the indirect method of cash flow analysis. This approach isn't just about tracking dollars and cents; it's about uncovering the stories those numbers tell about your company's operational heartbeat and strategic health. Imagine yourself as a financial detective, piecing together clues from various corners of your business to construct a cohesive picture of its financial well-being.

Crafting a Strategic Tapestry

Think of the indirect method as an artisan weaving a tapestry, where each thread represents a different financial activity or adjustment—depreciation, changes in inventory, accounts receivable, and payable. When woven together, these threads create a vivid portrayal of your company's operational performance and its impacts on cash flow. This narrative extends beyond mere transactions to illustrate how your business's operational decisions and financial strategies intertwine, offering a panoramic view of your financial landscape.

Forging Operational Synergy

By adopting the indirect method, you illuminate the interconnectedness of your business operations. Imagine adjusting the gears of a complex machine; a tweak here can influence the mechanism there. Similarly, a change in your sales collection period or inventory turnover can resonate throughout your financial statements, affecting cash flow and, by extension, strategic decision-making.

This method encourages a symphonic approach to management, where different departments and functions are orchestrated to play in harmony, mindful of how their individual actions contribute to the financial whole. It fosters a culture of strategic integration, where decisions made in silos give way to collaborative choices informed by their collective impact on the company's financial health.

Navigating with Insight and Foresight

In the realm of business, where unpredictability is the only certainty, the indirect method of cash flow analysis equips you with the insight and foresight to navigate with confidence. It transforms financial review sessions from retrospective examinations into strategic forums, where insights gleaned from past performance inform proactive decisions about the future.

In embracing the indirect method, you're not just tallying numbers; you're engaging with a powerful analytical tool that deciphers the financial implications of your operational strategies, illuminates potential challenges before they arise, and highlights opportunities for strategic enhancement. It's a commitment to understanding the financial undercurrents that shape your business's journey, empowering you to steer your enterprise toward sustainable growth and long-term success.

Connection to Profitability

- **Profit-Cash Dichotomy:** Unveil the sometimes elusive correlation between profitability and cash availability. The indirect method elucidates why profitable operations don't always equate to positive cash flow and vice versa, demystifying scenarios where profits on paper don't align with bank balances.
- **Strategic Forecasting:** By understanding this connection, you can better anticipate how changes in operational efficiency, cost management, and revenue growth will influence your cash flow, enabling you to craft strategies that enhance both profitability and liquidity.

Embark on a journey to unravel the intricate dance between profitability and cash flow, two pivotal indicators of your business's financial health that don't always move in harmony. The indirect method of cash flow analysis serves as your guide, illuminating the nuanced relationship between earning profits and maintaining a healthy cash reserve. This exploration is akin to deciphering a complex musical composition, where understanding the interplay between different elements reveals the true essence of the piece.

Understanding the Profit-Cash Dichotomy

Imagine your business as a flourishing garden. Profitability can be likened to the growth and blooming of your plants—a visible sign of health and vigor. However, the availability of cash is akin to the garden's water supply, essential for sustaining life, even if the plants are already thriving. Just as a garden can appear lush but still wilt without adequate water, a business can be profitable yet struggle due to insufficient cash flow.

The indirect method peels back the layers of your financial operations, showing you why a robust profit margin doesn't automatically ensure a strong cash position. It highlights non-cash factors like depreciation, changes in working capital, and deferred revenues that can create discrepancies between net income and actual cash available. Understanding these distinctions is crucial, as it helps you navigate the complexities of financial management, ensuring that profitability translates into liquidity, securing your business's operational resilience and strategic flexibility.

Leveraging Strategic Forecasting

Armed with the insights gleaned from the indirect method, you can transform raw data into strategic foresight. This approach enables you to anticipate how various operational maneuvers—be it streamlining production processes, tightening credit terms, or optimizing inventory management—will resonate through your cash flow.

By integrating this understanding into your strategic planning, you can synchronize your efforts to boost profitability with initiatives that ensure cash availability. It's about orchestrating your business decisions in a way that harmonizes profit generation with liquidity enhancement, ensuring that your company not only thrives on paper but also in its tangible financial reality.

In essence, mastering the connection between profitability and cash flow empowers you to steer your business with greater wisdom and foresight. It's a commitment to not just celebrating the blooms of success but also to nurturing the roots that sustain them. Embrace this nuanced understanding, and you'll be equipped to craft strategies that foster a robust, resilient, and financially sound enterprise, ready to flourish in today's dynamic economic landscape.

Analytical Depth

- **Forward-Looking Insights:** The indirect method's ability to identify non-cash factors and working capital adjustments provides a springboard for forward-looking financial analysis. Utilize these insights to predict how current trends and decisions will shape future cash flows, preparing your business to meet tomorrow's challenges with today's decisions.
- **Sustainability Assessment:** Dive deep into the workings of your business to assess the sustainability of your operational practices. Are increases in cash flow driven by genuine operational improvements, or are they merely the result of temporary working capital optimizations? The indirect method helps you distinguish between short-term fluctuations and long-term trends, guiding you toward sustainable financial practices.

By integrating the indirect method into your financial analysis repertoire, you transition from a reactive to a proactive stance, equipped to navigate your business's financial future with acumen and agility. This approach not only enhances your strategic planning but also deepens your understanding of the financial levers at your disposal, fostering a culture of informed decision-making and financial excellence within your organization.

Embark on a journey to elevate your financial foresight, harnessing the indirect method of cash flow analysis as a beacon, guiding your business towards a prosperous and sustainable future. This method, with its nuanced examination of your financial operations, acts as a powerful lens, magnifying the undercurrents that shape your company's fiscal landscape and offering a clear vision of the path ahead.

Cultivating Forward-Looking Insights

Imagine standing atop a watchtower, surveying the terrain before you. The indirect method equips you with a similar vantage point, enabling you to survey your business's financial terrain with clarity and breadth. It allows you to peer beyond the immediate horizon, interpreting today's financial data to forecast tomorrow's cash flows. By dissecting non-cash elements and working capital adjustments, you glean insights into how current operations, market conditions, and strategic decisions intertwine to influence future financial health.

This foresight is invaluable. It empowers you to anticipate potential cash shortfalls or surpluses, adjust strategies in response to emerging trends, and make informed decisions that steer your business toward long-term growth and stability. It's about transforming raw data into strategic foresight, enabling you to navigate your business's journey with confidence and precision.

Assessing Operational Sustainability

Venture deeper into the heart of your business, where the indirect method serves as your guide, illuminating the true drivers of cash flow changes. This exploration is crucial for distinguishing the ephemeral from the enduring. Are you witnessing a genuine enhancement in operational efficiency, or are the positive cash flow trends merely a facade, propped up by short-term working capital maneuvers?

This discernment is at the core of sustainability assessment. It challenges you to look beyond surface-level financial performance, probing the robustness and resilience of your operational practices. The goal is to ensure that your business is not just thriving in the moment but is built on foundations strong enough to endure the tests of time.

Embracing Proactive Financial Stewardship

By weaving the indirect method into the fabric of your financial analysis, you transition from merely reacting to financial outcomes to actively shaping them. This approach fosters a proactive financial culture within your organization, where decisions are informed by deep insights and strategic foresight.

In doing so, you empower yourself and your team to act not as mere participants in your business's financial narrative but as its authors, crafting a story of sustained success and resilience. You cultivate a landscape where every financial choice is a step toward a future defined by stability, growth, and financial excellence.

In summary, the indirect method of cash flow analysis is not just a tool but a compass, guiding you through the complexities of financial decision-making. It encourages a holistic view, where every number tells a story, and every story informs a strategy, enabling you to lead your business toward a future marked by foresight, sustainability, and enduring success.

Cultivating a Strategic Mindset:

Understanding and utilizing both direct and indirect cash flow analyses empower you to navigate your financial landscape with greater confidence and strategic acumen. Here's how you can leverage these insights:

In the intricate world of financial management, employing both the direct and indirect methods of cash flow analysis equips you with a dual lens through which to view your business's financial narrative, enabling nuanced strategy formulation, adept decision-making, and effective stakeholder engagement.

Imagine yourself as the captain of a ship sailing across the vast financial ocean, where the waters are constantly changing, influenced by market trends, operational shifts, and external economic conditions. To navigate these waters successfully, you need a comprehensive understanding of your ship's condition and the environment it operates in, which is where the dual approach of direct and indirect cash flow analyses comes into play.

Harnessing Dual Perspectives for Comprehensive Insights

Employing both direct and indirect cash flow analyses is akin to using two navigational tools: a telescope and a map. The direct method (the telescope) allows you to zoom in on the immediate cash transactions, offering clarity on the day-to-day operational cash flows. It's as if you're observing the waves that rock your boat, understanding their immediate impact and tracing their origins.

Conversely, the indirect method (the map) provides a broader view of your financial journey, showing how your operational earnings and working capital adjustments contribute to the overall cash flow. This method helps you understand the underlying currents and wind patterns that propel or hinder your financial progress.

Formulating Nuanced Strategies

With insights from both analyses at your disposal, you can craft strategies that are both reactive and proactive. The direct method's granular view helps you optimize day-to-day operations and manage short-term liquidity efficiently. It enables you to address leaks immediately and capitalize on favorable winds without delay.

The indirect method, on the other hand, informs your long-term strategy. By understanding the broader financial trends and their implications, you can make informed decisions about investments, expansions, or cost optimizations that ensure sustainable growth and stability.

Enhancing Decision-Making and Stakeholder Engagement

Armed with a dual perspective, you can communicate with stakeholders—be it investors, partners, or employees—with greater authority and credibility. You can explain not only what is happening within your business but also why it's happening, linking operational activities to financial outcomes.

This comprehensive understanding fosters trust and confidence among stakeholders, ensuring that they are more likely to support your strategic decisions and initiatives. It also empowers you to engage in more meaningful discussions about the company's financial direction, facilitating collaboration and alignment across different areas of the business.

Embracing Continuous Learning and Adaptation

Finally, cultivating a strategic mindset through these analyses is an ongoing journey. The financial landscape is ever-evolving, and so should your approach to financial analysis and strategy formulation. Regularly revisiting your cash flow analyses, staying attuned to new insights, and being willing to adjust your strategies in response to emerging information will keep your business agile and resilient in the face of change.

In summary, by leveraging both direct and indirect cash flow analyses, you position yourself not just as a navigator but as a master strategist, adept at steering your business through the financial ebbs and flows toward a prosperous and sustainable future. Embrace this dual approach, and you'll cultivate a strategic mindset that transforms financial data into actionable wisdom, guiding your business toward long-term success.

Scenario Planning

Dual-Faceted Approach: Utilize the direct method to gain immediate, actionable insights into your cash flow status, identifying specific areas for quick adjustments or highlighting urgent financial needs. Simultaneously, the indirect method offers a broader perspective, revealing underlying trends and long-term implications of your current financial activities, which is invaluable for strategic planning.

Comprehensive Scenarios: By integrating both methods, you can construct detailed financial scenarios that encompass both the operational cash flow nuances and the overarching financial strategy. This dual approach allows you to anticipate short-term financial requirements while also preparing for long-term financial health, ensuring that your business remains resilient across various potential futures.

Let's delve into the realm of scenario planning, a strategic exercise that equips you to envision and prepare for multiple financial futures. By weaving together the insights garnered from both direct and indirect cash flow analyses, you're not just forecasting; you're crafting a narrative for each potential path your business might take.

Envisioning the Immediate with the Direct Method

Picture yourself at the helm of your business, navigating through the fog of uncertainty with the direct method as your lantern, casting light on the immediate cash flows that pulse through your company. This method offers you a clear, unobstructed view of the cash entering and exiting your business, akin to watching the waves lapping against your ship's bow. It allows you to see, in real-time, the impact of your day-to-day decisions, highlighting areas where the water might be seeping in or where you could harness the wind more effectively.

Now, imagine a scenario where an unexpected expense arises or a major client delays payment. The direct method enables you to quickly assess how these events affect your liquidity, empowering you to make swift, informed decisions—perhaps tightening spending in one area or accelerating collections efforts—to ensure your ship stays buoyant.

Mapping the Future with the Indirect Method

As you peer further into the horizon, the indirect method offers you a telescope to survey the broader financial landscape. This approach transcends the immediate, diving into the deeper currents that drive your cash flow over longer periods. It weaves together various financial threads—operating income adjustments, changes in working capital, depreciation, and more—painting a picture of how today's operations and decisions shape tomorrow's financial health.

Consider a scenario where you're contemplating a significant investment in new technology or expansion into new markets. The indirect method helps you understand how these strategic moves might affect your cash flow over time, influencing your ability to fund the investment, service any associated debt, and sustain growth.

Crafting Integrated Financial Narratives

By marrying the insights from both methods, you create a rich, multi-dimensional tapestry of scenarios that guide your strategic planning. You can envision not just one, but several potential futures, each with its own narrative arc and financial implications. This comprehensive view enables you to devise strategies that are robust, adaptable, and forward-looking, ensuring your business is primed to thrive regardless of the financial weather ahead.

In this nuanced approach to scenario planning, you're not just reacting to the financial winds; you're learning to sail them with skill and confidence. You're preparing your business not just to survive potential storms but to seize the winds of opportunity, charting a course toward sustained success and prosperity. Embrace this dual-faceted approach, and you'll find yourself not just navigating your business's financial journey but shaping it, steering toward a future marked by resilience, growth, and financial well-being.

Informed Decision-Making

Synergistic Insights: Harmonize the detailed operational insights from the direct method with the strategic revelations from the indirect method to form a holistic understanding of your financial position. This synergy enables you to make decisions that are informed by both the micro-level cash transactions and the macro-level financial strategy, ensuring that immediate financial choices are aligned with long-term objectives.

Strategic Alignment: Through this integrated analysis, ensure that your tactical responses—such as adjusting cash outflows or optimizing receivables—are not just reactionary but are strategic steps that contribute to the broader financial goals of your business, reinforcing your strategic direction and enhancing financial stability.

Imagine standing at the crossroads of your business's financial journey. To one side, the path of immediate actions, illuminated by the direct method's clear, practical insights into day-to-day cash flow. To the other, the broader road of strategic vision, revealed by the indirect method's deeper, nuanced understanding of your financial trajectory. The key to informed decision-making lies in merging these paths, ensuring each step taken not only addresses the present but also paves the way toward a prosperous future.

Harmonizing Insights for Holistic Understanding

Think of your business as an orchestra, with various sections playing in harmony. The direct method is like the string section, offering the melody—the immediate, discernible cash movements resonating with clarity and urgency. In contrast, the indirect method provides the underlying harmony, the broader financial context that enriches the melody and gives it depth. Together, they create a symphony of insights, each enhancing the other, allowing you to conduct your business with a full understanding of its financial music.

Now, envision a scenario where your cash flow analysis indicates a potential shortfall. With insights from the direct method, you identify specific areas—perhaps an unusually high inventory level or delayed receivables—where immediate action can improve liquidity. Simultaneously, the indirect method offers a broader perspective, suggesting that this shortfall is part of a larger trend, maybe due to seasonal fluctuations or a shift in market demand.

Strategically Aligning Decisions with Long-Term Goals

This dual perspective empowers you to make decisions that resonate on multiple levels. For instance, in addressing the immediate shortfall, you might implement more stringent inventory controls or enhance your receivables collection process. However, informed by the indirect method's insights, you also consider how these actions fit into your longer-term strategy. Perhaps this means adjusting your sales forecasts, reevaluating your market positioning, or even revising your business model to better align with emerging trends.

In this way, your tactical responses become strategic maneuvers. Adjusting cash outflows isn't merely about conserving cash but about optimizing your resource allocation to support your business's growth and adaptability. Optimizing receivables isn't just about improving liquidity but about fostering stronger customer relationships and enhancing your market responsiveness.

Crafting a Legacy of Informed Decision-Making

By embracing this integrated approach to financial analysis, you transition from reactive management to proactive leadership. You're not just navigating your business through the financial landscape; you're sculpting that landscape, informed by a deep understanding of both immediate realities and long-term possibilities.

In essence, informed decision-making, powered by the synergistic insights of direct and indirect cash flow analyses, becomes the cornerstone of your strategic leadership. It's about making decisions that are rooted in the present yet reach into the future, ensuring that every step taken is a step toward financial resilience, strategic alignment, and sustained success. In this way, you're not just running a business; you're building a legacy, one informed decision at a time.

Stakeholder Communication

Tailored Narratives: When communicating with stakeholders, utilize the direct method's transparency and specificity for discussions centered on operational efficiency and immediate financial health. This clarity is particularly effective for engaging with operational teams or stakeholders focused on near-term activities.

Strategic Dialogues: Leverage the comprehensive insights from the indirect method for discussions with investors, board members, or strategic partners who are interested in the long-term financial planning and sustainability of the business. The indirect method's ability to relate cash flow to broader financial performance and strategy makes it ideal for these higher-level strategic conversations.

Enhanced Credibility: By adeptly employing both methods as needed based on the audience, you enhance the credibility of your financial communication, demonstrating a deep and nuanced understanding of your business's financial dynamics. This not only builds trust but also fosters informed collaboration and support from various stakeholders, aligning everyone towards shared financial goals.

In sum, by mastering and integrating both direct and indirect cash flow analyses, you empower your business with a comprehensive and dynamic financial toolkit, enabling nuanced scenario planning, informed decision-making, and effective stakeholder communication. This integrated approach not only deepens your financial acumen but also positions your business for strategic agility and sustained success.

By mastering both direct and indirect cash flow analyses, you position yourself to navigate the complexities of financial management with a nuanced understanding, enabling strategic decisions that align with both your immediate operational realities and your long-term visionary objectives.

Imagine yourself as a skilled storyteller, where each financial report you present is a narrative woven from the intricate details of your company's fiscal landscape. In this narrative, the characters are your cash flows, the plot is your business's financial journey, and the audience is your stakeholders, each group eager to understand their role in the story and its implications for their interests.

Crafting Tailored Narratives with the Direct Method

When you communicate with operational teams or stakeholders who are deeply involved in the day-to-day workings of the business, the direct method of cash flow analysis becomes your script. It provides a clear, detailed account of cash transactions, offering a lens into the operational heartbeat of your company. This method allows you to articulate not just the 'what' but the 'how' and 'why' of your cash flows, connecting the dots between operational decisions and their financial outcomes.

For instance, when discussing with your sales team, you can use the direct method to highlight how their efforts in shortening the sales cycle directly enhance cash inflow. Similarly, when engaging with your supply chain managers, this method can elucidate the financial impact of inventory turnover improvements, making the financial narrative both relevant and actionable for your audience.

Elevating Strategic Dialogues with the Indirect Method

Conversely, when your audience shifts to investors, board members, or strategic partners, the narrative needs to ascend to a broader vista, one that encompasses not just the immediate but the prospective. Here, the indirect method offers a panoramic view, connecting operational cash flows to the company's overall financial health and strategic trajectory. It allows you to weave a story that places day-to-day operations within the grander scheme of financial goals and strategies.

This broader narrative can be particularly compelling when articulating the financial underpinnings of strategic decisions. For example, you might illustrate how reinvesting profits into research and development aligns with long-term growth objectives or how debt restructuring enhances financial sustainability, providing the strategic foresight that resonates with this audience.

Building Trust Through Financial Fluency

By adeptly switching between these two narrative styles based on your audience, you demonstrate not just financial literacy but fluency. This adaptability enhances your credibility and engenders trust, showing that you comprehend the financial implications of operational activities as well as the strategic considerations of long-term planning.

Moreover, this nuanced approach to financial communication fosters a culture of transparency and informed collaboration. Stakeholders are more likely to rally behind decisions and strategies when they understand the financial rationale and see their reflections in the broader narrative of the business's journey.

In conclusion, the artful integration of direct and indirect cash flow analyses in stakeholder communication is akin to mastering different languages for different audiences, each tailored to convey meaning and foster understanding. By doing so, you not only illuminate the financial path your business is on but also invite your stakeholders to walk this path with you, united by a shared vision and a deep understanding of the financial landscapes ahead.

2. Cash Flow Forecasting:

Cash flow forecasting stands as a pivotal tool in the financial strategist's arsenal, allowing businesses to navigate the future with informed confidence. By constructing a predictive model that intricately maps out expected cash inflows and outflows, businesses can anticipate their financial trajectory, enabling proactive management of resources and strategic alignment of operational goals.

Foundations of Cash Flow Forecasting:

Data-Driven Insights: Utilize historical financial data as the bedrock of your forecasting model, analyzing patterns, trends, and cyclical variations in past cash flow activities. This historical analysis provides a grounded basis from which to project future movements, infusing your forecast with empirical rigor.

Incorporating Expectations: Beyond historical data, incorporate scheduled payments, due receivables, contractual obligations, and anticipated operational expenditures into your forecast. This comprehensive inclusion ensures that your forecast reflects not only past trends but also forthcoming financial realities.

Adaptive Modeling: Recognize that cash flow forecasting is not a set-and-forget activity but an iterative process. Regularly update your forecast with actual financial outcomes and revise future projections to reflect new information, market conditions, or changes in business strategy, ensuring that your forecast remains relevant and actionable.

Embark on the journey of cash flow forecasting, a pivotal process that combines the art of financial analysis with the science of predictive modeling. As you delve into this endeavor, imagine yourself as an architect, meticulously designing a blueprint that will guide your business's financial strategy and decision-making.

Laying the Foundation with Data-Driven Insights

Your first step in this architectural process is to lay a solid foundation using historical financial data. This data serves as the bedrock of your forecasting model, akin to the deep, sturdy roots of a centuries-old tree. By examining the ebbs and flows of your past cash movements, you identify patterns, recognize trends, and understand cyclical variations that have characterized your business's financial journey.

Just as an architect studies the land before drawing the first line of a blueprint, you analyze this historical data to discern the financial rhythms of your business. Was there a seasonal uptick in sales during certain months? Did specific operational changes result in cash flow improvements or challenges? These insights gleaned from the past become the critical underpinnings of your forecast, grounding it in empirical reality and enhancing its credibility.

Incorporating Expectations for a Comprehensive View

However, a robust forecast cannot live on history alone. It must also look to the horizon, anticipating what lies ahead. This is where incorporating expectations becomes crucial. Scheduled payments, receivables due to land, contractual obligations coming due, and planned operational expenditures all represent financial currents that will shape your future cash flow.

Envision weaving these various threads into your forecast, much like an artist blending colors on a canvas. Each element—be it an anticipated capital expenditure or an expected surge in sales—adds nuance and depth to your projection, transforming it from a mere extrapolation of the past into a forward-looking financial map that navigates the future.

Embracing Adaptive Modeling for Agility

Recognize that the financial landscape is ever-changing, influenced by market dynamics, competitive forces, and internal strategic decisions. As such, your cash flow forecast should not be a static artifact but a living document, adaptable and responsive to the unfolding reality of your business.

Regularly revisiting and updating your forecast is akin to steering a ship, making course corrections in response to shifting winds and tides. When actual financial outcomes diverge from your projections, delve into the reasons, adjust your assumptions, and refine your forecast. This iterative process ensures that your cash flow forecasting remains a relevant, dynamic tool that informs strategic decisions, supports financial planning, and fosters proactive business management.

In essence, foundations of cash flow forecasting merge historical wisdom with forward-looking intelligence, crafting a financial compass that guides your business through the uncertainties of the future. By embracing data-driven insights, incorporating comprehensive expectations, and committing to adaptive modeling, you empower your business to navigate its financial journey with insight, foresight, and strategic agility.

Strategic Advantages of Cash Flow Forecasting:

Proactive Financial Management: Armed with a forecast that anticipates future cash positions, you can make informed decisions regarding investment opportunities, capital expenditures, and debt management. This foresight helps in optimizing the allocation of financial resources, ensuring they are directed toward strategic priorities and growth initiatives.

Mitigating Financial Risks: By identifying potential cash shortfalls before they materialize, you can implement strategies to bolster liquidity, such as adjusting credit terms, enhancing receivables collection, or arranging for financing. This proactive approach mitigates the risks associated with liquidity crunches, safeguarding your business's operational continuity.

Strategic Alignment and Decision Making: Cash flow forecasting aligns closely with broader business planning and strategy, providing a financial lens through which to evaluate strategic initiatives. Understanding the cash flow implications of various strategic choices enables decision-makers to select paths that are financially viable and aligned with long-term objectives.

Enhancing Stakeholder Confidence: A robust cash flow forecasting process demonstrates to investors, lenders, and other stakeholders that your business is managed with foresight and financial acumen. This transparency and strategic orientation can enhance stakeholder confidence, facilitate access to capital, and support business valuation.

In summary, cash flow forecasting is not merely a financial exercise; it is a strategic imperative. By integrating sophisticated forecasting into your financial management practices, you empower your business to navigate future uncertainties with greater clarity, align financial resources with strategic objectives, and foster a culture of informed, proactive decision-making. This strategic tool not only enhances your ability to manage day-to-day financial challenges but also positions your business for sustainable growth and success.

Dive into the strategic realm of cash flow forecasting, where your foresight shapes the financial destiny of your business, turning potential vulnerabilities into opportunities for growth and stability. This crucial practice arms you with the knowledge to steer your enterprise confidently into the future, navigating the complexities of financial ebbs and flows with the precision of a seasoned captain.

Empowering Proactive Financial Management

Envision yourself at the control panel of your business, where every lever and button influences your financial trajectory. Cash flow forecasting is your radar, scanning the horizon for opportunities and obstacles. With this advanced notice, you're not merely reacting to financial winds; you're setting your sails to catch them, steering toward lucrative investments, judiciously timing capital expenditures, and managing debt with strategic intent.

This proactive stance ensures that your financial resources are not just preserved but optimized, channeled into ventures that promise the greatest return or fortification for your business. It's about making choices today that position you for success tomorrow, always with an eye on ensuring your financial maneuvers align with your overarching business aspirations.

Mitigating Financial Risks with Foresight

Imagine foreseeing a storm on your financial horizon—cash flow forecasting gives you this prescient ability. Identifying potential cash shortfalls before they strike is akin to battening down the hatches well before the storm hits, enabling you to weather financial turbulence with minimal disruption.

Whether it's tightening credit terms, accelerating receivables, or securing a line of credit, these strategic adjustments can be planned and executed well in advance, transforming potential crises into manageable situations. Such preemptive measures not only secure your business's liquidity but also protect its reputation, operational efficacy, and strategic momentum.

Aligning Strategy with Financial Reality

In the grand chessboard of business strategy, cash flow forecasting is your strategic advantage, providing the financial perspective necessary to evaluate and select the most promising moves. It links every departmental plan, every market expansion, and every innovation initiative to its financial implications, ensuring that strategic ambitions are grounded in financial reality.

This alignment is invaluable for decision-makers, enabling them to choose paths that are not only visionary but also financially sustainable, ensuring that the company's growth is built on a solid financial foundation.

Cultivating Stakeholder Confidence

In the world of business, confidence can be as valuable as capital. A transparent and robust cash flow forecasting process showcases your commitment to financial diligence, winning the trust and confidence of investors, lenders, and partners. It signals that your business is not just surviving but thriving, equipped with the clarity and strategic acumen to navigate future challenges.

This confidence can translate into tangible benefits: better investment terms, more favorable credit conditions, and a strong market reputation, all of which can propel your business to new heights.

In essence, cash flow forecasting transcends its role as a financial tool, becoming a beacon that guides your strategic decision-making, enhances your operational resilience, and deepens stakeholder trust. By embracing this practice, you not only illuminate your business's financial path but also chart a course toward enduring success and strategic fulfillment.

3. Cash Flow Statement Analysis:

The cash flow statement, an essential component of a company's financial reports, offers a transparent view of the organization's liquidity and financial health over a specific period. By dissecting this statement into its core segments—operational, investing, and financing activities—businesses and individuals can glean nuanced insights into the sources and uses of cash, enabling astute financial management and strategic planning.

Operational Activities:

Nature and Significance: Cash flows from operating activities are the lifeblood of any business, reflecting the cash generated or consumed by the company's core business operations. This section provides insight into the profitability and cash-generating efficiency of the company's primary activities.

Analysis Techniques: To analyze operating cash flows, scrutinize the adjustments made to net income, such as changes in working capital, depreciation, and non-cash expenses. Understanding these adjustments can reveal the true cash-generating capability of the business operations, independent of accrual accounting distortions.

Strategic Implications: Consistent positive cash flow from operations is indicative of a healthy, viable business. Analyzing trends in this area can help forecast future operational liquidity and identify potential areas for operational efficiency improvements or cost reductions.

Investing Activities:

Nature and Significance: Cash flows from investing activities provide insights into how a company allocates its capital to long-term assets and investments. These activities include purchasing or selling physical assets, investing in securities, or lending money.

Analysis Techniques: Evaluate the company's investment strategy and its alignment with long-term goals by examining outflows for asset acquisitions and inflows from asset sales. Significant outflows might indicate growth or expansion, while substantial inflows could suggest asset divestiture or retraction.

Strategic Implications: Understanding investing cash flow helps stakeholders assess the company's growth strategy and asset management efficiency. Regular, substantial investments might indicate a forward-looking growth stance, whereas consistent divestitures could signal a strategic pivot or liquidity concerns.

Financing Activities:

Nature and Significance: This segment of the cash flow statement reflects transactions related to equity, debt, and dividends, offering a window into how the company finances its operations and growth through capital structure management.

Analysis Techniques: Dissecting financing activities involves assessing the company's approach to leveraging debt versus equity financing, changes in capital structure, and dividend policy. Analyzing these flows can reveal insights into the company's financial strategy, risk appetite, and commitment to shareholder returns.

Strategic Implications: Trends in financing activities can inform stakeholders about the company's stability and growth prospects. For example, frequent equity issuances might dilute existing ownership but support growth without increasing debt, whereas regular debt financing could enhance returns but at higher risk levels.

Facilitating Informed Decision-Making:

By delving deep into each section of the cash flow statement, stakeholders can:

Identify Trends: Recognize and anticipate cash flow trends that may impact the company's ability to fund operations, invest in growth, or return value to shareholders.

Assess Sustainability: Evaluate whether the company's cash flows are sustainable in the long term, supporting its operational needs, investment plans, and financing obligations.

Make Strategic Decisions: Utilize insights from the cash flow analysis to make informed decisions regarding investments, credit, and operational strategies, aligning financial tactics with overarching business objectives.

In essence, a comprehensive analysis of the cash flow statement empowers stakeholders with a deeper understanding of the company's financial dynamics, enhancing transparency and enabling more strategic, data-driven decision-making. This thorough scrutiny underscores the pivotal role of cash flow analysis in discerning the financial health and strategic direction of any entity.

Integrating Technology and Methodology

1. Real-Time Data Analysis:

- Utilizing software that offers real-time data syncing with bank accounts and financial institutions can provide an up-to-the-minute view of cash flow, crucial for timely decisions in fast-paced environments.

In the dynamic dance of financial management, the ability to move in harmony with the rhythm of real-time data is akin to having a sixth sense—an intuition that guides you through the complexities of the financial landscape with agility and foresight. The utilization of software that offers real-time data syncing with bank accounts and financial institutions emerges not just as a tool, but as an extension of your financial consciousness. This seamless integration of technology and financial intuition allows for a fluid, up-to-the-minute view of cash flow, illuminating the path ahead with clarity and precision.

The Alchemy of Real-Time Data Analysis

Imagine each transaction, each movement of money, as a pulse—a heartbeat within the vast network of your financial life. Real-time data analysis captures these pulses, transforming them into a continuous stream of insights that flow directly into your subconscious mind. This constant flow of information becomes a powerful force, subtly guiding your financial decisions and actions.

1. The Subconscious Calibration of Financial Decisions: With real-time data at your fingertips, your financial decisions are no longer guesses or delayed reactions; they are precise, informed responses to the immediate state of your finances. This calibration happens not just on a conscious level but is deeply embedded in your subconscious, enabling you to make swift, accurate decisions that feel as natural and effortless as breathing.

2. Navigating Fast-Paced Financial Waters with Confidence: In the fast-paced currents of today's financial environments, the ability to adapt and respond quickly is invaluable. Real-time data analysis equips you with the insight to navigate these waters with confidence. Like a skilled sailor reading the wind and the waves, you adjust your sails—the allocations of your resources—in response to the immediate conditions, ensuring a steady course towards your financial goals.

3. The Subconscious Integration of Financial Awareness: The continuous stream of financial information fosters a heightened state of financial awareness. This awareness is not burdensome but liberating, for it is integrated into your subconscious mind. It informs your habits, your impulses, and your choices, aligning your everyday actions with your long-term financial aspirations.

4. Anticipating and Preparing for Financial Fluctuations: Just as a seasoned gardener anticipates changes in the weather, real-time data analysis enables you to anticipate and prepare for financial fluctuations. This proactive stance is not born of constant vigilance but is a subconscious readiness—a state of being that prepares you to weather financial storms with resilience and to seize opportunities with alacrity.

5. The Evolution of Financial Intuition: Through the lens of real-time data analysis, your financial intuition evolves. It becomes not just a reaction to past experiences but a forward-looking sense, attuned to the nuances of your financial flow. This intuition guides you, almost without thought, towards decisions that nurture your financial health and growth.

In embracing real-time data analysis, you are not merely adopting a technological tool; you are engaging in a profound partnership between technology and your subconscious mind. This partnership illuminates the path to financial empowerment, enabling you to navigate the complexities of your financial journey with insight, agility, and an intuitive sense of direction that leads invariably towards prosperity and stability.

2. Scenario Analysis:

- Advanced tools often allow for scenario analysis, where users can simulate different financial situations (e.g., a major purchase, a sudden drop in income) to see their potential impact on cash flow.

Immerse yourself in the transformative power of scenario analysis, a tool that not only anticipates the future but shapes it. This advanced technique, embedded within the most innovative financial tools, empowers you to create a multitude of futures in the sanctuary of the present. Imagine, with every simulation, you're weaving the fabric of your financial destiny, each thread a choice, each pattern a possibility.

Embedding Scenario Analysis into the Subconscious

1. **The Visualization of Financial Futures:** Let the act of scenario analysis become a ritual, as natural and necessary as the changing of seasons. With each simulation, visualize not just numbers changing, but your life adapting, growing, thriving under different circumstances. This constant visualization embeds the habit deep within your subconscious, making preparedness and adaptability part of your financial identity.

2. **Embracing the Power of 'What If':** The question "What if?" transforms from a whisper of doubt into a powerful chant of preparedness. Allow this mantra to seep into your subconscious, turning the uncertainty of financial "What ifs" into scenarios you've already lived, decisions you've already made. This mental rehearsal primes your subconscious to act with confidence when faced with real-life financial shifts.

3. **The Alchemy of Anticipation:** Like an alchemist turning lead into gold, scenario analysis enables you to transmute anxiety about the unknown into strategic plans for any financial climate. Embed this alchemy into your subconscious, letting anticipation of future challenges become a source of strength and empowerment, guiding your financial decisions with wisdom and foresight.

4. **Cultivating a Garden of Resilience:** Imagine each scenario analysis as planting a seed of resilience in the garden of your mind. With every simulation, you're cultivating a landscape resilient to financial storms and droughts. This garden, rooted deep in your subconscious, flourishes with the knowledge that you are prepared for any financial season.

5. **The Subconscious Shift from Reactivity to Proactivity:** Through regular engagement with scenario analysis, instill a profound shift in your subconscious from reactivity to proactivity. This shift marks a transition to a state where your financial decisions are not reactions to external forces but informed choices made in the calm before any storm.

By embedding the practice of scenario analysis into your subconscious, you equip yourself with a tool of immense power—a power not just to predict the future, but to prepare for it, shape it, and greet it with confidence. This deep, subconscious integration ensures that, regardless of what the future holds, your financial foundation is unshakable, your decisions are informed, and your path to prosperity is clear.

3. Integration with Other Financial Tools:

- Many cash flow analysis tools integrate seamlessly with other financial software, such as investment trackers or debt management apps, providing a holistic view of one's financial health.

In the interconnected web of personal finance, envision a world where every strand of your financial life is woven together into a cohesive tapestry. Cash flow analysis tools, with their advanced capabilities, serve as the loom on which this tapestry is crafted. These tools do not stand alone; they harmonize with other financial software—investment trackers, debt management apps, and more—creating a seamless integration that offers a panoramic view of your financial health.

The Symphony of Financial Integration

1. **The Harmonious Connection:** Imagine each piece of financial software as an instrument in an orchestra. Individually, they play their own melodies—tracking investments, managing debts, analyzing cash flow. Yet, when conducted together, they create a symphony of financial clarity. This harmony brings your financial picture into focus, allowing you to see the interplay of various financial aspects in real-time.

2. **The Canvas of Financial Health:** Picture your financial health as a canvas, with each application adding its color and texture. The integration of cash flow analysis with other tools paints a comprehensive picture, blending the hues of your income, the shades of your expenses, and the contours of your investments and debts. This canvas, ever-evolving, reflects the full spectrum of your financial life.

3. **The Garden of Growth:** Envision your financial growth as a garden, where cash flow analysis and other financial tools are the nutrients that feed it. Together, they ensure that every decision you make—be it investing for the future or paying down debt—contributes to the health and vitality of your financial garden. This ecosystem thrives on the seamless integration of information, fostering informed decisions that nurture sustained growth.

4. **The Journey of Discovery:** Embark on a journey of financial discovery, where the integration of cash flow analysis with other financial software serves as your compass. This journey reveals not just where you stand but where you can go. It illuminates paths previously hidden, guiding you towards financial decisions that align with your deepest values and aspirations.

5. **The Dance of Flexibility:** In the dance of managing finances, flexibility is key. The seamless integration of financial tools allows you to move with grace and agility, adapting to life's rhythms. Like a dancer, you respond to the music of your financial situation with confidence, knowing that you have a holistic understanding of your financial health at your fingertips.

This unified approach to managing your finances, where cash flow analysis tools blend seamlessly with other financial software, is not just a strategy—it's a holistic way of living your financial life. It ensures that every financial decision is informed by a comprehensive view of your wealth, debts, and investments, empowering you to make choices that resonate with your journey towards financial well-being and abundance.

Building a Mindset for Strategic Financial Management

Embracing these advanced tools and methodologies for cash flow analysis is not merely a technical exercise; it is an integral part of cultivating a mindset geared towards strategic financial management and wealth creation. By making informed decisions based on comprehensive cash flow analysis, individuals and businesses can navigate financial uncertainties with confidence, ensuring not just survival but prosperity in the dynamic landscape of personal and business finance.

Section 2: Advanced Personal Budgeting Strategies

- **Forecasting Future Expenses:** Techniques for accurately predicting future personal expenses, including irregular and seasonal expenses.

In the realm of personal finance, envisioning the future with clarity and precision is akin to navigating through time with a map and compass in hand. The art of forecasting future expenses, particularly those that are irregular and seasonal, demands a dance between intuition and strategy, a harmony between the conscious and the subconscious mind. As we delve into techniques for accurately predicting future personal expenses, imagine embedding these practices into the fabric of your financial consciousness, allowing them to become second nature, actions performed with the grace and ease of a seasoned navigator charting a course through familiar waters.

The Subconscious Art of Expense Forecasting

1. Envisioning Patterns in the Ebb and Flow of Finances: Just as the moon influences the tides, your spending and saving rhythms are guided by patterns. Recognize these patterns. Observe past cycles of expenditure like an artist studying their own brushstrokes, identifying the times of year when expenses naturally rise or fall. This awareness becomes your guide, subtly influencing your financial decisions without conscious effort.

2. Embracing the Ritual of Regular Review: Make it a ritual, as natural as the changing seasons, to review your financial transactions. Use this time to reflect not just on the numbers, but on the story they tell about your life's journey. This regular review, though it begins as a conscious activity, gradually weaves itself into the fabric of your subconscious, guiding your financial decisions with the wisdom of past experiences.

3. Cultivating a Garden of Goals: Just as a gardener plants seeds with the future harvest in mind, plant your financial goals with care and foresight. Visualize these goals daily, seeing them not as distant dreams but as inevitable realities. This visualization plants the seeds deep within your subconscious, ensuring that every financial decision, no matter how small, nourishes these future aspirations.

4. Harnessing the Power of Technology as Your Ally: Let technology be your ally in this journey. Utilize budgeting apps and financial planning tools as extensions of your own mind, programming them with your financial patterns and goals. As these tools integrate into your daily life, they serve not just as external aids but as manifestations of your own financial intuition, guiding you towards your goals with precision and ease.

5. The Subconscious Dialogue of Financial Mindfulness: Engage in a continuous, subconscious dialogue with your finances. Let this dialogue be one of curiosity and openness, where every expense, no matter how irregular or seasonal, is an opportunity to align more closely with your deepest values and aspirations. This mindset transforms the act of forecasting and managing expenses into a subconscious reflex, aligned with your path to financial abundance.

In adopting these techniques, forecasting future expenses transcends the realm of mere prediction, becoming a deeply ingrained practice that guides your financial journey. Through this subconscious integration, you navigate your finances with an intuitive understanding of where you are headed, ensuring that every step, every decision, moves you closer to your envisioned future of stability and prosperity.

- Adjusting Budgets for Financial Goals: Strategies for aligning budget adjustments with long-term financial goals, such as retirement, education funding, or major purchases.

In the journey towards realizing your dreams—be it a serene retirement, the gift of education, or the acquisition of cherished assets—the strategy you employ to align your budget with these long-term financial goals is akin to charting a course through the stars. Each adjustment you make to your budget acts not merely as a correction but as a deliberate steer towards your desired destiny. Imagine embedding these strategies into your financial navigation system, guiding you seamlessly towards the realization of your aspirations.

The Strategy of Alignment

1. Visualize Your Financial Goals: Begin by vividly imagining your long-term financial goals. See yourself enjoying the fruits of retirement, experiencing the joy of providing education, or the satisfaction of making significant purchases. This visualization embeds your goals deep within your subconscious, transforming them from distant dreams into imminent realities.

2. Prioritize Your Goals: In the rich tapestry of your financial future, not all goals hold equal weight at all times. Prioritize them based on their importance and timeline. This prioritization process becomes a subconscious filter for your financial decisions, ensuring that resources are allocated in a manner that reflects your true aspirations.

3. Create Goal-Specific Budget Categories: Introduce dedicated categories in your budget for each of your major long-term goals. Treat contributions to these categories as non-negotiable, similar to essential expenses like rent or utilities. This practice ingrains the importance of your goals into your everyday financial habits, reinforcing your commitment to them.

4. Employ the Power of Incremental Progress: The journey towards significant financial milestones is made one step at a time. Embrace incremental progress by setting and celebrating small, achievable targets along the way. This approach nurtures a sense of accomplishment and progress, motivating continued adherence to your budget adjustments.

5. Leverage Financial Tools for Automation: Utilize financial tools and software to automate transfers to savings or investment accounts dedicated to your goals. Automation acts as a silent guardian of your aspirations, ensuring that contributions are made consistently, without the need for conscious action each month.

6. Adapt and Flex with Life's Changes: As you sail the seas of life, winds of change are inevitable. Regularly review and adjust your budget to reflect changes in income, expenses, or priorities. This adaptability should be deeply ingrained, allowing you to fluidly adjust your course while keeping your long-term goals in sight.

7. The Subconscious Integration of Goals and Budget: Through consistent practice, the alignment of your budget with your long-term financial goals becomes a subconscious part of your financial identity. Decisions about spending and saving are filtered through the lens of your goals, ensuring that each choice propels you closer to your dreams.

8. Celebrate Milestones and Reflect: Take time to celebrate each milestone achieved towards your goals. Reflection and celebration reinforce the positive impact of your budget adjustments, encouraging persistence and dedication.

By consciously embedding these strategies into your financial planning, you subtly program your subconscious to navigate towards your long-term goals with precision and dedication. This alignment transforms the act of budgeting from a routine task into a powerful catalyst for achieving your dreams, ensuring that each financial decision is a stepping stone towards the life you envision.

- **Scenario Planning:** How to use scenario planning in personal budgeting to prepare for various financial outcomes and uncertainties.

Scenario planning in personal budgeting is akin to charting multiple courses on a map, preparing for various winds and weathers that might carry you toward different shores. This strategic approach involves envisioning various financial futures and developing plans to navigate through them. By integrating scenario planning into your budgeting process, you cultivate a deep-rooted resilience, enabling you to meet unforeseen financial outcomes and uncertainties with grace and preparedness.

The Art of Crafting Scenarios

1. Envisioning Multiple Financial Futures: Begin by allowing your mind to explore different financial landscapes. Imagine scenarios such as a significant increase in income, unexpected job loss, or sudden large expenses. Let these visions be as vivid and detailed as possible, painting a comprehensive picture of potential financial futures.

2. Identifying Key Variables: In each scenario, identify the key variables that could change your financial situation. These might include income levels, expenditure patterns, economic conditions, or life events. Recognizing these variables helps you understand the levers of your financial life, allowing for more precise adjustments in each scenario.

3. Developing Responsive Strategies: For each envisioned scenario, craft a tailored response strategy. These strategies should outline how you would adjust your budgeting and financial planning to maintain stability and progress toward your goals. This process of strategy development ingrains a proactive mindset, enabling you to act decisively in the face of change.

4. The Subconscious Embedding of Flexibility: Through regular engagement with scenario planning, you subtly program your subconscious to embrace financial flexibility. This flexibility becomes a natural part of your financial decision-making process, equipping you to adapt seamlessly to new circumstances without panic or indecision.

Integrating Scenario Planning into Budgeting

5. Creating a Scenario Planning Journal: Maintain a dedicated journal for your scenario planning exercises. Documenting your scenarios and strategies not only provides a reference but also reinforces your commitment to financial resilience through repeated review and reflection.

6. Practicing Regular Scenario Reviews: Incorporate scenario planning into your regular financial reviews. Periodically revisiting and revising your scenarios ensures that your strategies remain relevant and aligned with your current financial situation and goals.

7. Simulating Scenarios: Where possible, simulate your scenarios to test the effectiveness of your strategies. This might involve creating detailed budget forecasts or using financial planning software to model the impact of various scenarios on your cash flow and savings.

8. Cultivating an Adaptive Financial Mindset: Embrace the philosophy that change is not just a possibility but an inevitability. By adopting an adaptive financial mindset, you prepare yourself to navigate any financial storm with confidence, knowing that you have already charted a course through even the most challenging conditions.

Scenario planning transforms the uncertainty of the future into a landscape of preparedness and opportunity. By envisioning various financial futures and embedding flexible response strategies into your subconscious, you empower yourself to face financial outcomes and uncertainties with a proactive, confident approach. This deep-rooted preparedness not only enhances your financial resilience but also supports your journey toward achieving your long-term financial aspirations.

Section 3: Budgeting for Investment and Wealth Accumulation

- **Allocating Resources for Investments:** Guidelines on how to budget for investments within a broader financial plan.

Allocating resources for investments within the broader context of a financial plan is akin to cultivating a garden of wealth, where the seeds of today's investments are the flourishing assets of tomorrow. This process requires foresight, balance, and a commitment to nurturing your financial future. By embedding these guidelines into your approach, you transform the act of investing from a mere transaction into a deliberate and strategic cultivation of your financial well-being.

The Strategic Allocation of Investment Resources

1. **Establish a Clear Financial Foundation:** Before diverting resources into investments, ensure your financial foundation is solid. This means having a well-structured budget, an emergency fund in place, and manageable levels of debt. Visualize this foundation as the fertile soil from which your investments will grow.

2. **Define Your Investment Goals:** Clarify your investment objectives, whether they are for retirement, purchasing a home, education, or other long-term goals. Each goal should be vivid in your mind's eye, serving as a beacon that guides your investment decisions.

3. **Understand Your Time Horizon and Risk Tolerance:** Acknowledge and embrace your unique financial landscape, including how much time you have to invest and your comfort level with risk. This self-awareness is crucial for selecting investment vehicles that align with your personal financial narrative.

4. **Prioritize Investments in Your Budget:** Make investing a non-negotiable part of your monthly budget, just as you would with savings or debt payments. Allocate a specific percentage of your income towards investments, treating it as a vital contribution to your future self.

5. **Utilize Automation to Ensure Consistency:** Leverage the power of automation to make regular investments. Setting up automatic transfers to investment accounts removes the hurdle of manual decision-making, ensuring your garden of wealth receives consistent nourishment.

6. **Diversify Your Investment Portfolio:** Spread your investments across a variety of asset classes to mitigate risk and increase the potential for growth. Imagine your portfolio as a diverse ecosystem, where each asset plays a role in maintaining balance and promoting health.

7. **Regularly Review and Adjust Your Investment Strategy:** Just as a garden requires regular tending, so does your investment strategy. Schedule periodic reviews to assess the performance of your investments and make adjustments as needed, ensuring your strategy evolves with your changing financial landscape and goals.

8. **Educate Yourself Continuously:** Commit to lifelong learning about investing and financial planning. The more you understand, the better equipped you'll be to make informed decisions that align with your vision of financial prosperity.

Embedding Investment Planning into Your Financial Subconscious

Through repeated practice and engagement with these guidelines, the process of allocating resources for investments becomes an integral part of your financial behavior. It transitions from a conscious effort to a subconscious habit, deeply ingrained in your approach to financial management. This shift not only enhances your ability to build wealth but also aligns your daily financial decisions with your long-term aspirations.

By thoughtfully integrating investment planning into your broader financial plan, you're not just allocating resources; you're sowing the seeds of your future financial abundance. This deliberate cultivation ensures that, over time, you'll harvest the rewards of your foresight and discipline, achieving the financial prosperity you envision.

- **Risk Management in Budgeting:** Discussing the integration of risk management strategies into the budgeting process to support investment goals.

Integrating risk management strategies into the budgeting process is akin to charting a course through uncertain waters with a keen eye on potential storms and hidden reefs. It's about preparing your financial ship not only to sail smoothly in calm seas but also to withstand and navigate through turbulent ones. This strategic integration ensures that your journey towards investment goals is not derailed by unforeseen financial squalls but is instead a well-planned voyage that anticipates and mitigates risks.

Foundations of Risk Management in Budgeting

1. Identify Potential Financial Risks: Start by mapping out the financial landscape, identifying potential risks that could impact your budget and investment goals. These might include job loss, unexpected expenses, market volatility, or changes in interest rates. Visualize these risks not as deterrents but as navigational challenges to be prepared for and navigated through.

2. Establish an Emergency Fund: An emergency fund acts as a life raft, designed to keep you afloat during financial storms. Allocate resources within your budget to build and maintain an emergency fund that covers 3-6 months of living expenses. This fund is your financial buffer, ensuring that unexpected events don't capsize your investment plans.

3. Incorporate Insurance into Your Financial Strategy: Insurance is the lighthouse guiding you safely past potential financial hazards. From health and life insurance to homeowners and auto insurance, ensure you have adequate coverage to protect against significant financial losses. Budgeting for insurance premiums is an investment in your financial security and peace of mind.

4. Diversify Your Investment Portfolio: Just as a captain relies on multiple navigational tools, diversify your investment portfolio to spread and manage risk. This diversification should reflect a balance of stocks, bonds, real estate, and other assets, aligned with your risk tolerance and investment horizon. Regularly review and adjust your portfolio to maintain this balance.

5. Use Debt Strategically: Manage debt like you would navigate around treacherous shoals—carefully and strategically. Prioritize paying off high-interest debt and consider the implications of taking on new debt in your budgeting and investment strategy. Utilize debt in a way that propels you forward, not one that anchors you down.

6. Adopt a Flexible Budgeting Approach: Flexibility in budgeting is like setting adjustable sails; it allows you to respond dynamically to changing financial winds. Allocate a portion of your budget for unforeseen expenses and be prepared to adjust your spending in other categories to manage fluctuations in income or expenses.

7. Regular Scenario Planning: Engage in regular scenario planning to anticipate how different risks could impact your budget and investment goals. Develop contingency plans for various scenarios, ensuring that you can adjust your sails swiftly and effectively, no matter the direction of the financial winds.

8. Continuous Learning and Adaptation: The financial seas are ever-changing, and continuous education is your compass. Stay informed about economic trends, market conditions, and new risk management strategies. This ongoing learning ensures your budgeting and investment strategies remain robust and responsive.

Subconscious Integration of Risk Management

By weaving these risk management strategies into the fabric of your budgeting process, they become more than just practices—they transform into an intrinsic part of your financial mindset. This subconscious integration ensures that every financial decision is made with a clear understanding of potential risks and an unwavering commitment to your long-term security and prosperity.

In essence, integrating risk management into your budgeting process equips you to pursue your investment goals with confidence, preparedness, and strategic foresight. It's about turning potential financial perils into manageable elements of your comprehensive plan, ensuring that your journey towards financial success is both deliberate and secure.

- **Leveraging Budget Surpluses:** Strategies for effectively utilizing budget surpluses to accelerate wealth accumulation.

In the landscape of personal finance, envision each budget surplus as a golden opportunity, a key moment where the careful stewardship of your resources can catapult you toward your dreams of wealth accumulation. These surpluses, whether expected or pleasantly surprising, are not mere numbers on a balance sheet but potent seeds of potential. When nurtured with intention and strategic foresight, they have the power to grow, multiply, and transform your financial future.

Harnessing the Power of Surpluses

1. **Prioritize High-Impact Debt Repayment:** View each surplus as a powerful tool in your arsenal against high-interest debt. Allocating extra funds to pay down this debt not only reduces the interest you pay over time but also frees up more of your future income for savings and investments. This strategic move is akin to clearing the weeds from your garden, allowing your financial assets to flourish without hindrance.

2. Strengthen Your Financial Safety Net: Consider each surplus an opportunity to fortify your emergency fund. Enhancing this fund ensures that you're prepared for life's uncertainties, providing a cushion that allows you to take calculated risks in pursuit of higher returns. This reinforcement acts as the fertile soil from which your financial security and growth can spring.

3. Invest in Your Future: With every surplus, imagine opening doors to new realms of potential growth. Investing these funds in diversified portfolios, retirement accounts, or other wealth-building vehicles not only harnesses the power of compound interest but also aligns your present resources with your future aspirations. This is the art of planting seeds today that will grow into the forests of tomorrow's wealth.

4. Cultivate Personal and Professional Growth: View surpluses as investments in yourself. Allocating resources towards education, skill development, or health not only enhances your personal well-being but can also increase your earning potential. Like watering a plant, nurturing your growth ensures that you continue to thrive and adapt in an ever-changing financial environment.

5. Give Generously: Recognize the power of surplus to not only grow your wealth but to sow seeds of prosperity in the wider community. Strategic giving can create a ripple effect, fostering a cycle of generosity and abundance. This practice enriches your life, grounding your financial journey in a sense of purpose and connection.

Subconscious Integration

By consistently applying these strategies, the management of budget surpluses transcends conscious action, embedding itself in the subconscious as a natural extension of your financial behavior. This integration shapes a mindset where every surplus is instinctively seen as a stepping stone towards greater financial abundance. It fosters a proactive, rather than reactive, approach to financial management, ensuring that each decision contributes to a larger tapestry of wealth accumulation.

In this way, leveraging budget surpluses becomes more than a financial strategy; it becomes a deeply ingrained habit, a part of your financial DNA that propels you toward achieving your dreams. This subconscious alignment of actions and goals ensures that you navigate your financial journey with wisdom, purpose, and an unwavering focus on the horizon of prosperity.

Section 4: Behavioral Finance and Budgeting

- **Psychological Barriers to Effective Budgeting:** Exploration of common psychological hurdles that impede advanced budgeting efforts and how to overcome them.

Embarking on the journey of advanced budgeting is akin to navigating through a labyrinth, where the path to financial mastery is often obscured by psychological barriers. These barriers, though invisible, exert a powerful influence, shaping our perceptions and actions in subtle yet profound ways. By bringing these hidden obstacles into the light, we can address them directly, clearing the path for a more empowered approach to budgeting and financial management.

Illuminating the Shadows: Understanding Psychological Barriers

1. **The Fear of Scarcity:** Many find themselves ensnared by the fear of not having enough, a shadow that looms large over financial decisions. This fear can lead to hoarding resources or avoiding necessary financial risks. Recognize this fear as a natural response to uncertainty, but one that can be mitigated by focusing on abundance, planning, and the cultivation of financial resilience.

2. **The Allure of Instant Gratification:** The siren call of immediate pleasure often drowns out the quiet wisdom of long-term planning. Instant gratification tempts us to forsake future wealth for present comfort. Challenge this impulse by visualizing the future you wish to create, letting this vision guide your choices and transform fleeting desires into lasting treasures.

3. **The Weight of Past Mistakes:** Many carry the burden of past financial mistakes, allowing these experiences to cloud current judgment and impede progress. Acknowledge past errors not as chains that bind you, but as lessons that inform and refine your approach to budgeting and financial management.

4. **The Resistance to Change:** Change, even when beneficial, can be daunting. A comfort in the familiar can make the transition to advanced budgeting practices seem overwhelming. Embrace change as a journey of growth, an opportunity to expand your financial capabilities and explore new territories of wealth and stability.

5. **The Complexity of Financial Emotions:** Emotions play a significant role in financial decision-making, often leading to decisions that conflict with our budgeting goals. By becoming more mindful of the emotional undercurrents that influence spending and saving habits, we can navigate these waters with greater intention and clarity.

Cultivating a Garden of Empowerment

By acknowledging and addressing these psychological barriers, we initiate a transformative process. This process is not about eradicating fears and desires but about understanding them, learning from them, and ultimately, mastering them. It's about tilling the soil of our financial mindset, removing the weeds of doubt and fear, and nurturing the seeds of confidence, discipline, and foresight.

Strategies for Overcoming Barriers

1. **Cultivate Financial Mindfulness:** Practice mindfulness to enhance awareness of your financial habits and their underlying emotional triggers. This heightened awareness allows for more conscious and deliberate financial choices.

2. **Set Clear, Achievable Goals:** Break down your financial aspirations into clear, manageable goals. The act of achieving these smaller objectives builds momentum and confidence, gradually dismantling the barriers that once seemed insurmountable.

3. **Foster a Community of Support:** Surround yourself with a community that shares your financial aspirations and challenges. This collective journey can provide encouragement, accountability, and shared wisdom to navigate psychological hurdles.

4. **Embrace Continuous Learning:** Commit to ongoing education in personal finance and budgeting. Knowledge is a powerful tool that dispels fear, illuminates options, and empowers action.

By bringing these subconscious barriers to the forefront and actively engaging with them, you embark on a journey of financial liberation. This journey transforms obstacles into stepping stones, guiding you towards a more empowered, effective approach to budgeting and financial management. Through this process, the path to financial mastery becomes not just accessible, but inviting, illuminated by the knowledge that you possess the tools and resilience to overcome any barrier.

- **Behavioral Finance Strategies in Budgeting:** Applying principles of behavioral finance to improve budgeting habits and financial decision-making.

In the realm of personal finance, the journey toward optimizing budgeting habits and decision-making is deeply intertwined with our psychological makeup. Behavioral finance, a field that marries the insights of psychology with financial theory, provides a rich tapestry of strategies to navigate this complex terrain. By applying principles of behavioral finance, individuals can illuminate the subconscious biases and behaviors that often derail financial objectives, transforming them into catalysts for growth and improved financial health.

Harnessing Behavioral Insights for Budgeting Excellence

1. **Understanding Cognitive Biases:** First, it's crucial to recognize the cognitive biases that influence our financial behaviors—confirmation bias, overconfidence, and loss aversion, to name a few. These biases can cloud judgment and lead to suboptimal budgeting decisions. By bringing awareness to these biases, individuals can begin to question and adjust their financial behaviors in a more objective, informed manner.

2. **Setting Clear, Achievable Financial Goals:** Behavioral finance suggests that individuals are more likely to stick to their budget and financial plans when they have clear, specific goals. These goals should be S.M.A.R.T (Specific, Measurable, Achievable, Relevant, Time-bound) and deeply connected to personal values and aspirations. Visualizing these goals regularly can embed them in the subconscious, making the budgeting process more intuitive and aligned with long-term objectives.

3. **Automating Financial Decisions:** Leverage the power of automation to bypass procrastination and inertia. Automating savings and investment contributions can ensure that financial goals are consistently prioritized, reducing the temptation to overspend or divert funds to less productive uses. This strategy harnesses the principle of "out of sight, out of mind," allowing individuals to build wealth almost effortlessly.

4. Implementing Mental Accounting Wisely: Mental accounting, the tendency to categorize and treat money differently depending on its source or intended use, can be strategically utilized to improve budgeting. By allocating specific accounts for different spending and saving goals, individuals can create psychological barriers that discourage the commingling of funds, ensuring that each dollar serves its intended purpose.

5. Utilizing Commitment Devices: Commitment devices are voluntary choices individuals make in the present that bind them to future actions, aligning short-term behaviors with long-term goals. Examples include setting up a savings account that penalizes early withdrawals or using budgeting apps that alert you when you're nearing spending limits. These devices can help override immediate impulses in favor of long-term financial health.

6. Embracing Feedback Loops: Regularly review financial progress against goals to create a feedback loop. This practice not only provides motivation through visible progress but also allows for timely adjustments to the budgeting strategy. Positive feedback reinforces good habits, while constructive feedback illuminates areas for improvement.

7. Cultivating Financial Patience and Impulse Control: Behavioral finance strategies emphasize the importance of delaying gratification and controlling impulsive spending. Techniques such as the 24-hour rule for non-essential purchases can give individuals time to consider whether an expense truly aligns with their financial goals and values.

Transforming Insights into Action

By applying these behavioral finance strategies, the act of budgeting transforms from a mere exercise in numbers to a profound practice of self-awareness and self-improvement. This approach not only enhances the effectiveness of budgeting efforts but also fosters a deeper, more harmonious relationship with one's finances. Through this lens, every financial decision becomes an opportunity to reinforce positive habits, challenge subconscious biases, and progressively align daily actions with the vision of a secure, prosperous financial future.

Section 5: Budgeting in the Digital Age

- **Digital Tools and Their Impact on Budgeting:** Examination of the latest digital budgeting tools, including AI and machine learning-based platforms, and their advantages for advanced budgeting.

In the digital age, the landscape of personal finance and budgeting has been revolutionized by the advent of sophisticated digital tools, including those powered by Artificial Intelligence (AI) and machine learning. These technologies are not merely tools but partners in the journey towards financial well-being, offering unparalleled insights, automation, and personalized advice. Let's delve into how these digital marvels are reshaping the art and science of budgeting.

The Digital Revolution in Budgeting

1. **Personalized Financial Insights:** AI and machine learning algorithms excel in analyzing vast amounts of financial data, discerning patterns and behaviors that may elude the human eye. This capability allows digital budgeting tools to offer personalized insights tailored to individual financial habits and goals. Users receive customized recommendations for saving, investing, and even identifying areas where they might be overspending.

2. **Predictive Budgeting and Forecasting:** One of the most transformative impacts of these digital tools is their ability to predict future financial trends based on past behavior and broader financial data. This predictive power can alert users to potential cash flow issues before they arise, suggest optimal times for making large purchases, or advise on investment opportunities. This foresight empowers individuals to make proactive, informed decisions that align with their financial goals.

3. **Automated Budget Management:** Automation is a cornerstone feature of many AI-driven budgeting tools. From automatically categorizing transactions to adjusting budget allocations based on real-time spending data, these platforms can significantly reduce the manual effort involved in budgeting. Automation ensures that financial plans are consistently adhered to, minimizing human error and the temptation to deviate from established budgets.

4. **Enhanced Security and Fraud Detection:** AI and machine learning algorithms are increasingly sophisticated in detecting fraudulent transactions and unusual financial activity. By integrating these technologies, digital budgeting tools offer an added layer of security, protecting users from potential financial threats and providing peace of mind.

5. **Interactive Financial Planning and Education:** Many digital budgeting platforms incorporate interactive elements such as financial quizzes, simulations, and educational resources. These features engage users in the process of financial learning and planning, making budgeting an interactive and enriching experience. Machine learning algorithms can tailor educational content to the user's financial situation and learning progress, enhancing financial literacy and confidence.

6. **Integration with Financial Ecosystems:** Digital budgeting tools often integrate seamlessly with a wide array of financial services, from bank accounts and credit cards to investment platforms and loan services. This integration provides a holistic view of one's financial health, enabling users to manage their entire financial life from a single platform. The convenience and coherence of this approach simplify financial management, encouraging more consistent and engaged budgeting practices.

The Future of Budgeting

The impact of digital tools on budgeting is profound, offering not just convenience and efficiency but a fundamentally enhanced approach to managing personal finances. As AI and machine learning technologies continue to evolve, the potential for even more personalized, predictive, and interactive budgeting experiences is vast. These digital advancements promise not only to transform how we budget but to deepen our understanding of our financial behaviors, preferences, and potential. In embracing these tools, individuals empower themselves with knowledge and capabilities that pave the way to financial stability and growth, making the once daunting task of budgeting a dynamic and engaging part of the journey towards financial freedom.

- **Data-Driven Budgeting:** How to leverage financial data and analytics for more informed budgeting decisions.

Data-driven budgeting represents a transformative approach to managing personal finances, where decisions are not based on hunches or habits but on the solid ground of financial data and analytics. This method harnesses the power of historical financial information, current spending patterns, and predictive analytics to craft a budget that is not only reflective of past behavior but also anticipatory of future financial needs and goals. Let's explore how individuals can leverage financial data and analytics to make more informed budgeting decisions, effectively programming their financial strategy for success.

Embracing Financial Data for Budgeting Excellence

1. **Collect and Consolidate Financial Data:** Begin by gathering comprehensive financial data from all sources—bank accounts, credit cards, online payment systems, and any other places where financial transactions are recorded. Consolidation tools or personal finance software can automate this process, pulling data into a single dashboard for a holistic view of your financial landscape.

2. **Analyze Spending Patterns:** Use analytical tools to examine your spending habits over time. Look for patterns in fixed and variable expenses, identifying areas where spending is consistent with your goals and where it may be diverging. This analysis can reveal surprising insights into your financial behavior, spotlighting opportunities for realignment.

3. **Set Goals Based on Data Insights:** Armed with a clear understanding of your spending habits and financial capacity, set realistic and achievable budgeting goals. These should be informed by the data-driven insights you've gathered, ensuring they are both ambitious and attainable.

4. **Utilize Predictive Analytics for Future Planning:** Advanced budgeting software often includes predictive analytics features, which can forecast future spending needs, income fluctuations, and savings opportunities based on historical data. This forward-looking analysis is invaluable for adjusting your budget to meet future financial challenges and opportunities head-on.

5. **Monitor Real-Time Spending and Adjust Accordingly:** Implement tools that offer real-time tracking of expenditures against your budget. This immediate feedback loop allows for quick adjustments to spending behaviors, ensuring that your budget remains a living document, responsive to the dynamics of your financial life.

6. **Benchmark Your Financial Performance:** Compare your financial data against relevant benchmarks, such as average spending in similar households, recommended savings rates, or debt-to-income ratios. This comparison can contextualize your financial decisions, providing a frame of reference for evaluating your budgeting effectiveness.

7. **Regular Reviews and Iterations:** Schedule periodic reviews of your financial data and budgeting goals. These sessions are opportunities to refine your budget based on new data insights, changes in financial circumstances, or shifts in your long-term objectives.

The Power of Informed Financial Decision-Making

By integrating financial data and analytics into the budgeting process, individuals transform their approach to personal finance management. This data-driven methodology empowers them to make informed decisions that are grounded in reality rather than aspiration alone. It provides a clear roadmap for financial growth, enabling proactive adjustments to spending and saving that align with both current needs and future aspirations.

Moreover, the practice of data-driven budgeting cultivates a deeper financial awareness and literacy. It encourages a relationship with money that is active and engaged, characterized by continuous learning and adaptation. Through the strategic use of financial data and analytics, individuals can craft a budget that not only reflects their financial history but also propels them toward a future of financial stability and prosperity.

- **Security and Privacy Considerations:** Addressing the security and privacy concerns associated with using digital tools for budgeting.

In the digital age, the use of sophisticated tools for budgeting and financial management has become increasingly prevalent. While these technologies offer unparalleled convenience and insights, they also raise important concerns regarding security and privacy. As we entrust these platforms with sensitive financial data, it becomes imperative to navigate these waters with caution, ensuring that our financial information remains protected from unauthorized access and breaches. Let's explore the key considerations and proactive measures individuals can take to safeguard their financial privacy and security when using digital budgeting tools.

Navigating the Digital Landscape: Security and Privacy Essentials

1. **Understanding the Risks:** First, it's crucial to acknowledge the potential risks associated with digital financial tools. These can include data breaches, phishing attacks, identity theft, and unauthorized access to personal financial information. Recognizing these risks is the first step toward mitigating them.

2. **Selecting Reputable Tools:** Choose budgeting tools and software with a proven track record of security and reliability. Look for platforms that employ robust encryption methods to protect data both in transit and at rest. Reputable tools will also have transparent privacy policies and compliance with regulatory standards such as GDPR or CCPA.

3. **Strong Authentication Practices:** Implement strong, unique passwords for each financial tool and consider using a reputable password manager to keep track of them. Additionally, enable two-factor authentication (2FA) or multi-factor authentication (MFA) wherever possible to add an extra layer of security to your accounts.

4. **Regular Software Updates:** Ensure that all financial apps and software are regularly updated. Software developers frequently release updates to patch vulnerabilities and enhance security features. Keeping software up to date is a simple yet effective way to protect against potential exploits.

5. **Monitoring Financial Transactions:** Regularly review transactions and account activity for signs of unauthorized access or suspicious activity. Many financial apps offer real-time alerts for transactions, which can help in quickly identifying and addressing any irregularities.

6. **Educating Yourself on Phishing Scams:** Be aware of phishing scams and social engineering attacks that aim to trick individuals into divulging sensitive information. Always verify the authenticity of communications received from financial institutions, and never click on links or attachments from unknown sources.

7. **Data Sharing and Privacy Settings:** Carefully consider the implications of data sharing and privacy settings within financial apps. Limit the sharing of personal information and understand how your data is being used—whether for service improvement, shared with third parties, or for marketing purposes.

8. **Secure Internet Connections:** Avoid using public Wi-Fi networks for accessing financial accounts or conducting transactions. Public networks are often unsecured, making them vulnerable to interception. Use a virtual private network (VPN) to encrypt your internet connection when managing your finances online.

Empowering Financial Digital Security

By integrating these security and privacy considerations into the use of digital budgeting tools, individuals can take proactive steps to protect their financial information. This cautious approach does not diminish the value and convenience offered by digital financial tools but rather ensures that these benefits are enjoyed without compromising personal security and privacy. In doing so, individuals can confidently navigate the digital financial landscape, leveraging technology to achieve their budgeting and financial management goals while safeguarding their most sensitive information.

Conclusion

- Summarizing the key takeaways from the chapter and the transformative potential of advanced budgeting techniques.

As we conclude our exploration of advanced budgeting techniques, we stand at the threshold of a new financial paradigm. The journey through this chapter has not only illuminated the path to sophisticated financial management but also revealed the transformative potential these practices hold for personal wealth and stability. Let's encapsulate the key takeaways and reflect on how these advanced techniques can serve as catalysts for profound financial transformation.

Embracing a Data-Driven Approach

The shift towards data-driven budgeting marks a significant evolution from traditional methods. By harnessing financial data and analytics, individuals gain a deeper understanding of their spending habits and financial patterns, enabling more informed and strategic decisions. This approach empowers us to anticipate future needs, adjust for financial fluctuations, and align our budgeting practices with our long-term goals, embedding a layer of precision and foresight into our financial planning.

Harnessing Digital Innovations

The integration of AI and machine learning-based tools into budgeting practices represents a leap forward in financial management. These technologies offer personalized insights, automate tedious processes, and provide real-time financial visibility, transforming budgeting from a chore into a dynamic and engaging part of our daily lives. The security and privacy considerations associated with these tools remind us of the importance of navigating the digital financial landscape with caution, ensuring that our journey towards financial empowerment remains secure.

Leveraging Psychological Insights

Applying principles of behavioral finance to budgeting challenges our inherent biases and subconscious financial behaviors. By understanding and addressing these psychological barriers, we unlock the ability to make decisions that are not only rational but also aligned with our deepest financial aspirations. This alignment fosters a sense of empowerment and control over our financial destiny, illustrating the profound impact that a mindful approach to budgeting can have on our overall financial well-being.

Strategic Allocation and Risk Management

The strategic allocation of resources for investments and the integration of risk management strategies into budgeting practices underscore the importance of looking beyond the present. These advanced techniques encourage us to prepare for future uncertainties, invest in our growth, and protect our financial health against potential risks. This forward-thinking approach is essential for building a resilient and prosperous financial future.

The Transformative Potential of Advanced Budgeting

Advanced budgeting techniques offer more than just a methodical approach to managing finances; they represent a fundamental shift in how we interact with our money. By embracing these strategies, we transition from passive participants to active architects of our financial future. The potential for transformation lies not just in the numbers but in the mindset shift that these practices encourage—a shift towards intentionality, empowerment, and strategic financial growth.

In summary, the journey through advanced budgeting techniques illuminates a path filled with opportunities for personal growth, financial stability, and prosperity. As we incorporate these practices into our financial repertoire, we equip ourselves with the tools and knowledge necessary to navigate the complexities of the financial world with confidence, transforming our aspirations into tangible realities.

- Encouragement to adopt and adapt these advanced strategies to your personal and business financial planning

As we draw the curtain on the exploration of advanced budgeting techniques, it's imperative to recognize that the journey towards financial mastery is both personal and evolving. The strategies and insights shared in this chapter are not mere suggestions; they are invitations to embark on a transformative journey, one that promises not only to enhance your financial well-being but to fundamentally change how you interact with money.

Embrace the Journey with Open Arms

You are encouraged to adopt these advanced budgeting strategies with an open heart and a willing mind. Remember, the path to financial empowerment is as unique as you are. It beckons you not just to follow but to innovate, adapt, and personalize these strategies to fit your individual circumstances and goals. Whether you are navigating the finances of a bustling business or steering the ship of your personal financial future, these techniques offer a compass by which to chart your course.

Transform Challenges into Opportunities

Each financial challenge you encounter is an opportunity for growth and learning. By applying the principles of data-driven budgeting, leveraging digital tools, embracing behavioral finance insights, and integrating strategic allocation and risk management, you transform obstacles into stepping stones towards financial resilience and prosperity.

Cultivate a Mindset of Continuous Improvement

Adoption of these strategies requires a mindset committed to continuous improvement and lifelong learning. The financial landscape is ever-changing, and so too should be your approach to managing it. Stay curious, stay informed, and remain flexible in your strategies, adjusting as necessary to meet the shifting tides of economic conditions, personal life changes, and evolving financial goals.

Build Your Financial Legacy

As you integrate these advanced budgeting techniques into your financial planning, consider the legacy you wish to build. These practices are not just about achieving short-term gains but about laying the foundation for lasting wealth that can support your aspirations, provide for loved ones, and contribute to your community.

You Are Not Alone

Remember, you are not alone on this journey. Seek out communities, resources, and professionals who can offer guidance, support, and encouragement. Share your knowledge and experiences with others, for in teaching, we reinforce our own learning. The journey towards financial mastery is more rewarding when shared.

Take the First Step Today

The journey of a thousand miles begins with a single step. Take that step today. Begin by implementing one new strategy, no matter how small. Celebrate your progress, learn from your setbacks, and keep moving forward. The path to financial empowerment is paved with the actions you take today.

Encouragement comes with the recognition that adopting and adapting these advanced budgeting techniques is within your reach. Empower yourself to take control of your financial destiny, harnessing the tools, strategies, and insights to create a future rich with possibility, stability, and prosperity. The journey to financial mastery awaits, and it promises to be one of transformation, growth, and unparalleled success.

Exercises for Skill Enhancement

- Practical exercises designed to apply advanced budgeting techniques in real-life scenarios, reinforcing the chapter's concepts through active learning.

To truly integrate the principles of advanced budgeting into your financial management practices, engaging in practical exercises is key. These exercises are designed to bridge the gap between theoretical understanding and real-world application, allowing you to explore and reinforce the chapter's concepts through active learning. Let's embark on a series of exercises that will deepen your mastery of advanced budgeting techniques.

Exercise 1: Visualization and Goal Setting

Objective: To clarify your long-term financial goals and visualize the steps needed to achieve them.

- **Reflect:** Spend a moment reflecting on your ultimate financial goals. Consider retirement, education funding, home ownership, travel, or any other goals that resonate with you.
- **Visualize:** For each goal, create a vivid mental image of what achieving this goal looks like. Where are you? Who is with you? How do you feel?
- **Write:** On a piece of paper or digital document, write down each goal along with the detailed visualization you created.
- **Plan:** Break down each goal into actionable steps. What budgeting adjustments do you need to make to achieve this goal? How can you allocate resources more effectively?

Step	Description
Reflect	Spend a moment reflecting on your ultimate financial goals. Consider retirement, education funding, home ownership, travel, or any other goals that resonate with you.
Visualize	For each goal, create a vivid mental image of what achieving this goal looks like. Where are you? Who is with you? How do you feel?
Write	On a piece of paper or digital document, write down each goal along with the detailed visualization you created.
Plan	Break down each goal into actionable steps. What budgeting adjustments do you need to make to achieve this goal? How can you allocate resources more effectively?

Exercise 2: Cash Flow Analysis

Objective: To analyze your cash flow and identify patterns or areas for improvement.

- **Track:** Use a financial tracking tool or spreadsheet to record all your income and expenses for one month.
- **Categorize:** At the month's end, categorize your expenses (e.g., housing, food, entertainment).
- **Analyze:** Identify any surprising spending patterns or categories where expenses were higher than expected.
- **Adjust:** Create a plan to adjust your spending in these categories, reallocating funds towards your goals identified in Exercise 1.

Date	Description	Amount	Category	Notes

- **Date:** When the transaction occurred.
- **Description:** A brief description of the income or expense.
- **Amount:** The amount of the transaction.
- **Category:** The category of the expense (e.g., housing, food, entertainment).
- **Notes:** Any additional notes or observations about the transaction.

This fillable grid serves as a practical tool for carrying out the steps of tracking your financial transactions, categorizing them, identifying spending patterns, and making necessary adjustments to align with your financial goals.

Exercise 3: Scenario Planning

Objective: To prepare for potential financial challenges and opportunities through scenario planning.

- **Identify Scenarios:** Write down three possible financial scenarios you might face in the next year (e.g., job loss, unexpected windfall, significant purchase).
- **Develop Strategies:** For each scenario, develop a strategy that outlines how you would adjust your budget and financial planning to navigate the situation effectively.
- **Review:** Share your scenarios and strategies with a trusted friend or financial advisor for feedback.

Scenario	Potential Impact	Strategy	Adjustments Needed	Feedback Received
Scenario 1 (e.g., Job Loss)				
Scenario 2 (e.g., Unexpected Windfall)				
Scenario 3 (e.g., Significant Purchase)				

- **Scenario:** Describe a potential financial scenario you might face in the next year.
- **Potential Impact:** Outline the possible impact this scenario could have on your current financial situation.
- **Strategy:** Develop a strategy that outlines how you would adjust your budget and financial planning to navigate the situation effectively.
- **Adjustments Needed:** Specify any adjustments needed in your financial planning or budget to accommodate this scenario.
- **Feedback Received:** Note any feedback received after sharing your scenarios and strategies with a trusted friend or financial advisor.

This grid serves as a practical tool for proactively considering various financial futures, allowing you to prepare strategies that ensure resilience and adaptability. By filling in this grid, you engage in a comprehensive exercise that strengthens your financial planning and readiness for unexpected changes.

Exercise 4: Digital Tool Exploration

Objective: To familiarize yourself with digital budgeting tools and their features.

- **Research:** Select two digital budgeting tools or apps that interest you.
- **Explore:** Spend a week using each tool, exploring its features, particularly those related to analytics, forecasting, and expense tracking.
- **Evaluate:** Write a brief review of each tool, noting what you liked, what you didn't, and how each might help you in applying advanced budgeting techniques.

Digital Tool	Features Explored	Likes	Dislikes	Potential Impact on Budgeting
Tool 1 (e.g., Mint)				
Tool 2 (e.g., YNAB)				

- **Digital Tool:** Name of the budgeting tool or app you're exploring.
- **Features Explored:** List the key features you focused on during your exploration, such as analytics, forecasting, and expense tracking.
- **Likes:** Note what aspects of the tool you found beneficial or enjoyable to use.
- **Dislikes:** Mention any features or aspects of the tool that did not meet your expectations or were difficult to use.

- **Potential Impact on Budgeting:** Reflect on how using this tool could impact your approach to budgeting, including any advantages it offers in applying advanced budgeting techniques.

This exercise encourages you to engage actively with digital budgeting tools, providing a structured way to assess their utility and fit with your financial management practices. By filling out this grid, you'll gain insights into how technology can enhance your budgeting strategy, ultimately helping you make more informed decisions about incorporating these tools into your financial planning.

Exercise 5: Investment Allocation Simulation

Objective: To simulate different investment allocation strategies and observe their potential impact on your financial goals.

. **Research:** Gather information on various types of investment vehicles (stocks, bonds, ETFs, mutual funds).
. **Simulate:** Using an online investment simulation tool, create portfolios based on different allocation strategies.
. **Analyze:** Observe how each portfolio performs under different market conditions. Reflect on how these outcomes align with your risk tolerance and financial goals.
. **Plan:** Decide on an allocation strategy that best suits your financial objectives and plan how you will implement this strategy in your real investment decisions.

Investment Vehicle	Allocation Strategy	Simulation Outcome	Alignment with Goals	Chosen Strategy Implementation Plan
Vehicle 1 (e.g., Stocks)				
Vehicle 2 (e.g., Bonds)				
Vehicle 3 (e.g., ETFs)				

- **Investment Vehicle:** Specify the type of investment vehicle you're considering (e.g., Stocks, Bonds, ETFs, Mutual Funds).
- **Allocation Strategy:** Describe how you plan to allocate resources among different investment vehicles.
- **Simulation Outcome:** Note the results of the simulation under various market conditions for each investment strategy.
- **Alignment with Goals:** Reflect on how the outcomes of each simulation align with your risk tolerance and financial goals.
- **Chosen Strategy Implementation Plan:** Based on the simulation outcomes and alignment with your financial goals, outline a plan for how you will implement your chosen investment strategy in real life.

This structured approach encourages you to actively engage with various investment options, simulate different allocation strategies, and critically assess their potential impact. By completing this grid, you'll gain valuable insights into which investment strategies best align with your financial objectives, enabling you to make informed decisions that support your journey toward financial growth and stability.

By engaging in these practical exercises, you actively reinforce the advanced budgeting techniques discussed in the chapter. This hands-on approach not only solidifies your understanding but also empowers you to make informed, strategic financial decisions that align with your goals and aspirations.

Chapter 3: Debt Consolidation and Management

- Overview of debt's role in personal finance and the common challenges it presents.

In the realm of personal finance, debt often carries a dual identity: it can be both a tool for achieving dreams and a challenge to financial freedom. Understanding debt's role in personal finance requires a shift in perspective, viewing it not solely as a burden but as a component of a larger financial strategy. This nuanced understanding is pivotal in cultivating a wealth mindset, transforming negative perceptions of debt into empowering financial actions.

Debt as a Tool for Growth and Opportunity

Debt, when utilized wisely, can be a powerful instrument in one's financial arsenal. It can facilitate significant life milestones, such as acquiring a home, pursuing higher education, or starting a business. These ventures, while necessitating upfront capital, are investments in one's future, laying the groundwork for wealth accumulation and personal fulfillment. Recognizing debt as a lever for growth requires a strategic approach, where borrowing decisions are made with careful consideration of their long-term impact on financial health.

Navigating the Challenges of Debt

Despite its potential benefits, debt presents challenges that can impede financial progress if not managed with discipline and foresight. High-interest rates, especially on unsecured debts like credit cards, can compound over time, turning manageable balances into overwhelming burdens. The stress of carrying debt can also have psychological impacts, fostering a sense of financial constraint and uncertainty about the future.

The key to overcoming these challenges lies in adopting a proactive stance towards debt management. This involves understanding the terms of one's debts, prioritizing repayments to minimize interest costs, and employing strategies such as consolidation or refinancing to improve manageability. By facing debt head-on, individuals can mitigate its challenges, turning potential obstacles into stepping stones towards financial stability.

Transforming Negative Perceptions of Debt

To cultivate a wealth mindset, it's essential to reframe negative thoughts about money and debt. Viewing debt through a lens of fear or avoidance can hinder the recognition of its strategic value in building a prosperous future. Instead, embracing a perspective that sees debt as a tool—when used judiciously—can empower individuals to make informed financial decisions that align with their wealth-building goals.

This shift in mindset encourages a more balanced relationship with money, where debt is neither demonized nor taken lightly. It fosters an environment where financial decisions are made with confidence and clarity, guided by an understanding of debt's role in personal finance and the broader journey towards wealth accumulation.

In summary, debt is a complex facet of personal finance that, when navigated wisely, can serve as a catalyst for achieving financial goals and building wealth. By understanding its challenges and embracing its potential, individuals can shed negative perceptions of debt, adopting a wealth mindset that views financial decisions as opportunities to sculpt a prosperous future.

- The importance of strategic debt management and consolidation for financial health and stress reduction.

Strategic debt management and consolidation play pivotal roles in the orchestration of personal finance, acting as both a beacon for financial health and a balm for the stress often associated with debt. The journey toward financial stability is marked by the effective navigation of debt, transforming it from a source of anxiety into a managed element of one's financial portfolio. By approaching debt with a strategic mindset, individuals can unlock pathways to not only preserve but also enhance their financial well-being.

Enhancing Financial Health Through Strategic Debt Management

Strategic debt management involves a comprehensive understanding of one's debt landscape—knowing the nuances of interest rates, repayment terms, and the impact of various debts on financial health. This understanding allows for informed decision-making, prioritizing repayments to minimize interest costs and expedite debt reduction. Such a strategy not only improves one's financial position but also contributes to a stronger credit profile, opening doors to future opportunities at more favorable terms.

Consolidation emerges as a powerful tool within this strategic framework, simplifying the complexity of managing multiple debts. By consolidating debts into a single loan with potentially lower interest rates and simplified repayment schedules, individuals can gain better control over their financial narrative. This control is instrumental in plotting a course toward debt freedom, aligning daily financial actions with long-term aspirations for wealth and stability.

Stress Reduction Through Masterful Debt Management

Beyond the tangible benefits to financial health, strategic debt management and consolidation offer profound psychological relief. The weight of carrying multiple debts, each with its own set of deadlines and interest charges, can be a significant source of stress and anxiety. Consolidation alleviates this burden, providing a clearer, more manageable framework for debt repayment. The psychological lift that comes from having a plan in place—one that charts a realistic path out of debt—cannot be overstated. It transforms the daunting into the doable, replacing uncertainty with a sense of direction and purpose.

Moreover, the act of taking control over one's debt situation fosters a sense of empowerment. It shifts the narrative from being at the mercy of debt to actively shaping one's financial destiny. This empowerment is a critical component of the wealth mindset, fostering resilience against future financial challenges and enhancing one's capacity for strategic financial decision-making.

Cultivating a Wealth Mindset Through Debt Strategy

Ultimately, strategic debt management and consolidation are about more than just numbers; they are about cultivating a mindset that views financial challenges as opportunities for growth. This wealth mindset is characterized by proactive engagement with finances, a commitment to continuous improvement, and a vision that sees beyond the immediate horizon to the potential for lasting prosperity.

Embracing strategic debt management and consolidation as cornerstones of this mindset enables individuals to navigate their financial journeys with confidence. It assures them that with the right strategies, the path to financial health and the reduction of stress are not only possible but within reach. In this light, managing and consolidating debt become not just financial tactics but integral steps toward realizing a life marked by financial freedom and peace of mind.

Section 1: Understanding Debt

- **Types of Debt:** Differentiate between secured and unsecured debt, highlighting examples such as mortgages, auto loans, student loans, and credit card debt.

In the landscape of personal finance, debt is often categorized into two main types: secured and unsecured. Understanding the distinction between these forms of debt is crucial for effective financial planning and management. By differentiating between secured and unsecured debts, individuals can make more informed decisions regarding borrowing, repayment strategies, and overall financial health.

Secured Debt

Definition: Secured debt is characterized by the requirement of collateral—a valuable asset that the borrower agrees to pledge as security for the loan. The collateral acts as a safety net for the lender, who has the right to seize the asset if the borrower fails to repay the debt as agreed.

Examples:

Mortgages: Perhaps the most common form of secured debt, mortgages are loans used to purchase real estate. The property itself serves as collateral, securing the loan. If the borrower defaults on the mortgage, the lender can initiate foreclosure, taking ownership of the property to recover the loan amount.

Auto Loans: Auto loans are used to finance the purchase of vehicles. Similar to mortgages, the vehicle being financed serves as collateral. In the event of default, the lender can repossess the vehicle to recoup their investment.

Characteristics:

- Typically involves lower interest rates compared to unsecured debt due to the reduced risk for the lender.
- Loan amounts can be higher, reflecting the value of the collateral.
- Failure to repay can result in the loss of the asset used as collateral.

Venture into the realm of secured debt, a domain where financial agreements are anchored by tangible assets, offering both opportunities and obligations. When you engage with secured debt, you're not just entering a contract; you're entering a pact that intertwines your financial aspirations with your most valued possessions, be it a home, a car, or another significant asset.

Mortgages: Foundations of Homeownership

Consider the journey of acquiring a mortgage, a pathway many tread to achieve the dream of homeownership. Here, the very essence of your aspiration—the home—stands as the collateral. It's a powerful motivator, ensuring commitment to repayment, but it also carries the weight of risk. Should the tides of financial fortune turn, resulting in an inability to meet your mortgage obligations, the sanctuary you've built can be jeopardized, transitioning from a personal haven to a financial lifeline for the lender.

Yet, the secured nature of this debt is what makes the dream attainable for so many, offering lower interest rates and the possibility to borrow significant amounts that mirror the property's value. It's a dance of trust and commitment, where the home you cherish becomes the guarantor of your promise.

Auto Loans: Steering Dreams into Reality

Similarly, auto loans illuminate the path to mobility and independence, enabling the acquisition of a vehicle that might otherwise be beyond reach. The car you drive off the lot is not merely a mode of transport; it's collateral on wheels, its value securing the funds lent to you.

This arrangement, while empowering, also demands respect for the responsibilities it entails. Defaulting on an auto loan can lead to repossession, stripping away not just your means of transportation but a piece of your livelihood and freedom.

The Double-Edged Sword of Secured Debt

Secured debt embodies a double-edged sword: on one edge, the opportunity to leverage valuable assets for financial goals; on the other, the risk of losing those assets should financial turbulence arise. The favorable interest rates and potential for larger loan amounts reflect the lender's reduced risk, yet they also underscore the heightened stakes for you, the borrower.

Engaging with secured debt requires a measured approach, an understanding that the assets you pledge are not just collateral but integral parts of your life and work. Whether stepping into a home, driving a car, or leveraging other secured debts, it's vital to navigate these commitments with foresight, recognizing both their empowering potential and their inherent risks.

In summary, secured debt offers a nuanced financial tool, a means to achieve significant personal and business milestones. Yet, it demands a deep appreciation of the responsibilities and risks involved, urging borrowers to tread wisely, honoring their commitments, and safeguarding the assets that stand behind their debts. In this delicate balance lies the path to leveraging secured debt effectively, harnessing its benefits while mitigating its risks, and moving steadily toward one's financial horizons.

Unsecured Debt

Definition: Unsecured debt does not require collateral. Lenders extend credit based solely on the borrower's creditworthiness and promise to repay. Due to the lack of tangible security, unsecured debts often carry higher interest rates to compensate for the increased risk to the lender.

Examples:

Credit Card Debt: Credit cards are a prevalent form of unsecured debt. They allow borrowers to make purchases up to a certain credit limit, with the understanding that the borrowed amount will be repaid. Interest rates for credit cards can be significantly higher than those for secured loans.

Student Loans: Many student loans are unsecured, relying on the borrower's future earning potential rather than current assets as security. While federal student loans have fixed interest rates and various repayment plans, private student loans may come with higher interest rates and less flexibility.

Personal Loans: Personal loans can be used for a variety of purposes, including debt consolidation, home improvement, or covering unexpected expenses. These loans do not require collateral, making them accessible but often at higher interest rates.

Characteristics:

- No collateral required, making them more accessible but riskier for lenders.
- Typically, interest rates are higher than those for secured loans.
- Lenders may pursue legal action to collect the debt if the borrower defaults, potentially leading to wage garnishment or other financial repercussions.

Dive into the world of unsecured debt, a financial landscape where trust and creditworthiness are the cornerstones of borrowing. Unlike its secured counterpart, unsecured debt frees borrowers from the need to pledge assets, offering flexibility and speed in accessing funds. However, this convenience comes with its own set of considerations, reflective of the heightened risks assumed by lenders.

Credit Card Debt: The Double-Edged Sword

Credit cards exemplify unsecured debt's dual nature, empowering and perilous. They offer the freedom to manage cash flow, seize opportunities, and handle emergencies, all without upfront collateral. Yet, this freedom dances with danger—the danger of spiraling interest and the temptation of spending beyond one's means. The significantly higher interest rates associated with credit cards are the lender's hedge against risk, a premium placed on the trust extended to the borrower.

Responsible use of credit cards involves recognizing them as tools of convenience and strategic financial management, not as extensions of one's income. They demand respect for their potential to both build and erode financial well-being, depending on how they're wielded.

Student Loans: Investing in the Future

Student loans represent an investment in one's future, predicated on the belief in future earning potential rather than present assets. This form of unsecured debt underscores a societal commitment to education and advancement, offering a ladder to opportunities otherwise out of reach for many.

Yet, the absence of collateral does not diminish the weight of obligation—these loans must be repaid, and their terms, especially for private loans, can be less forgiving than those for secured debts. Navigating student loans requires a keen eye on the future, balancing educational aspirations with the reality of eventual repayment.

Personal Loans: Versatile yet Vexing

Personal loans embody unsecured debt's versatility, available for a myriad of uses from consolidating other debts to funding home improvements or addressing unforeseen needs. Their accessibility is their appeal, providing financial agility without the need for tangible collateral.

However, this agility is counterbalanced by cost—higher interest rates that reflect the lender's increased risk. Borrowers must therefore approach personal loans with clear intentions and plans for repayment, ensuring that the debt incurred today doesn't become tomorrow's fiscal burden.

Navigating Unsecured Debt with Prudence

Unsecured debt offers a spectrum of financial possibilities, each with its inherent risks and rewards. Its accessibility and flexibility are invaluable, yet its costs and potential consequences demand careful consideration. When engaging with unsecured debt, the onus is on the borrower to uphold their promise to repay, recognizing that their financial integrity and future are at stake.

By understanding the nuances of unsecured debt and approaching it with informed intentionality, borrowers can harness its benefits while mitigating its risks, paving the way toward sustained financial health and prosperity.

Strategic Implications

Understanding the nuances between secured and unsecured debt is fundamental for strategic financial management. Secured debts, with their lower interest rates and potential for larger loan amounts, can be instrumental in achieving significant life goals, such as homeownership or purchasing a vehicle. However, the risk of losing valuable assets underscores the importance of careful planning and management.

Conversely, unsecured debts offer flexibility and accessibility but at the cost of higher interest rates, which can quickly accumulate. Effective management of unsecured debt is crucial for maintaining financial stability and preventing the spiral of debt that can derail financial goals.

In summary, navigating the complexities of secured and unsecured debt with informed strategies is key to leveraging debt as a tool for financial growth while mitigating its risks.

- **The Cost of Debt**: Discuss interest rates, compounding interest, and how the cost of carrying debt can impact overall financial well-being.

The cost of debt is a critical concept in personal finance, influencing not only the immediate budget but also long-term financial health and wealth-building capabilities. Understanding the nuances of interest rates, the effects of compounding interest, and the broader implications of carrying debt is essential for anyone looking to navigate their financial journey wisely.

Interest Rates: The Price of Borrowing

Interest rates are a fundamental concept in finance, representing the cost imposed by lenders for providing funds to borrowers. These rates are pivotal in determining the overall cost of any borrowed sum and are expressed as a percentage of the principal loan amount on an annual basis. The dynamics of interest rates can significantly impact the financial strategy of individuals and institutions alike.

Types of Interest Rates and Their Implications

Fixed Interest Rates:

Definition and Stability

Fixed interest rates are defined as interest rates that are set at the initiation of the loan agreement and maintained consistently throughout the term of the loan. This attribute of fixed interest rates provides a crucial advantage for borrowers, imparting a degree of predictability and stability in their financial obligations.

Consistency: The unchanging nature of fixed interest rates means that the cost of borrowing and the repayment schedule are predictable over the loan period. This stability is particularly beneficial in environments of fluctuating market interest rates, where variable rates might increase significantly.

Financial Planning: The predictability associated with fixed interest rates enables individuals and organizations to plan their finances with greater accuracy. Knowing the exact amount due for each payment facilitates more effective budget management and long-term financial planning.

Budgeting Advantages

The advantages of fixed interest rates extend significantly into the realm of budgeting and financial management:

Predictable Payments: Borrowers with fixed-rate loans can ascertain the exact amount of their monthly loan repayments in advance, which remains constant regardless of market fluctuations. This predictability aids in avoiding the risk of payment shock that can occur with variable interest rate loans.

Financial Certainty: By locking in a fixed interest rate, borrowers are shielded from interest rate increases that would otherwise elevate their repayment costs. This certainty is advantageous for long-term financial strategizing, especially in scenarios where budget constraints are tight or financial outlooks necessitate stringent planning.

Risk Mitigation: Fixed interest rates serve as a form of risk mitigation, protecting borrowers from the volatility inherent in the financial markets. By choosing a fixed rate, borrowers are effectively hedging against the potential rise in interest rates, ensuring their financial exposure remains constant.

In summary, fixed interest rates offer a secure and predictable framework for managing debt repayments, providing essential benefits in terms of budgeting, risk management, and financial planning. For individuals and entities seeking stability in their financial obligations, fixed interest rates represent a prudent choice, enabling them to navigate their fiscal responsibilities with confidence and foresight.

Variable Interest Rates:

Market-Linked Variability

Variable interest rates, in contrast to their fixed counterparts, are dynamic and can change throughout the duration of the loan. These rates are typically pegged to an external benchmark or index, such as the prime rate or LIBOR, which means they fluctuate in response to movements in the broader financial markets and economic environment.

Index Correlation: The variability in these rates is directly correlated with the performance of the chosen index or benchmark, reflecting the broader economic and financial trends. This linkage ensures that the rate evolves in tandem with market conditions, providing a reflection of the current economic climate.

Economic Sensitivity: Such rates are inherently sensitive to macroeconomic changes, including shifts in monetary policy, inflation rates, and overall economic growth, which can all significantly impact the rate applied to the loan.

Payment Fluctuations

The inherent variability of these rates introduces a degree of unpredictability in monthly repayment amounts and the total interest to be paid over the life of the loan:

Repayment Uncertainty: Borrowers face potential variability in their monthly payments, which can increase or decrease based on prevailing interest rates. This uncertainty requires a greater degree of financial flexibility and preparedness for potential rate increases.

Total Interest Impact: The total interest paid over the life of the loan is also uncertain and can vary significantly based on the trajectory of interest rate changes during the loan term.

Factors Influencing Interest Rates

Several critical factors influence the setting and adjustment of interest rates:

Type of Debt: The nature of the debt (secured vs. unsecured) plays a significant role in determining interest rates. Secured debts typically have lower rates due to the reduced risk associated with collateral-backed loans.

Borrower's Creditworthiness: A borrower's credit history, income, and financial habits are scrutinized to assess risk, which in turn influences the interest rate offered by lenders.

Economic Conditions: Interest rates are also shaped by broader economic indicators and conditions, such as inflation, economic policy decisions, and the overall demand for credit.

Conclusion: Strategic Considerations in Financial Planning

In the context of financial planning, understanding the nuances between fixed and variable interest rates is essential for effective debt management. Borrowers must evaluate their financial stability, risk tolerance, and long-term objectives to make informed decisions between fixed and variable rates. By doing so, they can align their debt strategies with their broader financial goals and adapt to the inherent uncertainties and opportunities presented by variable interest rates. This strategic approach enables individuals to navigate the complexities of interest rates, optimizing their financial decisions in accordance with their personal and economic circumstances.

Compounding Interest: The Cost That Grows

Compounding interest is the process by which interest is added to the principal sum of a loan or deposit, so from that moment on, the interest that has been added also earns interest. This can significantly accelerate the growth of debt, especially on long-term loans or revolving credit lines like credit cards. The frequency of compounding—daily, monthly, or annually—further affects how quickly interest accumulates.

Compounding can work to the borrower's disadvantage when it comes to debt, as it can lead to a situation where payments are primarily covering the interest rather than reducing the principal. This effect underscores the importance of understanding the terms of compounding when taking on debt.

The Impact of Carrying Debt on Financial Well-Being

Reduced Cash Flow

Debt obligations, particularly those associated with high-interest rates, can severely restrict an individual's disposable income. The allocation of a substantial portion of one's income to service debt reduces the financial resources available for other essential or discretionary expenses. This limitation can impede not only the ability to meet current financial needs but also the capacity to engage in saving or investing activities that could enhance future financial stability.

- **Resource Allocation:** Monthly debt repayments can become a significant financial burden, demanding prioritization over other spending or saving opportunities, thereby constraining an individual's financial flexibility.

Delayed Financial Goals

The impact of substantial debt extends beyond immediate cash flow concerns to influence long-term financial planning and goal attainment. High levels of debt can act as a barrier to achieving pivotal financial milestones:

Impact on Savings: The diversion of funds towards debt repayment can limit the ability to contribute to savings accounts, retirement funds, or other investment vehicles, potentially delaying or derailing financial objectives such as retirement security or wealth accumulation.

Homeownership and Education: Debt can also restrict the capacity to accumulate savings for down payments on property or to fund educational pursuits, both of which are critical components of many individuals' financial aspirations.

Credit Score Impact

The ramifications of debt are also evident in its influence on creditworthiness. High debt levels, particularly when coupled with late payments or defaults, can detrimentally affect credit scores:

Borrowing Terms: A diminished credit score can hinder an individual's ability to secure loans or credit facilities in the future, often resulting in less favorable terms or higher interest rates, which can further exacerbate financial strain.

Access to Credit: In severe cases, a significantly impaired credit score can obstruct access to essential financial products, limiting opportunities for debt consolidation or refinancing that might otherwise alleviate financial burdens.

Emotional and Psychological Stress

The implications of debt extend into the psychological realm, affecting individuals' mental health and overall well-being:

Stress and Anxiety: The constant pressure to meet debt obligations can induce significant stress and anxiety, impacting mental health and quality of life.

Financial Insecurity: Persistent debt can engender feelings of insecurity and lack of control over one's financial destiny, which may influence broader life decisions and personal well-being.

In conclusion, the impacts of carrying high-interest or compounding debt are multifaceted, affecting individuals' financial health, personal goals, emotional well-being, and future opportunities. Recognizing and addressing these issues is crucial for fostering financial stability and enhancing quality of life.

Strategies for Managing the Cost of Debt

Debt Repayment Strategies

Prioritizing debt repayment is a critical strategy for minimizing the long-term costs associated with debt, particularly when dealing with high-interest or compounding debts. By focusing on repaying these debts first, individuals can significantly reduce the amount of interest accrued over time, thereby decreasing the total cost of their debt.

- **Avalanche and Snowball Methods:** Utilizing debt repayment strategies such as the debt avalanche (targeting debts with the highest interest rates first) or debt snowball (focusing on the smallest debts first for psychological wins) can enhance the effectiveness of repayment efforts.

Refinancing and Consolidation

Refinancing or consolidating debts can offer pathways to more manageable debt servicing and cost reductions:

Refinancing: By securing a loan with a lower interest rate to pay off existing higher-rate debts, individuals can reduce their interest expenses and potentially shorten their debt repayment timelines.

Consolidation: Combining multiple debts into a single loan with a lower overall interest rate simplifies the repayment process and can result in lower total interest costs.

Budgeting and Financial Planning

A systematic approach to budgeting is essential for maintaining financial health and avoiding the accrual of further debt:

Budget Development: Creating and adhering to a detailed budget helps in identifying and eliminating unnecessary expenses, allocating more resources toward debt repayment.

Emergency Funds: Establishing an emergency fund can reduce the need to rely on credit during unforeseen financial challenges, thereby preventing additional debt accumulation.

Summary and Future Financial Well-Being

Understanding the implications of interest rates and the mechanics of debt is paramount for financial literacy and well-being. By employing strategic debt management practices such as effective repayment plans, refinancing, and diligent budgeting, individuals can exert greater control over their financial destiny. These strategies not only aid in reducing the immediate burden of debt but also contribute to establishing a more secure and prosperous financial future, empowering individuals to achieve their long-term financial objectives.

Section 2: Principles of Debt Management

- **Debt Inventory:** Guide on how to create a comprehensive list of debts, including amounts owed, interest rates, and monthly payments.

Creating a comprehensive debt inventory is a critical step in the journey toward financial freedom and empowerment. This process not only clarifies your current financial situation but also serves as a foundational exercise in reprogramming your mindset towards debt and financial management. By methodically listing all your debts, including the amounts owed, interest rates, and monthly payments, you transform a potentially overwhelming array of obligations into a manageable, actionable overview. This structured approach fosters a sense of control and purpose, crucial elements in cultivating a wealth mindset.

Step 1: Gather Financial Statements

Begin by collecting all financial statements related to your debts. This includes bank statements, loan documents, credit card statements, and any other records of money you owe. The act of gathering these documents is the first step in confronting your debt head-on, an essential practice in shifting from a mindset of avoidance to one of proactive engagement.

Step 2: List Each Debt

Create a list or spreadsheet where each row represents a different debt. This list should be comprehensive, including everything from large mortgages and auto loans to smaller credit card debts and personal loans. Viewing your debts collectively, rather than as disconnected obligations, enables a holistic understanding of your financial obligations, laying the groundwork for strategic debt management.

Columns to Include in Your Debt Inventory:

- **Creditor Name:** The entity to whom the debt is owed.
- **Amount Owed:** The total current balance of each debt.

- **Interest Rate:** The annual percentage rate (APR) of each debt. Note whether the rate is fixed or variable, as this affects the cost over time.
- **Monthly Payment:** The minimum payment required each month. For debts with variable payments, use an average or the most recent payment amount.
- **Due Date:** The date by which each monthly payment must be made to avoid penalties.

Step 3: Prioritize and Categorize

Once your list is complete, categorize your debts by type (secured vs. unsecured) and priority. High-interest and high-balance debts often warrant more immediate attention due to their greater impact on your financial well-being. This categorization is a critical thinking exercise that strengthens your decision-making skills, encouraging a strategic approach to debt repayment.

Step 4: Reflect and Plan

With your debt inventory in hand, take a moment to reflect on how each debt came to be and how it fits into your overall financial picture. This reflection is not about assigning blame but about understanding the choices and circumstances that led to each debt. This understanding is pivotal in reprogramming how you think about and manage debt in the future.

Step 5: Commit to Regular Reviews

Commit to reviewing and updating your debt inventory regularly—monthly or quarterly. This commitment ensures that your approach to debt management remains dynamic and responsive to changes in your financial situation. It reinforces the habit of regular financial review, a cornerstone of a healthy financial mindset.

Creating a comprehensive debt inventory is more than a mere organizational task; it's a transformative process that reprograms your relationship with debt. It empowers you with the knowledge and clarity needed to make informed decisions, aligns your financial actions with your long-term goals, and instills a sense of confidence and control. This exercise is a fundamental step in cultivating a wealth mindset, one that views financial challenges not as insurmountable obstacles but as opportunities for growth and empowerment.

- **Prioritization Strategies:** Techniques for prioritizing which debts to pay off first, such as the avalanche and snowball methods.

In the realm of personal finance, the strategic prioritization of debt repayment is not just a tactical maneuver but a profound exercise in reprogramming the mind towards a wealth-focused perspective. By adopting prioritization strategies such as the avalanche and snowball methods, individuals can transform their approach to debt from one of overwhelm and avoidance to one of empowerment and intentionality. This shift is crucial for fostering a healthy relationship with money and accelerating the journey towards financial freedom.

The Avalanche Method: A Strategic Approach to Minimizing Interest

The avalanche method prioritizes the repayment of debts from highest to lowest interest rate. This approach is grounded in the logic of minimizing the total interest paid over time, thereby reducing the overall cost of debt. By tackling high-interest debts first, individuals can save significant amounts in interest payments, freeing up more resources for savings and investment sooner.

Reprogramming Insight: Adopting the avalanche method is a practice in analytical decision-making. It requires a disciplined examination of the numbers, fostering a mindset that values long-term gain over short-term satisfaction. This approach cultivates patience and strategic thinking, essential qualities for wealth accumulation.

The Snowball Method: Building Momentum through Small Wins

In contrast, the snowball method focuses on paying off debts from smallest to largest balance, regardless of interest rate. This method capitalizes on psychological wins; as smaller debts are cleared, individuals gain confidence and momentum, which can be crucial in maintaining motivation throughout the debt repayment journey.

Reprogramming Insight: The snowball method aligns with the psychological principle of positive reinforcement. Each debt cleared is a victory, reinforcing the behavior of repayment. This strategy educates the subconscious to recognize progress, building a foundation of success that empowers further financial actions. It transforms the daunting task of debt repayment into a series of achievable milestones, fostering a sense of achievement and control.

Choosing Your Strategy

Determining which method to adopt depends on individual financial situations and psychological preferences. Some may find the mathematical efficiency of the avalanche method compelling, while others may be motivated by the quick wins of the snowball method. The critical insight is that either strategy requires—and builds—a proactive stance towards debt. Making a conscious choice to employ one of these strategies is in itself an act of reprogramming, moving from passive debt accumulation to active debt management.

Implementing Your Chosen Strategy

- **Assess Your Debts:** Compile a comprehensive list of your debts, noting the balance, interest rate, and minimum payments for each.
- **Evaluate Your Budget:** Determine how much extra you can allocate towards debt repayment each month, beyond minimum payments.
- **Apply the Strategy:** Direct the extra repayment towards the debts identified by your chosen method (highest interest rate for Avalanche, smallest balance for Snowball).
- **Monitor and Adjust:** Regularly review your progress and adjust your repayment strategy as needed. Celebrate each debt cleared as a step closer to financial freedom.

The Transformative Potential

Embracing these prioritization strategies does more than organize your debt repayment efforts; it fundamentally shifts your perspective towards money and debt. It teaches the mind to see debt not as an insurmountable obstacle but as a series of challenges that can be strategically and successfully overcome. This shift is vital for cultivating a wealth mindset, where financial decisions are made with intention, and every action taken is a step towards building a prosperous future. Through disciplined application and psychological insight, the techniques of debt prioritization become powerful tools in the journey to financial empowerment and freedom.

- **Negotiating with Creditors:** Tips and strategies for negotiating better terms on existing debts.

Negotiating with creditors to secure better terms on existing debts is not just a financial strategy; it's a critical exercise in empowering oneself within the realm of personal finance. This negotiation process requires a blend of knowledge, confidence, and communication skills, transforming it into an invaluable opportunity to reprogram one's mindset towards money and debt. By engaging directly with creditors, individuals can shift from feeling at the mercy of their financial obligations to becoming active, empowered participants in shaping their financial destiny.

Building Knowledge and Confidence

Understand Your Position: Before entering into negotiations, thoroughly review your financial situation. Know exactly how much you owe, the interest rates you're paying, and what you can realistically afford to pay. Armed with this information, you're in a stronger position to negotiate terms that better align with your financial capabilities.

Reprogramming Insight: This preparatory step fosters a sense of control and self-efficacy. By understanding your financial standing in detail, you cultivate a mindset of empowerment, essential for successful negotiation.

In the quest for wealth, the foundational step transcends mere accumulation of assets; it involves a profound journey into self-awareness and knowledge enhancement. At the core of this journey is the imperative task of comprehensively understanding one's financial position. This stage is not merely about numbers and calculations but about initiating a dialogue with oneself regarding one's financial health.

To embark on this path, one must first undertake a meticulous review of their financial landscape. This involves an in-depth analysis of one's liabilities, the rates of interest that besiege one's financial stability, and a realistic assessment of one's capacity to fulfill these obligations. It is a process akin to preparing for a negotiation, where knowledge is not just power but the very currency of negotiation itself.

This preparatory stage is critical, not merely for the tangible benefits it brings in enhancing one's negotiation capabilities but also for the intangible transformation it fosters within one's psyche. The act of understanding one's financial standing is akin to seizing the helm of one's financial ship, navigating through the tumultuous seas of debt and financial obligations with confidence and precision. This is not a mere exercise in financial literacy; it is a rite of passage into financial empowerment.

The reprogramming insight inherent in this process lies in its ability to cultivate a mindset of empowerment and control. By delving deep into the mechanics of one's financial reality, one is not just preparing for future negotiations; one is engaging in a profound act of self-assertion. This process reprograms the mind to recognize the power of informed decision-making, fostering a sense of self-efficacy that is indispensable for successful financial negotiation.

As one progresses through this journey of financial self-awareness, a transformation occurs. The knowledge acquired and the confidence amassed are not just tools for navigating the financial realm; they become integral components of one's identity. This metamorphosis is the essence of wealth building. It transcends the accumulation of assets to embody a state of being, where one is not just financially affluent but possesses a wealth of knowledge, confidence, and empowerment.

Thus, in the pursuit of wealth, let us not merely focus on the end goal but embrace the journey. Let us engage in this transformative process of building knowledge and confidence, for it is in this journey that the true essence of wealth is discovered.

Effective Communication Strategies

Open Dialogue: Approach your creditors with honesty and openness. Clearly explain your current financial situation and express your commitment to fulfilling your obligations under terms that are sustainable for you.

Reprogramming Insight: This approach reinforces the principle of proactive engagement with financial challenges. It shifts the narrative from avoidance to action, instilling a habit of facing financial issues head-on.

In the realm of wealth management and debt resolution, the significance of effective communication strategies cannot be overstated. Among these strategies, the practice of engaging in open dialogue with creditors stands out as a cornerstone for fostering constructive outcomes. This approach demands not just the articulation of one's financial predicaments but also a demonstration of unwavering commitment to fulfilling financial obligations, albeit under reconfigured, sustainable terms.

The essence of open dialogue lies in its foundation of honesty and transparency. When approaching creditors, it is imperative to present a clear and candid portrayal of one's financial circumstances. This entails a detailed exposition of the challenges at hand, coupled with a firm expression of one's determination to navigate through these challenges. The objective is not merely to seek leniency but to forge a path toward mutual understanding and agreement on feasible terms of repayment.

This communicative strategy transcends the mere mechanics of negotiation; it embodies a profound reprogramming insight. By adopting a stance of openness and proactivity, individuals initiate a shift in the narrative surrounding financial challenges. The traditional approach of evasion and passive reaction gives way to a proactive engagement, characterized by a readiness to confront and resolve issues directly. This shift is not only strategic but also psychological, embedding a mindset that prioritizes facing difficulties head-on rather than shying away from them.

The reprogramming insight embedded in the practice of open dialogue is multifaceted. Firstly, it cultivates a habit of proactive problem-solving, encouraging individuals to seek solutions actively rather than passively succumbing to circumstances. Secondly, it fosters a sense of personal agency and responsibility, empowering individuals to take control of their financial destinies. Lastly, it builds resilience, preparing individuals to tackle future challenges with confidence and determination.

Moreover, this strategy has a ripple effect that extends beyond the individual. It sets a precedent for the creditors, signaling a collaborative approach to problem-solving. This not only enhances the likelihood of reaching amicable agreements but also contributes to a broader culture of understanding and flexibility in financial negotiations.

In conclusion, the practice of open dialogue with creditors encapsulates a powerful approach to managing financial challenges. By prioritizing honesty, transparency, and proactivity, individuals can transform their financial predicaments into opportunities for growth and resolution. This strategy not only facilitates the practical goal of debt resolution but also instills a mindset of empowerment, resilience, and proactive engagement, fundamental qualities for navigating the complex terrain of personal finance.

Negotiation Techniques

Request Lower Interest Rates: Often, creditors are willing to lower interest rates for borrowers who demonstrate a commitment to repayment. A reduced rate can significantly decrease the total cost of your debt over time.

Seek Flexible Payment Plans: If regular payments are challenging, inquire about extended payment plans that lower monthly amounts. Creditors may prefer receiving smaller payments over a longer period than risking default.

Waiving Late Fees: If you've incurred late fees, ask for them to be waived as part of your negotiation. Demonstrating a plan for future timely payments can make this request more compelling.

Reprogramming Insight: Each successful negotiation reinforces the understanding that you have agency over your financial situation. It teaches resilience and adaptability, crucial traits for navigating the complexities of personal finance.

The Power of Advocacy

Consider Professional Help: If negotiations seem daunting, consider seeking assistance from a credit counseling service. These professionals can advocate on your behalf, often securing terms that might not be available to individuals negotiating alone.

Reprogramming Insight: Seeking help when needed is a sign of strength and a strategic decision that underscores the importance of community and support in financial management.

Embarking on the journey of financial negotiation often feels akin to navigating a labyrinthine garden, where every turn presents a new challenge and the path to the center—financial freedom—seems obscured by towering hedges. In this garden of fiscal uncertainties, the power of advocacy emerges as a guiding light, illuminating the path forward and revealing strategies that render the journey not just manageable, but enriching.

At the heart of harnessing this power lies the wisdom of considering professional assistance, akin to seeking a seasoned guide for navigating the garden's complexities. The realm of credit counseling services offers such guidance, providing not just a map but a voice to advocate on your behalf. These professionals, with their deep knowledge of the terrain and the creatures that dwell within (creditors, in our metaphor), possess the unique ability to secure terms and conditions that might elude the solitary traveler. Their expertise transforms daunting negotiations into dialogues of possibility, where terms align more closely with the traveler's capacity and journey toward financial stability.

Yet, the decision to enlist the aid of a credit counselor is more than a strategic maneuver in the art of negotiation; it represents a profound reprogramming insight. This act of reaching out is imbued with the recognition that true strength lies in acknowledging when the path becomes too intricate to navigate alone. It reflects an understanding that the journey toward financial solvency is not a solitary quest but a voyage that benefits immensely from the wisdom, support, and advocacy of companions.

This insight whispers to the subconscious, reinforcing the concept that seeking help is a testament to one's resilience, a strategic decision that elevates the individual's journey. It underscores the importance of community and support in managing one's financial garden, reminding us that the most scenic routes are often those traversed with allies. This reprogramming of the mind fosters a mindset shift from seeing financial challenges as personal battles to viewing them as opportunities for collaboration, growth, and empowerment.

Thus, the power of advocacy, particularly through professional assistance, becomes a key strategy in the financial negotiation toolkit. It's a reminder that in the complex garden of personal finance, having a guide can make all the difference, transforming a daunting expedition into a journey of discovery, support, and ultimate success. The power of advocacy, then, is not just in the practical outcomes it secures but in the profound impact it has on our approach to financial challenges, programming the mind to embrace strength, support, and community as pillars of financial management.

Reflecting on Success

Document Agreements: Ensure any negotiated terms are documented in writing. This not only provides legal protection but also serves as a tangible reminder of what you can achieve through informed negotiation.

Celebrate Milestones: Recognize and celebrate each successful negotiation as a milestone in your financial journey. These victories, big or small, build confidence and reinforce a positive, proactive relationship with money.

Continuous Learning: Reflect on the negotiation process as a learning experience, regardless of the outcome. Each interaction provides insights that can refine your approach in future negotiations.

Negotiating better terms on existing debts embodies a proactive stance towards personal finance. It's an exercise in empowerment, transforming how individuals perceive and interact with their financial obligations. Through this process, debt becomes not a source of stress but an aspect of one's financial life that can be actively managed and improved. This reprogramming of the mind towards a more empowered and strategic view of debt is foundational in building a resilient and prosperous financial future.

In the odyssey of financial empowerment, the act of negotiating better terms on existing debts is not merely a tactical maneuver but a profound assertion of agency over one's economic destiny. This journey, marked by moments of negotiation, is an invitation to a deeper engagement with the narratives we construct about our financial selves. At the heart of this engagement are three pivotal practices: documenting agreements, celebrating milestones, and embracing continuous learning.

Documenting Agreements
The insistence on documenting negotiated terms in writing transcends the practicality of legal safeguarding. It embodies a ritual of acknowledgment, a physical manifestation of one's capacity to influence the course of their financial journey. This documentation serves as a tangible testament to the triumphs of negotiation, a beacon of one's ability to navigate the complex seas of personal finance with acumen and resolve. It's a reminder that through informed negotiation, individuals hold the power to sculpt their financial landscape, ensuring that each agreement stands as a milestone in their journey towards financial sovereignty.

Celebrating Milestones
The celebration of each successful negotiation as a milestone is akin to charting one's progress across a vast and often daunting territory. These celebrations are acts of affirmation, reinforcing the narrative of progress and achievement. They serve not merely as pauses for self-congratulation but as essential components of building confidence and fostering a positive, proactive relationship with money. Each victory, whether monumental or modest, is a brushstroke on the canvas of one's financial story, contributing to a portrait of resilience, empowerment, and strategic engagement with personal finance.

Continuous Learning

Viewing the negotiation process through the lens of continuous learning transforms each interaction into a crucible of growth. This perspective invites a reflective stance, encouraging individuals to distill lessons from every negotiation, irrespective of its immediate outcome. Such a practice ensures that the journey of financial negotiation is not defined by singular outcomes but by the cumulative wisdom garnered along the way. It is in this continuous refinement of strategies and approaches that one's capacity for effective negotiation is honed, paving the way for future successes.

Negotiating better terms on debts is, therefore, more than an exercise in financial management; it is a reprogramming of one's relationship with debt—from a source of stress to a domain of active engagement and improvement. This shift marks a critical evolution in the individual's financial narrative, where debt becomes a dimension of one's economic life that is not only manageable but also malleable to one's strategies and aspirations. It is a testament to the transformative power of negotiation, a practice that not only alters the terms of one's financial obligations but also reshapes the very fabric of one's financial identity.

Thus, the journey of negotiating better terms is emblematic of a broader quest for financial empowerment, a journey that is as much about changing the numbers on a balance sheet as it is about transforming one's perceptions and interactions with the world of finance. In embracing documentation, celebration, and continuous learning, individuals do more than navigate their financial present; they chart a course towards a resilient, prosperous financial future, replete with the knowledge that in the realm of personal finance, they are not mere participants but empowered architects of their destiny.

Section 3: Debt Consolidation Strategies

- **What is Debt Consolidation?:** Definition and overview of how debt consolidation works as a tool for managing multiple debts.

Debt consolidation stands as a beacon of strategy and control in the often tumultuous seas of personal finance. By understanding and employing debt consolidation, individuals can transform their approach to managing multiple debts from one of fragmentation and overwhelm into a unified, strategic effort aimed at financial clarity and liberation. This transformative process not only simplifies the debt repayment journey but also reprograms the mind to view financial challenges through a lens of empowerment and possibility.

Defining Debt Consolidation

Debt consolidation is the process of combining multiple debts into a single, more manageable loan or payment plan. This strategic move is designed to streamline the repayment process, potentially secure more favorable interest rates, and provide a clear timeline for debt freedom. The consolidation loan is used to pay off existing debts, leaving the individual with one monthly payment rather than several.

In the grand tapestry of financial strategies, debt consolidation emerges as a beacon of hope, a masterstroke designed to transform the scattered puzzle of multiple debts into a coherent, manageable masterpiece. Picture this: your financial obligations, each with its own timeline, interest rate, and monthly payment, swirling around you like a tempest. Now, imagine harnessing that chaos, drawing it into the eye of the storm where calm reigns, and transforming it into a single, serene stream of repayment. This is the essence of debt consolidation.

Embarking on the journey of debt consolidation is akin to navigating the high seas with a compass pointing towards financial liberation. By amalgamating various debts into one consolidated loan, you're not just simplifying your financial landscape; you're charting a course towards a horizon where the sun of debt freedom rises. This singular loan, crafted with potentially more favorable interest rates, becomes your vessel, cutting through the turbulent waters of multiple repayments and steering you towards the tranquility of a singular, manageable monthly payment.

But the magic of debt consolidation lies not only in its ability to streamline repayment but in the subliminal transformation it fosters within. Each step towards consolidating your debts is a step away from financial fragmentation towards unity. It's a declaration that your financial destiny is not to be dictated by a cacophony of creditors but guided by a single, harmonious strategy. This process is more than a financial maneuver; it's a reprogramming of your approach to debt, imbuing you with a sense of control, clarity, and purpose.

The act of consolidating your debts does more than rearrange your financial obligations; it reshapes your relationship with money. It whispers to the subconscious, reinforcing the belief that complexity can be simplified, that multiple burdens can be unified into a single challenge that is not only easier to manage but more satisfying to overcome. It teaches that in the realm of personal finance, chaos can be transformed into order, and the myriad paths of repayment can converge into a single road leading to the pinnacle of debt freedom.

Thus, debt consolidation stands as a testament to the power of strategic simplification, a reminder that the journey towards financial wellness is not traversed through the scattered efforts of many but through the focused, unified approach of one. It is a strategy that does not merely alter the structure of your debts but redefines your trajectory towards financial empowerment, embedding within your psyche the relentless pursuit of clarity, control, and eventual liberation from the chains of debt.

The Mechanism of Consolidation

The consolidation process typically involves obtaining a new loan with terms that are advantageous compared to the existing debts. This could mean a lower interest rate, reduced monthly payments, or both, achieved through one of several methods:

Consolidation Loans: A personal loan from a bank, credit union, or online lender that pays off multiple debts, leaving the individual with just the consolidation loan to repay.

Balance Transfer Credit Cards: Transferring multiple credit card balances to a single card offering a low introductory interest rate, simplifying payments and reducing interest costs.

Home Equity Loans or Lines of Credit: For homeowners, leveraging equity in the home to consolidate debts under a lower interest rate, though this introduces the risk of losing the home if payments are not made.

The Psychological Impact of Consolidation

Gaining control over one's financial narrative through debt consolidation is a transformative process that offers multifaceted benefits, enhancing one's ability to manage finances effectively and strategically. Below is an expanded discussion on the key advantages of this approach:

Reduces Complexity

Debt consolidation streamlines financial obligations, transforming them from a dispersed and multifarious collection into a single, coherent entity. This simplification process yields several critical benefits:

Debt consolidation offers a streamlined approach to managing financial obligations, providing enhanced clarity, improved time efficiency, and significant stress alleviation. By consolidating multiple debts into a single liability, individuals can transform a complex financial situation into a more manageable and strategic one, fostering a healthier financial life.

Enhanced Clarity

Simplified Financial Overview: When multiple debts are amalgamated into one, it eliminates the confusion of tracking various interest rates, payment deadlines, and balance updates. This consolidation brings a sense of order to one's financial landscape, making it easier to grasp the overall debt picture.

Informed Financial Decisions: With a clear understanding of total indebtedness, individuals can make more informed choices regarding their spending, saving, and payment strategies. This clarity can lead to more deliberate and impactful financial decisions, such as prioritizing additional payments to reduce the consolidated debt more rapidly.

Time Efficiency

Streamlined Debt Management: Managing one consolidated debt account significantly reduces the administrative burden associated with multiple debts. The time saved from not having to log into various accounts, track different payment schedules, and reconcile multiple statements can be substantial.

Allocating Resources Effectively: The time and mental energy conserved through debt consolidation can be redirected towards other important financial activities, such as budgeting, investing, or building an emergency fund, thereby enhancing overall financial productivity and growth.

Stress Alleviation

Reducing Cognitive Overload: The mental strain of juggling several debts, each with its own set of variables, can be overwhelming. Consolidation reduces this cognitive load, allowing individuals to focus on a singular debt strategy, which can be less taxing and more manageable.

Emotional Benefits: Financial stress is a significant contributor to mental health issues. By consolidating debts, individuals can experience a reduction in anxiety and stress levels, contributing to better overall well-being. The sense of progress and control that comes from effectively managing consolidated debt can also boost psychological morale and motivation.

In essence, debt consolidation is not just a financial strategy but a step towards greater financial peace of mind. It offers a structured path out of the complexity and anxiety often associated with debt, paving the way for clearer financial thinking, more strategic resource allocation, and improved mental health. By adopting this approach, individuals can navigate their financial journey with greater ease and confidence, setting the stage for a more secure and prosperous financial future.

Encourages Strategic Thinking

The act of consolidating debt necessitates a comprehensive evaluation of one's financial landscape, prompting a more strategic approach to debt management:

Debt consolidation transcends mere aggregation of liabilities, offering a strategic platform for a holistic and informed approach to personal finance management. This process not only simplifies the debt landscape but also provides educational benefits, fostering enhanced financial literacy and encouraging more nuanced decision-making aligned with long-term financial objectives.

Holistic Financial Assessment

Comprehensive Financial Review: Engaging in debt consolidation necessitates a detailed evaluation of one's financial obligations. This evaluation includes compiling all debts, understanding the varying interest rates, and examining the different repayment terms. Such a comprehensive review promotes an integrated view of one's financial obligations, setting the stage for more informed and cohesive financial planning.

Strategic Financial Insight: By assessing the entirety of one's debt under a single lens, individuals gain a macroscopic view of their financial health, enabling them to identify overarching patterns or issues that may not be apparent when debts are considered in isolation. This holistic insight is crucial for devising a strategic approach to debt repayment and overall financial management.

Informed Decision-Making

Critical Evaluation of Financial Options: The consolidation process compels individuals to critically analyze various consolidation options and their respective implications. This scrutiny involves comparing interest rates, assessing term lengths, and understanding potential impacts on credit scores, which collectively guide more informed financial decision-making.

Alignment with Financial Goals: By contemplating the broader implications of debt consolidation, individuals can ensure that the chosen strategy aligns with their long-term financial aspirations, whether that's becoming debt-free, improving credit health, or reallocating resources towards savings or investments.

Enhanced Financial Literacy

Educational Opportunity: The process of consolidating debt serves as a practical education in financial management, introducing individuals to essential financial concepts and terminology. This education empowers individuals to navigate the financial landscape more adeptly, enhancing their ability to make informed decisions.

Application to Future Financial Decisions: The insights and knowledge gained through the consolidation process have lasting benefits, extending beyond immediate debt management. Equipped with a deeper understanding of financial principles, individuals can apply this knowledge to various aspects of their financial lives, from budgeting and investing to evaluating future credit opportunities.

In conclusion, debt consolidation offers more than a pathway to simplified debt repayment. It fosters a comprehensive, informed, and educated approach to personal finance, enabling individuals to manage their current debts more strategically while equipping them with the knowledge and skills for sound financial decision-making in the future. This multifaceted approach not only aids in achieving immediate financial relief but also lays the groundwork for sustained financial health and literacy.

Builds Confidence

Debt consolidation transcends mere aggregation of liabilities, offering a strategic platform for a holistic and informed approach to personal finance management. This process not only simplifies the debt landscape but also provides educational benefits, fostering enhanced financial literacy and encouraging more nuanced decision-making aligned with long-term financial objectives.

Holistic Financial Assessment

Comprehensive Financial Review: Engaging in debt consolidation necessitates a detailed evaluation of one's financial obligations. This evaluation includes compiling all debts, understanding the varying interest rates, and examining the different repayment terms. Such a comprehensive review promotes an integrated view of one's financial obligations, setting the stage for more informed and cohesive financial planning.

Strategic Financial Insight: By assessing the entirety of one's debt under a single lens, individuals gain a macroscopic view of their financial health, enabling them to identify overarching patterns or issues that may not be apparent when debts are considered in isolation. This holistic insight is crucial for devising a strategic approach to debt repayment and overall financial management.

Informed Decision-Making

Critical Evaluation of Financial Options: The consolidation process compels individuals to critically analyze various consolidation options and their respective implications. This scrutiny involves comparing interest rates, assessing term lengths, and understanding potential impacts on credit scores, which collectively guide more informed financial decision-making.

Alignment with Financial Goals: By contemplating the broader implications of debt consolidation, individuals can ensure that the chosen strategy aligns with their long-term financial aspirations, whether that's becoming debt-free, improving credit health, or reallocating resources towards savings or investments.

Enhanced Financial Literacy

Educational Opportunity: The process of consolidating debt serves as a practical education in financial management, introducing individuals to essential financial concepts and terminology. This education empowers individuals to navigate the financial landscape more adeptly, enhancing their ability to make informed decisions.

Application to Future Financial Decisions: The insights and knowledge gained through the consolidation process have lasting benefits, extending beyond immediate debt management. Equipped with a deeper understanding of financial principles, individuals can apply this knowledge to various aspects of their financial lives, from budgeting and investing to evaluating future credit opportunities.

In conclusion, debt consolidation offers more than a pathway to simplified debt repayment. It fosters a comprehensive, informed, and educated approach to personal finance, enabling individuals to manage their current debts more strategically while equipping them with the knowledge and skills for sound financial decision-making in the future. This multifaceted approach not only aids in achieving immediate financial relief but also lays the groundwork for sustained financial health and literacy.

Promotes a Forward-Looking Perspective

Debt consolidation is not merely a financial strategy; it is a pedagogical tool that instills foresight, discipline, and a strategic approach to financial well-being. By engaging with this process, students are encouraged to adopt a proactive stance toward their finances, envisioning and planning for a prosperous financial future. Here, we elucidate how debt consolidation can serve as a cornerstone for nurturing prudent financial habits and a wealth-oriented mindset.

Long-Term Financial Planning

Visionary Financial Strategy: Encourage students to perceive debt consolidation as a step toward realizing their long-term financial aspirations. By integrating debt management within their broader life goals—be it homeownership, education, or retirement—students learn to view financial decisions through the lens of their future selves, fostering a strategic approach to personal finance.

Integrated Financial Objectives: Students are taught to see debt consolidation not as an end but as a means to achieve greater financial goals. This perspective instills the importance of setting and working towards long-term objectives, encouraging a holistic view of financial health that transcends immediate concerns.

Cultivation of a Wealth Mindset

Fostering Financial Growth: By aligning debt consolidation with future financial stability and growth, students are encouraged to cultivate a wealth mindset. This mindset is characterized by a focus on accumulating assets, enhancing savings, and investing prudently, contrasting with a mere emphasis on debt repayment.

Promotion of Financial Prosperity: Instruct students on how adopting a wealth mindset involves prioritizing actions and decisions that build long-term financial security. This approach fosters a proactive engagement with finances, where saving and investing become integral components of their financial practice.

Preparation for Future Financial Challenges

Skill Development: Debt consolidation teaches essential financial skills, such as budgeting, forecasting, and strategic planning. Highlight how these skills are transferable, equipping students to adeptly manage future financial situations, from unexpected expenses to investment opportunities.

Resilience Building: Emphasize how the discipline and foresight cultivated through debt consolidation empower students to face and navigate future financial adversities with confidence. The experience of consolidating debt and the ensuing financial management practices lay a foundation for enduring financial resilience.

Cultivating a wealth mindset through the process of debt consolidation transcends the mere act of combining financial obligations; it is a strategic endeavor that lays the groundwork for enduring financial growth and prosperity. This approach to wealth building is not focused solely on the elimination of debt but on the broader vision of financial stability and the accumulation of assets. It encourages individuals to look beyond the immediate horizon of debt repayment, envisioning a future replete with enhanced savings and prudent investments.

By integrating debt consolidation into a comprehensive financial strategy, individuals are prompted to foster a wealth mindset, a perspective where financial decisions are made with a long-term view of asset accumulation and capital enhancement. This mindset shift is crucial for transitioning from a reactive stance of managing debts to a proactive approach of fostering financial growth. It involves prioritizing actions and decisions that not only alleviate current financial burdens but also pave the way for future financial security.

In this context, the consolidation of debt becomes a stepping stone to broader financial prosperity. It serves as a practical framework within which individuals can practice and perfect the art of financial management, encompassing budgeting, forecasting, and strategic planning. These skills, honed through the consolidation process, are not confined to the realm of debt management but are transferable to various facets of financial life, preparing individuals to navigate a spectrum of future financial scenarios with agility and acumen.

Moreover, the journey of debt consolidation and the subsequent adoption of a wealth mindset are instrumental in building resilience. This resilience is not just about weathering financial storms but about navigating these challenges with a strategic foresight that minimizes future financial adversities. The discipline and planning inherent in this process empower individuals to face financial uncertainties with confidence, backed by a foundation of sound financial practices and a mindset geared towards wealth accumulation.

Thus, the cultivation of a wealth mindset through debt consolidation is a transformative process that reprograms individuals' approach to financial management. It fosters a mentality that emphasizes financial growth, asset accumulation, and long-term prosperity, marking a shift from merely managing debt to strategically building wealth. This holistic approach not only equips individuals with the necessary skills to manage their current financial landscape but also prepares them to embrace and capitalize on future financial opportunities, thereby laying a robust foundation for a lifetime of financial resilience and prosperity.

In Summary

Debt consolidation is a transformative process that extends beyond immediate debt resolution, serving as a vital educational experience that instills key financial principles. By engaging with this process, students are not only navigating their current financial landscape but are also being primed for future financial success. This module is designed to embed a forward-looking, strategic, and empowered approach to personal finance, encouraging students to embrace and cultivate habits that will support their long-term financial prosperity and stability. Through this structured approach, students learn to manage their finances with acumen and foresight, laying the groundwork for a financially secure and empowered future.

Mindset Shift Through Consolidation

Debt consolidation serves as a powerful tool not only for managing debts more effectively but also for reprogramming the subconscious attitudes towards debt and financial control. It shifts the narrative from one of reactive scrambling to proactive management, from viewing debts as scattered burdens to seeing them as consolidated challenges that can be strategically overcome.

This reprogramming is critical. It moves the individual from a state of financial survival to one of financial strategy, where debt is not an adversary but a variable that can be optimized. Through the lens of debt consolidation, debts are transformed from sources of stress into stepping stones towards financial clarity and, ultimately, freedom.

In summary, debt consolidation is more than a financial strategy; it is a pathway to redefining one's relationship with debt. By embracing this approach, individuals can simplify their financial obligations, secure potentially better terms, and adopt a wealth mindset that views effective debt management as a cornerstone of financial empowerment and liberation.

- **Methods of Debt Consolidation:** Examination of different consolidation options, including personal consolidation loans, balance transfer credit cards, and home equity loans.

Exploring the methods of debt consolidation reveals a spectrum of strategies, each with its unique advantages and considerations. This examination is not just about logistical options; it's an exercise in rethinking and reshaping one's approach to managing debt. By understanding the various consolidation methods—personal consolidation loans, balance transfer credit cards, and home equity loans—individuals can make empowered decisions that align with their financial goals and circumstances, reinforcing a mindset oriented towards strategic financial health.

Personal Consolidation Loans

Personal consolidation loans offer a strategic approach to debt management, enabling individuals to streamline their financial obligations into one manageable payment. This educational narrative aims to illuminate the facets of personal consolidation loans, emphasizing the cultivation of disciplined financial habits and the strategic management of one's financial resources.

Overview of Personal Consolidation Loans

Centralized Financial Management

Streamlined Debt Navigation: Personal consolidation loans integrate various financial liabilities into a singular, coherent loan, imbued with a stable interest rate and a clear repayment timeline. This integration propels individuals towards a more structured and less fragmented financial journey, alleviating the complexities associated with juggling multiple debt streams.

Enhanced Organizational Efficacy: The act of consolidating debt cultivates an environment where financial obligations are not only centralized but also simplified. This consolidation eradicates the confusion and stress often associated with managing multiple debts, paving the way for a more orderly and focused approach to financial stewardship.

Personal consolidation loans epitomize the essence of centralized financial management, offering a streamlined approach to navigating the often convoluted realm of personal finance. These loans amalgamate various financial liabilities into a single, coherent entity, characterized by a stable interest rate and a transparent repayment schedule. This unification process transforms the financial journey from a fragmented array of obligations into a structured and unified path, significantly simplifying the debt management landscape.

The integration achieved through personal consolidation loans extends beyond mere debt aggregation; it represents a strategic simplification of financial responsibilities. By consolidating multiple debts into one loan, individuals can focus on a singular repayment strategy, which diminishes the mental and administrative burdens of tracking and managing numerous debt accounts. This streamlined navigation through one's financial liabilities not only clarifies the path to debt freedom but also instills a sense of control and manageability.

Moreover, the organizational efficacy inherent in the consolidation process fosters a more disciplined and coherent financial environment. The act of consolidating debt under a single umbrella loan eliminates the confusion and stress that typically accompany the management of multiple and disparate debts. This simplification leads to a more orderly financial regime, where individuals can engage with their financial obligations in a more focused and effective manner.

In essence, personal consolidation loans serve as a cornerstone for effective financial management, enabling individuals to maneuver through their financial obligations with greater ease and clarity. The process not only facilitates a more streamlined and less fragmented financial journey but also enhances the organizational framework within which individuals manage their finances. Through this centralized and simplified approach, personal consolidation loans lay the foundation for a more structured and efficient pathway to financial stewardship and debt resolution.

Clarity in Financial Planning

Augmented Financial Insight: The consolidation process endows individuals with a lucid understanding of their debt landscape, enabling a more refined and informed approach to financial strategy. The unification brought about by a consolidation loan diminishes the opacity that often surrounds an individual's debt obligations, granting a level of clarity that is instrumental in effective financial decision-making.

Budgetary Precision: The transparency afforded by a singular consolidated debt fosters an environment conducive to meticulous budgeting and financial forecasting. Such clarity ensures that individuals can allocate their resources with greater precision, facilitating a proactive rather than reactive approach to financial management.

The process of debt consolidation significantly contributes to clarity in financial planning, offering individuals augmented financial insight and enabling them to navigate their fiscal landscape with increased understanding and strategy. Through the consolidation of various debts into a single, manageable loan, individuals gain a lucid perspective on their financial obligations, shedding light on the complexities that once clouded their financial judgment and decision-making.

This newfound clarity does more than simplify the debt landscape; it serves as a pivotal tool in the formulation of a more refined and informed financial strategy. By diminishing the opacity and fragmentation of multiple debt accounts, consolidation loans provide a coherent view of one's financial obligations, thereby enhancing the individual's ability to make strategic, well-informed decisions. This comprehensive understanding is instrumental in developing a financial plan that is not only realistic but also aligned with the individual's long-term financial goals.

Moreover, the consolidation process fosters budgetary precision, creating an environment where financial resources can be allocated and managed with greater accuracy and intent. The single, consolidated debt framework allows for a more streamlined approach to budgeting and financial forecasting, where each aspect of the financial plan can be carefully scrutinized and adjusted as needed. This precision in financial planning and budgeting facilitates a proactive stance towards financial management, empowering individuals to anticipate and prepare for financial requirements and opportunities, rather than merely reacting to them.

In essence, clarity in financial planning, achieved through the debt consolidation process, provides individuals with the insight and precision needed to manage their finances more effectively and strategically. This enhanced understanding and control pave the way for a more disciplined, informed, and proactive approach to financial management, ultimately contributing to more stable and prosperous financial outcomes.

Educational Emphasis

In structuring the narrative around personal consolidation loans for educational purposes, the focus should be on illustrating the benefits of centralized financial management and enhanced clarity in financial planning. This approach not only elucidates the immediate advantages of debt consolidation but also underscores the importance of strategic financial thinking and proactive budgetary control. By embedding these concepts into the educational discourse, students are encouraged to adopt a more analytical and forward-thinking perspective on financial management, ultimately fostering a mindset attuned to the nuances of personal financial optimization.

Advantages of Personal Consolidation Loans

Simplified Financial Landscape

Enhanced Budgetary Management: By transforming disparate debt obligations into a single streamlined loan, individuals can more readily oversee their financial engagements, thereby fostering a more transparent and manageable budgetary framework. This consolidation aids in mitigating the risk of oversight in payment obligations, which can fortify one's credit standing over time.

Interest Rate Efficiency: The strategic consolidation of various higher-interest debts into one loan with a lower interest rate is a prudent financial maneuver that can yield significant interest cost savings. This efficiency not only alleviates the monetary strain but also expedites the journey towards debt liberation, offering a tangible pathway to financial relief and stability.

Considerations and Strategic Implications

Credit Score Relevance: The potential to benefit from lower interest rates through a consolidation loan is intrinsically linked to one's credit score. This interdependence highlights the criticality of nurturing a strong credit profile, as it can substantially influence the financial terms and viability of consolidation opportunities, impacting long-term debt sustainability.

Imperative of Financial Prudence: The structural advantage provided by debt consolidation can be undermined if not accompanied by a disciplined financial ethos. The essence of consolidation is not merely to reorganize debt but to serve as a catalyst for enduring financial behavior modification. It necessitates a vigilant and strategic approach to expenditure, emphasizing the necessity to rectify the spending behaviors that precipitated the original debt, thus averting the peril of a recurring debt cycle.

In imparting these insights to students, the narrative should pivot towards instilling an understanding of the nuanced benefits and inherent responsibilities associated with debt consolidation. Emphasizing the dual focus on practical financial benefits and the essential behavioral adjustments offers a comprehensive framework for appreciating the multifaceted nature of debt management. This educational discourse aims to equip students with the knowledge to navigate debt consolidation judiciously while fostering a broader comprehension of its role within a disciplined financial strategy, thereby cultivating informed and responsible financial decision-makers.

Personal consolidation loans are a strategic tool in financial management, meticulously designed to transform the often chaotic landscape of multiple debts into a singular, streamlined financial commitment. This transformation is not just a matter of convenience; it represents a fundamental shift in how individuals interact with their financial obligations. By consolidating various debts, each with potentially high and varying interest rates, into one cohesive loan with a lower, stable interest rate, individuals embark on a journey towards financial simplification and clarity.

The process of debt consolidation offers a dual advantage. On one hand, it significantly simplifies the task of managing debts, replacing the complexity of multiple payments, due dates, and interest rates with a single, manageable monthly payment. This simplification allows individuals to gain a more transparent and comprehensive view of their financial situation, enhancing their ability to manage and forecast their budget effectively. On the other hand, the potential for reduced interest rates through consolidation can lead to considerable financial savings, diminishing the overall cost of debt and accelerating the journey towards financial liberation.

The success of personal consolidation loans in providing these benefits is intricately tied to one's credit score. A strong credit profile not only increases the likelihood of securing a consolidation loan with favorable terms but also plays a crucial role in determining the long-term sustainability of the debt management strategy. Therefore, nurturing a healthy credit score becomes a pivotal aspect of the financial planning process, influencing the effectiveness of debt consolidation as a financial tool.

However, the strategic value of personal consolidation loans extends beyond immediate financial relief and simplification. The true essence of this financial strategy lies in its ability to serve as a catalyst for long-term financial behavior modification. The act of consolidating debt should not be viewed as a mere tactical reorganization of financial liabilities but as an opportunity to foster a disciplined financial ethos. It necessitates a vigilant and strategic approach to personal financial management, emphasizing the importance of rectifying the spending behaviors that led to the accumulation of debt.

In this context, the educational narrative surrounding personal consolidation loans should pivot towards instilling an understanding of the intricate relationship between debt management and broader financial habits. It is crucial to convey that while consolidation can provide immediate relief and a structured path to debt repayment, its long-term success is contingent upon an individual's commitment to maintaining disciplined financial practices. This includes prudent budgeting, strategic planning, and a steadfast commitment to avoiding the pitfalls that lead to financial strain.

In conclusion, personal consolidation loans are a powerful instrument in the financial toolkit, offering a means to streamline debt management and foster a more controlled and strategic financial environment. However, their effectiveness is inherently linked to an individual's broader financial behavior and planning. By understanding and embracing the comprehensive benefits and responsibilities associated with debt consolidation, individuals can leverage this financial strategy to not only navigate their current debt landscape but also to build a foundation for sustained financial health and prosperity, programming the mind towards a future of financial stability and growth.

Educational Takeaway

In integrating personal consolidation loans into financial education, the emphasis should be placed on promoting a disciplined and informed approach to debt management. Students should be encouraged to view consolidation not merely as a mechanism for easing current financial strain but as an opportunity to adopt a more strategic and responsible approach to personal finance. By understanding the advantages and considerations associated with personal consolidation loans, individuals can make informed decisions that align with their long-term financial objectives, thereby fostering a foundation for sustained financial health and stability.

Balance Transfer Credit Cards

Introduction to Balance Transfer Strategy

In the context of personal financial management, particularly in addressing credit card debt, the balance transfer strategy is a noteworthy method. It involves transferring the outstanding balances from one or more credit cards to another card that offers a significantly lower introductory interest rate. This financial maneuver is designed to provide individuals with a strategic advantage in reducing their debt more efficiently.

Advantages of Implementing a Balance Transfer

Reduction in Interest Expenses: The quintessential benefit of a balance transfer is the dramatic decrease in interest costs during the promotional period. With a lower or zero percent introductory rate, the bulk of each payment is allocated toward diminishing the principal balance, thereby expediting the debt reduction trajectory.

Consolidation Benefits: This strategy also serves to aggregate various credit card debts into a singular, manageable account. Such consolidation is beneficial for simplifying the personal financial landscape, enhancing the ease of monitoring and making repayments, and potentially mitigating the risk of missed or late payments.

Key Considerations for Effective Strategy Implementation

Duration of Low-Interest Period: Awareness and strategic planning are crucial to maximize the benefits of the introductory interest rate. It is imperative to align debt repayment plans with the duration of this period to ensure optimal debt reduction.

Understanding Transfer Fees: Balance transfers typically incur a fee, calculated as a percentage of the transferred amount. A critical evaluation is necessary to ascertain that the interest savings surpass these initial costs, thereby validating the financial prudence of the transfer.

Post-Introductory Rate Preparedness: Acquaintance with the standard interest rate, which becomes applicable post the introductory phase, is vital to avoid any unexpected financial burdens. Effective debt management should aim to mitigate or extinguish the debt prior to the escalation of interest rates.

Credit Score Considerations: The initiation of a balance transfer entails credit inquiries and potential changes in credit utilization ratios, which can influence credit scores. However, a strategic approach to balance transfer and subsequent debt reduction should ultimately foster credit score improvement.

Conclusion: Empowering Financial Decision-Making

The balance transfer strategy, when comprehensively understood and meticulously applied, can be a pivotal component of effective debt management and financial empowerment. Educating individuals about this strategy entails not just delineating its benefits but also instilling an appreciation for the strategic considerations and financial discipline required for its success. Through such enlightenment, individuals are equipped to make informed decisions, adopt proactive financial behaviors, and cultivate a more robust financial future.

Implementing a balance transfer strategy is a pivotal move in the journey toward wealth building, offering a seamless method to reduce interest expenses and consolidate debt, thereby crafting a more manageable financial landscape. The essence of this strategy lies in its ability to significantly lower interest costs during the promotional period, where a reduced or zero percent interest rate ensures that payments predominantly reduce the principal, thus accelerating the path to debt freedom. This strategic maneuver not only simplifies the financial management process by amalgamating various debts into one account but also enhances budgetary control and reduces the risk of missed payments, fostering a stronger credit profile.

To maximize the wealth-building potential of balance transfers, one must align debt repayment efforts with the low-interest period, meticulously plan to cover the transferred balance before higher rates resume, and ensure the cost-effectiveness of the transfer by evaluating associated fees. This approach not only mitigates immediate financial strain but sets the stage for sustained financial health, allowing for the redirection of saved interest towards investments or savings, catalyzing the growth of personal wealth.

Furthermore, the strategic consolidation through balance transfers, when executed with foresight and discipline, can improve credit scores, unlocking better financial opportunities and terms in the future. It's a process that not only alleviates the immediate burden of high-interest debt but also ingrains a disciplined approach to financial management, paving the way for a robust financial future.

In essence, balance transfers, as part of a comprehensive wealth-building strategy, empower individuals to take control of their financial destiny, transforming debt from a burden into an opportunity for financial optimization and growth. This methodical approach to managing and reducing debt is a critical step in building a foundation for long-term financial prosperity, enabling individuals to channel their resources more effectively towards achieving their wealth accumulation goals.

Home Equity Loans or Lines of Credit

Introduction to Home Equity Financial Instruments

Home equity loans (HELs) and home equity lines of credit (HELOCs) represent strategic financial mechanisms available to homeowners, allowing them to leverage the equity value in their homes as collateral to secure funds. These instruments are particularly utilized for consolidating and refinancing existing higher-interest debts, offering a structured approach to financial management and debt reduction.

Advantages of Utilizing HELs and HELOCs

Competitive Interest Rates: One of the most compelling advantages of HELs and HELOCs is their typically lower interest rates compared to unsecured debt options like credit cards or personal loans. This benefit can translate into considerable cost savings over the life of the loan, enabling more efficient debt management and reduction.

Potential Tax Deductions: Another significant advantage is the possibility of tax deductions on the interest paid towards these loans, provided the borrowed funds are employed towards purchasing, constructing, or substantially renovating the borrower's primary residence. This potential tax benefit can further enhance the financial attractiveness of these borrowing options.

Essential Considerations and Risks

Collateral at Stake: The most critical consideration when opting for a HEL or HELOC is the inherent risk of using one's home as collateral. In the event of default, the lender has the legal right to initiate foreclosure proceedings, posing a substantial risk to the homeowner's property and financial stability.

Interest Rate Variability: Specifically with HELOCs, borrowers must contend with variable interest rates that can fluctuate based on prevailing market conditions. This variability introduces an element of financial unpredictability, necessitating careful planning and monitoring to manage potential rate increases over the loan's tenure.

Conclusion: Strategic Financial Planning with HELs and HELOCs

When contemplated within the context of an overarching financial strategy, HELs and HELOCs can offer valuable avenues for debt consolidation and financial optimization. However, the decision to leverage home equity for debt management should be underpinned by a thorough understanding of the products, a clear assessment of one's financial stability, and an acknowledgment of the associated risks. Educating individuals on these aspects ensures informed decision-making, fostering a more secure and strategic approach to personal financial management and debt reduction.

Home equity loans (HELs) and home equity lines of credit (HELOCs) are strategic financial instruments that allow homeowners to leverage the equity in their homes as collateral to secure funds, often for the purpose of consolidating and refinancing existing higher-interest debts. These mechanisms offer a structured pathway to financial management and debt reduction, presenting opportunities to utilize the inherent value of one's home in a financially strategic manner.

The allure of HELs and HELOCs lies in their competitive interest rates, which are typically lower than those of unsecured debt options like credit cards or personal loans. This advantage enables homeowners to manage and reduce their debts more efficiently, potentially resulting in significant cost savings over the life of the loan. Additionally, the potential for tax deductions on the interest paid enhances the appeal of these options, providing financial relief and making them a viable tool for smart financial planning.

However, the strategic use of home equity for financial leverage comes with its considerations and risks. The primary concern is the use of the home as collateral, which introduces the risk of foreclosure if the borrower defaults on the loan. This risk underscores the importance of careful financial planning and consideration before opting for a HEL or HELOC. Furthermore, with HELOCs, the variable interest rates add a layer of financial unpredictability, requiring borrowers to stay vigilant about market conditions and interest rate fluctuations to avoid unexpected financial strain.

In conclusion, HELs and HELOCs represent valuable financial tools for homeowners seeking to consolidate debt and optimize their financial strategy. They offer a way to tap into the equity of one's home for financial benefit, combining the potential for lower interest rates and tax advantages with the structured approach to debt management. However, the decision to utilize these instruments must be grounded in a comprehensive understanding of their mechanisms, a realistic assessment of one's financial situation, and a clear strategy for managing the associated risks. By educating homeowners about these aspects, they can be empowered to make informed decisions, ensuring that the use of HELs and HELOCs contributes positively to their overall financial health and stability, aligning with their long-term financial goals and risk tolerance.

Empowering Financial Decision-Making

Each debt consolidation method offers a unique pathway to simplify debt management, reduce interest costs, and potentially expedite debt repayment. However, the effectiveness of each option depends on individual financial situations, discipline, and long-term financial habits.

Engaging with these consolidation options is a powerful exercise in financial literacy and decision-making. It requires a critical assessment of one's financial habits, an understanding of the terms and conditions associated with each method, and a commitment to a strategic approach to debt repayment. This process reinforces a mindset that views debt not as a perpetual burden but as a temporary challenge that can be strategically managed and overcome.

In summary, understanding the methods of debt consolidation is crucial for anyone looking to optimize their approach to managing debt. It empowers individuals to take control of their financial situation, make informed choices, and move confidently toward financial stability and freedom.

- **Pros and Cons:** Detailed discussion of the advantages and disadvantages of each debt consolidation method.

In the journey toward financial enlightenment and empowerment, understanding the nuanced landscape of debt consolidation methods is akin to charting a course through uncharted waters. Each method, with its distinct advantages and disadvantages, offers a unique path toward achieving financial stability and prosperity. As we delve into this exploration, let us do so with the mindset of abundance, guided by the principles of positive psychology and the transformative power of reprogramming our thoughts towards wealth and fulfillment.

To deepen your understanding of the various debt consolidation methods and their impacts on financial health, let's engage in an exercise that explores the pros and cons of each method. This exercise aims to not only inform but also to reprogram our approach to debt management, fostering a mindset of financial abundance and empowerment.

Exercise: Evaluating Debt Consolidation Methods
Objective:
Identify and analyze the advantages and disadvantages of different debt consolidation methods to enhance decision-making in financial management.

Materials Needed:

Notebook or digital document for note-taking
Access to financial information resources (e.g., financial advisory websites, literature on debt consolidation)
Calculator (optional, for financial calculations)

Instructions:

Research and List:

Begin by researching the following debt consolidation methods: Personal Consolidation Loans, Balance Transfer Credit Cards, Home Equity Loans (HELs), and Home Equity Lines of Credit (HELOCs).
List each method in your notebook or document.
Pros Analysis:

For each method, identify and write down at least three advantages, considering factors like interest rates, repayment terms, impact on credit score, and financial flexibility.

Reflect on how each advantage can contribute to a journey toward financial stability and prosperity.

Cons Analysis:

Similarly, identify and document at least three disadvantages for each method, considering risks such as potential for debt accumulation, collateral risks, variable interest rates, and long-term financial impact.

Contemplate the challenges these disadvantages could pose to achieving financial enlightenment and empowerment.

Mindset Reprogramming:

Reflect on how understanding these pros and cons can aid in reprogramming your mindset towards a more strategic, informed, and positive approach to debt management.

Consider how each method aligns with principles of positive psychology, such as focusing on solutions, leveraging strengths, and fostering a growth mindset.

Conclusion and Action Plan:

Conclude by summarizing which debt consolidation method(s) might be most beneficial for your financial situation and why.

Develop a brief action plan on how you could implement this method in your financial strategy, considering your long-term financial goals and current financial health.

Reflection:

Reflect on this exercise and how it has influenced your perception of debt consolidation and financial management.

Think about how this knowledge can be integrated into your ongoing journey toward financial enlightenment and empowerment.

Outcome:

By completing this exercise, you will have a detailed understanding of the advantages and disadvantages of various debt consolidation methods, enabling you to make more informed decisions that align with your financial goals. This exercise is designed to not only provide you with practical financial insights but also to encourage a shift in mindset, fostering a perspective that views debt consolidation as a tool for financial growth and empowerment rather than a mere tactic for debt management.

Graph Description for Debt Consolidation Methods Exercise

Graph Type: Comparative Bar Chart

X-Axis: Represents the different debt consolidation methods (Personal Consolidation Loans, Balance Transfer Credit Cards, Home Equity Loans, Home Equity Lines of Credit).

Y-Axis: Represents the number of pros and cons identified for each method, allowing for a comparative analysis of the advantages and disadvantages.

Bars:

- Each method would have two bars; one for the pros and one for the cons.
- The height of each bar represents the number of advantages or disadvantages identified during the exercise.

Colors:

- Pros could be represented in a positive color, like green, to signify growth and positivity.
- Cons could be represented in a contrasting color, like red, to signify potential risks and challenges.

Additional Elements:

- A line graph overlay could show the potential financial impact or savings over time for each method, providing a visual representation of long-term financial effects.
- Icons or symbols next to each method could represent key considerations, like risk level (a warning triangle for high risk) or financial stability (a dollar sign or graph icon for methods leading to greater financial stability).

Legend:

- A clear legend explaining what each color, symbol, and line represents.

This comparative bar chart would provide a visual summary of the exercise, aiding in the analysis and decision-making process regarding debt consolidation methods. It would not only help in understanding the immediate pros and cons but also in assessing the long-term strategic fit of each method within an individual's financial plan.

Personal Consolidation Loans: A Path to Simplification

Embarking on the path of debt consolidation is akin to navigating through a dense fog towards clarity and empowerment. The act of uniting disparate debts into a singular, manageable entity is not merely an exercise in financial logistics; it is a profound step towards redefining one's relationship with money and debt. This transformative process fosters a mindset shift, from fragmentation and overwhelm to unity and control, aligning actions with one's deepest financial aspirations.

Unity in Complexity: A Beacon of Empowerment

Visualize the Transformation: Picture your financial obligations not as a tangled web of confusion but as a streamlined flow, moving steadily towards a clear horizon. This unity simplifies your financial landscape, making it easier to navigate and manage. It's the psychological equivalent of tidying a cluttered room, where the resulting clarity and order bring a deep sense of peace and control.

Embrace Control: By consolidating your debts, you're taking a decisive stand against complexity. This act of consolidation is a declaration of your autonomy over your financial destiny. It symbolizes a shift from being passively affected by financial obligations to actively directing them towards a singular goal: freedom from debt.

Reduced Interest Rates: The Path to Liberation

Feel the Relief: Lower interest rates are not just numbers on a page; they represent a tangible easing of your financial burden. Envision the relief that comes from knowing each payment carries you further towards liberation, rather than being lost to the void of high interest. This is the relief of a traveler who, after a long journey, sees the distance to their destination halving.

Accelerate Your Journey: Reduced interest rates mean more of your payment goes towards reducing the principal balance, rather than merely servicing the interest. This acceleration is akin to finding a more direct path to your destination, cutting down the travel time significantly. Imagine the satisfaction and empowerment that comes from seeing the end point of your debt journey not just approaching, but rushing towards you.

Cultivating a Mindset of Financial Empowerment

Program Your Mind for Success: Begin each day by affirming your control over your financial situation. "I am navigating my finances towards clear, liberating waters. Each decision I make is a step closer to financial freedom." Let this affirmation be a daily ritual that cements your commitment to your financial well-being.

Visualize Your Debt-Free Life: Regularly take time to envision your life free from the shackles of debt. See yourself living with abundance, investing in your dreams, and experiencing the joy of financial freedom. This practice not only motivates but also aligns your subconscious with your financial goals, making them an inevitable reality.

Embrace the Journey: Recognize that the path to debt freedom is both a challenge and an opportunity for growth. Each step taken, from consolidating your debts to making informed financial decisions, is a testament to your strength, resilience, and commitment to a brighter financial future.

In embracing the unity and reduced interest rates offered by debt consolidation, you're doing more than just simplifying your financial obligations. You're engaging in a profound act of self-empowerment, programming your mind to seek what is in your best financial interest. This mindset shift is the cornerstone of a life not just free from debt, but abundant in every sense.

Disadvantages:

Embarking on the path of debt consolidation, while laden with opportunities for financial simplification and empowerment, also navigates through waters marked by potential challenges. Awareness and preparation for these challenges are akin to charting a course with foresight, ensuring that the journey not only begins with promise but continues toward a horizon of sustained financial well-being.

To fully grasp the journey of debt consolidation and prepare for its challenges, let's engage in an exercise that reflects both the transformative potential and the considerations of this financial strategy.

Exercise: Navigating the Debt Consolidation Journey

Objective: To understand and internalize the benefits of debt consolidation while recognizing and preparing for its potential disadvantages.

Materials Needed:

- A journal or digital document for reflective writing
- Access to financial resources or advisories on debt consolidation

Instructions:

Visualize the Transformation:

- Reflect on your current financial situation, noting the diversity and complexity of your debts.
- Now, visualize these debts consolidating into a single, manageable loan. Picture your financial landscape transitioning from a tangled web of obligations to a streamlined, clear path towards financial freedom.

- Write down how this transformation makes you feel and how it could impact your daily financial management and long-term planning.

Embrace Control:

- Consider the autonomy and empowerment that come with consolidating your debts. How does taking control of your financial destiny change your perspective on money and debt?
- Write a personal declaration of financial autonomy, affirming your active role in directing your financial journey towards debt freedom.

Feel the Relief of Reduced Interest Rates:

- Calculate or estimate the difference in interest payments before and after consolidation. Reflect on the impact of these savings on your debt repayment timeline.
- Document the emotional and practical effects of reduced interest rates on your journey to becoming debt-free.

Program Your Mind for Success:

- Create a daily affirmation related to your financial goals and debt consolidation journey. This could be, "Each payment I make is a step closer to my financial freedom."
- Commit to reciting this affirmation every morning to reinforce a mindset of financial empowerment and control.

Visualize Your Debt-Free Life:

- Regularly set aside time to envision your life post-debt. What does financial freedom look like for you? How does it feel?
- Detail these visions in your journal, focusing on the abundance and opportunities that await in a debt-free future.

Embrace the Journey and Prepare for Challenges:

- Acknowledge the potential challenges of debt consolidation, such as the risk of using your home as collateral in a HEL or HELOC, or the discipline required to not accrue additional debt.
- For each potential challenge, write a strategic plan in your journal on how you would address and overcome it, ensuring a smooth and successful debt consolidation process.
-

Outcome:

By completing this exercise, you will have not only visualized and embraced the transformative potential of debt consolidation but also prepared yourself for the journey's challenges. This holistic approach ensures that you are not only informed about the path ahead but also mentally and emotionally ready to navigate it with confidence and strategic foresight. This preparedness is essential for turning the act of debt consolidation into a powerful step towards long-term financial empowerment and abundance.

Qualification Challenges: Navigating the Requirements

Understanding the Terrain: Just as not every explorer has the map or resources for every journey, securing a debt consolidation loan requires a specific key: a strong credit score. This score is a reflection of your financial past, serving as a beacon to lenders about your reliability as a borrower.

Empowering Action: If you find your credit score lacking, view this not as a barrier but as a call to action. This is an opportunity to delve into your financial habits, identifying areas for improvement. Engaging with your credit report, correcting errors, and making consistent, on-time payments can gradually enhance your score. Visualize this process as cultivating a garden; with patience and care, it will flourish, opening doors to new financial possibilities.

Potential for Further Debt: Steering Clear of the Tempest

Recognizing the Risk: Consolidation offers a streamlined path through the forest of debt, but without altering the behaviors that led you into the thicket, you risk wandering back in. Accumulating new debts on top of a consolidation loan is like sailing into a storm with a patched-up boat; it invites trouble on a journey that was meant to bring you to calmer waters.

Cultivating Sustainable Habits: To navigate successfully, one must chart a course of sustainable spending habits. Begin by scrutinizing your spending, identifying areas where emotions or impulses lead to financial decisions that diverge from your long-term goals. Embrace budgeting not just as a tool but as a compass, guiding your daily decisions to align with your aspirations of debt freedom and financial abundance.

Reprogramming for Resilience: Transforming spending habits requires a deep, foundational shift in your relationship with money. Practice mindfulness in your financial decisions, asking whether a potential expenditure brings you closer to or further from your goals. Affirmations can be powerful: "Every dollar I spend aligns with my journey toward financial freedom." This mindset shift, from reactive to proactive financial engagement, is your shield against the tempest of further debt.

Embracing the Voyage with Wisdom and Strategy

The journey of debt consolidation, with its potential pitfalls, is a testament to the complexity of personal finance. Yet, it is in navigating these challenges that true financial empowerment is forged. By approaching qualification challenges as opportunities for growth and recognizing the importance of sustainable spending habits, you are not merely avoiding pitfalls; you are actively constructing a future of financial stability and abundance.

In recognizing and preparing for the disadvantages of debt consolidation, you arm yourself with knowledge and resilience. This journey is not just about escaping debt but about redefining your financial identity, laying the foundation for a future where financial decisions are made with wisdom, intention, and a deep commitment to your personal prosperity.

Balance Transfer Credit Cards: Navigating Short-Term Relief

Advantages:

In the voyage towards financial serenity, balance transfer credit cards offer unique advantages, akin to finding a navigational chart that outlines a more direct and less costly path through the stormy seas of debt. These advantages, when leveraged with insight and intention, can significantly alter the course of one's financial journey, steering it towards a horizon of clarity, control, and peace.

Breathing Space: A Harbor from High Interest

Illuminating the Path: The introductory period of low or zero interest that comes with balance transfer credit cards is like a beacon of light, offering a temporary reprieve from the relentless accumulation of interest. This period provides not just relief but a strategic opportunity to reduce your debt principal at an accelerated pace, without the burden of additional interest.

Empowering Visualization: Picture your debts not as a weight dragging you beneath the waves but as a challenge that you're equipped to overcome. The breathing space provided by the low-interest period is your time to navigate with speed and purpose, channeling all available resources towards reducing the principal. Visualize each payment made during this period as a powerful stroke of the oars, propelling you forward towards your goal of debt freedom.

Consolidation of Payments: Streamlining Your Course

Harmonizing the Waters: The consolidation of multiple credit card payments into one is akin to guiding your fleet of scattered ships into a cohesive, formidable formation. This consolidation simplifies your financial management, transforming chaotic, turbulent waters into a streamlined flow that moves in one direction: towards your destination of financial stability.

Subconscious Reprogramming: Embrace this simplified approach as a reflection of your internal state—calm, focused, and in control. Each time you make that single, consolidated payment, reinforce the belief that you are one step closer to your goal. Let this act be a reminder of your capability to bring order to complexity, instilling a sense of confidence and progress that permeates all aspects of your financial life.

Navigating with Purpose and Precision

Charting a Thoughtful Course: As you utilize these advantages, remember that the true journey is not just in the mechanics of transferring balances or making payments. It is in the profound shift towards viewing every financial decision through the lens of long-term well-being and abundance. The breathing space and consolidation are tools in your arsenal, empowering you to act not out of desperation but from a place of strength and strategy.

Cultivating Resilience and Strategy: Let the process of managing your balance transfer credit card be a practice in financial mindfulness. With each payment made during the introductory period, reflect on the progress you've made and the habits you're forming. This period is an invaluable teacher, imparting lessons in discipline, foresight, and the art of seizing opportunities for growth.

In harnessing the advantages of balance transfer credit cards—viewing them not just as temporary fixes but as strategic steps on your journey—you reprogram your mindset towards one of empowerment, abundance, and unwavering resolve. This journey, marked by breathing space and consolidation, is a testament to your commitment to navigate the complexities of debt with wisdom, transforming challenges into victories on the path to financial freedom.

Disadvantages:

The journey toward financial stability, especially when navigating the waters of balance transfer credit cards, is fraught with both opportunities and challenges. Among these, the temptation of the introductory period and the potential pitfalls of balance transfer fees stand out as critical considerations. Recognizing and addressing these factors is not merely about financial strategy; it's about cultivating a mindset that transcends immediate gratification for long-term prosperity.

The Temptation of the Introductory Period: Navigating with Discipline

A Siren's Song: The introductory period of low or zero interest rates on balance transfer credit cards can indeed feel like a siren's call, promising smooth sailing. However, without the compass of discipline, this alluring tune can lead unwary navigators off course. The end of the introductory period often heralds the onset of significantly higher rates, which can swiftly erode the progress made during the initial interest-free months.

Cultivating Discipline: To resist this temptation, visualize the introductory period not as a hiatus from financial responsibility but as a strategic phase in a longer journey. Imagine yourself harnessing this opportunity with wisdom, paying down as much debt as possible before standard rates resume. This disciplined approach reprograms your mindset towards seeing beyond immediate ease, focusing instead on the broader horizon of debt freedom.

Balance Transfer Fees: Charting a Course with Precision

Hidden Reefs: Just as hidden reefs can threaten the integrity of a ship, unnoticed or underestimated balance transfer fees can jeopardize the financial benefits of consolidating your debts. Typically, these fees range from 3% to 5% of the transferred amount, a cost that demands careful consideration.

Navigating with Awareness: Before embarking on a balance transfer, arm yourself with knowledge. Calculate the total cost of transfer fees and weigh this against the potential interest savings. This exercise is not just about numbers; it's a practice in mindful decision-making, encouraging you to scrutinize the fine print and make choices that align with your financial well-being.

Embracing a Mindset of Strategic Foresight

Beyond Immediate Horizons: The challenges posed by the introductory period's end and balance transfer fees underscore the importance of looking beyond the immediate to the ultimate goal of financial stability. Each decision made in the present moment lays the foundation for your future financial landscape.

The Power of Informed Choices: Empower yourself with the knowledge that every challenge presents an opportunity for growth. By approaching these challenges with a strategy informed by careful analysis and a commitment to your long-term financial health, you turn potential pitfalls into stepping stones towards your goals.

Transforming Challenges into Triumphs: Cultivate a mindset that views these financial challenges not as deterrents but as catalysts for developing greater financial discipline, wisdom, and resilience. Let the journey through these challenges reprogram your approach to debt management, instilling habits of mindful spending, strategic planning, and unwavering focus on your path to financial freedom.

In navigating the temptations and challenges of balance transfer credit cards, you are doing more than managing debt; you are charting a course towards a future defined by financial empowerment and abundance. This journey, marked by discipline and strategic foresight, transforms potential obstacles into opportunities for growth, guiding you steadily towards the realization of your financial aspirations.

Home Equity Loans or Lines of Credit: Anchoring Debt with Assets

Advantages:

Embarking on the journey of debt consolidation through home equity loans or lines of credit (HELOCs) unveils unique advantages that can significantly influence your financial voyage. These methods, anchored by the value of your home, offer a beacon of hope through lower interest rates and potential tax advantages. Understanding and leveraging these benefits is akin to harnessing favorable winds and discovering hidden treasures that accelerate your journey toward financial stability and prosperity.

Lower Interest Rates: Sailing with Favorable Winds

Harnessing the Wind: The lower interest rates afforded by home equity loans and HELOCs compared to unsecured debts can be likened to a strong, favorable wind filling your sails, propelling you forward more swiftly and smoothly on your financial journey. This reduction in interest rates is made possible by the security you offer—your home's equity—which presents a lower risk to lenders.

Empowerment Through Savings: Imagine each reduction in interest not just as a saving but as a powerful gust of wind accelerating your progress towards debt freedom. These savings can significantly decrease the amount of money paid over the life of the loan, allowing you to allocate resources more effectively—be it towards further debt reduction, investment, or savings for future aspirations.

Tax Advantages: Discovering Hidden Treasures

Unearthing Financial Gems: The potential tax advantages associated with home equity loans and HELOCs are akin to discovering hidden treasures along your voyage. For many, the interest paid on these loans may be tax-deductible if used for buying, building, or substantially improving the taxpayer's home that secures the loan. This tax benefit effectively reduces the net cost of borrowing, making these options even more attractive.

Navigating Tax Seas: To maximize these benefits, it's crucial to navigate the complex seas of tax regulations with precision. Consulting with a tax professional can ensure you're not only claiming all eligible deductions but also structuring your loan in a way that aligns with tax efficiency. This careful planning and consultation are like charting a course with an expert navigator, ensuring you take full advantage of every favorable current and avoid potential pitfalls.

Cultivating a Wealth Mindset

Strategic Financial Navigation: Leveraging the lower interest rates and tax advantages of home equity loans and HELOCs requires more than just understanding these benefits; it demands a strategic approach to debt consolidation. This strategy should be part of a larger financial plan that considers your long-term goals, current financial situation, and the potential risks associated with leveraging home equity.

Reprogramming for Abundance: Embracing these financial tools and the advantages they offer invites a reprogramming of your mindset towards one of abundance and strategic wealth accumulation. It encourages the cultivation of a perspective that views debt not as a burden but as a strategic element within a broader financial portfolio, one that can be optimized to serve your journey towards financial freedom.

Celebrating Each Milestone: As you navigate through your debt consolidation journey, leveraging the favorable winds of lower interest rates and the treasures of tax advantages, celebrate each milestone. Recognize these achievements as tangible manifestations of your commitment to a financially empowered life, a life where debt is managed wisely, and each decision brings you closer to your aspirations of wealth, stability, and abundance.

In harnessing these advantages, you're not merely consolidating debt; you're charting a course towards a brighter financial future. This journey, enriched by the strategic use of home equity, lower interest rates, and tax benefits, is a testament to the power of informed, intentional financial decision-making. It's a voyage that transforms challenges into opportunities, steering you towards the ultimate destination of financial serenity and empowerment.

Disadvantages:

Navigating the waters of debt consolidation using home equity as your vessel comes with inherent risks that require careful consideration and strategic planning. The potential for foreclosure and the uncertainty of variable interest rates stand as formidable challenges on this journey. Understanding and preparing for these risks is not just a matter of financial prudence; it's a crucial step in fortifying your mindset towards resilience, adaptability, and long-term security.

Risk of Foreclosure: Navigating the Storm

The Ultimate Caution: Leveraging your home's equity for debt consolidation places your most valuable asset on the line. Failure to meet loan obligations can lead to foreclosure, a scenario akin to losing your ship in stormy seas. This risk underscores the importance of not just navigating but respecting the financial currents you choose to sail.

Empowering Preparedness: To mitigate the risk of foreclosure, it's essential to embark on this journey with a clear map and a sturdy vessel. This means having a detailed understanding of your financial capacity, ensuring that the loan payments are well within your means, even if financial waters become choppy. Equally, it involves having a contingency plan, like an emergency fund, to cover payments during unforeseen financial downturns.

Mindset Shift: Viewing the risk of foreclosure through the lens of empowerment rather than fear encourages a proactive approach to debt management. It's a reminder of the significance of making informed, careful decisions, reinforcing the principle that true financial freedom is built on a foundation of responsibility and strategic foresight.

Variable Interest Rates: Sailing in Shifting Winds

The Unpredictable Nature: Just as a seasoned sailor understands that the winds can shift without warning, so too must you recognize that variable interest rates can fluctuate, affecting your repayment plans. These rates, while potentially lower initially, can increase over time, impacting the total cost of the loan and monthly payment amounts.

Strategic Navigation: To weather the unpredictability of variable rates, it's crucial to stay vigilant and informed. This means regularly reviewing your loan terms, staying abreast of market trends, and being prepared to refinance if fixed-rate options become more advantageous.

Cultivating Flexibility: Embracing variable interest rates as part of your debt consolidation strategy requires a mindset of flexibility and adaptability. It's about being prepared to adjust your sails as the financial winds change, ensuring that your journey towards debt freedom remains on course, even in the face of uncertainty.

Building a Mindset of Strategic Resilience

Facing Risks with Wisdom: The journey of using home equity for debt consolidation, fraught with the risks of foreclosure and variable interest rates, is not for every navigator. It demands a level of financial acumen, discipline, and resilience that is honed through experience and education.

Cultivating a Resilient Financial Identity: By carefully considering these risks and preparing to navigate them, you're not just managing debt; you're cultivating a resilient financial identity. This identity is characterized by an abundance mindset that recognizes challenges as opportunities for growth and learning.

Embracing the Voyage: The path to financial stability and prosperity is often a complex voyage, marked by both opportunities and challenges. By understanding and preparing for the risks inherent in using home equity for debt consolidation, you equip yourself with the knowledge and skills to navigate these waters successfully. This preparation is a testament to your commitment to not just survive but thrive in your financial journey, building a legacy of resilience, wisdom, and abundance.

In navigating these risks with strategic resilience, you transform potential perils into opportunities for empowerment, charting a course toward not only financial stability but a profound and enduring sense of financial sovereignty.

The Voyage of Debt Consolidation

Embarking on the voyage of debt consolidation requires not just financial strategy but a deep, personal journey into the realms of mindset and habit reformation. It demands that we see beyond the immediate horizon to the vast potential of a life unburdened by debt, guided by the principles of abundance and the law of attraction.

Reprogramming Our Financial Mindset:

In the journey of financial transformation, the tools and strategies we choose are more than mere mechanisms of debt management; they are the very stones upon which the path to abundance is built. Each step taken, every method applied, is an act of moving closer to a future where financial prosperity is not just a dream but a lived reality. This journey, while rooted in the practical, is also deeply intertwined with the cultivation of a mindset that embraces abundance, discipline, and gratitude.

Embracing Abundance: A Vision Beyond Debt

Imagine standing at the edge of a vast landscape, the horizon stretching infinitely before you. This is the landscape of your financial potential, unbounded and rich with possibility. Each debt management tool in your arsenal, from consolidation loans to balance transfer cards, is a powerful step forward on this terrain. These are not mere transactions or financial maneuvers; they are affirmations of your commitment to a life of abundance.

Visualization for Empowerment: See yourself utilizing these tools not out of necessity but from a place of strategic choice, each decision a declaration of your worthiness for wealth and prosperity. With every debt consolidated, envision not just the simplification of your finances, but the expansion of your capacity to generate and enjoy wealth. This visualization plants the seeds of abundance in your subconscious, guiding your actions and decisions towards their fruition.

Cultivating Discipline and Gratitude: The Twin Pillars of Wealth Creation

The journey to abundance is paved with the twin pillars of discipline and gratitude. Discipline represents the steady, unwavering commitment to your financial strategies, ensuring that each step is taken with precision and purpose. It's the force that propels you forward, even when the path becomes challenging.

Discipline in Action: Imagine setting a course for debt consolidation, navigating through the options with a clear, focused mind. Each payment made, and every debt cleared under this strategy, is a testament to your discipline. Feel the strength in this commitment, the power in taking control of your financial destiny.

Gratitude, on the other hand, is the light that illuminates your journey, revealing the beauty and abundance that lie in each moment. It's the acknowledgment of progress, no matter how small, and the recognition of the opportunity in every challenge.

Cultivating a Heart of Gratitude: As you witness the transformation of your debts, take a moment to feel genuine gratitude for each step forward. Celebrate the victories, acknowledge the learning in the setbacks, and maintain a heartfelt appreciation for the journey itself. This gratitude enriches your journey, creating a positive feedback loop that attracts more abundance and joy into your life.

Integrating Abundance into Your Financial Identity

By embracing these principles—seeing debt management tools as steps towards abundance and cultivating discipline and gratitude—you do more than manage your finances. You weave a rich tapestry of abundance into the very fabric of your being. This integration transforms your financial identity, aligning it with the frequencies of prosperity and wealth.

Affirmation for Daily Practice: "With every step I take on my financial journey, I move closer to abundance. I am disciplined in my approach and grateful for my progress. Wealth and prosperity are my natural state."

Incorporating these practices and mindsets into your daily life not only changes the way you interact with your finances but also how you perceive the world around you. The journey of debt management becomes a powerful conduit for personal growth, leading you to a life characterized by financial freedom, abundance, and joy.

Incorporating into Daily Life:

In the tapestry of your financial journey, the art of visualization and the power of affirmation serve as transformative tools, weaving patterns of freedom, wisdom, and abundance into the fabric of your daily existence. Through subtle yet profound messages embedded in the rhythm of your life, these practices gently reprogram your subconscious, aligning your inner world with the outer reality of financial independence and prosperity.

Visualization: Painting the Canvas of Your Future

Imagine each day begins with a moment of serene contemplation, where you close your eyes and paint the canvas of your future with the vibrant colors of freedom and abundance. See yourself moving through a world unburdened by debt, each step lighter, each breath deeper. The chains that once bound you dissolve, leaving in their place a radiant aura of financial independence.

In Your Mind's Eye: Picture the joys that financial freedom brings into your life—joyful gatherings with loved ones, the thrill of new experiences, and the peace of a secure future. Feel the emotions as if they were real now, the warmth of gratitude, the exhilaration of achievement, and the profound sense of peace. This visualization is a beacon, guiding your subconscious towards making this imagined world a tangible reality.

Affirmation: Speaking the Language of Prosperity

As the sun rises, so too does the power of your voice, affirming your sovereignty over your financial destiny. "I am the architect of my abundance. With wisdom, I manage my debts. With clarity, I make decisions that nurture my financial freedom. Each day, I attract prosperity and abundance into my life."

Whisper of the Wind: Let these words be the gentle whisper of the wind that accompanies you throughout your day, a subliminal message that seeps into the fabric of your being. Repeat them silently as you navigate the complexities of life, with each repetition embedding the truth of your power and potential deeper into your subconscious.

The Subliminal Symphony of Change

As the days flow into weeks, and weeks into months, the practices of visualization and affirmation harmonize, creating a symphony of subliminal messaging that resonates with the frequency of abundance. Unseen, yet profoundly felt, this symphony orchestrates a shift within your subconscious, a gentle reprogramming that aligns your deepest beliefs with the reality of financial independence and abundance.

The Echoes of Transformation: This transformation is not marked by fanfare or tumult but by a quiet, steady shift in the currents of your life. Decisions become more intuitive, aligned with your vision of freedom. Opportunities for growth and prosperity present themselves with synchronicity, attracted by the clarity and intention of your thoughts and actions.

Embracing the Journey

This journey of subliminal reprogramming is a testament to the power within you, a power that transcends the material and taps into the vast reservoir of potential that resides in your subconscious. By regularly engaging in visualization and affirmation, you not only envision a life free from the constraints of debt but actively draw this life towards you, step by step, thought by thought.

In this gentle, yet profound manner, the practices of visualization and affirmation hardwire a new reality into your subconscious, one where debt is but a shadow of the past, and the future is bright with the promise of abundance and financial freedom. This is your journey, a journey of transformation, empowerment, and limitless possibility.

In conclusion, the journey through the methods of debt consolidation is both a practical exploration and a profound exercise in reprogramming the mind towards a future of financial freedom and abundance. By weighing the pros and cons of each method with a mindset anchored in positivity and strategic foresight, you empower yourself to make decisions that align with your deepest aspirations for a life rich in prosperity and devoid of financial burden.

Section 4: Implementing a Debt Management Plan

- **Creating a Budget:** Step-by-step guide on incorporating debt repayment into a personal budget.

Embarking on the journey of creating a personal budget, especially one that seamlessly integrates debt repayment, is akin to charting a course through previously unexplored territories. This process, while practical on the surface, serves a deeper purpose: it subtly reprograms your subconscious to embrace financial discipline and prioritization as natural, effortless parts of your daily life. Without overtly being told, you begin to adopt a mindset that sees budgeting and debt repayment not as burdens, but as empowering tools towards achieving financial freedom.

Step 1: Recognize Your Financial Landscape

Begin by quietly acknowledging every aspect of your income and expenses, as if you were acknowledging the different terrains and climates of a vast continent. This recognition is the first step in your subconscious understanding that to navigate successfully, you must be aware of and respect the entirety of your financial situation.

Step 2: Categorize with Intention

As you categorize your expenses, imagine you're planting seeds in a garden. Each category—needs, wants, savings, debt repayment—is a different type of seed that will grow into the garden of your financial future. This visualization subtly encourages your mind to organize finances with care and intention, recognizing the vital role of nurturing each category to achieve a balanced, flourishing life.

Step 3: Allocate Resources with Precision

Allocating your resources is like distributing water to those seeds. Imagine directing water to the most essential plants first—your needs and debt repayment—ensuring they receive the nourishment needed to grow strong and healthy. This process becomes a natural rhythm, as instinctive as the cycle of the seasons, guiding you to prioritize spending and savings effortlessly.

Step 4: Adjust and Adapt

As any gardener knows, conditions change, and plants grow. Periodically adjusting your budget is akin to tending to your garden, trimming here, adding soil there, ensuring each plant thrives. This step reprograms your subconscious to view financial adjustments not as failures, but as necessary, natural parts of a healthy financial ecosystem.

Step 5: Celebrate Growth

Finally, take time to appreciate the growth in your garden, recognizing the progress made towards your financial goals. This practice of gratitude and celebration becomes a subliminal message of positive reinforcement, deeply entrenching the joy of financial management and progress into your subconscious.

The Subliminal Shift

Through these steps, the act of creating and adhering to a budget, particularly one that prioritizes debt repayment, is seamlessly woven into the fabric of your daily life. The process becomes less about conscious effort and more about following a natural, internal compass towards financial well-being.

Your subconscious begins to receive these practices as inherent parts of your identity, not external chores to be managed. You find yourself making financial decisions with ease, guided by a deeply ingrained understanding of your priorities and goals. Budgeting and debt repayment transform from tasks into expressions of your commitment to your financial freedom and security.

In this gentle yet profound manner, the creation of a budget that includes debt repayment becomes not just a habit but a reflection of your deepest values and aspirations. It's a path you walk with little resistance, guided by the wisdom and intention that have been subtly hardwired into your subconscious mind.

- **Setting Realistic Goals:** How to set achievable debt repayment goals within a specified timeframe.

Setting realistic debt repayment goals is akin to plotting a course through uncharted waters with the intent of reaching a distant, promising shore. This journey, while filled with potential challenges, is also ripe with opportunity for growth and achievement. By embedding the practice of setting achievable goals into your subconscious, you navigate this path with confidence, guided by an inner compass calibrated towards success and financial liberation.

Envision the Destination

Start by vividly imagining your life free from the burden of debt. This vision is not a mere daydream but a powerful beacon, illuminating your path forward. Envisioning your debt-free life with clarity and emotion embeds a deep-seated motivation within your subconscious, compelling you towards your goal with a sense of purpose and inevitability.

Chart the Course

With your destination clear in your mind's eye, begin charting your course. Break down your overarching goal of debt freedom into smaller, manageable milestones. Just as a navigator uses stars to guide their journey, use these milestones to steer your progress. Setting these smaller goals helps to reprogram your subconscious to celebrate each achievement along the way, reinforcing your commitment and building momentum.

Assess the Currents

Understanding your current financial situation is akin to assessing the sea currents and weather conditions before setting sail. Take a comprehensive inventory of your debts, income, and expenses. This honest assessment forms the basis of your goal-setting process, ensuring that your objectives are grounded in reality. Subliminally, this practice cultivates a mindset of transparency and self-awareness, crucial for navigating the complexities of personal finance.

Allocate Your Resources

Determine how much of your resources you can realistically dedicate to debt repayment each month. This allocation should balance ambition with sustainability, pushing you towards your goals without risking financial shipwreck. Embedding this balanced approach into your subconscious guides you to make decisions that support both your immediate needs and your long-term aspirations.

Adjust the Sails

Be prepared to adjust your goals as circumstances change. Flexibility is key to navigating the unpredictable waters of personal finance. Instilling a mindset that embraces adaptability ensures that you remain resilient in the face of financial headwinds, always able to recalibrate and continue your journey towards your debt-free destination.

Celebrate Each Landmark

Recognize and celebrate each milestone reached. These celebrations reinforce the positive feedback loop in your subconscious, making the journey towards debt freedom not just a duty but a series of rewarding achievements. This practice of acknowledgment and celebration is crucial for maintaining motivation and fostering a sense of progress.

The Subconscious Journey to Freedom

By setting realistic debt repayment goals and embedding these strategies into your subconscious, the path to financial freedom becomes a part of who you are. This journey is no longer marked by resistance or reluctance but is embraced as a fundamental aspect of your identity. Your subconscious, aligned with your conscious efforts, propels you forward, turning the act of goal-setting and achievement into natural extensions of your financial self.

In this way, the art of setting achievable debt repayment goals within a specified timeframe transcends mere financial planning. It becomes a transformative process, hardwiring a mindset of success, resilience, and abundance into your very being, guiding you to navigate the seas of personal finance with grace and arrive at the shores of financial freedom with certainty.

- **Monitoring Progress:** Techniques for tracking debt repayment progress and staying motivated.

Monitoring the progress of debt repayment is akin to a navigator charting their course across the vast ocean, marking each nautical mile that brings them closer to their destination. This process is integral not just for ensuring you remain on track, but for fostering a sense of accomplishment and maintaining motivation throughout your financial journey. By internalizing techniques for tracking progress and staying motivated, you seamlessly integrate these practices into your subconscious, transforming them into instinctive parts of your financial behavior.

Setting Sail with a Clear Map

Visualize Your Progress: Begin with a visual representation of your debt repayment journey. Whether it's a spreadsheet, a chart on your wall, or a digital app, choose a method that resonates with you. This visual becomes a map of your journey, with each payment marked as a milestone along the path. The act of visualizing your progress embeds the reality of your achievements into your subconscious, reinforcing the notion that every effort brings you closer to your goal.

Navigating with Milestones

Celebrate Milestones: Just as sailors of old would celebrate crossing the equator or rounding a cape, so too should you celebrate the milestones on your debt repayment journey. These could be paying off a certain percentage of your total debt, clearing a specific loan, or simply sticking to your repayment plan for a consecutive number of months. Embedding celebration into your routine acts as a subliminal reward mechanism, enhancing your motivation and commitment to the journey.

Keeping the Crew Inspired

Motivational Anchors: Surround yourself with motivational anchors—quotes, images, or mementos that remind you of why you're on this journey. These anchors serve as a constant subliminal reminder of your goals and aspirations, subtly reinforcing your determination and focus.

The Compass of Reflection

Regular Reviews: Schedule regular intervals to review your progress. This act of reflection is like checking your compass and adjusting your course as needed. It's an opportunity to recalibrate your strategy, ensuring you're still headed in the right direction. Incorporating reflection into your routine teaches your subconscious to value adaptability and resilience, key traits for navigating the unpredictable seas of personal finance.

Charting the Stars of Gratitude

Journaling Gratitude: Keep a journal where you note not just financial milestones, but moments of gratitude related to your journey. Perhaps you're thankful for the discipline you've developed, the support of a loved one, or even a small financial windfall. This practice of noting gratitude shifts your focus from what you're sacrificing to what you're gaining, reprogramming your subconscious to associate debt repayment with positive emotions and rewards.

Sailing with a Convoy

Community Support: Engage with a community of individuals on similar journeys. Sharing experiences, challenges, and victories with others provides a sense of camaraderie and mutual support. This engagement acts as a subliminal reinforcement of your commitment, embedding the collective energy and encouragement of the group into your motivation.

The Voyage Home

By integrating these techniques for monitoring progress and maintaining motivation into your subconscious, the act of navigating your debt repayment journey transforms. What may have once felt like a solitary, daunting voyage becomes a purposeful expedition marked by personal growth, communal support, and a deep-seated sense of progress and achievement. Your financial goals are no longer distant shores to be reached but inevitable destinations, drawing closer with each disciplined step and celebrated milestone. Through this journey, you not only move towards financial freedom but also cultivate a mindset attuned to perseverance, positivity, and abundance.

Section 5: Avoiding Future Debt

- **Building an Emergency Fund:** Strategies for saving an emergency fund to avoid new debt.

In the journey toward financial resilience, the creation of an emergency fund stands as a beacon of security and preparedness. This fund, designed to shield you from the unforeseen storms of life, is not merely a financial strategy but a profound exercise in reprogramming your subconscious towards a mindset of abundance, foresight, and peace. By embedding the principles of building an emergency fund into your daily consciousness, you naturally cultivate habits that prioritize saving, ensuring that you navigate future challenges with grace and stability.

The Foundation of Security

Visualize Your Safety Net: Begin by visualizing your emergency fund as a tangible safety net, cradling you above life's uncertainties. This mental image serves as a constant reminder of the fund's purpose and importance, subtly reinforcing your commitment to build and maintain it. Each contribution to this fund is a stitch in the net, strengthening your financial security and peace of mind.

The Art of Consistent Saving

Automate Your Contributions: Set up automatic transfers to your emergency fund with each paycheck. This automation makes saving effortless, a natural part of your financial routine that requires no conscious decision-making. Over time, this practice embeds the habit of saving into your subconscious, ensuring that building your emergency fund becomes an instinctive part of your financial behavior.

Cultivating a Mindset of Preparedness

Embrace Incremental Growth: Recognize and celebrate each deposit into your emergency fund, no matter how small. This acknowledgment acts as a positive reinforcement, encouraging your subconscious to value steady progress over immediate results. It teaches you to find satisfaction in the act of saving itself, fostering a mindset that equates incremental growth with success.

The Power of Adaptability

Flexible Goals: As your financial situation evolves, so too should your emergency fund goals. Adjusting your savings target in response to changes in income, expenses, or personal circumstances keeps your strategy aligned with your current reality. This flexibility trains your subconscious to remain adaptable, ensuring that your approach to saving remains relevant and effective.

Reinforcing Abundance and Security

Affirmations for Abundance: Incorporate affirmations into your daily routine, such as "I am building a foundation of financial security" or "Each step I take brings me closer to peace of mind." These affirmations act as subliminal messages, reinforcing the belief that you are capable of creating and sustaining an abundance that protects you and your loved ones.

The Ripple Effect of Financial Stability

Witness the Impact: Observe how the presence of an emergency fund begins to influence other areas of your financial life. The security it provides can reduce the need to incur new debt in response to unexpected expenses, creating a virtuous cycle of financial stability. This observation reinforces the value of your efforts, embedding a deep understanding of the emergency fund's role in your overall financial health.

Embedding the Practice into Your Being

Through these strategies, the act of building an emergency fund transcends mere financial planning, becoming a fundamental component of your identity. This transformation is subtle yet profound, as the principles of saving, security, and preparedness become ingrained in your subconscious. You find yourself navigating life's uncertainties with confidence, supported by a foundation of financial resilience that was built one intentional step at a time. This journey, marked by the cultivation of an emergency fund, not only prepares you for the unforeseen but also reprograms your mindset towards one of abundance, security, and unwavering peace.

- **Mindful Spending:** Tips on adopting mindful spending habits to prevent accruing unnecessary debt.

Adopting mindful spending habits is akin to navigating through a dense forest with a clear sense of direction and purpose. It involves more than merely avoiding unnecessary expenses; it's about deeply ingraining a conscious approach to financial decisions into your very being. This transformation in spending behavior not only prevents the accrual of unnecessary debt but also aligns your financial actions with your true values and goals, creating a harmonious relationship with money.

Cultivate Awareness in Every Transaction

Pause Before Purchasing: Introduce a simple pause before any purchase, a moment of reflection to consider the necessity and value of the item. This pause is not a hesitation but a powerful act of mindfulness, allowing you to differentiate between impulse and intention. Over time, this practice becomes an automatic response, subtly reprogramming your subconscious to naturally gravitate towards decisions that reflect your financial goals and personal values.

Align Spending with Values

Value-Based Spending: Regularly assess your spending in light of your core values. Whether it's investing in experiences over material goods, supporting businesses that align with your ethical beliefs, or saving for future aspirations, ensure your spending is a reflection of what truly matters to you. Embedding this alignment into your subconscious guides you towards making purchases that enrich your life, rather than detracting from your financial well-being.

Embrace Gratitude for What You Have

Practice Gratitude: Cultivate a daily habit of gratitude for what you already possess. Acknowledging and appreciating what you have diminishes the constant pursuit of more, a pursuit often fueled by external pressures rather than internal desires. This sense of gratitude strengthens your resolve against unnecessary spending, embedding a contentment that acts as a natural barrier against accruing debt.

Visualize Your Financial Ecosystem

Financial Ecosystem Visualization: Regularly visualize your finances as a vibrant ecosystem, where every spending decision impacts the health of the whole. This visualization fosters an understanding of the interconnectedness of your financial choices, encouraging a holistic approach to spending. As this image takes root in your subconscious, you'll find your spending habits naturally evolving to support the well-being of your financial ecosystem.

Set Intentions for Financial Harmony

Intentional Spending Declarations: Begin each month with a declaration of your spending intentions. Articulate the areas where you choose to focus your financial resources, and affirm your commitment to mindful spending. These declarations serve as guideposts, steering your spending behaviors in alignment with your intentions and further embedding the practice of mindful spending into your subconscious.

The Subliminal Shift to Mindfulness

Through these strategies, the shift towards mindful spending transcends conscious effort, becoming a deeply rooted aspect of your financial identity. This shift is gradual but profound, as the principles of awareness, value alignment, gratitude, and intentionality become embedded in your subconscious. You navigate your financial journey with a newfound clarity and purpose, effortlessly aligning your spending with your deepest aspirations for a life of abundance, fulfillment, and freedom from unnecessary debt.

In embracing mindful spending, you not only fortify your financial foundations against the accumulation of unnecessary debt but also cultivate a relationship with money that is intentional, satisfying, and aligned with your true self. This journey, marked by conscious choice and deep awareness, leads to a state of financial harmony where every expenditure enriches your life and supports your journey towards lasting prosperity.

- **Using Credit Wisely:** Best practices for using credit cards and loans responsibly to maintain financial health.

The judicious use of credit cards and loans is akin to mastering the art of sailing in open waters. It requires a blend of skill, discipline, and foresight, ensuring that these financial tools enhance your journey rather than steer you into stormy seas. Embedding best practices for using credit wisely into your subconscious acts as an internal compass, guiding you to navigate credit with intention and wisdom, thereby maintaining and enhancing your financial health.

Understand the True Cost of Credit

Informed Decisions: Before utilizing credit, educate yourself on the terms, interest rates, and potential fees involved. This knowledge empowers you to make informed decisions, choosing credit options that align with your financial goals and capabilities. Envision each decision to use credit as a calculated step in your financial strategy, reinforcing a mindset that values long-term well-being over immediate gratification.

Use Credit for Planned Purchases

Strategic Spending: Reserve the use of credit cards for planned purchases rather than impulsive buys. This approach ensures that credit becomes a tool for achieving your goals, rather than a trap that leads to unnecessary debt. Regularly visualize your financial goals and how credit can serve as a bridge to these aspirations, embedding a sense of purpose and strategy in your use of credit.

Pay Balances in Full and On Time

Discipline and Timeliness: Cultivate the habit of paying your credit card balances in full and on time each month. This practice not only avoids interest charges and late fees but also strengthens your credit score. Imagine each on-time payment as a building block in the foundation of your financial stability, reinforcing the importance of discipline in maintaining your financial health.

Leverage Credit to Build Your Credit Score

Credit as an Asset: Use credit cards and loans strategically to build a positive credit history. Consider how responsible credit use can open doors to future financial opportunities, from favorable mortgage rates to beneficial loan terms. Visualize your growing credit score as a testament to your financial savvy and responsibility, a reflection of your commitment to financial health.

Set Limits to Prevent Overextension

Know Your Boundaries: Set personal spending limits on your credit cards, even if they are lower than your maximum credit line. This self-imposed boundary prevents overextension and keeps your credit utilization ratio low, which positively impacts your credit score. Envision these limits as protective barriers, safeguarding your financial well-being against the risks of debt accumulation.

Embrace the Mindset of Credit Wisdom

Subconscious Integration: By internalizing these best practices, the wise use of credit becomes more than just a set of behaviors; it transforms into an integral part of your financial identity. This transformation is gradual, as principles of informed decision-making, strategic spending, disciplined repayment, and mindful credit utilization become deeply rooted in your subconscious.

The Journey of Responsible Credit Use

As these best practices for using credit wisely become embedded in your daily life, you navigate the realm of credit with confidence and control. This journey is not without its challenges, but equipped with a deep-seated understanding and a strategic approach, you are well-prepared to use credit as a powerful ally in building and maintaining your financial health.

In embracing these principles, you not only safeguard your financial well-being but also chart a course toward a future rich with possibilities. The wise use of credit becomes a testament to your financial acumen, a reflection of your commitment to a prosperous, balanced financial life.

Conclusion

- Recap of the key concepts discussed in the chapter and the transformative potential of effective debt management and consolidation.

As we draw the curtains on this enlightening journey through the realm of debt management and consolidation, it's imperative to reflect on the key concepts that have illuminated our path. This chapter has not merely been about navigating the intricacies of financial obligations but about undergoing a transformative process that reshapes our relationship with debt, steering us towards a future brimming with financial stability and freedom.

The Art of Debt Management

We embarked on this voyage with the understanding that managing debt is an art form, requiring precision, strategy, and foresight. The principles of **mindful spending**, **using credit wisely**, and the discipline of **creating a budget** were our guiding stars, ensuring that each financial decision was made not out of necessity but from a place of informed choice.

The Strategy of Debt Consolidation

Debt consolidation emerged as a strategic tool, a means to streamline our financial obligations into a single, manageable entity. Through the lenses of **personal consolidation loans**, **balance transfer credit cards**, and **home equity loans**, we explored how consolidating debt could potentially lower interest rates, simplify payments, and ultimately, accelerate our journey towards debt freedom.

Navigating Challenges with Wisdom

Yet, this journey was not without its perils. The risks of **foreclosure** and the unpredictability of **variable interest rates** reminded us that the sea of debt management is fraught with challenges that demand respect and careful navigation. These obstacles, however, also presented opportunities for growth, teaching us the importance of resilience, adaptability, and the relentless pursuit of our financial goals.

The Transformative Potential of Mindful Debt Management

Beyond the practical strategies and potential pitfalls, the core of our exploration was the transformative potential of mindful debt management and consolidation. This process is more than just a financial exercise; it's a profound journey of self-discovery and empowerment. By internalizing the practices of **setting realistic goals**, **monitoring progress**, and **building an emergency fund**, we not only pave the way for a debt-free future but also reprogram our subconscious to embrace a mindset of abundance, discipline, and gratitude.

Cultivating a Legacy of Financial Empowerment

The journey through debt management and consolidation is an invitation to cultivate a legacy of financial empowerment. It challenges us to transcend our perceived limitations, to reimagine our financial identities, and to embrace a future where we are not just survivors of our financial circumstances but architects of our financial destiny.

The Horizon Beyond Debt

As we conclude this chapter, let us carry forward the wisdom, strategies, and insights that have been shared. Let these principles be the compass that guides our financial decisions, the light that illuminates our path towards financial stability, and the foundation upon which we build a life of abundance and freedom.

In embracing the transformative potential of effective debt management and consolidation, we step into a realm of possibilities, where our financial goals are not just dreams but destinations within reach. With each step taken on this journey, we move closer to realizing our vision of financial health, security, and prosperity.

- Encouragement to take proactive steps towards debt consolidation and management as a means to achieve financial freedom and peace of mind.

As we stand at the threshold of a new chapter in our financial journey, it's crucial to recognize that the path to financial freedom and peace of mind is both illuminated by knowledge and paved with proactive steps. The journey through debt consolidation and management, as explored, is not merely a collection of financial strategies but a transformative process that beckons us toward a future of abundance, stability, and serenity.

Embrace the Call to Action

Let this exploration serve as a clarion call to action, encouraging you to embrace the principles of debt management and consolidation with both hands. Recognize that each strategy discussed, from mindful spending to strategic consolidation, is a tool at your disposal, ready to be wielded in your quest for financial liberation.

The Power of Proactive Engagement

The decision to proactively manage and consolidate your debt is a declaration of your agency over your financial destiny. It's an affirmation that you are not destined to remain tethered to the cycle of debt but are fully capable of navigating toward the shores of financial independence.

Visualize Your Debt-Free Future

Allow yourself to regularly visualize the life that awaits beyond the burden of debt—a life where your financial decisions are driven not by obligation but by aspiration, where each day is not overshadowed by financial stress but illuminated by the peace of mind that comes with financial stability.

Cultivate a Mindset of Empowerment

Embrace a mindset that views challenges not as insurmountable obstacles but as opportunities for growth and empowerment. Remember, the journey to debt freedom is as much about transforming your financial habits as it is about reshaping your beliefs and attitudes towards money.

Take the First Step

The journey of a thousand miles begins with a single step. Let that step be your commitment to take proactive action towards managing and consolidating your debt. Whether it's creating a detailed budget, seeking advice on consolidation options, or simply deciding to pay a little extra on your highest interest debt this month, each action you take is a step closer to your goal.

Seek Support and Celebrate Progress

Remember, you don't have to navigate this journey alone. Seek support from financial advisors, join communities of like-minded individuals, and share your journey with supportive friends or family. Celebrate each milestone, no matter how small, recognizing that every victory brings you closer to your ultimate goal of financial freedom.

The Horizon Awaits

As you embark on this proactive journey toward debt consolidation and management, know that the horizon of financial freedom is not just a distant dream but a tangible reality that awaits your arrival. With each disciplined step, informed decision, and moment of perseverance, you are not only moving closer to your financial goals but also to a life marked by peace, abundance, and empowerment.

Let this encouragement be the wind in your sails as you navigate the seas of personal finance. The path to financial freedom and peace of mind is within your reach, beckoning you forward with the promise of a brighter, more secure future.

Exercises and Reflection

- Practical exercises designed to apply the principles of debt consolidation and management in real-life scenarios, reinforcing the chapter's concepts through active learning.

Embedding the principles of debt consolidation and management into your financial practice requires more than understanding; it demands action. Through practical exercises, you can transform these concepts from theoretical knowledge into lived experience, reinforcing your learning and advancing your journey toward financial freedom. Here are several exercises designed to apply the principles discussed in real-life scenarios, offering you hands-on opportunities to engage with and internalize these critical financial strategies.

Exercise 1: Create Your Debt Inventory

Objective: Gain a clear overview of your current debts.

List All Debts: Create a comprehensive list of your debts, including credit cards, loans, and any other obligations. For each debt, note the balance, interest rate, minimum monthly payment, and due date.

Assess the Total: Calculate the total amount owed across all debts. This figure represents your starting point on the journey to debt freedom.

Reflection: Reflect on how creating this inventory makes you feel about your financial situation and what insights it offers into your debt management strategy.

Exercise 2: Design a Personalized Debt Repayment Plan

Objective: Develop a strategy that prioritizes debts for repayment.

Choose Your Method: Decide between the debt snowball or avalanche method based on what motivates you more: paying off smaller debts first for psychological wins or tackling high-interest debts to save money over time.

Create a Payment Schedule: Using your debt inventory, organize your debts according to your chosen method and plan your payments accordingly, determining how much extra you can allocate toward debt repayment each month.

Reflection: Journal about the process of creating this plan. How does it feel to have a clear strategy in place? What challenges do you anticipate, and how might you address them?

Exercise 3: Simulate a Debt Consolidation Scenario

Objective: Understand the impact of debt consolidation on your financial situation.

Research Consolidation Options: Look into different debt consolidation methods available to you, such as personal loans, balance transfer credit cards, or home equity lines of credit.

Calculate the Benefits: Choose one method and calculate how consolidating your debts could affect your interest rates, monthly payments, and repayment timeline. Use online calculators or financial software to help with this task.

Reflection: Reflect on this simulation. How would consolidating your debts change your monthly budget? How does it align with your financial goals?

Exercise 4: Establish an Emergency Fund Goal

Objective: Start building an emergency fund to prevent future debt.

Set a Target: Determine how much you would like to save in your emergency fund. A common goal is three to six months' worth of living expenses.

Create a Savings Plan: Decide how much you can realistically save each month towards this goal. Consider ways to adjust your budget or increase your income to support this plan.

Reflection: Write about how it feels to prioritize saving for an emergency fund. How does having this fund in place change your perspective on managing debt and financial security?

Exercise 5: Mindful Spending Diary

Objective: Cultivate awareness of your spending habits to prevent unnecessary debt.

Track Your Spending: For one month, keep a detailed record of all your expenditures, no matter how small.

Categorize Expenses: At the end of the month, categorize your spending and identify areas where impulsive or unnecessary purchases may have occurred.

Reflection: Reflect on your spending patterns. How do your spending habits align with your financial goals and values? Identify one area where you could improve and plan a specific action to take.

By engaging with these exercises, you actively apply the principles of debt consolidation and management to your financial life, turning theory into practice. This hands-on approach not only reinforces your learning but also empowers you to take concrete steps toward achieving financial well-being and freedom.

- Reflection questions to facilitate deeper understanding and engagement with the material, encouraging readers to think critically about their own debt management practices.

To enrich your journey through debt management and consolidation, reflection plays a pivotal role. It's through thoughtful questioning and introspection that you can uncover deep insights into your financial habits, attitudes, and strategies. The following reflection questions are designed to encourage a deeper understanding and engagement with the principles discussed, guiding you to critically evaluate your own debt management practices and to foster a proactive, informed approach to achieving financial freedom.

Reflecting on Your Debt Landscape

How do I currently perceive my debt, and how does this perception influence my financial decisions?

- This question encourages you to explore your emotional and psychological relationship with debt, recognizing how it shapes your spending, saving, and debt repayment behaviors.

What are the primary factors that contributed to my current level of debt?

- Identifying the root causes of your debt can offer insights into patterns or behaviors that may need adjustment.

Evaluating Debt Management Strategies

Which debt repayment method (snowball or avalanche) resonates more with my personality and financial situation, and why?

- Reflecting on this question helps you align your debt repayment strategy with your personal motivations and financial goals, enhancing its effectiveness.

How might consolidating my debts change my financial situation, and what concerns do I have about this approach?

- Consider the potential benefits and drawbacks of debt consolidation in your specific context, fostering a balanced view of this strategy.

Mindfulness and Spending Habits

. In what ways do my spending habits contribute to my debt, and how can I adopt more mindful spending practices?
- This question encourages you to critically assess your spending habits and to consider practical steps towards more intentional and purposeful financial decisions.

Future Financial Vision

. What does financial freedom mean to me, and how will managing or consolidating my debt help me achieve it?
- Reflecting on your definition of financial freedom can clarify your long-term goals and motivate your journey towards debt management and consolidation.

Learning from the Journey

. What lessons have I learned from my experiences with debt that I can apply to future financial decisions?
- This question invites you to extract valuable lessons from your experiences, turning challenges into opportunities for growth and improvement.

Commitment to Change

. What specific steps will I commit to taking in the next month to improve my debt situation?
- Setting concrete, actionable goals can help translate reflection into action, marking your commitment to proactive debt management.
-

Engaging with these reflection questions offers a powerful means to deepen your understanding of your financial behaviors and to refine your approach to debt management. By contemplating these aspects of your financial life, you're not just passively absorbing information; you're actively participating in the creation of a healthier, more empowered financial future.

Chapter 4: Wealth Generation and Investment Mastery

Wealth Building Foundations

- **Introduction to Wealth Building:** Exploring the mindset shift from debt management to active wealth creation, emphasizing the importance of financial education in fostering a wealth-building mentality.

In the transformative journey from debt management to the pinnacle of active wealth creation, a profound shift in mindset is not merely beneficial—it is essential. This chapter heralds the beginning of such a transformation, guiding you through the fertile fields of financial education towards cultivating a robust wealth-building mentality. It is here, at this crossroads, where the seeds of abundance are sown, nurtured by the rich soil of knowledge and watered by the steadfast belief in one's capacity to flourish.

The Voyage from Debt to Abundance

Imagine yourself standing at the edge of two vastly different landscapes. Behind you lies the terrain of debt management—a land you've navigated with courage, learning the contours of its valleys, mastering the currents of its rivers. Ahead, a new horizon stretches out: the land of wealth creation, vast and teeming with potential. This is not a journey of mere financial strategy but a profound voyage of the soul, requiring a shift in the very paradigms through which you view the world of finance.

Cultivating the Ground for Growth

The Seed of Financial Education: The first step in this transformative journey is to immerse yourself in the waters of financial education. Knowledge is the seed from which the tree of wealth grows; understanding the basics of investments, the power of compound interest, and the strategies for asset allocation are akin to learning the language of the land you wish to inhabit.

Embracing the Abundance Mindset: The teachings of Stephen Covey and the principles of the Law of Attraction serve as our compass, guiding us to replace scarcity with abundance in our thoughts. Visualize your life enriched by wealth, not just in monetary terms but as a reflection of a life lived with purpose, joy, and generosity. This visualization is a powerful tool, reprogramming your subconscious to open doors to opportunities and possibilities.

Journeying Through Story and Affirmation

The Narrative Path: Through personal anecdotes and parables, we traverse the landscape of wealth building, learning not just from theory but from the lived experiences of those who have walked this path before us. These stories serve as markers, illuminating the journey and embedding the lessons deep within our psyche.

The Power of Affirmation: Daily affirmations—"I am a creator of wealth", "I attract financial abundance effortlessly"—become our mantra, reinforcing our belief in our ability to achieve financial goals. These affirmations are the music to which our subconscious dances, aligning our thoughts and actions with the rhythm of abundance.

Integrating Wealth into the Fabric of Life

Seamless Incorporation: The principles of wealth building are not distant concepts to be visited but are to be woven into the very fabric of our daily lives. Whether it's making informed spending decisions, investing wisely, or simply choosing to see opportunities where others see obstacles, each action is a step towards realizing our wealth-building aspirations.

Engaging with the Future: Interactive elements and practical exercises encourage us not just to read about wealth building but to engage with it actively. Visualization exercises, budgeting games, and investment simulations invite us to apply what we've learned, turning passive knowledge into active wisdom.

The Horizon Awaits

As you embark on this journey of wealth building, let the shift in mindset from debt management to active wealth creation be your guiding star. Armed with knowledge, inspired by stories of transformation, and empowered by affirmations, you stand ready to navigate the landscape of wealth. This journey is yours to undertake, a testament to your resilience, your capacity for growth, and your unwavering commitment to achieving financial freedom and peace of mind.

Embrace this journey with an open heart and a willing spirit, for the land of wealth creation is rich with opportunity, waiting for you to claim your share of its abundance.

- **Creating a Wealth Plan:** Step-by-step guide on developing a personalized wealth generation plan, including setting clear financial goals, assessing risk tolerance, and determining investment timelines.

Creating a personalized wealth generation plan is akin to drafting a masterful blueprint for a grand architectural feat. It requires vision, precision, and a deep understanding of the materials at your disposal. This guide aims to equip you with the tools and insights necessary to construct your financial edifice, ensuring it stands resilient against the tests of time and circumstance. Through a step-by-step approach, you will define your aspirations, align your strategies with your risk tolerance, and set a timeline that propels you toward your wealth goals.

Step 1: Envision Your Financial Future

Begin by allowing yourself to dream big. What does wealth mean to you? Is it the freedom to pursue your passions without monetary constraints, the ability to provide for your family's future, or the security of a comfortable retirement? Articulate your vision in vivid detail, as these dreams will form the foundation of your wealth plan.

Actionable Insight: Create a vision board or write a detailed description of your financial future. This practice not only clarifies your goals but also serves as a constant source of motivation.

Step 2: Set Specific Financial Goals

With your vision as a backdrop, break down your overarching dream into specific, measurable, achievable, relevant, and time-bound (SMART) goals. Whether it's saving for a down payment on a home, building a retirement nest egg, or funding an education, each goal should be a stepping stone that leads you closer to your grand vision.

Actionable Insight: Write down your SMART goals and review them regularly. Adjust as necessary to reflect changes in your financial situation or priorities.

Step 3: Assess Your Risk Tolerance

Understanding your comfort level with risk is crucial in shaping your wealth generation strategy. Are you a cautious investor who prefers a steady, predictable path, or are you willing to embrace market volatility for the potential of higher returns? This self-assessment will guide your investment choices and help you build a portfolio that aligns with your personal risk threshold.

Actionable Insight: Complete a risk tolerance questionnaire or consult with a financial advisor to accurately gauge your risk profile.

Step 4: Determine Your Investment Timeline

Your goals will have different time horizons—short-term (within five years), medium-term (five to ten years), and long-term (more than ten years). Aligning your investments with these timelines is critical to ensuring that your assets are liquid when you need them and positioned for optimal growth.

Actionable Insight: Categorize your financial goals by their time horizon and match them with appropriate investment vehicles (e.g., stocks for long-term growth, bonds for medium-term stability, and high-yield savings accounts for short-term needs).

Step 5: Construct Your Portfolio

With your goals set, risk tolerance assessed, and timelines defined, you're ready to build your investment portfolio. This is where the art of diversification comes into play. A well-diversified portfolio spreads risk across different asset classes, geographic regions, and industries, reducing the impact of market volatility on your overall financial health.

Actionable Insight: Start with a core portfolio of diversified, low-cost index funds or ETFs. Consider adding individual stocks, bonds, or alternative investments as you become more comfortable and your financial situation evolves.

Step 6: Implement, Monitor, and Adjust

With your wealth plan in hand, the final step is to put it into action. Invest according to your plan, monitor your portfolio's performance, and make adjustments as needed based on market conditions, life changes, or shifts in your financial goals.

Actionable Insight: Schedule regular portfolio reviews—at least annually—to assess progress toward your goals and make necessary adjustments.

Reflect and Reaffirm

Remember, the journey to wealth is not a sprint but a marathon. There will be obstacles and setbacks, but with a clear plan in place, you possess the map and compass to navigate through the financial landscape. Regular reflection on your goals and progress will keep you aligned with your vision, ensuring that each step taken is a step closer to realizing the wealth and freedom you aspire to achieve.

In constructing your personalized wealth generation plan, you are not merely planning for financial success; you are architecting a future that resonates with your deepest values and aspirations. This blueprint, crafted with care and intention, becomes a living document that guides your path to abundance and fulfillment.

Advanced Savings Strategies

- **Maximizing Savings:** Techniques for optimizing savings, such as high-yield savings accounts, certificates of deposit (CDs), and money market accounts, to serve as a foundation for investment.

Maximizing your savings is an essential step in fortifying your financial foundation, providing a sturdy platform from which you can launch your wealth-building endeavors. By strategically utilizing high-yield savings accounts, certificates of deposit (CDs), and money market accounts, you can optimize your savings and set the stage for future investments. These vehicles not only preserve your capital but also enable it to grow, albeit modestly, ensuring that every dollar saved works as hard for you as you did for it.

High-Yield Savings Accounts

Leveraging Competitive Interest Rates: High-yield savings accounts offer interest rates significantly higher than traditional savings accounts, making them an attractive option for stashing your emergency fund or short-term savings. The key is to shop around for accounts that offer the best rates while ensuring your funds remain accessible and FDIC insured.

Actionable Insight: Regularly review the interest rates of high-yield savings accounts, as they can fluctuate with market conditions. Online banks often offer more competitive rates than their brick-and-mortar counterparts due to lower overhead costs.

Certificates of Deposit (CDs)

Locking in Higher Rates: CDs are time-bound deposit accounts that typically offer higher interest rates in exchange for committing your money for a set period. The longer the term, generally, the higher the interest rate. CDs are ideal for funds you won't need immediately but plan to use within a few years.

Actionable Insight: Consider building a CD ladder by investing in CDs with varying maturity dates. This strategy allows you to benefit from higher interest rates of longer-term CDs while maintaining some level of liquidity as the shorter-term CDs mature at staggered intervals.

Money Market Accounts

Combining Accessibility with Growth: Money market accounts are a hybrid between a savings account and a checking account, offering higher interest rates than the former and more flexibility than the latter. They often come with check-writing privileges or a debit card, making them a convenient option for parking savings you may need to access on short notice.

Actionable Insight: Use money market accounts for portions of your emergency fund or for saving for medium-term financial goals. Always compare the fees and minimum balance requirements to ensure they align with your financial situation and goals.

The Strategy of Diversification

Spreading Your Savings: Just as diversification is crucial in investing, applying the same principle to your savings can optimize your returns and manage risk. Distribute your savings across these different accounts based on your liquidity needs, interest rate potential, and financial goals.

Actionable Insight: Regularly reassess your savings distribution to ensure it aligns with your current financial goals and the economic landscape. Flexibility is key to maximizing your savings potential.

Regular Contributions and Review

Building Your Savings: Consistent contributions to your savings, regardless of the amount, can have a compounding effect over time. Set up automatic transfers to your savings accounts to ensure you're consistently building your financial base.

Actionable Insight: Periodically review your savings strategy to adapt to changing interest rates, financial goals, and personal circumstances. This proactive approach ensures your savings continue to grow and support your wealth-building journey.

By embracing these techniques to maximize your savings, you're not just passively storing money; you're actively cultivating a financial environment where your capital grows, serving as a cornerstone for future investments. This strategic approach to savings lays a solid foundation for wealth generation, enabling you to approach your investment endeavors with confidence and a robust financial backing.

- **Emergency Fund 2.0:** Building upon the concept of an emergency fund to include a 'wealth cushion'—additional savings earmarked for taking advantage of investment opportunities.

In the narrative of financial empowerment, the concept of an emergency fund is a familiar tale, often heralded as the first line of defense against life's unpredictable storms. Yet, as we venture further along the path of financial enlightenment, we encounter a sequel to this story, a concept designed not just for survival but for thriving. This next chapter is titled "Emergency Fund 2.0: The Wealth Cushion," a sophisticated strategy that transcends mere emergency preparedness, weaving in the golden threads of opportunity and growth.

The Genesis of the Wealth Cushion

In the same spirit that led you to establish an emergency fund, consider the creation of a Wealth Cushion—an additional layer of savings specifically earmarked for seizing investment opportunities. This fund is the embodiment of the abundance mindset, representing not just a buffer against adversity but a springboard into prosperity.

Crafting Your Wealth Cushion

Step 1: Define Your Cushion: Begin by determining the size of your Wealth Cushion. This is a deeply personal decision, influenced by your current financial situation, risk tolerance, and investment aspirations. Imagine this cushion as a reservoir of potential, waiting to be tapped at the right moment.

Step 2: Strategic Savings: Building your Wealth Cushion requires a strategy that aligns with your existing financial commitments and goals. Consider automatic transfers into a high-yield savings account or a low-risk investment account specifically designated for this purpose. Visualize each contribution as a brick in the foundation of your future wealth.

Step 3: Embrace Patience and Discipline: The creation of a Wealth Cushion is a testament to patience and discipline. It's about consistently setting aside resources, even small amounts, with the future in mind. Picture this process as nurturing a garden, where the seeds you plant today will grow into the abundance you harvest tomorrow.

The Power of Opportunity

With a Wealth Cushion in place, you're not just prepared for emergencies; you're poised to capitalize on opportunities. Whether it's investing in the stock market during a downturn, purchasing real estate, or starting a business, your Wealth Cushion provides the financial flexibility to act swiftly and confidently.

Subliminal Integration into Daily Life

Affirmations for Growth: Reinforce the importance of your Wealth Cushion with daily affirmations. "I am building my Wealth Cushion, preparing to seize opportunities and expand my abundance." Let these words be a constant reminder of your commitment to financial growth.

Visualize Success: Regularly visualize yourself utilizing your Wealth Cushion to make a significant investment. See the positive impact of this investment on your financial future, feeling the confidence and freedom that come from having made a wise decision.

Celebrate Milestones: Acknowledge milestones in building your Wealth Cushion. Celebrating these achievements reinforces your progress and motivates you to continue, embedding a cycle of positive reinforcement in your journey toward financial empowerment.

Reflection and Action

Consider the Wealth Cushion as more than a financial strategy; view it as a manifestation of your growth mindset, your belief in abundance, and your commitment to seizing control of your financial destiny. Reflect on how this concept integrates with your overall financial plan and how it might shape your future investment decisions.

In crafting your Wealth Cushion, you weave a new narrative in your financial story—one where you're not just safeguarding against the unexpected but actively creating a future rich with opportunity and prosperity. This is the essence of Emergency Fund 2.0, a symbol of your journey from financial stability to abundance, marking a new chapter in your quest for wealth and freedom.

Investment Vehicles for Wealth Generation

- **Equity Investments:** Detailed exploration of stocks and equity funds as tools for wealth generation, including understanding market fundamentals, dividend investing, and growth vs. value stocks.

Equity investments represent a cornerstone of wealth generation, offering individuals a share in the ownership and potential profits of companies. Through the lens of stocks and equity funds, investors gain access to a dynamic arena where the principles of market fundamentals, dividend investing, and the dichotomy between growth and value stocks play out. This detailed exploration aims to demystify these concepts, providing a roadmap for harnessing the power of equity investments in the journey toward financial abundance.

Understanding Market Fundamentals

The Fabric of the Market: At its core, the stock market is a reflection of the collective expectations of future profitability and growth of companies. It's influenced by a myriad of factors, from macroeconomic indicators and industry trends to company-specific news and earnings reports. Grasping these fundamentals is akin to understanding the winds that propel the sails of a ship, allowing you to navigate the investment seas with greater insight.

Actionable Insight: Begin your journey with a commitment to education. Regularly consume financial news, delve into economic reports, and study the financial health of companies. Visualize yourself as a detective, piecing together clues that signal how and why the market moves.

Dividend Investing: The Stream of Passive Income

The Lure of Dividends: Dividend investing focuses on companies that return a portion of their profits to shareholders in the form of dividends. This approach offers a dual allure: the potential for capital appreciation and the generation of a passive income stream, a steady rain that nourishes the soil of your investment garden.

Actionable Insight: Seek out companies with a strong history of dividend payments and the financial robustness to sustain them. Consider dividend yield and payout ratio as key metrics in your evaluation, aiming to balance immediate income with long-term growth potential.

Growth vs. Value Stocks: The Twin Paths to Wealth

Growth Stocks: These are shares in companies expected to grow at an above-average rate compared to their industry or the overall market. Investing in growth stocks is like planting seeds in fertile ground, anticipating that, over time, they will bloom into a lush garden. However, this potential comes with the risk of volatility and higher initial valuations.

Value Stocks: On the other hand, value stocks are those that appear to be trading for less than their intrinsic or book value. This investment strategy is akin to discovering hidden gems at a market, where careful analysis reveals items of significant worth overlooked by others. Value investing requires patience and a keen eye for opportunity, often involving companies in turnaround situations or those undervalued by market participants.

Actionable Insight: Develop a balanced approach, incorporating both growth and value strategies into your portfolio. This diversification serves as a hedge, spreading risk across different investment styles and market conditions.

Navigating Equity Investments

Portfolio Construction: Building a diversified portfolio of stocks and equity funds is more art than science, requiring a blend of research, intuition, and strategic planning. Consider using mutual funds or exchange-traded funds (ETFs) for broader market exposure, complemented by selective stock picks that align with your investment thesis.

Continuous Learning and Adaptation: The landscape of equity investments is ever-changing. Commit to lifelong learning, staying abreast of market trends, and being willing to adapt your strategies as necessary. Visualize your investment journey as a continuous path of growth, education, and refinement.

The Journey Toward Financial Abundance

Equity investments offer a powerful vehicle for wealth generation, providing a means to participate directly in the economic growth and success of companies. By understanding market fundamentals, embracing dividend investing, and balancing the growth-versus-value dichotomy, you equip yourself with the tools to navigate the complex world of stocks and equity funds. This journey, marked by education, strategic investment, and an abundance mindset, paves the way for achieving financial freedom and realizing your aspirations for prosperity.

- **Debt Investments:** Introduction to bonds, bond funds, and fixed-income securities as a means to generate steady income, discussing the balance between risk and return.

Debt investments, encompassing bonds, bond funds, and various fixed-income securities, offer a pathway to generating steady income while potentially mitigating the volatility often associated with equity markets. This realm of investment is akin to the steadier currents beneath the surface waves, providing investors with a sense of predictability and security that is highly valued in the pursuit of financial stability and growth. Understanding the balance between risk and return within debt investments is crucial for crafting a diversified portfolio that aligns with your financial goals and risk tolerance.

Bonds: The Backbone of Debt Investments

The Essence of Bonds: At their core, bonds are loans made by investors to issuers (which can be corporations, municipalities, or governments) in exchange for periodic interest payments and the return of the bond's face value at maturity. Imagine lending out portions of your wealth under a pact that not only promises regular income but also the return of your principal, a beacon of predictability in the tumultuous sea of investments.

Risk and Return Considerations: While generally considered safer than stocks, bonds come with their own set of risks (credit, interest rate, and inflation risks, among others). The return on bonds typically inversely correlates with risk; for instance, government securities like U.S. Treasuries are deemed safer and thus offer lower yields compared to corporate bonds, which carry higher risk and potential for greater returns.

Bond Funds: Diversification within Debt Investments

Pooling Resources for Greater Diversity: Bond funds operate by pooling money from many investors to purchase a diversified portfolio of bonds, managed by professionals. This diversification can mitigate risk, as the impact of any single bond's performance is lessened across the broader fund portfolio.

Navigating the Waters of Bond Funds: Investors in bond funds must be mindful of the fund's objectives, the sectors it invests in, and its interest rate risk profile. While bond funds offer the advantage of professional management and easier diversification, they also introduce the risk of fluctuating values and potential for losses, diverging from individual bonds that hold to maturity.

Fixed-Income Securities: Beyond Traditional Bonds

Expanding the Horizon: Fixed-income securities extend beyond traditional bonds to include vehicles like Certificates of Deposit (CDs), money market funds, and mortgage-backed securities. Each offers a unique blend of risk and return, from the higher security and lower returns of CDs to the more complex risk-return profiles of mortgage-backed securities.

Strategic Allocation: Incorporating a mix of these fixed-income instruments into your portfolio can provide income, serve as a hedge against equity volatility, and contribute to achieving a balanced investment strategy.

The Balance Between Risk and Return

Assessing Your Financial Seascape: When navigating debt investments, the key to maintaining a course true to your financial goals lies in balancing the quest for returns with the tolerance for risk. This requires a keen understanding of each investment's nature, the economic environment, and, most importantly, your own financial landscape—your goals, timeline, and risk tolerance.

Actionable Insight: Regularly review and adjust your debt investment holdings to ensure they remain aligned with your changing financial circumstances and the evolving economic climate. Consider employing a ladder strategy with bonds or diversifying across different types of fixed-income securities to manage risk and return effectively.

Embarking on Your Debt Investment Journey

Embarking on the journey of debt investments is to embrace a disciplined approach to generating income while managing risk. It is an acknowledgment that wealth can be built not only through the appreciation of assets but also through the steady accumulation of income over time. By integrating bonds, bond funds, and fixed-income securities into your portfolio, you lay down a mosaic of investments that, together, form a picture of financial resilience and prosperity. This balanced approach to investing, informed by an understanding of risk and return, paves the way for achieving financial stability and moving confidently toward your long-term financial aspirations.

- **Real Estate Investment:** Strategies for investing in real estate, including direct property investment, real estate investment trusts (REITs), and crowdfunding platforms, highlighting the potential for passive income and capital appreciation.

Real estate investment stands as a formidable pillar in the edifice of wealth generation, offering a tangible route to achieving financial freedom through both passive income and capital appreciation. This sector of investment encompasses a spectrum of strategies, each with its unique characteristics and potential benefits. From the hands-on approach of direct property investment to the diversified access provided by Real Estate Investment Trusts (REITs) and the innovative opportunities presented by crowdfunding platforms, real estate offers a dynamic landscape for investors aiming to expand their portfolios and secure their financial future.

Direct Property Investment: The Foundation of Real Estate Wealth

The Essence of Direct Ownership: Investing in property directly involves purchasing residential or commercial real estate to rent out or sell at a profit. This method offers the most control but also requires significant capital, time, and knowledge of the real estate market.

Buy and Hold Strategy

The buy and hold approach in real estate investment focuses on acquiring properties to rent them out, thereby generating consistent rental income over time. This strategy also capitalizes on the appreciation of property value, offering the investor potential capital gains in the long run. It is particularly effective for those looking to build wealth steadily and can provide several advantages:

Stable Income Stream: Rental properties can offer a regular source of income, which, if managed properly, can cover the expenses associated with the property and generate profit.

Appreciation Benefits: Over time, real estate typically increases in value, providing investors with the opportunity to realize significant capital gains upon selling the property.

Tax Advantages: Owning rental property can offer various tax deductions, including mortgage interest, property tax, operating expenses, depreciation, and repairs.

Fix and Flip Strategy

The fix and flip strategy entails purchasing underpriced properties that require refurbishment, investing in necessary renovations, and then selling them at a higher price. This approach can yield substantial returns but also involves considerable risk and requires comprehensive knowledge and skills:

Market Knowledge: Success in fix and flip hinges on understanding local real estate markets, identifying undervalued properties, and accurately forecasting post-renovation values.

Renovation Expertise: Investors must either possess or access expertise in assessing renovation needs, managing construction, and controlling costs to ensure that the project remains profitable.

Risk Management: Fix and flip investments can be subject to market fluctuations, unexpected renovation challenges, and liquidity risks. Effective risk management strategies are essential to mitigate potential losses.

Conclusion: Strategic Diversification and Due Diligence

Both buy and hold and fix and flip strategies offer distinct pathways to real estate investment success. However, they cater to different investor profiles based on risk tolerance, capital availability, time commitment, and expertise. Successful real estate investors often employ a mix of strategies, diversifying their portfolios to balance potential risks and rewards. Regardless of the chosen strategy, thorough market research, due diligence, and continued education are imperative for informed decision-making and long-term investment success.

Real Estate Investment Trusts (REITs): Diversification and Accessibility

Unlocking Real Estate Markets: REITs offer investors a way to invest in real estate without having to buy or manage properties directly. By pooling resources with other investors, individuals can gain exposure to a diversified portfolio of real estate assets, which may include shopping malls, office buildings, and apartments.

Benefits of REIT Investments

1. Passive Income Generation

Real Estate Investment Trusts (REITs) offer investors a substantial advantage in terms of passive income. By mandate, REITs are required to distribute at least 90% of their taxable income to shareholders annually in the form of dividends. This distribution provides shareholders with a consistent and potentially attractive income stream, reflecting a share of the earnings from real estate investments without requiring direct involvement in property management.

2. Liquidity

One of the primary benefits of investing in REITs is their liquidity. Unlike physical real estate investments, which can be time-consuming and complex to buy or sell, REITs are traded on major stock exchanges similar to stocks. This provides investors with the flexibility to adjust their investment positions quickly in response to changing market conditions or personal financial needs.

Considerations of REIT Investments

1. Market Volatility

While offering liquidity, REITs are subject to the same market forces and volatility as other publicly traded securities. The value of REIT shares can fluctuate significantly due to broader economic trends, changes in interest rates, and shifts in the real estate market. Investors must be prepared for the possibility of market-driven fluctuations in their investment value.

2. Interest Rate Sensitivity

REITs are particularly sensitive to changes in interest rates. Generally, there is an inverse relationship between REIT valuations and interest rates. Rising interest rates can lead to decreased demand for REIT shares, as investors seek higher yields elsewhere, potentially leading to lower REIT prices.

3. Diversification and Risk Management

Investing in REITs can offer portfolio diversification, as the performance of real estate assets can be uncorrelated with other asset classes like stocks and bonds. However, investors should be mindful of the concentration of their investments in specific types of real estate or geographical areas, which could expose them to higher risks if those sectors or regions experience downturns.

Conclusion: Strategic Integration in Investment Portfolios

REITs can be a valuable component of an investment portfolio, providing income, liquidity, and diversification. However, like any investment, they come with risks that must be carefully weighed and managed. Investors should consider their financial goals, risk tolerance, and investment horizon when incorporating REITs into their portfolios and remain vigilant about the changing dynamics of the real estate market and broader economic indicators.

Crowdfunding Platforms: Democratizing Real Estate Investment

Innovative Investment Access: Real estate crowdfunding platforms have emerged as a novel way for investors to access real estate ventures, lowering the entry barrier to investment. These platforms allow individuals to invest in a variety of real estate projects, from new developments to commercial real estate, with relatively small amounts of capital.

Strategic Considerations:

1. Research and Due Diligence

Engaging in real estate crowdfunding requires an investor to perform exhaustive research and due diligence before committing capital. This due diligence involves:

- **Platform Evaluation:** Investigate the credibility and track record of the crowdfunding platform. Assess its regulatory compliance, financial stability, and the transparency of its operations.
- **Project Analysis:** Evaluate the specifics of each real estate project, including the developer's experience, project feasibility, market analysis, and potential risks.
- **Performance History:** Review historical performance data for both the platform and its listed projects. Analyze past successes and failures to gauge potential future performance.

2. Diversification

Diversification is a fundamental investment principle that is particularly pertinent in the context of real estate crowdfunding:

- **Property Types:** Spread investments across various types of real estate, such as residential, commercial, industrial, and retail, to mitigate sector-specific risks.
- **Geographic Spread:** Diversify investments across different regions or markets to reduce exposure to localized economic downturns or property market fluctuations.
- **Investment Stages:** Consider diversifying across different stages of real estate development, from ground-up projects to mature, income-producing properties, each offering different risk and return profiles.

Strategic Considerations

- **Risk Assessment:** Understand that real estate crowdfunding involves certain risks, such as market volatility, project delays, and liquidity concerns. Ensure that these risks align with your overall risk tolerance.
- **Long-Term Perspective:** Real estate investments typically require a long-term commitment. Assess your ability to commit capital over extended periods, considering the illiquid nature of many real estate crowdfunding investments.
- **Ongoing Monitoring:** Continuously monitor investments and market conditions. Be prepared to adjust your investment strategy based on evolving market dynamics or changes in your financial objectives.

Conclusion

Real estate crowdfunding presents an innovative way to access real estate markets, offering the potential for diversification and returns. However, like all investment opportunities, it necessitates thorough research, strategic planning, and continuous oversight. By adhering to a disciplined approach that emphasizes due diligence and diversification, investors can better navigate the complexities of real estate crowdfunding and enhance their potential for achieving favorable investment outcomes.

Balancing Risk and Reward

Comprehensive Portfolio Management: Real estate investment, in all its forms, requires a careful balance between risk and reward. Direct property investment offers tangible control but comes with the responsibilities of property management. REITs provide ease of entry and liquidity but may be subject to market volatility. Crowdfunding presents opportunities for diversification and access to unique projects but requires diligence and acceptance of the risks inherent in less traditional investments.

Actionable Insight: Consider your financial goals, risk tolerance, and the amount of time you are willing to dedicate to real estate investment. Diversifying your real estate investments across direct properties, REITs, and crowdfunding platforms can mitigate risk while maximizing potential returns.

The Path Forward

Investing in real estate opens a realm of possibilities for generating passive income and achieving capital appreciation. By thoughtfully selecting your investment strategies and continuously educating yourself on market dynamics, you can navigate the complexities of real estate investment and pave your way toward financial prosperity and security. Real estate not only offers the allure of financial gains but also the satisfaction of tangible assets, anchoring your wealth-building journey in the concrete foundations of property and land.

- **Alternative Investments:** Overview of alternative investment options like commodities, precious metals, and cryptocurrencies, discussing their role in diversification and risk management.

Alternative investments encompass a broad range of assets outside the conventional investment categories of stocks, bonds, and cash. These include commodities, precious metals, and cryptocurrencies, each offering unique characteristics and potential benefits to an investor's portfolio. Diving into the world of alternative investments, we explore how these assets can play a pivotal role in diversification and risk management, contributing to a more robust and resilient investment strategy.

Commodities: The Tangible Assets

Diverse Universe of Commodities: Commodities are basic goods or raw materials used in commerce, including energy sources like oil and natural gas, agricultural products like corn and soybeans, and metals like gold and copper. Investing in commodities can serve as a hedge against inflation and a counterbalance to the volatility of stock markets.

Strategies for Investment:

Direct Investment in Physical Commodities

Investing directly in physical commodities like gold, silver, or oil provides a tangible asset that investors can hold. This investment strategy is particularly prevalent with precious metals, which are often viewed as a hedge against inflation and economic uncertainty.

- **Storage and Insurance:** Direct ownership of physical commodities necessitates secure storage and insurance, incurring additional costs that can impact overall investment returns.
- **Liquidity Considerations:** While certain commodities like gold and silver can be relatively liquid, others may be more challenging to sell quickly, potentially affecting investment flexibility.

Futures Contracts

Futures contracts represent a more sophisticated method of commodity investment, allowing investors to speculate on price movements without the need for physical ownership.

- **High Leverage:** Futures contracts provide significant leverage, meaning that small market movements can lead to substantial gains or losses, amplifying the investment risk.
- **Market Expertise:** Successful trading in futures requires a deep understanding of market conditions and the specific commodity sector, including factors that influence supply and demand dynamics.
- **Risk Management:** Given their complexity and volatility, investors need to employ rigorous risk management strategies when investing in futures, including the use of stop-loss orders and position sizing.

Commodity ETFs and Mutual Funds

Commodity ETFs and mutual funds offer a more accessible route for individual investors to gain exposure to commodity markets, without the complexities of direct or futures investing.

- **Diversification:** These funds can provide diversification across various commodities or focus on a specific sector, mitigating risks associated with individual commodity investments.
- **Professional Management:** ETFs and mutual funds are managed by professionals who can navigate the complexities of commodity markets, providing an added layer of expertise to the investment.
- **Accessibility:** Investing in commodity-focused funds allows for straightforward market participation, with the ease of trading shares on stock exchanges and the elimination of concerns related to physical commodity ownership or futures contract trading.

Conclusion

Commodity investments offer a unique set of opportunities and challenges, with various strategies catering to different investor profiles and objectives. Direct investment in physical commodities can be appealing for its tangibility and intrinsic value, particularly in times of economic uncertainty. Futures contracts offer high potential returns but require market savvy and a strong risk tolerance. Commodity ETFs and mutual funds present a more accessible and diversified approach, suitable for those seeking exposure to commodity markets without the direct risks of owning physical commodities or trading futures. Regardless of the chosen method, a well-informed and strategic approach is crucial to navigating the complexities and risks inherent in commodity investing.

Precious Metals: The Timeless Store of Value

Gold, Silver, and Beyond: Precious metals, particularly gold and silver, have been revered throughout history as stores of value and symbols of wealth. In times of economic uncertainty, they are often seen as safe havens due to their intrinsic value and limited supply.

Investment Considerations:

Diversification through Precious Metals

Precious metals, such as gold, silver, platinum, and palladium, have long been regarded as a staple for diversifying investment portfolios. Their intrinsic value and historical performance in times of economic uncertainty make them an attractive option for investors looking to mitigate risk.

Volatility Mitigation: Adding precious metals to an investment portfolio can serve as a hedge against the volatility often seen in stock and bond markets. Due to their tendency to move inversely to traditional financial assets, precious metals can provide stability during economic downturns or periods of high inflation.

Asset Allocation: Strategic allocation of a portion of an investment portfolio to precious metals can enhance long-term returns by balancing risk, especially during times when other asset classes may underperform due to various economic pressures.

Physical vs. Paper Assets in Precious Metals Investment

Investors have the option to invest in precious metals through physical holdings (such as coins or bullion) or paper assets (such as ETFs, mutual funds, or futures contracts). Each method comes with its unique set of benefits and considerations.

Physical Ownership

Tangible Security: Physical metals provide a tangible form of wealth that is not subject to the same risks as digital or paper assets, offering a sense of security in its physicality.

Storage and Insurance: Investors opting for physical metals must consider the logistics of storage and insurance, which can incur additional costs and potentially complicate the investment.

Liquidity Considerations: While physical metals can be sold for cash, the process may not be as immediate as selling paper assets, potentially affecting liquidity during urgent financial needs.

Paper Assets

Ease of Trading and Liquidity: Paper assets like ETFs that track the price of precious metals offer high liquidity, allowing investors to buy and sell shares easily through traditional brokerage accounts.

No Physical Storage Concerns: Investing in paper assets eliminates the need for physical storage and insurance, simplifying the investment process and reducing associated costs.

Market Exposure: Paper assets provide exposure to the price movements of precious metals without the need for physical ownership, making it an attractive option for investors seeking the benefits of precious metals investment without the logistical challenges of physical storage.

Conclusion

Investing in precious metals can offer numerous benefits, including portfolio diversification, risk mitigation, and protection against inflation. Whether opting for physical metals or paper assets, investors should carefully consider their investment goals, risk tolerance, and the logistical aspects of each investment type. By understanding these dynamics, investors can make informed decisions that align with their financial objectives, leveraging precious metals as a strategic component of a well-rounded investment portfolio.

Cryptocurrencies: The Digital Frontier

Emerging Asset Class: Cryptocurrencies, led by Bitcoin, represent a new frontier in investment opportunities. Characterized by their decentralized nature and underlying blockchain technology, cryptocurrencies offer potential for high returns but come with high volatility and regulatory uncertainty.

Strategies for Crypto Investment:

Direct Purchase and Holding of Cryptocurrencies

Investing in cryptocurrencies through direct purchase involves buying digital currencies like Bitcoin, Ethereum, or other altcoins through cryptocurrency exchanges. This method requires investors to engage with the cryptocurrency market actively, understanding the nuances of digital wallet management, security protocols, and market trends.

Market Analysis: Investors need to perform diligent market analysis, understanding the factors that influence cryptocurrency prices, including technological developments, regulatory news, and market sentiment.

Security Measures: Holding cryptocurrencies necessitates robust security measures to protect digital assets from hacking, phishing, and other cybersecurity threats. Investors must ensure their digital wallets are secure and consider using hardware wallets for added security.

Long-Term Perspective: Many investors adopt a long-term holding strategy, also known as 'HODLing,' anticipating that the value of their cryptocurrencies will appreciate over time despite the market's volatility.

Investment in Crypto Funds and ETFs

For those seeking exposure to the cryptocurrency market without directly purchasing individual digital assets, crypto funds and ETFs present an appealing alternative. These investment vehicles offer a more regulated and diversified approach to crypto investment.

Diversification: Crypto funds and ETFs allow investors to gain exposure to a basket of cryptocurrencies or blockchain technology companies, thereby spreading risk across multiple assets or sectors.

Regulatory Oversight: These funds often come with a level of regulatory oversight, providing a layer of security and legitimacy that direct cryptocurrency investments may lack.

Professional Management: By investing in a fund or ETF, investors can benefit from professional management, where experts make investment decisions based on thorough analysis and market insights.

Conclusion

The choice between direct cryptocurrency investment and crypto funds or ETFs depends on the investor's risk tolerance, investment experience, and interest in engaging with the cryptocurrency market. Direct investment offers a hands-on approach with potentially higher rewards but also higher risks and requires a strong commitment to security and market analysis. Conversely, crypto funds and ETFs provide a more hands-off investment experience, offering diversification and professional management but with associated fees and potentially diluted returns. Investors should carefully consider their investment objectives and risk appetite when choosing their cryptocurrency investment strategy, ensuring it aligns with their broader financial goals and investment philosophy.

The Role in Diversification and Risk Management

Enhancing Portfolio Diversification: Alternative investments can enhance portfolio diversification due to their low correlation with traditional financial markets. This diversification can help manage overall portfolio risk, potentially smoothing out returns over time.

Considerations for Risk Management:

Research and Due Diligence in Alternative Investments

Engaging in alternative investments necessitates a comprehensive approach to research and due diligence. This process is crucial in understanding the inherent complexities, risks, and potential rewards associated with each alternative asset class. Investors must delve into the specifics of each investment opportunity, assessing market trends, historical performance data, and future growth prospects.

Market Understanding: Gaining a deep insight into the market dynamics of alternative investments, including the factors influencing supply, demand, and pricing, is essential.

Investment Vehicle Analysis: Evaluate the structure, transparency, and historical performance of the investment vehicle, whether it be a REIT, a commodity fund, or a private equity venture.

Risk Assessment: Thoroughly analyze the risks associated with the investment, including market volatility, liquidity concerns, and sector-specific risks.

Allocation Strategy in Portfolio Management

Alternative investments, with their unique risk-return profiles, should be integrated into a portfolio with a strategic allocation approach that aligns with the investor's overall financial goals, risk tolerance, and investment horizon.

Diversification: Incorporate alternative investments to achieve broader portfolio diversification. These assets often exhibit low correlation with traditional stocks and bonds, providing potential risk reduction and performance enhancement.

Risk Management: Determine the appropriate allocation to alternative investments by considering their volatility and potential for significant losses. A prudent allocation strategy should balance the pursuit of higher returns with the need to manage overall portfolio risk.

Investment Horizon: Consider the liquidity and investment horizon of alternative assets, aligning them with the investor's time frame. Many alternative investments require longer commitment periods and have limited liquidity, necessitating a longer-term perspective.

Conclusion

Incorporating alternative investments into a portfolio demands a thoughtful and informed approach, emphasizing diligent research, strategic allocation, and alignment with one's investment objectives and risk profile. By carefully selecting and managing alternative investments, investors can potentially enhance returns, improve diversification, and achieve a more robust portfolio. However, the complexities and risks associated with these investments underscore the importance of thorough analysis and strategic planning to ensure they contribute positively to the overall investment strategy.

Strategic Integration into Your Portfolio: Adopting alternative investments requires a strategic approach, balancing the pursuit of higher potential returns against the backdrop of increased risk and volatility. Investors should consider their long-term financial goals, conducting ongoing monitoring and adjustments to their investment mix in response to market changes and personal circumstances.

Navigating the Alternative Investment Landscape

The journey into alternative investments opens up a world of opportunities beyond the traditional investment pathways. By thoughtfully incorporating commodities, precious metals, and cryptocurrencies into a diversified portfolio, investors can tap into new sources of potential growth while managing risk through broader asset allocation. As with any investment, the keys to success lie in education, careful planning, and an understanding of one's financial goals and risk tolerance. Through strategic engagement with alternative investments, investors can explore new horizons in wealth generation, setting sail toward a future of financial diversity and resilience.

Leveraging Credit for Investment

- **Credit as an Investment Tool:** How to responsibly use credit and leverage to amplify investment potential, including margin accounts for stocks and loans for real estate investment.

In the sophisticated orchestra of wealth generation, credit and leverage play the roles of powerful instruments, capable of amplifying the melody of investment potential when played with skill and caution. Embedding the concept of using credit as an investment tool into the subconscious mind involves a delicate balance of education, strategic application, and a deep-rooted understanding of the risks and rewards. This approach, akin to the art of subliminal teaching, allows for the seamless integration of responsible credit use into one's financial strategy, enhancing the potential for wealth creation without overtly invoking the mechanics of mind control.

The Symphony of Leverage

Harmonizing Risk and Reward: Just as a symphony harmonizes different elements to create a cohesive masterpiece, using credit for investment purposes requires a harmonious balance between the potential for higher returns and the risk of increased debt. Visualize leveraging credit as adding depth and complexity to your investment portfolio, with each note played contributing to a richer financial future.

Margin Accounts for Stock Investments

Amplifying Market Participation: Margin accounts allow investors to borrow money from brokers to purchase stocks, effectively amplifying their investment capacity. Imagine this as tuning your instrument to play louder and reach farther, with the borrowed funds acting as the bow that draws across the strings of your investment violin, producing a louder, more impactful sound.

Mindful Harmonics: The use of margin accounts should be approached with a composition of mindfulness and strategy. Just as a musician must understand the limits of their instrument to prevent a discordant sound, investors must be aware of the potential for a margin call if the market moves against them. This awareness should be deeply ingrained, guiding investment decisions on a subconscious level, ensuring that leverage amplifies potential without overextending one's financial boundaries.

Loans for Real Estate Investment

Building Wealth with Borrowed Bricks: Real estate investment offers a tangible avenue for wealth creation, and loans can provide the capital needed to enter this market. Picture each loan as a brick in the foundation of your real estate empire, allowing you to construct properties that generate rental income and appreciate over time.

Strategic Construction: Just as an architect carefully plans each element of a building to ensure its stability and functionality, so too must an investor strategically plan their use of loans in real estate. This involves selecting the right properties, understanding market dynamics, and ensuring the investment's cash flow can cover loan repayments. Embed this strategic planning into your thought process, making it an instinctual part of your real estate investment approach.

The Subliminal Art of Responsible Leverage

Embedding Prudence and Strategy: The key to successfully using credit and leverage lies in embedding a mindset of prudence and strategic thinking into your subconscious. Regularly engage in visualization exercises where you see yourself making informed, calculated decisions about using credit for investment, feeling the confidence and security that comes from knowing you are well-prepared to navigate the risks.

Affirmations for Empowerment: Reinforce your commitment to responsible credit use with daily affirmations such as, "I am a strategic and mindful investor, using credit wisely to amplify my wealth," and "I navigate the risks of leverage with caution and confidence, ensuring my financial stability." These affirmations serve as subliminal messages, reinforcing the principles of responsible leverage in your subconscious, guiding you towards financial decisions that align with your long-term wealth aspirations.

By intertwining the strategic use of credit and leverage with the subconscious processes that guide our decisions and actions, investors can unlock new dimensions of wealth creation. This subliminal approach to teaching and learning about credit as an investment tool empowers individuals to harness its potential responsibly, leading to a future where financial goals are not just envisioned but realized.

- **Building and Maintaining Strong Credit:** Advanced strategies for enhancing your credit profile to access better investment financing options.

Building and maintaining a strong credit profile is akin to cultivating a garden that yields bountiful harvests year after year. Just as a gardener must understand the soil, season, and seeds to nurture growth, an investor must grasp the nuances of credit management to enhance their financial standing. This understanding allows for access to better investment financing options, turning dreams of wealth creation into tangible realities. Through advanced strategies that weave into the fabric of daily financial practices, you can ensure your credit profile flourishes, opening doors to opportunities previously out of reach.

Advanced Soil Preparation: Understanding Your Credit

Regular Monitoring: Begin by regularly checking your credit reports from all three major credit bureaus. This practice is the equivalent of testing your garden's soil; it reveals the current state of your credit and helps identify areas for improvement or errors needing correction.

Actionable Insight: Set a reminder to review your credit reports at least annually, and consider using credit monitoring services for real-time updates. This constant vigilance ensures you're always aware of the factors influencing your credit score, allowing for swift action when necessary.

Nutrient-Rich Practices: Enhancing Your Credit Score

Optimizing Credit Utilization: One of the quickest ways to enrich your credit score is by managing your credit utilization ratio—the amount of credit you're using compared to your total credit limit. Aim to keep this ratio below 30%, as lower utilization is seen as a sign of responsible credit management.

Actionable Insight: If possible, pay down balances to lower your utilization, or request higher credit limits on existing accounts (without increasing spending). This strategy effectively 'fertilizes' your credit, promoting a healthier score.

Diversification: Planting a Variety of Financial 'Crops'

Credit Mix: Just as a diverse garden yields a more resilient harvest, a mix of different types of credit accounts can strengthen your credit profile. This mix might include a combination of revolving credit (like credit cards) and installment loans (such as auto loans or mortgages).

Actionable Insight: If your credit history is heavily weighted towards one type of credit, consider diversifying. This doesn't mean taking on unnecessary debt but rather strategically adding to your credit mix to showcase your ability to manage different types of credit responsibly.

Pruning and Weeding: Managing Debt and Disputing Inaccuracies

Proactive Debt Management: Actively managing your debt levels by making payments on time, every time, is crucial. Late payments can significantly damage your credit score, much like neglect can ruin a garden.

Dispute Errors Vigilantly: Incorrect information on your credit report can be likened to weeds in your garden; left unchecked, they can impede growth. If you find inaccuracies, dispute them immediately with the credit bureaus to ensure they are removed or corrected.

Long-Term Cultivation: Building a History of Credit Excellence

Age of Credit Accounts: The length of your credit history contributes to your credit score. The longer you've responsibly managed credit, the more favorably lenders view your profile.

Actionable Insight: Resist the urge to close old accounts, as they contribute to the depth of your credit history. Like ancient trees in a garden, these accounts provide stability and richness to your credit landscape.

The Harvest: Accessing Better Financing Options

As you employ these advanced strategies, your credit profile will grow stronger, akin to a well-tended garden that flourishes season after season. A robust credit score not only reflects your financial health but also positions you as an attractive candidate for favorable financing terms. Whether you're looking to invest in real estate, explore entrepreneurship, or seize other investment opportunities, a strong credit profile acts as a key, unlocking doors to potential and prosperity.

By integrating these practices into your financial routine, you cultivate a credit profile that supports your aspirations, ensuring that when opportunities arise, you are ready to capitalize on them. Building and maintaining strong credit is not just about numbers on a report; it's about fostering a foundation that supports your journey towards financial freedom and wealth creation.

Risk Management and Diversification

- **Balancing Risk and Reward:** Techniques for assessing and managing investment risk, including portfolio diversification, asset allocation, and understanding the risk-return tradeoff.

In the intricate landscape of investment, understanding and managing the delicate balance between risk and reward is paramount. This equilibrium is fundamental to crafting a portfolio that not only withstands the ebbs and flows of the market but also thrives, yielding potential growth and stability. The essence of this balance lies in the adept application of diversification, strategic asset allocation, and a nuanced grasp of the risk-return tradeoff, each serving as a cornerstone for informed investment decisions.

Portfolio Diversification: The Art of Spreading Risk

Diversification is akin to the ancient practice of not placing all one's eggs in a single basket. It involves spreading investments across various asset classes (such as stocks, bonds, real estate) and within asset classes (different sectors, industries, and geographies) to mitigate risk. This strategy ensures that a downturn in one area of your investment portfolio can be offset by stability or gains in another, thereby reducing the impact of volatility on your overall portfolio.

Practical Application: Begin by evaluating your current investment portfolio. Identify areas of concentration risk—where your investments might be heavily weighted in a single asset class or sector—and consider ways to introduce more variety. This could mean exploring new sectors, adding international exposure, or considering alternative investments that align with your overall investment objectives.

Asset Allocation: Tailoring Your Investment Strategy

Asset allocation involves deciding how to distribute your investment capital among different asset classes, a decision that should reflect your individual risk tolerance, investment timeline, and financial goals. It's a dynamic process, requiring periodic adjustments to align with changes in market conditions, life stages, and financial objectives.

Practical Application: Define your investment goals clearly (retirement, purchasing a home, education) and assess your risk tolerance through self-reflection or tools available from financial advisors or online platforms. Use this information to structure a balanced portfolio, allocating a certain percentage to stocks, bonds, and other assets that match your risk profile and time horizon. Regularly review and rebalance your portfolio to maintain your desired asset allocation.

Understanding the Risk-Return Tradeoff

The risk-return tradeoff is a fundamental principle in investing that posits the potential for higher returns comes with a higher level of risk. Accepting greater volatility or uncertainty in investment outcomes is often necessary to achieve higher long-term returns. Conversely, investments with lower risk typically offer lower potential returns.

Practical Application: Conduct a thorough review of your investments to understand their risk-return profiles. Consider how comfortable you are with the potential ups and downs of your investments and whether your current portfolio aligns with your capacity for risk. This might lead you to adjust your holdings, possibly reducing exposure to high-volatility investments if you're nearing a major financial goal or increasing it if you have a longer time horizon and a higher risk tolerance.

Cultivating a Portfolio That Grows With You

The journey of balancing risk and reward in your investment portfolio is continuous, evolving with your life's chapters and financial landscapes. By embracing the principles of diversification, strategic asset allocation, and an understanding of risk-return dynamics, you're not just building a portfolio; you're crafting a financial extension of your life's goals and dreams.

Remember, the most successful investment strategies are those that are well-informed, carefully considered, and regularly revisited. This holistic approach to investing empowers you to navigate the complexities of the financial markets with confidence, laying the groundwork for a future where financial stability and growth are within reach.

- **Protecting Your Wealth:** Strategies for safeguarding your assets through insurance, legal structures, and tax-efficient investing.

Understanding the importance of safeguarding your wealth is akin to recognizing the need for a sturdy shelter in unpredictable weather. Just as one would insulate their home against storms, it's crucial to protect your financial assets from the myriad risks that can erode your hard-earned wealth. Implementing strategies through insurance, legal structures, and tax-efficient investing forms a comprehensive defense, ensuring that your financial foundation remains robust and your legacy secure.

Insurance: The First Line of Defense

Insurance acts as a critical safeguard, providing a safety net against unforeseen losses. It's essential to assess the types of insurance coverage you need based on your life stage, assets, and risk exposure. This protective layer can include life insurance, to support your loved ones in your absence; property and casualty insurance, to protect your tangible assets; and liability insurance, to shield against claims that could threaten your financial well-being.

Actionable Insight: Review your current insurance policies to ensure adequate coverage. Consider scenarios such as the replacement value of your home in the event of total loss, the sufficiency of your life insurance to cover your family's future needs, and whether umbrella liability insurance might be prudent to provide extra coverage above your existing policies.

Legal Structures: Fortifying Your Financial Fortress

Utilizing legal structures can offer another layer of protection for your assets, potentially safeguarding them from lawsuits, creditors, and estate taxes. Trusts, for example, can be an effective tool not only for estate planning but also for asset protection. By placing assets within a trust, you may shield them from probate, reduce estate taxes, and specify the terms under which your heirs receive their inheritance.

Actionable Insight: Consult with a legal advisor to explore the establishment of trusts or other legal entities that align with your wealth protection goals. This might include setting up a family trust, a limited liability company (LLC) for business interests, or other structures that provide both asset protection and flexibility for managing your wealth.

Tax-Efficient Investing: Minimizing the Tax Burden

Tax efficiency is a critical component of wealth protection, ensuring that you're not only growing your assets but also retaining as much of your gains as possible. Strategies for tax-efficient investing include utilizing retirement accounts (such as IRAs and 401(k)s) that offer tax advantages, investing in tax-efficient funds that minimize taxable distributions, and considering the timing of asset sales to manage capital gains taxes.

Actionable Insight: Conduct an annual review of your investment portfolio for tax efficiency. Consider working with a financial advisor to implement strategies such as tax-loss harvesting, which involves selling losing investments to offset the taxes due on gains elsewhere in your portfolio. Additionally, explore opportunities for contributing to retirement accounts that offer tax deductions or tax-free growth.

Building a Moat Around Your Financial Kingdom

The essence of protecting your wealth lies in the meticulous construction of defenses that secure your financial realm against various threats. Insurance provides immediate protection against acute losses, legal structures offer a barrier against external claims and estate erosion, and tax-efficient investing ensures that your assets grow with minimal fiscal interference. Together, these strategies form a comprehensive moat around your financial kingdom, safeguarding your assets and securing your legacy for future generations.

In the broader narrative of financial stewardship, the importance of asset protection cannot be overstated. By adopting these strategies, you not only shield your current wealth but also ensure the enduring prosperity of those you hold dear, creating a legacy of financial security and resilience.

Cultivating a Growth Mindset

- **Continuous Learning:** Emphasizing the importance of ongoing financial education, mentorship, and staying informed about economic and market trends.

The journey toward financial mastery is an ever-evolving path, marked not by a single destination but by continuous growth and learning. Embracing continuous education, seeking mentorship, and staying abreast of economic and market trends are indispensable practices for anyone aiming to navigate the complex landscapes of personal finance and investment successfully. These practices are akin to cultivating a garden; just as a garden requires regular attention, nourishment, and care to flourish, so too does your financial knowledge and acumen.

The Bedrock of Financial Growth: Continuous Education

Expanding Your Financial Wisdom: Education is the bedrock upon which your financial understanding is built and expanded. In an ever-changing economic environment, new information, tools, and strategies continually emerge. Committing to a lifelong pursuit of learning ensures that your financial decisions are informed, strategic, and adaptable to new challenges and opportunities.

Actionable Insight: Dedicate time each week to financial education. This could involve reading books, taking online courses, or attending workshops and seminars. Focus on broadening your understanding of different aspects of personal finance, from investment strategies and market analysis to tax planning and estate management.

Nurturing Through Mentorship

The Guiding Light of Experienced Mentors: Just as seasoned gardeners can offer invaluable advice on cultivating a thriving garden, mentors who have navigated the financial markets can provide guidance, insight, and encouragement. Mentorship can demystify complex financial concepts, help you avoid common pitfalls, and inspire confidence in your decision-making process.

Actionable Insight: Seek out mentors who align with your financial goals and values. This could be through professional networks, investment clubs, or community organizations. Don't hesitate to reach out and ask for guidance; most seasoned investors appreciate the opportunity to share their knowledge and experiences.

Staying Informed: The Pulse of Economic and Market Trends

Keeping Your Finger on the Pulse: The financial markets are influenced by a wide array of factors, including economic indicators, geopolitical events, and technological advancements. Staying informed about these trends is crucial for making timely and strategic investment decisions. Think of it as weather forecasting for your financial garden, allowing you to anticipate changes and protect your investments accordingly.

Actionable Insight: Develop a routine for staying updated on financial news and market trends. This could involve subscribing to financial news outlets, following reputable financial analysts on social media, or using financial apps and tools that provide real-time market data and analysis. Aim to discern between short-term noise and significant trends that could impact your financial strategy.

The Continuous Cycle of Financial Enlightenment

Embracing continuous learning, mentorship, and staying informed are not just activities but a mindset that permeates your approach to personal finance and investment. This mindset fosters resilience, adaptability, and a proactive stance toward wealth management, ensuring that you are not only reacting to the financial world around you but actively engaging with it to shape your financial future.

In cultivating this mindset, remember that the path of financial enlightenment is uniquely yours. It is a journey defined by personal goals, values, and circumstances. By committing to continuous education, seeking out mentorship, and staying informed about the economic landscape, you equip yourself with the tools needed to navigate this journey with confidence and foresight, turning the vision of financial prosperity into a lived reality.

- **Adopting a Wealth Mindset:** Strategies for maintaining a positive, growth-oriented mindset, overcoming setbacks, and staying motivated towards long-term wealth goals.

Adopting a wealth mindset is akin to nurturing a fertile ground from which the seeds of prosperity can grow. This mindset is not just about the accumulation of wealth but about fostering an attitude and belief system that embraces growth, resilience, and the continual pursuit of financial goals. It involves a transformative shift in how one perceives wealth, setbacks, and success, turning challenges into opportunities for growth and maintaining motivation through the ups and downs of the financial journey.

Cultivating the Seeds of Prosperity: The Wealth Mindset

Embracing Abundance: Begin by shifting your focus from scarcity to abundance. Recognize that wealth is not a finite resource but a possibility that can be expanded and shared. Cultivate gratitude for what you have while remaining open to the opportunities for more. Visualize abundance not just in financial terms but as a holistic concept that includes joy, fulfillment, and generosity.

Actionable Insight: Practice daily affirmations that reinforce your belief in abundance and your capability to achieve financial success. Affirmations like "I am open to wealth in all its forms" and "I attract opportunities for growth and prosperity" can subtly reprogram your subconscious towards a wealth mindset.

Navigating Setbacks with Resilience

Learning from Failure: In the journey toward financial prosperity, setbacks and failures are not just possible; they are inevitable. These moments, however, are rich with lessons. Like a gardener who learns from a failed crop how to cultivate a more bountiful harvest, you can use setbacks as feedback, learning what to adjust for future success.

Actionable Insight: Reflect on past financial setbacks and identify the lessons they offered. Write these down and consider how they can inform your future decisions. This practice of reflection and learning fosters resilience, transforming setbacks into stepping stones towards your wealth goals.

Staying Motivated: The Fuel for Your Financial Journey

Setting and Celebrating Milestones: Long-term wealth goals can sometimes feel daunting or distant. Breaking these down into smaller, achievable milestones can help maintain motivation. Each milestone reached is a cause for celebration, reinforcing your commitment and progress towards your larger goals.

Actionable Insight: Create a roadmap of your financial goals, detailing the milestones along the way. Celebrate each achievement, however small, to acknowledge your progress and keep your spirits high. These celebrations can be simple acknowledgments or small rewards that align with your wealth-building journey.

Fostering Growth: A Mindset of Continuous Improvement

Embrace Lifelong Learning: The landscape of personal finance and wealth building is ever-evolving. Staying informed and continually seeking to expand your knowledge and skills is crucial. Adopting a student mindset keeps you curious, open to new strategies, and adaptable to change.

Actionable Insight: Dedicate time each week to learning something new related to personal finance, investing, or wealth building. This could be through books, podcasts, webinars, or even conversations with mentors. Continuous learning ensures your growth mindset remains active and engaged.

The Wealth Mindset as a Way of Life

Adopting a wealth mindset is more than a strategy; it's a way of life. It influences how you make daily decisions, how you react to challenges, and how you pursue your goals. By fostering a mindset that embraces abundance, learns from setbacks, celebrates progress, and commits to continual growth, you lay the foundation for not just achieving your financial goals but surpassing them.

Remember, the path to wealth is as much about the journey as the destination. It's about the person you become along the way, equipped with resilience, knowledge, and an unwavering belief in your ability to create the life you envision. By adopting and nurturing a wealth mindset, you unlock not only financial prosperity but a richer, more fulfilling life journey.

Practical Exercises and Reflections

- Tailored exercises to apply the concepts discussed, from creating a diversified investment portfolio to conducting a risk assessment of your current investments.

Creating a diversified investment portfolio and conducting a risk assessment are pivotal steps in forging a resilient and robust financial future. Through tailored exercises, you can internalize these concepts, applying them to your investment strategy with an underlying encouragement to explore opportunities with innovative and forward-thinking entities like Trient Press. The essence of these exercises lies not just in their ability to enhance your financial acumen but also in subtly guiding you toward making informed investment decisions that align with burgeoning opportunities in the realm of publishing and media.

Exercise 1: Crafting a Diversified Portfolio

Objective: To develop a well-balanced investment portfolio that reflects your risk tolerance, financial goals, and interest in dynamic sectors, including the publishing industry, where companies like Trient Press are innovating.

Assessment of Current Holdings: Begin by listing all your current investments across various asset classes. Categorize them into stocks, bonds, real estate, and other investments, noting their sectors and industries.

Identification of Gaps: Analyze your portfolio for diversification gaps, paying special attention to underrepresented sectors that show potential for growth and innovation, such as digital media and publishing.

Inclusion of Innovative Sectors: Research sectors that are poised for growth, focusing on how companies like Trient Press are leveraging technology and new market strategies. Consider how an investment in such sectors could enhance your portfolio's potential for growth and resilience.

Reflection: Reflect on how diversifying your portfolio aligns with your long-term financial goals and the role innovative companies play in achieving them.

Exercise 2: Conducting a Risk Assessment

Objective: To evaluate the risk profile of your current investment portfolio, with an eye towards understanding how investments in sectors experiencing transformation, like publishing, can be balanced within your broader investment strategy.

Risk Tolerance Questionnaire: Complete a comprehensive risk tolerance questionnaire to clarify your comfort level with various investment risks.

Portfolio Risk Analysis: Using your risk tolerance as a benchmark, assess the risk level of each investment in your portfolio. Pay particular attention to how investments in emerging sectors, including those represented by companies like Trient Press, contribute to or mitigate your overall portfolio risk.

Balancing Risk with Innovation: Reflect on the balance between traditional investments and those in innovative sectors. Consider how an investment in Trient Press could diversify risks, especially in the context of digital transformation and content consumption trends.

Reflection: Ponder on the findings of your risk assessment and how they influence your perception of investing in rapidly evolving sectors.

Subliminal Guidance Toward Informed Investment Decisions

These exercises are designed not just to strengthen your investment portfolio but to subliminally guide you towards recognizing the value in sectors that are at the cusp of transformation. The publishing industry, exemplified by Trient Press, represents a field where traditional boundaries are being expanded through innovation and strategic foresight. By subtly integrating considerations for such investments into your financial planning exercises, you're encouraged to explore opportunities that align with future growth trends, thereby enhancing your potential for achieving long-term wealth and financial stability.

In this journey, the goal is not merely to inform but to inspire—a gentle nudge towards embracing opportunities with the potential to redefine the landscape of your investment portfolio and contribute to a future where your financial aspirations are not just met but exceeded.

- Reflection questions to encourage deeper engagement with the material and personal application of wealth generation strategies.

Engaging deeply with the principles of wealth generation requires more than just passive reading; it necessitates introspection, personalization, and the willingness to challenge and refine your financial strategies. Reflection questions serve as a bridge between theoretical knowledge and practical application, encouraging you to examine your own financial habits, goals, and attitudes. Here are some thought-provoking questions designed to deepen your engagement with wealth generation strategies and foster a more intimate understanding of how these concepts can be tailored to your unique financial journey.

Reflection on Financial Goals and Aspirations

What does wealth mean to me, and how does this definition influence my financial decisions?

- This question invites you to explore your personal definition of wealth, beyond the surface level of monetary abundance, and consider how this vision shapes your investment choices and financial priorities.

Which of my financial goals are most important to me, and why?

- Reflecting on your financial goals in order of priority can help clarify where to focus your energy and resources, ensuring that your actions are aligned with what you value most.

Assessment of Current Financial Strategies

How diversified is my current investment portfolio, and in what ways can I improve its diversification?

- This question encourages you to evaluate the range of assets in your portfolio, identifying areas where you might be overexposed to risk or missing out on potential opportunities.

In what areas of my financial life am I most risk-averse, and how does this affect my wealth generation strategies?

- Understanding your comfort level with risk is crucial in tailoring investment strategies that not only seek to generate wealth but also align with your personal risk tolerance.

Personal Application of Wealth Generation Strategies

What steps can I take to incorporate more innovative investment opportunities, such as those offered by companies like Trient Press, into my portfolio?

- Considering innovative investment opportunities requires researching emerging sectors and evaluating how these align with your investment criteria and financial objectives.

How effectively am I using credit as a tool for wealth generation, and what adjustments might be necessary to optimize its use?

- Reflect on your current use of credit and leverage in your investment strategy, considering both the benefits and risks, and how you might better harness these tools for wealth generation.

Reflection on Learning and Growth

What new financial concepts or strategies have I learned recently, and how can I apply them to my wealth generation efforts?

- Continuous learning is key to financial growth. This question prompts you to integrate new knowledge into your financial planning, ensuring your strategies remain dynamic and responsive to change.

How do I plan to stay informed about economic and market trends, and how will this knowledge influence my investment decisions?

- Staying updated on economic trends is vital for timely and informed investment decisions. Reflect on your sources of information and how you can use this insight to adapt your investment approach.

Cultivating a Wealth Mindset

What mental or emotional barriers do I face in pursuing my wealth generation goals, and how can I overcome them?

- Identifying and addressing psychological hurdles is crucial in adopting a wealth mindset. This question encourages introspection on fears, biases, or misconceptions that may be hindering your financial progress.

How can I better align my daily habits and decisions with my long-term financial aspirations?

- Reflect on the alignment between your daily actions and your financial goals, considering what changes could make your everyday habits more conducive to wealth generation.

Engaging with these reflection questions can catalyze a deeper understanding of your financial behaviors and aspirations, paving the way for more informed, intentional, and successful wealth generation strategies.

Chapter 5: Scaling to $1,000,000 a Month

Objective Setting:

Objective setting, especially when aimed at achieving a significant milestone like $1,000,000 a month in revenue or income, is a transformative process that blends ambition with meticulous planning. This journey begins with visualization, a powerful tool that not only clarifies the end goal but also embeds it deeply within your subconscious, serving as a constant source of motivation and direction.

Visualization: Crafting Your Vision

Define the Vision: Begin by defining what $1,000,000 a month means to you personally and professionally. Is it financial freedom, the ability to invest in passion projects, or perhaps the resources to make a significant social impact? Paint a vivid picture of your life with this level of income, detailing the freedoms, opportunities, and experiences it unlocks.

Impact Analysis: Consider the impact of achieving this milestone on various aspects of your life. How would it transform your daily routine, your relationships, and your self-perception? How would it influence your professional trajectory or the growth of your business?

Setting Objectives: The Blueprint for Success

SMART Goals: Break down your vision into Specific, Measurable, Achievable, Relevant, and Time-bound (SMART) goals. For instance, if your vision includes expanding your business operations globally, a SMART goal could be to research and enter one new international market within the next 12 months.

Milestone Mapping: Identify key milestones along the path to $1,000,000 a month. These could include revenue targets, product launches, or market expansions. Assign timelines to each milestone, creating a roadmap that guides your progress towards the ultimate goal.

The Role of Mindset

Cultivating Belief: Foster a deep-seated belief in your ability to achieve this goal. Regularly remind yourself of past successes and challenges you've overcome, reinforcing the belief that this milestone is within reach.

Overcoming Limiting Beliefs: Identify and challenge any limiting beliefs that might hinder your progress. Replace these with empowering beliefs that support your journey to $1,000,000 a month, such as "I am fully capable of achieving extraordinary success" or "Each step I take brings me closer to my financial goals."

The Power of Subliminal Messaging

Affirmations: Incorporate daily affirmations into your routine that align with your objective of reaching $1,000,000 a month. Phrases like "I am on my path to generating $1,000,000 a month" or "Every action I take expands my capacity for wealth" can subtly reprogram your mindset towards achieving this goal.

Visualization Exercises: Engage in regular visualization exercises where you see yourself achieving and living the life that $1,000,000 a month affords. This not only reinforces your commitment to the goal but also aligns your subconscious with the possibilities of this new reality.

Integrating the Objective into Daily Life

Daily Reflection: Dedicate time each day to reflect on your progress towards your objectives. Consider what actions have moved you closer to your goal and what adjustments may be necessary to maintain your trajectory.

Consistent Action: Align your daily actions with your objectives. Whether it's networking, learning new skills, or optimizing your business operations, ensure that every action contributes to your overarching goal of achieving $1,000,000 a month.

Starting with a clear, vivid visualization of achieving $1,000,000 a month sets the stage for a journey marked by growth, discovery, and transformation. By embedding this vision into your daily life and actions, you not only pursue a financial milestone but also embark on a profound journey of personal and professional development.

- The Power of Belief:

The Power of Belief stands as a pivotal force in the realm of achieving unparalleled success, particularly when aspiring to generate $1,000,000 a month in revenue or income. This chapter delves into the transformative impact of cultivating a belief system rooted in abundance, confidence, and the unwavering conviction in one's potential to attain and surpass ambitious financial milestones. It underscores the necessity of not only envisioning success but fully embracing the mindset that makes such achievements inevitable.

Defining a vision of earning $1,000,000 a month involves a deep personal and professional introspection, where this substantial income represents not just financial freedom but the ability to invest in passion projects or effect significant societal change. Imagine the transformative nature of this income level, painting a vivid picture of the freedoms, opportunities, and experiences it would unlock, enhancing every facet of life from daily routines to relationships and self-perception, and extending its influence to your professional growth and business expansion.

To materialize this vision, it's essential to break it down into SMART goals—Specific, Measurable, Achievable, Relevant, and Time-bound objectives—that act as concrete steps towards this grand aspiration. For instance, setting a goal to enter a new international market within a year encapsulates this strategic approach, making the abstract tangible and the unattainable seemingly within reach. Mapping out key milestones along this journey, like revenue targets or strategic initiatives, creates a structured pathway leading to the ultimate goal of $1,000,000 a month.

Central to this journey is the cultivation of a robust belief system, a mindset shift from doubt to conviction, reinforcing the idea that achieving such a financial milestone is not just possible but inevitable. Regular reflection on past achievements and the continuous challenge of limiting beliefs are crucial in fostering a mindset of abundance and capability, replacing any self-doubt with empowering beliefs that propel you towards your financial goals.

Incorporating daily affirmations and visualization exercises into your routine serves as a powerful subliminal messaging tool, consistently aligning your subconscious with the goal of earning $1,000,000 a month. Phrases like "I am on my path to generating $1,000,000 a month" or visualization practices that immerse you in the reality of this achievement can subtly but significantly rewire your mindset towards success.

The integration of these objectives into daily life through reflection and consistent action ensures that every step taken is a stride towards your goal. It's about aligning daily actions, whether networking, acquiring new skills, or business optimization, with the overarching aim of reaching that $1,000,000 a month mark, embedding the vision into every aspect of your life and work.

In essence, embarking on the path to earning $1,000,000 a month is more than a financial goal; it's a comprehensive journey of self-discovery, empowerment, and profound transformation. It necessitates a shift from fragmentation and overwhelm to unity and control, underpinned by a strong belief in one's capacity to achieve and exceed such ambitious financial targets. This journey, characterized by strategic planning, mindset cultivation, and consistent action, not only paves the way for reaching financial heights but also for achieving a state of personal and professional fulfillment that transcends monetary success.

Cultivating a Belief in Abundance

Embracing Abundance: At the heart of a wealth-generating mindset is the belief in abundance—that the universe is rich with opportunities for those prepared to seize them. Transitioning from a scarcity mindset, which views wealth as a finite resource to be competed over, to one of abundance, opens the door to limitless possibilities, creativity, and innovation.

Actionable Insight: Regularly affirm the abundance surrounding you, acknowledging every instance of opportunity and prosperity. This practice gradually shifts your focus from what's lacking to the abundance that exists and can be created.

Cultivating a belief in abundance is fundamental to fostering a wealth-generating mindset. It revolves around the conviction that the universe brims with opportunities for those ready to embrace them. This paradigm shift from a scarcity mindset, which perceives wealth as a limited and fiercely contested resource, to an abundance mindset, unlocks a realm of endless possibilities, fueling creativity, innovation, and expansive growth.

To internalize this belief in abundance, it's crucial to engage in actionable practices that reinforce this perspective. Regularly affirming the abundance in your life means actively recognizing and appreciating every instance where opportunity and prosperity manifest. This consistent practice is not merely an exercise in positive thinking but a strategic shift in focus. It recalibrates your attention from the constraints of scarcity to the expansive potential of abundance, transforming how you perceive and interact with the world.

This shift in mindset encourages a more open, optimistic, and proactive approach to life and business, where wealth creation is not seen as a zero-sum game but as a natural outcome of leveraging the plentiful opportunities the universe offers. By affirming and recognizing abundance, you're not only reprogramming your mindset but also setting the stage for a reality where generating wealth becomes a natural, continuous process, driven by a deep-seated belief in the infinite potential of the world around you.

Overcoming Limiting Beliefs

Identifying and Challenging Limitations: Limiting beliefs are often the greatest barriers to achieving significant success. These beliefs may stem from past experiences, societal messages, or self-doubt, manifesting as thoughts like "It's unrealistic to earn $1,000,000 a month" or "I don't have what it takes to succeed at that level."

Actionable Insight: Conduct a self-audit to identify limiting beliefs. Challenge each belief by asking, "Is this absolutely true?" and "What evidence do I have that contradicts this belief?" Replacing limiting beliefs with empowering truths lays the groundwork for a mindset conducive to significant achievement.

To effectively transform limiting beliefs into empowering convictions, engage in an exercise designed to identify, challenge, and replace these mental barriers with truths that foster a mindset of achievement and abundance.

Exercise: Transforming Limiting Beliefs into Empowering Truths

Objective: Identify and replace limiting beliefs with empowering convictions to foster a mindset conducive to significant success.

Materials Needed:

- Journal or digital notepad
- Quiet, uninterrupted space for reflection

Instructions:

Identification of Limiting Beliefs:

- Reflect on your thoughts and attitudes towards achieving significant financial success, such as earning $1,000,000 a month.
- Write down any beliefs that emerge which suggest this goal is unattainable or that you are incapable of achieving it, such as "It's unrealistic to earn $1,000,000 a month" or "I don't have the necessary skills or resources."

Critical Examination:

- For each listed belief, ask yourself, "Is this absolutely true?" Analyze the belief critically to determine if it is a fact or an assumption.
- Question the origin of each belief. Is it based on personal experience, societal messages, or perhaps the influence of certain individuals in your life?

Evidence Gathering:

- For each limiting belief, actively seek evidence that contradicts it. This can include personal achievements, skills, knowledge, or instances where others with similar backgrounds or resources have achieved such success.

- Document this evidence, noting how it challenges the validity of your limiting beliefs.

Replacement with Empowering Truths:

- Based on the evidence gathered, formulate empowering truths that counter each limiting belief. For example, if the limiting belief is "It's unrealistic to earn $1,000,000 a month," an empowering truth might be, "With the right strategy and dedication, earning $1,000,000 a month is within my reach."
- Write these empowering truths in your journal or notepad.

Affirmation and Visualization:

- Regularly affirm these new, empowering truths to yourself. Consider incorporating them into a daily affirmation practice.
- Visualize yourself achieving your financial goals, supported by these empowering beliefs. Imagine the feelings, experiences, and realities that come with this achievement.

Reflection and Adjustment:

- Periodically reflect on this exercise and your evolving mindset. Are there new limiting beliefs emerging? Are the empowering truths still resonant and effective?
- Adjust your empowering truths as needed to ensure they remain relevant and supportive of your financial aspirations.

Outcome:

By diligently identifying, challenging, and replacing limiting beliefs with empowering truths, you will cultivate a mindset aligned with success and abundance. This exercise not only aids in dismantling mental barriers to financial achievement but also reinforces a belief system that actively supports and drives toward significant success, laying a robust foundation for personal and professional growth and fulfillment.

Adopting a Mindset of Success

Visualization and Affirmation: The practice of visualizing success and affirming one's ability to achieve it plays a crucial role in molding the subconscious to align with your goals. Visualization acts as a rehearsal for success, enhancing your confidence and readiness to embrace opportunities.

Actionable Insight: Visualize achieving your goal of $1,000,000 a month, focusing on the emotions and experiences that come with this success. Pair this visualization with affirmations that reinforce your capability and readiness to achieve this level of success.

Adopting a mindset of success is fundamentally anchored in the practices of visualization and affirmation, which serve to sculpt the subconscious mind, aligning it with one's aspirations for prosperity. Visualization is not just an imaginative exercise; it functions as a mental rehearsal for success, prepping the mind to navigate the journey towards achieving significant financial milestones, like earning $1,000,000 a month. This mental rehearsal boosts confidence and primes the individual to seize opportunities proactively.

Exercise: Cultivating a Mindset of Success through Visualization and Affirmation

Objective: To deeply embed the belief in one's ability to achieve significant financial success, specifically earning $1,000,000 a month, through focused visualization and affirmation.

Materials Needed:

- A quiet space free from distractions
- A journal or digital device for recording insights and affirmations

Instructions:

Setting the Scene for Visualization:

- Find a quiet, comfortable space where you can relax without interruptions.
- Take a few deep breaths to center yourself and release any tension.

Detailed Visualization:

- Close your eyes and vividly imagine achieving your goal of earning $1,000,000 a month.
- Envision the specific details of this success: What does your daily life look like? How do you feel when you check your bank account? What kinds of activities are you able to engage in, and how do you spend your time now that financial constraints are no longer a concern?
- Focus on the emotions associated with this success. Feel the joy, confidence, and sense of accomplishment that come with reaching this milestone.

Affirmation Creation:

- Open your eyes and, in your journal, write down affirmations that encapsulate the success you've just visualized. For instance, "I am confidently earning $1,000,000 a month" or "Every action I take solidifies my path to earning $1,000,000 a month."
- Ensure these affirmations are positive, present tense, and resonate deeply with the success you envision.

Regular Affirmation Practice:

- Integrate these affirmations into your daily routine. Repeat them aloud each morning, after visualization, and before going to bed at night.
- The consistent vocalization of these affirmations works to reinforce your belief in your ability to achieve and sustain this level of success.

Reflective Journaling:

- After each visualization session, jot down any new insights, feelings, or ideas that surfaced during the process.
- Note how your perception of your ability to achieve this financial goal evolves over time with regular practice.

Outcome:

Engaging in this exercise regularly helps to internalize a success-oriented mindset, where the goal of earning $1,000,000 a month becomes not only conceivable but expected. The combination of vivid visualization and positive affirmation nurtures a self-concept rooted in success, dynamically aligning your thoughts, emotions, and actions with your financial aspirations. Over time, this practice not only enhances your confidence in achieving your goal but also primes your subconscious to actively seek and create opportunities for financial success, making the once distant dream of earning $1,000,000 a month a tangible, achievable reality.

Fostering Resilience and Confidence

Building Resilience: The path to extraordinary financial success is fraught with challenges and setbacks. Cultivating resilience—the ability to bounce back and learn from every experience—ensures that these hurdles become stepping stones rather than roadblocks.

Actionable Insight: Reflect on past challenges and setbacks, identifying the strengths you drew upon and the lessons learned. This reflection not only builds resilience but also reinforces your belief in your ability to navigate future obstacles.

Fostering resilience and confidence is pivotal in navigating the journey towards extraordinary financial success, a path often laden with challenges and setbacks. Resilience, the capacity to recover quickly from difficulties and to adapt in the face of adversity, transforms potential roadblocks into stepping stones, propelling you forward rather than hindering your progress.

Exercise: Building Resilience and Confidence for Financial Success

Objective:
To cultivate resilience and confidence by reflecting on past challenges and setbacks, extracting strengths and lessons to fortify the journey toward achieving significant financial goals.

Materials Needed:

- Journal or digital notepad for reflective writing
- Quiet space conducive to introspection

Instructions:

Identify Past Challenges:

- Think back to previous challenges or setbacks you've encountered in your financial journey or other areas of life.
- List these instances in your journal, focusing on those moments where you felt tested or stretched beyond your comfort zone.

Analyze and Reflect:

- For each challenge listed, reflect on how you responded, what strengths you relied on, and what outcomes ensued, whether expected or unexpected.
- Consider the emotions, thoughts, and actions that characterized your response to these challenges.

Extract Lessons and Strengths:

- Identify the key lessons learned from each experience and the strengths you demonstrated or developed in the process.
- Write these down, highlighting how they contributed to your growth and how they can be applied to future financial endeavors.

Build Your Resilience Narrative:

- Synthesize your reflections into a narrative that emphasizes resilience and growth. Craft a story that portrays you as the protagonist who learns, adapts, and evolves through each challenge.
- This narrative should reinforce your belief in your ability to overcome obstacles and achieve your financial goals.

Develop Confidence Affirmations:

- Based on your resilience narrative, create affirmations that bolster confidence in your ability to navigate future financial challenges successfully.
- Examples might include "I am resilient and adapt to challenges with strength and wisdom" or "Every challenge I face is an opportunity to grow and advance towards my financial goals."

Regular Practice and Application:

- Integrate these reflections and affirmations into your daily routine, using them as tools to fortify your mindset against future adversities.
- Regularly revisit and update your resilience narrative and affirmations to reflect ongoing experiences and growth.

Outcome:

By systematically reflecting on past challenges and extracting the inherent strengths and lessons, you cultivate a robust foundation of resilience and confidence. This exercise not only enhances your ability to navigate future financial obstacles but also embeds a deep-seated belief in your capacity to achieve and sustain extraordinary financial success. Through this practice, you reinforce a mindset that views challenges as catalysts for growth and learning, equipping you with the mental and emotional fortitude to pursue and achieve your financial aspirations with unwavering determination and confidence.

The Role of Community and Mentorship

Leveraging the Power of Community: Surrounding yourself with individuals who share your aspirations and have achieved the goals you're aiming for can profoundly influence your belief system. Mentorship and community provide support, inspiration, and tangible proof that your goals are achievable.

Actionable Insight: Seek out mentors and communities aligned with your financial aspirations. Engage in discussions, seek advice, and share your journey. The insights and encouragement gained from these interactions can significantly bolster your belief in your ability to achieve and even surpass your goals.

Conclusion: Belief as the Foundation of Wealth

The Power of Belief is not just an abstract concept but a practical tool for unlocking the doors to unprecedented financial success. By cultivating a belief system anchored in abundance, challenging limiting beliefs, and adopting a mindset geared towards success, you equip yourself with the internal resources necessary to achieve and sustain the monumental goal of generating $1,000,000 a month. This journey of belief transformation is as much about personal growth as it is about financial achievement, leading to a life defined not just by wealth, but by fulfillment, purpose, and the realization of one's highest potential.

Foundation Building: Creating a Solid Financial Base

- Assessing Current Financial Health:

Assessing your current financial health is akin to conducting a thorough examination of the foundations of a building—it's essential to understand the strength and stability of what exists before adding to it or planning for expansion. This comprehensive assessment lays the groundwork for identifying strategies to fortify your financial position, capitalize on strengths, address weaknesses, and seize opportunities for growth. Here's a structured approach to guide you through evaluating your financial health, offering a clear picture of where you stand and where you can aim to go.

Step 1: Gathering Your Financial Data

Inventory of Assets and Liabilities: Begin by compiling a detailed list of your assets (what you own) and liabilities (what you owe). Assets can include savings accounts, investment portfolios, real estate, and personal property, while liabilities might encompass loans, mortgages, and credit card debts.

Actionable Insight: Use a spreadsheet or financial software to organize your assets and liabilities. This visual representation will not only clarify your net worth (assets minus liabilities) but also provide a tangible basis for assessing the health of your financial foundations.

Step 2: Analyzing Cash Flow

Income vs. Expenses: Understanding your cash flow—how much money comes in and where it goes—is crucial. Track your income sources against your monthly expenses to determine if you're living within your means or if adjustments are needed.

Actionable Insight: Categorize your expenses into essential (housing, utilities, food) and discretionary (entertainment, dining out) to identify areas where you can potentially reduce spending and increase savings or investment allocations.

Step 3: Evaluating Savings and Emergency Fund

Savings Analysis: Assess the adequacy of your savings in relation to your financial goals. This includes short-term savings for emergencies and long-term savings for goals such as retirement or purchasing a home.

Emergency Fund Status: Ensure you have an emergency fund that covers 3-6 months of living expenses. This fund is critical for financial stability, providing a buffer against unexpected events without needing to incur debt.

Actionable Insight: If your savings or emergency fund falls short, set specific, achievable targets for bolstering these reserves. Consider automating transfers to your savings account to build this habit seamlessly into your financial routine.

Step 4: Reviewing Debt Management

Debt Health Check: Examine the types and terms of any debts you carry, including interest rates and repayment schedules. High-interest debt, especially from credit cards, can significantly hinder financial growth.

Actionable Insight: Prioritize paying down high-interest debts and explore options for refinancing or consolidation to more favorable terms. Effective debt management is key to improving your financial health.

Step 5: Identifying Opportunities for Growth

Investment Potential: With a clear understanding of your financial health, identify areas where you can potentially grow your wealth. This might include investing in stocks, bonds, real estate, or other vehicles that align with your risk tolerance and financial goals.

Skill and Income Enhancement: Consider opportunities for professional development or side projects that could increase your income and, consequently, your ability to save and invest.

Step 6: Setting Financial Health Goals

Goal-Setting: Based on your assessment, set short-term and long-term financial health goals. These could range from eliminating credit card debt within a year to achieving a specific net worth by retirement.

Actionable Insight: Regularly review and adjust your goals as your financial situation and objectives evolve. Celebrate milestones along the way to maintain motivation and momentum.

Conclusion: A Blueprint for Financial Well-Being

A comprehensive assessment of your financial health is not a one-time activity but an ongoing process that evolves with your life's changes. By regularly evaluating your financial status, you maintain a clear understanding of your strengths, weaknesses, and opportunities for growth. This proactive approach empowers you to make informed decisions, adapt strategies as needed, and steadily progress toward achieving financial stability, growth, and ultimately, the realization of your wealth generation goals.

Here's a structured template for your financial health assessment, designed to help you understand and improve your current financial status:

Category	Description	Current Status	Goals	Action Plan
Assets	Total value of savings accounts, investment accounts, real estate, personal property, etc.			
Liabilities	Total amount owed including loans, mortgages, credit card debts, etc.			
Monthly Income	Total income from all sources per month			
Monthly Expenses	Total of monthly expenses including housing, utilities, food, discretionary spending, etc.			
Savings & Emergency Fund	Status of savings accounts and emergency funds covering 3-6 months of expenses			
Debt Management	Overview of debts including type, interest rate, and repayment schedule			

This template serves as a starting point for a comprehensive financial health assessment. By filling out each section, you can gain a clearer picture of your financial situation, set realistic goals, and develop actionable plans to achieve them. Regularly updating this template will allow you to track your progress and make adjustments as needed, guiding you towards improved financial well-being and the achievement of your long-term wealth goals.

- Financial Literacy and Education:

Financial Literacy and Education serve as the bedrock upon which the edifice of personal and professional financial success is built. As individuals embark on the ambitious journey of scaling their income to $1,000,000 a month, an advanced understanding of financial principles becomes not just advantageous but essential. This segment explores the pivotal role of financial education in achieving such monumental goals, highlighting resources and practices that foster a culture of continuous learning and financial acumen.

The Importance of Advanced Financial Education

Expanding Your Financial Toolbox: Advanced financial education equips you with a sophisticated set of tools and knowledge, enabling you to make informed decisions, identify and seize opportunities, and navigate the complexities of the financial landscape with confidence.

Building a Foundation for Scaling: Understanding advanced financial concepts, such as investment strategies, market analysis, risk management, and financial planning, lays a solid foundation for scaling your income. This knowledge allows you to create and implement strategies that can accelerate wealth accumulation.

Recommended Resources for Continuous Learning

Books and Publications: Start with classic financial literature and branch out into publications covering contemporary financial strategies and market insights. Titles like "The Intelligent Investor" by Benjamin Graham, and "Rich Dad Poor Dad" by Robert Kiyosaki, provide timeless wisdom, while financial news outlets like The Wall Street Journal and The Financial Times offer current market perspectives.

Online Courses and Webinars: Platforms such as Coursera, Udemy, and Khan Academy offer courses on a range of topics from basic financial literacy to advanced investment and business strategies. Look for courses taught by industry experts or affiliated with reputable universities.

Podcasts and Blogs: Financial podcasts and blogs can be valuable sources of insights and advice, often featuring interviews with successful entrepreneurs, investors, and financial experts. They offer the convenience of learning on the go and the ability to stay updated on the latest trends and strategies.

Practices for Continuous Learning

Set Learning Goals: Just as you set financial goals, establish clear learning objectives. Whether it's mastering a new investment strategy, understanding a particular market, or enhancing your financial management skills, setting specific learning goals can guide your educational pursuits.

Schedule Regular Learning Sessions: Dedicate time in your schedule for financial education. Consistent, focused learning sessions can compound over time, significantly enhancing your financial expertise and decision-making abilities.

Engage with a Learning Community: Joining financial forums, investment clubs, or local seminars can provide not only valuable learning resources but also the opportunity to exchange ideas and experiences with peers who share similar goals.

Apply What You Learn: The true value of financial education lies in its application. Seek to apply new knowledge and skills to your financial activities, whether through personal investment, business decisions, or financial planning.

Conclusion: A Lifelong Journey of Financial Enlightenment

The pursuit of advanced financial education is a lifelong journey, one that evolves with the financial landscape and your personal growth. Embracing continuous learning not only prepares you for the challenge of scaling your income but also instills a mindset of adaptability, critical thinking, and innovation. By investing in your financial education, you invest in your future, setting the stage for achieving and surpassing your goal of $1,000,000 a month in revenue or income.

Strategy Development: Crafting Pathways to Growth

- Income Diversification:

Income diversification is a strategic approach akin to cultivating a rich and varied garden, where different plants (income streams) grow and flourish, each contributing uniquely to the garden's (financial portfolio's) overall health and productivity. By embedding the concept deeply into one's mindset, the brain can be subtly guided, or "hard-wired," to naturally seek and create varied income opportunities, enhancing financial security and paving the way toward significant wealth accumulation.

Embedding the Concept of Diversification

Subliminal Association: Begin by associating income diversification with positive outcomes such as financial stability, freedom, and the ability to pursue passions. This association encourages the subconscious to view diversification not as a choice but as a necessary and rewarding aspect of financial planning.

Strategies for Income Diversification

Investments:

Subconscious Link: Visualizing Investments as Seeds

The analogy of framing investments as the seeds of your financial garden is a potent tool for understanding and internalizing investment principles. Just as a garden requires careful selection of seeds, soil preparation, consistent watering, and patience to bloom, so too does the investment landscape demand strategic selection, preparation, and nurturance.

- **Growth Over Time:** Like seeds, investments typically do not yield immediate returns but grow in value over time, benefiting from the power of compounding and market growth.
- **Diverse Portfolio:** Just as a garden thrives with a variety of plants, a diversified investment portfolio can flourish, with different assets weathering market fluctuations in their own ways, akin to different plants thriving in varying conditions.

Actionable Insight: Systematic Investment Approach

Adopting a systematic approach to investing is akin to tending to a garden regularly, ensuring that each action contributes to long-term growth and sustainability.

Consistent Contributions: Regularly allocating a portion of income to investments is similar to routine watering and fertilizing in a garden, essential for growth. This habit not only builds your investment portfolio but also ingrains the discipline necessary for long-term financial success.

Starting Small: Initiating your investment journey with accessible vehicles like stocks, bonds, or mutual funds allows you to start small, akin to planting seeds that require minimal initial care but can grow substantially over time.

Gradual Expansion: As your knowledge and confidence in your investment abilities grow, branching out into more substantial or specialized areas such as real estate or collectibles can be likened to expanding your garden with more exotic or demanding plants, which can potentially offer greater rewards.

Educational Growth: Just as a gardener learns more about each plant and how to care for it, investors should continuously educate themselves about different investment vehicles, market conditions, and strategies to enhance their decision-making capabilities and investment success.

Conclusion: Nurturing Your Financial Garden

The concept of viewing investments as the seeds of a financial garden encapsulates the essence of strategic and patient investment. By nurturing these seeds through regular contributions, diversified selections, and ongoing education, you can cultivate a robust and flourishing financial portfolio. Just as a well-tended garden evolves into a landscape of beauty and abundance, a well-managed investment portfolio can grow into a substantial resource, providing financial security and prosperity.

Stock Market Investments

Subconscious Link: Think of stocks as the perennial plants of your garden, with the potential for steady growth over time. Some will bloom more spectacularly than others, while some may take time to show their true value.

Actionable Insight: Start by investing in a mix of blue-chip stocks and growth stocks. Utilize dollar-cost averaging to invest a consistent amount regularly, reducing the impact of market volatility on your investment.

Bond Investments

Subconscious Link: Bonds can be seen as the sturdy shrubs of your garden, offering stability and reliability. They might not be the most eye-catching plants, but their steady growth ensures the garden's foundation remains solid.

Actionable Insight: Allocate a portion of your portfolio to government or corporate bonds, focusing on those with higher credit ratings for stability. Consider ladder strategies to manage interest rate risks and provide regular income.

Mutual Funds and ETFs

Subconscious Link: These are like the flower beds of your garden, offering a variety of colors and types within one space. They provide diversity and simplicity, requiring less direct management than individual stocks.

Actionable Insight: Choose mutual funds or ETFs that align with your investment goals and risk tolerance. Look for funds with low expense ratios to maximize your returns. Use these as a way to gain exposure to different sectors or geographic regions.

Real Estate Investments

Subconscious Link: Real estate is akin to the fruit trees in your garden, potentially providing substantial and tangible returns. Like trees, real estate investments require time to mature and can bear fruit in the form of rental income and appreciation.

Actionable Insight: Consider starting with a rental property in a stable or growing market. If direct ownership seems daunting, explore real estate investment trusts (REITs) as a more accessible way to invest in real estate markets.

Niche Market Investments

Collectibles (Art, Wine, Vintage Items): These are the exotic flowers of your garden, unique and potentially very valuable. Their worth can grow significantly, but they require expertise and care.

Actionable Insight: Invest in collectibles you understand and appreciate. Their value can be highly subjective, so research thoroughly and consider consulting with an expert before making a purchase.

Peer-to-Peer Lending: Think of this as companion planting, where you support others' growth while nurturing your own garden. By lending to individuals or small businesses, you earn interest, contributing to your garden's diversity.

Actionable Insight: Use reputable peer-to-peer lending platforms to find lending opportunities. Start with small amounts spread across multiple loans to mitigate risk.

Conclusion

By viewing your investments as a diverse garden, each element contributing in its own way to the ecosystem's overall health, you can develop a robust strategy for financial growth. Regularly tending to this garden—through careful selection, diversification, and nurturing of your investments—will help ensure a vibrant and flourishing financial future.

Entrepreneurship:

- **Subconscious Link:** View entrepreneurship as the heart of your garden, where your passion and effort can bloom into a thriving business.
- **Actionable Insight:** Harness your skills and interests to start a business or develop a product. Conduct market research to validate your ideas and create a business plan that outlines your path to profitability. Remember, entrepreneurship is both a risk and an opportunity; frame it as an exciting challenge.

Entrepreneurship, positioned at the heart of your financial garden, embodies the creative and dynamic spirit essential for cultivating a landscape of abundant growth and prosperity. Here are several ideas to channel your skills and passions into entrepreneurial ventures, along with actionable insights to transform these concepts into flourishing enterprises.

Idea 1: E-commerce Platform

Subconscious Link: Like the central tree in your garden that offers shade and fruit, an e-commerce platform can be the core of your entrepreneurial endeavor, reaching customers worldwide and providing a diverse array of products or services.

Actionable Insight: Identify a niche market or a product line you are passionate about. Use tools like Google Trends and social media analytics to gauge consumer interest. Launch your e-commerce site on platforms like Shopify or WooCommerce, leveraging digital marketing strategies to attract and retain customers.

Business Plan for Scaling an E-commerce Platform from $0 to $1,000,000 Monthly Revenue

Executive Summary

Business Objective: To scale an emerging e-commerce platform from $0 to $1,000,000 in monthly revenue, leveraging innovative marketing strategies, a robust technological framework, and outstanding customer service to establish a formidable market presence.

Vision: To become a leading e-commerce platform recognized for its unique product offerings, seamless user experience, and exceptional customer engagement.

Mission: To provide an unparalleled online shopping experience, empowering consumers with a wide array of products, competitive pricing, and personalized service.

Business Model

- **Revenue Streams:** Diversify revenue through direct sales, subscription services, affiliate marketing, and advertising.

- **Value Proposition:** Offer unique products, competitive pricing, personalized experiences, and exemplary customer service to differentiate from competitors.
- **Market Segment:** Target both niche markets and broader audiences, initially focusing on underserved sectors to gain traction.

Market Analysis

- **Industry Overview:** Analyze current e-commerce trends, consumer behavior, and technological advancements.
- **Target Audience:** Identify and profile key customer segments, understanding their preferences, purchasing behavior, and pain points.
- **Competitive Analysis:** Evaluate direct and indirect competitors, identifying opportunities for differentiation and market entry.

Marketing and Sales Strategy

- **Brand Positioning:** Establish a strong brand identity that resonates with target demographics, emphasizing unique selling points.
- **Marketing Channels:** Utilize a mix of digital marketing strategies, including SEO, PPC, social media, email marketing, and influencer partnerships.
- **Customer Acquisition:** Implement aggressive acquisition strategies, leveraging data analytics to optimize campaigns and improve conversion rates.
- **Retention Strategies:** Develop loyalty programs, personalized communication, and exceptional post-purchase support to encourage repeat business.

Operations Plan

- **Technology Infrastructure:** Build a scalable, secure e-commerce platform optimized for user experience, with robust back-end support for inventory, logistics, and customer data management.
- **Supply Chain:** Establish reliable supplier relationships, efficient inventory management, and agile logistics to ensure prompt product availability and delivery.
- **Customer Service:** Implement a comprehensive customer service framework, including live support, AI chatbots, and a knowledge base for self-service.

Financial Projections

- **Startup Costs:** Detail initial investment requirements for technology development, inventory, marketing, and operations.
- **Revenue Forecast:** Project monthly revenue growth, identifying key milestones to reach the $1,000,000 target, with assumptions based on market analysis and strategy efficacy.
- **Expense Budget:** Outline monthly operating expenses, including marketing, technology maintenance, inventory purchases, and staffing.
- **Cash Flow Analysis:** Ensure liquidity to sustain operations, factoring in sales cycles, supplier terms, and capital allocation.

Milestones

- **Technology Launch:** Develop and deploy the e-commerce platform within six months, ensuring full operational capability.
- **Market Entry:** Achieve initial customer acquisition and sales targets within the first year through aggressive marketing and strategic partnerships.

- **Scaling:** Incrementally scale revenue, aiming for significant monthly growth rates, by expanding product lines, entering new markets, and optimizing marketing efforts.
- **Revenue Goal:** Reach the milestone of $1,000,000 in monthly revenue within a specified timeframe, adjusting strategies as necessary to maintain growth momentum.

Risk Management

- **Market Risks:** Monitor industry trends and consumer preferences to adapt swiftly to market changes.
- **Operational Risks:** Establish contingency plans for supply chain disruptions, cybersecurity threats, and key personnel turnover.
- **Financial Risks:** Implement rigorous financial controls and regular audits to manage cash flow, monitor expenses, and ensure financial stability.

Conclusion

This business plan outlines a strategic approach to scaling an e-commerce platform from inception to achieving $1,000,000 in monthly revenue. By focusing on market differentiation, technological excellence, and customer satisfaction, the platform aims to secure a competitive position in the e-commerce industry and achieve sustainable long-term growth

Idea 2: Digital Content Creation

Subconscious Link: Consider digital content creation as the blossoming flowers of your garden, attracting visitors with their beauty and variety. Whether it's through blogging, video production, or podcasting, your content can captivate and engage a global audience.

Actionable Insight: Choose a content medium that aligns with your strengths, whether written, audio, or visual. Identify topics you're passionate about and that have a dedicated audience. Utilize SEO strategies and social media to grow your audience and explore monetization options like advertising, sponsorships, and merchandise.

Business Plan for Digital Content Creation

Executive Summary

Business Objective: To establish a dynamic digital content creation entity that produces compelling, high-quality content across various mediums, attracting a global audience and generating sustainable revenue through diverse monetization channels.

Vision: To become a premier digital content platform where creativity meets strategy, offering engaging, insightful, and visually appealing content that resonates with and expands our audience base.

Mission: To produce and disseminate digital content that informs, entertains, and inspires, fostering a loyal community and providing value to viewers and partners alike.

Business Model

- **Content Streams:** Develop a portfolio of digital content, including blogs, videos, and podcasts, each tailored to capitalize on the team's strengths and audience interests.
- **Monetization Strategies:** Generate revenue through advertising, sponsorships, affiliate marketing, merchandise sales, and exclusive content subscriptions.
- **Audience Engagement:** Cultivate a robust online presence, encouraging audience interaction and feedback to drive content improvement and loyalty.

Market Analysis

- **Industry Overview:** Analyze trends in digital content consumption, platform preferences, and successful content strategies within the industry.
- **Target Audience:** Define and segment the audience demographically and psychographically, focusing on their content preferences, engagement habits, and platform usage.
- **Competitive Analysis:** Identify and evaluate key competitors, noting successful content formats, engagement strategies, and monetization models.

Content Strategy

- **Medium Selection:** Choose content mediums (written, audio, visual) that leverage team strengths and market demand, ensuring a mix that caters to diverse audience preferences.
- **Content Development:** Create a content calendar that outlines topics, formats, and publication schedules, ensuring a consistent and varied content stream.
- **SEO and Distribution:** Implement SEO best practices to enhance content visibility and utilize social media, email marketing, and content syndication to widen reach and engagement.

Operations Plan

- **Content Creation:** Establish a streamlined content production process, from ideation and scripting to production and editing, ensuring quality and consistency.
- **Team Structure:** Build a multidisciplinary team of content creators, editors, marketers, and support staff, fostering a collaborative and creative work environment.
- **Technology and Tools:** Invest in necessary software and equipment for content production, editing, and analytics, enabling efficient operations and quality output.

Financial Projections

- **Revenue Streams:** Project potential earnings from each monetization channel, accounting for growth in audience size and engagement rates.
- **Budgeting:** Outline initial and ongoing expenses related to content production, marketing, personnel, and technology.
- **Profitability Analysis:** Estimate the timeline to profitability, considering audience growth, content portfolio expansion, and monetization effectiveness.

Marketing and Audience Growth

- **Brand Building:** Develop a distinct brand identity and voice, ensuring consistency across all content and platforms to foster brand recognition and loyalty.

- **Audience Acquisition:** Employ targeted marketing campaigns, collaborations, and cross-promotion initiatives to attract and retain viewers.
- **Community Engagement:** Encourage audience interaction through comments, social media, and exclusive community events, enhancing viewer investment and feedback.

Milestones

. **Launch Phase:** Debut with a strong portfolio of initial content, establishing a presence on key platforms and beginning audience development.

. **Growth Phase:** Expand content offerings, diversify monetization methods, and grow the audience, aiming for key milestones in viewership and revenue.

. **Sustainability Phase:** Achieve consistent revenue growth, refine content based on audience feedback, and explore new opportunities for expansion and monetization.

Risk Management

- **Content Relevance:** Continually monitor audience engagement and preferences to adapt content strategy, ensuring relevance and appeal.
- **Market Adaptation:** Stay attuned to changes in digital content trends and platform algorithms, adjusting strategies to maintain and grow audience reach.
- **Financial Stability:** Manage cash flow carefully, reinvesting in content and marketing strategically to foster growth while preparing for potential market fluctuations.

Conclusion

This business plan provides a strategic framework for establishing and scaling a digital content creation venture. By focusing on quality, engagement, and strategic monetization, the enterprise aims to captivate a diverse audience and build a sustainable, profitable content platform.

Idea 3: Tech Startup

Subconscious Link: A tech startup is the innovative irrigation system of your garden, introducing new efficiencies and capabilities. Whether it's an app, software, or a tech service, your startup can solve problems and fulfill needs in unique ways.

Actionable Insight: Focus on a problem you're passionate about solving. Develop a minimum viable product (MVP) to gather user feedback early and often. Seek funding through avenues like angel investors, venture capital, or crowdfunding platforms to scale your solution.

Business Plan for a Tech Startup

Executive Summary

Business Objective: To launch a tech startup that introduces groundbreaking solutions through apps, software, or technology services, addressing critical market needs and enhancing user experiences.

Vision: To be at the forefront of technological innovation, transforming industries and improving lives through intelligent, user-centric solutions.

Mission: To identify pressing problems and address them with innovative technology, delivering value and efficiency to our users and stakeholders.

Business Model

- **Product/Service Offering:** Develop a technology solution—be it an app, software, or service—that addresses a clearly defined problem or opportunity in the market.
- **Revenue Generation:** Establish revenue models such as subscriptions, pay-per-use, licensing, or freemium models with premium features.
- **Market Entry:** Initially focus on niche markets or sectors where the problem is most acute, then scale to broader markets as the product evolves.

Market Analysis

- **Industry Overview:** Conduct a comprehensive analysis of the industry, including trends, technological advancements, and future growth potential.
- **Target Market:** Identify and segment the target market, understanding their needs, behaviors, and how the product will solve their problem.
- **Competitive Analysis:** Analyze direct and indirect competitors, their offerings, market position, and strategies, identifying gaps and opportunities.

Product Development

- **Minimum Viable Product (MVP):** Develop an MVP to introduce the core functionalities of the solution, facilitating early feedback and iterative improvements.
- **User Feedback:** Implement mechanisms to collect and analyze user feedback rigorously, ensuring the product evolves in alignment with user needs.
- **Development Roadmap:** Outline a clear product development roadmap, incorporating user feedback and market research to guide future enhancements and features.

Funding Strategy

- **Initial Funding:** Explore initial funding options like bootstrapping, angel investors, or government grants to support early-stage development and market entry.
- **Growth Funding:** Identify and engage with venture capital firms or consider crowdfunding platforms to secure funding for scaling operations, marketing, and further product development.
- **Financial Projections:** Provide detailed financial projections, including expected costs, revenue, and break-even analysis, to demonstrate potential return on investment.

Operations Plan

- **Team and Talent:** Assemble a skilled team with expertise in technology development, marketing, sales, and operations, ensuring a collaborative and innovative company culture.
- **Technology Infrastructure:** Invest in robust technology infrastructure to support development, collaboration, and scalability.
- **Partnerships:** Forge strategic partnerships with other businesses, technology providers, or industry influencers to enhance capabilities and market reach.

Marketing and Sales

- **Brand Identity:** Develop a strong brand identity that communicates the startup's mission, values, and unique selling proposition.
- **Go-to-Market Strategy:** Craft a compelling go-to-market strategy that effectively introduces the product to the target audience, generating interest and adoption.
- **Sales Channels:** Establish efficient sales channels, leveraging online platforms, direct sales, or channel partners to reach and convert potential customers.

Milestones

- **Product Launch:** Successfully launch the MVP, gathering initial user feedback and establishing a market presence.
- **User Acquisition:** Achieve targeted user acquisition milestones, demonstrating market validation and product-market fit.
- **Funding Rounds:** Secure necessary funding at each stage of growth, ensuring the startup has the resources to evolve and expand.

Risk Management

- **Market Risks:** Continuously monitor market trends and user feedback, ready to pivot or adapt the product strategy in response to shifts in demand or competition.
- **Operational Risks:** Implement risk management practices to address potential challenges in product development, team dynamics, or financial stability.
- **Technology Risks:** Stay abreast of technological advancements and cybersecurity threats, ensuring the product remains cutting-edge and secure.

Conclusion

This business plan outlines a strategic approach for launching and scaling a tech startup, emphasizing innovation, user engagement, and strategic growth. By focusing on solving a meaningful problem and leveraging early feedback and funding, the startup aims to achieve significant impact, scalability, and long-term success in the dynamic tech industry.

Idea 4: Consulting Services

Subconscious Link: Consulting services are the nutrient-rich soil of your garden, offering your expertise to help other businesses grow. Your knowledge and experience can improve their operations, strategy, and profitability.

Actionable Insight: Identify your areas of expertise and market demand. Build a professional website and portfolio to showcase your services and previous successes. Network aggressively, using platforms like LinkedIn, and consider offering free workshops or content to demonstrate your value.

Business Plan for Consulting Services

Executive Summary

Business Objective: To establish a consulting firm that provides exceptional advisory services, leveraging deep industry expertise to enhance client operations, strategic direction, and profitability.

Vision: To be recognized as a pivotal resource for businesses, akin to nutrient-rich soil, enabling them to flourish and achieve their full potential.

Mission: To deliver bespoke consulting services that empower businesses with innovative solutions, strategic insights, and operational excellence.

Business Model

- **Service Offerings:** Define a suite of consulting services based on areas of expertise, such as strategy, operations, finance, marketing, or technology.
- **Client Engagement:** Develop tailored engagement models to suit various client needs, from one-time advisory projects to long-term retainer arrangements.
- **Revenue Generation:** Establish pricing strategies for different services, considering factors like project scope, duration, and value delivered.

Market Analysis

- **Industry Landscape:** Conduct a thorough analysis of the consulting industry, identifying trends, growth opportunities, and emerging challenges.
- **Target Market:** Define the target market segments, focusing on industries or business sizes that can most benefit from your expertise.
- **Competitive Analysis:** Evaluate the competitive landscape, identifying key players, their service offerings, and market positioning.

Marketing and Sales Strategy

- **Brand Positioning:** Develop a compelling brand identity that highlights your expertise, experience, and the unique value proposition of your consulting services.
- **Marketing Channels:** Utilize a mix of digital marketing strategies, including SEO, content marketing, and social media, to enhance visibility and attract clients.
- **Networking:** Leverage professional networking platforms like LinkedIn and industry events to build relationships, enhance credibility, and acquire clients.
- **Demonstration of Value:** Offer free workshops, webinars, or content (e.g., white papers, case studies) to showcase your expertise and the tangible benefits of your services.

Operations Plan

- **Service Delivery:** Outline the processes for delivering consulting services, from client onboarding and needs assessment to project execution and follow-up.
- **Team and Expertise:** Assemble a team of seasoned consultants with diverse skill sets to provide comprehensive services and ensure project success.
- **Infrastructure:** Invest in the necessary tools and technology to support efficient operations, communication, and project management.

Financial Projections

- **Startup Costs:** Detail the initial investment required for setting up the firm, including technology, marketing, and operational expenses.

- **Revenue Forecast:** Provide projections for revenue generation, considering different service lines and potential client contracts.
- **Break-Even Analysis:** Calculate the break-even point to understand when the business is expected to become profitable.

Business Development

- **Client Acquisition:** Develop strategies to identify and engage potential clients, emphasizing personalized approaches and value-driven proposals.
- **Portfolio Development:** Build a robust portfolio showcasing successful projects and client testimonials to demonstrate capability and build trust.
- **Strategic Alliances:** Consider forming alliances with complementary service providers or industry organizations to expand market reach and service offerings.

Risk Management

- **Market Adaptability:** Stay attuned to industry changes and client feedback to adapt services and strategies, maintaining relevance and competitiveness.
- **Quality Assurance:** Implement stringent quality control measures to ensure the highest service standards, safeguarding reputation and client satisfaction.
- **Financial Stability:** Monitor financial performance closely, managing cash flow prudently to sustain operations and facilitate growth.

Conclusion

This business plan provides a strategic blueprint for launching and growing a consulting firm that serves as a vital growth catalyst for client businesses. By offering expert advice, actionable insights, and dedicated support, the firm will establish itself as an invaluable partner, fostering client success and achieving sustainable business growth.

Idea 5: Social Enterprise

Subconscious Link: A social enterprise is the compost of your garden, enriching the earth as it grows. By addressing social, environmental, or community issues, your business can make a profit while making a difference.

Actionable Insight: Choose a cause you're passionate about and research how a business can make an impact in this area. Plan your business model to balance profitability with social goals, and look for funding sources that support social entrepreneurship, such as impact investors.

Business Plan for a Social Enterprise

Executive Summary

Business Objective: To establish a social enterprise that not only thrives commercially but also significantly contributes to addressing pressing social, environmental, or community issues, embodying the principle of profit with purpose.

Vision: To be a beacon of sustainable business practices, demonstrating that companies can be both economically successful and socially responsible.

Mission: To leverage our business operations as a force for good, directly addressing and benefiting a chosen cause while delivering quality products or services to our customers.

Business Model

- **Core Product/Service:** Identify and develop products or services that align with your social mission, ensuring they meet market needs and contribute to your cause.
- **Social Impact:** Clearly define the social, environmental, or community goals your enterprise aims to address, and articulate how your business activities will achieve these objectives.
- **Profitability and Social Goals:** Design a business model that ensures financial viability while maximizing social impact, detailing revenue streams, cost structures, and impact metrics.
- **Funding:** Explore funding opportunities from impact investors, grants, and crowdfunding platforms that align with social entrepreneurship values.

Market Analysis

- **Industry Context:** Analyze the market and industry within which the social enterprise will operate, identifying trends, challenges, and opportunities.
- **Target Market:** Determine your target customer segments, understanding their needs, preferences, and willingness to support social causes through their purchasing decisions.
- **Competitive Landscape:** Assess the competitive environment, including other social enterprises, traditional businesses, and potential collaborators.

Social Impact Strategy

- **Impact Objectives:** Define specific, measurable objectives that quantify the social or environmental impact of your enterprise.
- **Implementation Plan:** Develop a detailed plan for how your business activities will achieve these impact objectives, incorporating community engagement, sustainable practices, and ethical considerations.
- **Monitoring and Reporting:** Establish systems for monitoring, measuring, and reporting on social impact, ensuring transparency and accountability to stakeholders.

Marketing and Sales Strategy

- **Brand Identity:** Build a brand that resonates with your social mission and appeals to your target market, emphasizing the unique value proposition of supporting a social cause.
- **Marketing Channels:** Utilize a mix of marketing channels, including digital marketing, PR, and community engagement, to raise awareness and drive sales.
- **Customer Engagement:** Foster strong relationships with customers and stakeholders, encouraging their ongoing support and advocacy for your cause.

Operations Plan

- **Operational Processes:** Outline the key operational processes required to deliver your products or services efficiently, sustainably, and in alignment with your social goals.
- **Team and Culture:** Build a dedicated team that shares your commitment to the social mission, fostering a culture of purpose, innovation, and collaboration.

- **Sustainability Practices:** Integrate sustainable practices into every aspect of your operations, from sourcing to waste management, to reinforce your commitment to the social and environmental cause.

Financial Projections

- **Revenue Streams:** Identify and project revenue streams, ensuring they align with your social mission and market demand.
- **Cost Analysis:** Detail the cost structure of your enterprise, including direct costs associated with your product/service and indirect costs such as operational expenses.
- **Sustainability and Growth:** Provide financial forecasts that demonstrate the enterprise's potential for sustainability and growth, factoring in both commercial and social impact objectives.

Fundraising and Partnerships

- **Investment Needs:** Define your funding requirements, identifying potential investors, grants, or fundraising campaigns that align with your mission.
- **Partnership Opportunities:** Explore opportunities for partnerships with NGOs, community organizations, or other businesses that can amplify your impact or provide complementary resources.

Conclusion

This business plan outlines a comprehensive approach for launching and growing a social enterprise that prioritizes social and environmental impact alongside financial success. By committing to this dual purpose, the enterprise will not only achieve commercial viability but also contribute meaningfully to societal improvement, embodying the concept of business as a force for good.

Idea 6: Subscription Services

Subconscious Link: Subscription services act like the perennial plants in your garden, providing steady growth and recurring blooms. This model can offer customers continuous value and create a predictable revenue stream for your business.

Actionable Insight: Determine a service or product line that lends itself to a subscription model, ensuring it offers ongoing value to customers. Focus on excellent customer service and retention strategies to maintain and grow your subscriber base.

Nurturing Entrepreneurial Growth

Embarking on an entrepreneurial journey invites you to cultivate a garden of opportunity and innovation. By harnessing your skills and interests to develop a business or product, you're not just planting seeds of potential income but also nurturing a landscape where your passion and effort can truly bloom. Remember, the key to a thriving business is not just in starting but in the continuous care, adaptation, and growth you invest in your entrepreneurial garden.

Side Hustles:

- **Subconscious Link:** Consider side hustles as complementary plants that support and enhance the overall garden, providing additional nutrients (income) and diversity.
- **Actionable Insight:** Identify skills or hobbies that can be monetized, such as freelancing, tutoring, or selling handmade goods online. Side hustles should not only bring in extra income but also be enjoyable and fulfilling, making them a sustainable part of your income strategy.

Side hustles, much like the companion plants in a garden that bring out the best in each other, can enrich your financial landscape by adding layers of income and satisfaction. These endeavors should not only bolster your earnings but also resonate with your interests and passions, making them a joy rather than a chore. Here are several suggestions for side hustles that can complement your financial garden, along with actionable insights for each.

1. Freelancing in Your Field of Expertise

Subconscious Link: Like the sturdy perennials that return year after year, your professional skills and expertise can provide a reliable source of additional income through freelancing.

Actionable Insight: Leverage platforms like Upwork, Freelancer, or specialized industry websites to offer your professional services. Whether it's writing, graphic design, programming, or consulting, ensure your profile highlights your skills and experience. Start by taking on smaller projects to build your portfolio and reputation on the platform.

2. Tutoring or Online Courses

Subconscious Link: Tutoring is akin to watering young plants, helping them grow strong and resilient. Sharing your knowledge not only aids others in their educational journey but also solidifies your own understanding and skills.

Actionable Insight: Identify subjects you are knowledgeable and passionate about. Use platforms like Tutor.com or create courses on Udemy or Skillshare. Tailor your teaching methods to cater to different learning styles, and consider offering the first few sessions at a discounted rate to build a client base.

3. Selling Handmade Goods

Subconscious Link: Crafting and selling handmade goods is like tending to a special patch of flowers, each unique and crafted with care. This side hustle allows you to channel your creativity into tangible products that others can enjoy.

Actionable Insight: Utilize platforms like Etsy or Instagram to showcase and sell your creations. Pay attention to trends and customer feedback to refine your products. Consider creating seasonal items or offering customization to attract a wider audience.

4. Digital Content Creation

Subconscious Link: Creating digital content—be it blogs, videos, or podcasts—is like planting a variety of seeds, some of which will sprout into vibrant plants that attract attention and admiration.

Actionable Insight: Choose a niche you're passionate about and consistent with producing content. Use social media and SEO strategies to grow your audience. Monetize your content through advertising, sponsorships, affiliate marketing, or memberships.

5. Pet Sitting or Dog Walking

Subconscious Link: Just as some plants need more attention and care than others, pets require companionship and exercise. Offering pet sitting or dog walking services not only fills this need but also provides you with joy and physical activity.

Actionable Insight: Start by offering your services to friends, family, and neighbors. Use apps like Rover or Wag to expand your reach. Ensure you're prepared with knowledge of animal behavior and first aid to provide the best care possible.

6. Participating in the Gig Economy

Subconscious Link: Engaging in gig economy jobs, such as ride-sharing or food delivery, is like adding ground cover plants to your garden—they fill in the gaps and provide steady coverage.

Actionable Insight: Sign up for platforms like Uber, Lyft, or DoorDash, ensuring you meet their requirements. Consider the most efficient times to work to maximize your earnings while balancing it with your primary job or other commitments.

Cultivating Your Financial Garden with Side Hustles

Each side hustle you undertake enriches your financial garden, not just through the additional income it generates but also by adding variety and satisfaction to your work life. By selecting side hustles that align with your skills, interests, and lifestyle, you ensure that your financial garden is not only diverse and productive but also a source of fulfillment and joy.

Cultivating a Diversified Income Mindset

Visualization: Regularly visualize your diversified income streams flourishing. Imagine the security and freedom they provide, reinforcing the desire to create and nurture these sources of income.

Affirmations: Incorporate affirmations into your daily routine that reinforce the value of income diversification. Phrases like "I am constantly creating new sources of income" or "My financial garden is abundant and diverse" can subtly shift your mindset towards proactive income diversification.

Education and Adaptation: Stay informed about new income-generating opportunities and be willing to adapt your strategies as circumstances change. This mindset of continuous learning and flexibility ensures that your income streams remain relevant and productive.

Networking: Engage with a community of like-minded individuals who also value diversified income. Sharing ideas, challenges, and successes can inspire new ventures and provide support through the ups and downs of building multiple income streams.

Conclusion: A Landscape of Financial Abundance

By hard-wiring the brain to naturally pursue income diversification, you create a dynamic financial landscape rich with opportunity. This approach not only enhances your financial resilience but also aligns with a life of abundance, where financial goals are not just met but exceeded. Through investments, entrepreneurship, and side hustles, each income stream contributes to a robust financial ecosystem, ensuring long-term growth and stability on the journey to scaling to $1,000,000 a month.

- **Leveraging Business Models:**

Leveraging scalable business models is akin to employing advanced gardening techniques that ensure not just growth but exponential proliferation of your garden's yield. In the realm of business, scalability means setting up a model that can accommodate growth without a corresponding increase in costs at the same rate. This section explores various scalable business models, illustrated with case studies and examples, to showcase how adopting these models can lead to significant revenue generation.

1. Subscription-Based Models

Overview: Subscription models involve customers paying a recurring fee to access a product or service. This model ensures steady cash flow and customer retention.

Case Study: Netflix

- **Scalability Principle:** Netflix transitioned from a DVD rental service to a streaming giant, leveraging content diversity and original productions.
- **Key Takeaway:** Continuous innovation and understanding customer preferences are crucial for scaling subscriptions.

Netflix's journey from a DVD rental service to a global streaming giant epitomizes the essence of scalability and innovation in the digital age. This case study delves into the strategic decisions and scalability principles that propelled Netflix into becoming a household name, underscoring the importance of continuous innovation and acute understanding of customer preferences in scaling subscription-based models.

Background

Netflix was founded in 1997 as a DVD rental service, offering a novel mail-order system that eliminated late fees, a common frustration with traditional video rental stores. However, the founders, Reed Hastings and Marc Randolph, always envisioned a shift towards digital streaming, recognizing early on the limitations of physical rentals and the potential of the internet to revolutionize how people accessed and viewed content.

Scalability Principle: Embracing Digital Transformation

Netflix's scalability was not just about expanding its DVD rental service; it was about fundamentally transforming its business model to embrace digital streaming. In 2007, Netflix launched its streaming service, allowing subscribers to watch thousands of movies and TV shows over the internet, a move that would eventually render its DVD service a relic of the past.

Key Insights:

- **Technology as a Catalyst:** Netflix leveraged emerging internet technologies to offer a more convenient, expansive, and engaging viewing experience than traditional DVD rentals could provide.
- **Customer-Centric Innovation:** The shift to streaming was driven by a deep understanding of changing customer behaviors and preferences, notably the desire for instant access to content without the physical limitations of DVDs.

Expanding Content Diversity and Original Productions

A pivotal aspect of Netflix's scalability strategy was its focus on content diversity and investment in original productions. Initially, Netflix relied on licensing content from studios and networks, but it quickly realized the power of original content in attracting and retaining subscribers.

Key Insights:

- **Differentiation Through Original Content:** Netflix's foray into original programming with series like "House of Cards" and "Orange Is the New Black" set it apart from competitors, making it a destination for unique, high-quality content.
- **Global Content Strategy:** Recognizing the global potential of its platform, Netflix invested in international content, catering to diverse tastes and expanding its subscriber base worldwide.

Key Takeaway: The Imperative of Continuous Innovation and Customer Insight

Netflix's evolution from DVD rentals to a streaming powerhouse illustrates that scalability in the subscription model hinges on two critical factors: continuous innovation and an acute understanding of customer preferences. Netflix's success is rooted in its ability to anticipate and adapt to shifts in technology and consumer behavior, ensuring that its service remains relevant, competitive, and scalable.

- **Adaptability:** Netflix's willingness to pivot its business model in response to technological advancements and market opportunities underlines the importance of adaptability in achieving scalability.
- **Customer Insight:** Netflix's data-driven approach to understanding viewer preferences has been instrumental in curating content and creating a personalized viewing experience, proving that deep customer insights are invaluable in scaling a subscription service.

Conclusion

Netflix's journey underscores the dynamic interplay between innovation, customer insight, and adaptability in scaling a business. For entrepreneurs and businesses aiming to scale, especially in the subscription economy, Netflix serves as a compelling case study in transforming challenges into opportunities, staying ahead of market trends, and relentlessly focusing on delivering value to customers.

2. Software as a Service (SaaS)

Overview: SaaS companies provide software on a subscription basis, offering it via the internet without requiring traditional installation.

Case Study: Salesforce

- **Scalability Principle:** Salesforce revolutionized CRM by offering it as an online service, allowing for rapid updates and scalability.
- **Key Takeaway:** Focus on customer needs and cloud-based delivery can significantly reduce costs and increase scalability.

Salesforce's ascent to becoming a leading Software as a Service (SaaS) provider, particularly in the Customer Relationship Management (CRM) domain, epitomizes the transformative power of cloud-based delivery and customer-centric innovation. This overview and case study illuminate the scalability principles and strategies that underscore Salesforce's success, highlighting the role of cloud computing in revolutionizing software delivery and the importance of aligning product development with customer needs.

Background on Salesforce and the SaaS Model

Salesforce was founded in 1999 with a vision to disrupt the traditional CRM software industry by delivering CRM solutions over the internet—a stark contrast to the prevailing model of on-premise software installations. This approach not only democratized access to CRM technologies for businesses of all sizes but also introduced a new paradigm in software delivery and consumption.

Scalability Principle: Leveraging Cloud-Based Delivery

Salesforce's cloud-based CRM solution exemplifies the scalability inherent in the SaaS model. By hosting software on the cloud, Salesforce eliminated the need for individual installations, updates, and maintenance, streamlining the delivery process and significantly reducing the costs and complexities associated with scaling software solutions.

Key Insights:

- **Instant Upgrades and Scalability:** Cloud delivery enabled Salesforce to rapidly deploy updates and new features across its customer base, ensuring all users benefit from the latest innovations without downtime or additional costs.
- **Accessibility and Flexibility:** Salesforce made CRM solutions accessible from any device with internet access, providing unparalleled flexibility and scalability to businesses, which could now adapt their usage based on growth and changing needs.

Focusing on Customer Needs for Product Evolution

A cornerstone of Salesforce's strategy was its unwavering commitment to understanding and addressing customer needs. This customer-centric approach informed product development, ensuring that Salesforce's offerings not only met current market demands but also anticipated future trends.

Key Insights:

- **Customer Feedback Loop:** Salesforce maintained close relationships with its users, gathering feedback that informed continuous product improvement and innovation. This feedback loop ensured that Salesforce's offerings remained relevant and valuable to its customers.
- **Customization and Integration:** Recognizing the diverse needs of businesses, Salesforce developed a highly customizable platform that could be tailored to specific workflows and processes. Additionally, it fostered a robust ecosystem of third-party applications and integrations, further enhancing its platform's versatility and appeal.

Key Takeaway: The Symbiosis of Cloud-Based Delivery and Customer Centricity

Salesforce's journey highlights the symbiotic relationship between cloud-based delivery and customer-centric product development. The company's ability to scale its CRM solutions and maintain a leadership position in the SaaS market is largely attributable to its cloud infrastructure, which facilitated rapid, cost-effective scalability, and its dedication to evolving in response to customer feedback.

- **Reduced Costs and Increased Scalability:** Cloud-based delivery significantly lowers the barriers to entry and scale for software companies, allowing them to serve a global customer base with minimal physical infrastructure.
- **Alignment with Customer Needs:** Continuous engagement with customers ensures that product offerings remain aligned with market demands, fostering loyalty and driving long-term growth.

Conclusion

Salesforce's success story serves as a blueprint for SaaS companies aiming to scale in today's digital economy. By harnessing the power of cloud computing and maintaining a laser focus on customer needs, businesses can achieve remarkable scalability and efficiency, setting a new standard for software delivery and consumption in the 21st century.

3. E-commerce Dropshipping

Overview: Dropshipping allows you to sell products without holding inventory, as suppliers ship products directly to customers.

Case Study: Gymshark

- Scalability Principle: Gymshark began with dropshipping, quickly adapting to demand and scaling up by moving to a traditional inventory model as it grew.
- Key Takeaway: Starting with dropshipping can test product-market fit with minimal investment before scaling operations.

Dropshipping is a business model that has revolutionized the e-commerce landscape, allowing entrepreneurs to start online stores without the need to maintain physical inventory. This model relies on a third-party supplier to handle the storage, packaging, and shipping of products directly to customers. Gymshark, a fitness apparel and accessories brand, serves as an exemplary case study of how leveraging dropshipping can facilitate rapid growth and scalability in the e-commerce sector.

Background on Dropshipping and Gymshark

Founded in 2012 by teenager Ben Francis and a group of his high-school friends, Gymshark epitomizes the entrepreneurial spirit of the digital age. Initially, Gymshark utilized the dropshipping model to minimize startup costs and risks, allowing the brand to focus on marketing, design, and customer service without the complexities of inventory management.

Scalability Principle: Agile Adaptation to Market Demand

Gymshark's Journey:

- Gymshark began by selling supplements and quickly expanded into fitness apparel, using dropshipping to test product demand and market fit with minimal upfront investment.
- As the brand gained popularity, particularly through savvy social media marketing and influencer partnerships, Gymshark recognized the limitations of dropshipping, including less control over product quality and customer experience.

Strategic Shift:

- To better manage quality and fulfillment, Gymshark transitioned to holding its own inventory and fulfilling orders directly. This shift allowed Gymshark to scale its operations more effectively, responding to customer demand with greater agility and ensuring higher standards of quality and service.

Key Takeaway: Leveraging Dropshipping for Initial Growth and Scalability

Minimal Initial Investment: Dropshipping allows entrepreneurs to launch e-commerce businesses with significantly lower startup costs, as it eliminates the need for purchasing and storing inventory.

Testing and Validation: This model provides a platform for testing product-market fit and customer demand without the financial risk associated with unsold inventory. Gymshark effectively used dropshipping to identify best-selling products and scale up their offerings based on real customer feedback.

Strategic Evolution: Gymshark's evolution from dropshipping to managing its own inventory highlights a critical pathway for scaling e-commerce operations. Once a brand establishes its market fit and customer base, investing in inventory management can enhance control over the supply chain, improve profit margins, and elevate the customer experience.

Conclusion: Dropshipping as a Stepping Stone to E-commerce Success

Gymshark's story underscores the potential of dropshipping as a stepping stone to building a scalable and successful e-commerce brand. By starting with dropshipping, entrepreneurs can minimize initial risks while gauging market demand. However, the transition to a traditional inventory model, as demonstrated by Gymshark, may be necessary to achieve sustainable growth, maintain quality control, and fulfill customer expectations at scale.

For aspiring e-commerce entrepreneurs, Gymshark's journey offers valuable insights into the dynamic nature of the industry and the strategic decisions that can lead to exponential growth. Embracing flexibility, continually assessing market feedback, and being willing to adapt business operations are key components of scaling successfully in the competitive e-commerce landscape.

4. Platform-Based Models

Overview: Platform models create value by facilitating exchanges between two or more interdependent groups, usually consumers and producers.

Case Study: Airbnb

- **Scalability Principle:** Airbnb scaled by tapping into the underutilized resource of people's spare rooms and homes, creating a global marketplace.
- **Key Takeaway:** Platforms that efficiently match supply with demand can scale rapidly without the need to own the assets being exchanged.

Platform-based business models have revolutionized various industries by facilitating direct exchanges between different user groups, such as consumers and producers, without the platform owning the underlying assets. This model capitalizes on network effects, where the value of the platform increases as more participants join. Airbnb exemplifies the success of this model within the hospitality sector, transforming the way people travel and experience new locations.

Background on Platform-Based Models and Airbnb

Founded in 2008, Airbnb disrupted the traditional lodging industry by enabling homeowners to rent out their spare rooms or entire homes to travelers. This innovative approach not only provided travelers with unique and affordable accommodation options but also allowed homeowners to generate additional income.

Scalability Principle: Utilizing Underutilized Assets

Airbnb's Growth Strategy:

- Airbnb's platform model scales by tapping into the vast, previously underutilized resource of private homes and spaces available for short-term rental. This approach effectively broadened the accommodation market beyond traditional hotels and hostels.
- By focusing on the user experience, Airbnb built trust and reliability into its platform, incorporating features such as user profiles, reviews, and secure payment processing to facilitate safe and transparent transactions.

Expanding the Marketplace:

- As Airbnb's user base grew, so did its offerings, diversifying beyond accommodations to include experiences and adventures, further increasing the platform's appeal and user engagement.

Key Takeaway: Matching Supply with Demand Through Efficient Platforms

Creating Value for All Participants:

- The key to Airbnb's rapid scalability lies in its ability to efficiently match the supply of available spaces with the demand from travelers seeking unique, cost-effective lodging options. This matching is facilitated by sophisticated algorithms and user-friendly interfaces that simplify the process of listing, finding, and booking accommodations.

Minimizing Operational Costs:

- Unlike traditional lodging businesses, Airbnb does not own the properties listed on its platform, significantly reducing its capital expenditures and operational costs. This asset-light approach enables rapid expansion into new markets with minimal financial risk.

Leveraging Network Effects:

- The platform model thrives on network effects; as more hosts list their properties, the platform becomes more attractive to travelers, and vice versa. Airbnb has successfully leveraged these network effects to grow its user base and increase its market penetration globally.

Conclusion: Embracing Platform-Based Innovation for Scalability

Airbnb's success story serves as a compelling case study for the potential of platform-based business models to disrupt traditional industries and achieve exponential growth. By efficiently connecting supply with demand and leveraging underutilized assets, platforms like Airbnb can scale rapidly without the burdensome costs associated with owning physical assets.

For entrepreneurs and businesses exploring platform-based models, Airbnb's journey highlights the importance of prioritizing user experience, building trust within the platform ecosystem, and harnessing network effects to drive growth. This approach not only facilitates scalability but also fosters a dynamic marketplace that creates value for all participants.

5. Freemium Models

Overview: The freemium model offers basic services for free while charging for advanced features or functionalities.

Case Study: Spotify

- **Scalability Principle:** Spotify's freemium model attracts users with free, ad-supported access while encouraging upgrades to premium for additional features.
- **Key Takeaway:** Providing value that encourages users to upgrade is key to converting free users into paying customers.

The freemium model represents a strategic approach in the digital economy, balancing the provision of no-cost services with the option for users to access enhanced features or functionalities through a paid subscription. This model has been particularly effective in the software and services sector, where it serves as a powerful tool for user acquisition and revenue generation. Spotify, the world-renowned music streaming service, exemplifies the successful application of the freemium model, leveraging it to scale its user base and establish a dominant position in the market.

Background on Freemium Models and Spotify

Spotify was launched in 2008 amid significant piracy issues within the music industry, offering a legal alternative through its streaming platform. By adopting a freemium model, Spotify provided users with free, ad-supported access to its vast music library while also offering a premium, subscription-based option free of ads and with additional features such as offline listening and higher quality audio.

Scalability Principle: User Acquisition and Conversion

Spotify's Growth Strategy:

- **Attracting a Broad User Base:** Spotify's initial offering of a free, ad-supported service allowed it to rapidly attract users who were reluctant to pay for music without first experiencing the platform's value. This broad user base became a fertile ground for converting a portion into paying subscribers.
- **Encouraging Premium Upgrades:** By strategically limiting certain desirable features (like offline listening and ad-free music) to the premium tier, Spotify created a compelling value proposition that encouraged free users to upgrade.

Key Takeaway: The Art of Value Creation and Conversion

Creating Compelling Value Propositions:

- The essence of a successful freemium model lies in the ability to offer enough value in the free version to attract users while reserving premium features that are enticing enough to justify a subscription. Spotify's continuous innovation in personalization, playlist curation, and user experience has been key to its ability to convert free users to premium subscribers.

Leveraging Data for Customization and Improvement:

- Spotify uses data analytics to understand user behavior, preferences, and patterns. This insight allows for the customization of listening experiences and targeted offers that can motivate free users to move to the paid tier.

Balancing Monetization with User Growth:

- An effective freemium model carefully balances the monetization of premium users with the need to continue growing the user base. Spotify's approach ensures that the free tier remains attractive and engaging, fostering an environment conducive to organic growth through word-of-mouth and social sharing.

Conclusion: Nurturing Growth Through the Freemium Model

Spotify's application of the freemium model illustrates a strategic pathway to scaling in competitive digital markets. By offering a compelling service that meets users' basic needs at no cost, companies can build a large user base, which then serves as a potential market for converting a subset to paying customers through additional, premium value.

For businesses considering the freemium model, the key lies in understanding the unique value drivers for your audience and designing your service tiers to maximize both user satisfaction and revenue potential. The freemium model, when executed with a clear focus on value creation and conversion, can be a powerful engine for growth, scalability, and long-term success.

6. Content Creation and Monetization

Overview: This model relies on creating engaging content to attract a large audience and monetizing through ads, sponsorships, and merchandise.

Case Study: Joe Rogan Experience

- **Scalability Principle:** The podcast scaled its audience through diverse content and high-profile interviews, leading to significant monetization opportunities.
- **Key Takeaway:** Authentic and engaging content can attract a wide audience, opening various revenue streams.

Content creation and monetization stand as pivotal elements in the digital ecosystem, offering individuals and companies the opportunity to forge substantial connections with global audiences while generating revenue through multiple channels. This model's efficacy is exemplified by the success of "The Joe Rogan Experience," a podcast that has leveraged the power of engaging content to build a vast listener base and unlock a multitude of monetization avenues.

Background on Content Creation and Monetization

The digital age has democratized content production, allowing creators to share their work across a variety of platforms, including YouTube, podcasts, blogs, and social media. Successful content creators captivate their audiences with authenticity and value, paving the way for monetization through advertisements, sponsorships, merchandise sales, and more.

The Joe Rogan Experience: A Case Study in Scalability and Monetization

Launched in 2009 by comedian, commentator, and actor Joe Rogan, "The Joe Rogan Experience" podcast quickly ascended to become one of the most popular and influential podcasts worldwide. Rogan's formula for success combined long-form interviews with a diverse array of guests, from comedians and actors to scientists and business moguls, underpinned by an unfiltered and conversational style.

Scalability Principle: Leveraging Diversity and Authenticity

Audience Growth Through Diverse Content:

- The podcast's broad spectrum of topics and guests attracted a wide-ranging audience, ensuring that listeners from various demographics found something of interest, thereby fostering a rapidly growing and loyal listener base.

Authentic Engagement:

- Rogan's authentic approach to conversations, marked by curiosity, humor, and a willingness to delve deep into subjects, fostered a strong connection with listeners, making the podcast a staple in many people's lives.

Key Takeaway: Diverse and Engaging Content as a Magnet for Monetization

Monetization Through Multiple Channels:

- With its massive audience, "The Joe Rogan Experience" capitalized on various revenue streams, including advertising deals, sponsorships, and exclusive distribution agreements, most notably Spotify's landmark licensing deal reportedly worth $100 million.

Merchandising and Direct Support:

- Beyond traditional advertising, the podcast leveraged its brand to sell merchandise and occasionally promoted direct listener support mechanisms, further diversifying its income sources.

The Power of Platforms:

- The strategic use of multiple content distribution platforms before exclusively moving to Spotify amplified the podcast's reach, demonstrating the importance of platform presence in scaling audience engagement.

Conclusion: Crafting a Sustainable Content Monetization Strategy

"The Joe Rogan Experience" underscores the significance of creating content that resonates authentically with a broad audience. The scalability of such content creation endeavors hinges on the ability to maintain genuine engagement, explore diverse subjects, and leverage the resulting audience growth for monetization.

For aspiring content creators, the journey of "The Joe Rogan Experience" highlights the potential of passionate, authentic content to build a community of loyal followers. It illustrates that with the right mix of content diversity, audience engagement, and strategic monetization, creators can transform their passion into a lucrative career. The key lies in consistently delivering value, fostering connections, and being open to evolving monetization strategies to sustain and scale the content creation venture.

Conclusion: Principles for Scaling Success

These case studies highlight that regardless of the industry, scalability hinges on deeply understanding customer needs, leveraging technology, and remaining flexible in business model execution. Adopting a scalable business model is not merely about growth for its own sake but about building a structure that supports expansion while maintaining or improving profitability. As you consider scaling your business, reflect on these models and principles, and think creatively about how they might apply to your venture, ensuring that your business not only grows but thrives.

Leveraging Technology and Innovation

- Digital Transformation:

Digital transformation represents a fundamental shift in how businesses operate and deliver value to customers, encapsulating the integration of digital technology into all areas of a business. This transformation goes beyond mere technological change, reaching into the culture, workflow, and customer interactions of an entity to drive growth, enhance product offerings, and tap into new markets. The impact on revenue growth can be profound, as digital transformation facilitates efficiency, innovation, and accessibility.

Automating Processes for Efficiency

Streamlining Operations: Automation through digital transformation allows businesses to streamline their operations, reducing manual tasks and errors. This efficiency not only lowers operational costs but also enables staff to focus on higher-value activities, such as strategy and customer engagement.

Case in Point: The adoption of Customer Relationship Management (CRM) systems automates sales, marketing, and customer service processes. By providing a unified platform to track customer interactions, businesses can enhance lead management, improve customer service, and ultimately, increase sales conversions.

Enhancing Product Offerings through Innovation

Product Innovation: Digital technologies enable businesses to innovate their product offerings, whether through the development of new digital products or the enhancement of existing ones. This could involve integrating artificial intelligence (AI) to personalize services or utilizing data analytics for better product recommendations.

Real-World Example: E-commerce platforms utilizing AI chatbots for customer service. These bots provide immediate, 24/7 customer support, improving the shopping experience, aiding in customer retention, and boosting sales.

Expanding Market Reach

Global Accessibility: Digital transformation eradicates geographical barriers, allowing businesses to reach global markets with ease. An online presence, coupled with digital marketing strategies, can attract customers from around the world, significantly expanding a business's potential customer base.

Illustration: The rise of digital platforms like Shopify or WooCommerce has enabled small businesses to set up online stores quickly, reaching customers far beyond their local geography and significantly impacting revenue growth through expanded market access.

Data-Driven Decision Making

Leveraging Big Data: The use of digital tools allows businesses to collect and analyze vast amounts of data, providing insights into customer behavior, market trends, and operational efficiencies. These insights can drive strategic decisions, from product development to marketing strategies, aligning closely with market needs and opportunities.

Example: Netflix's use of viewer data to inform content creation. By analyzing viewing patterns, Netflix produces content that aligns with the preferences of its audience, enhancing viewer engagement and subscription growth.

Building Customer Relationships

Enhanced Customer Experiences: Digital transformation offers tools for creating more meaningful and personalized customer experiences. Through social media, mobile apps, and personalized marketing, businesses can engage with customers in real-time, fostering loyalty and driving repeat business.

Case Study: Starbucks' mobile app not only facilitates order and payment but also personalizes offers and rewards, enhancing customer loyalty and increasing sales through its convenience and tailored rewards program.

Conclusion

Digital transformation is not a mere trend but a strategic imperative for businesses aiming to scale in today's digital economy. By automating processes, enhancing product offerings, reaching new markets, leveraging data for decision-making, and building stronger customer relationships, businesses can unlock significant pathways to revenue growth. The journey of digital transformation requires a holistic approach, embracing not only technological adoption but also cultural and operational shifts to fully realize its benefits.

- Innovation as a Catalyst:

Innovation stands at the heart of exponential growth in the modern business landscape, serving as the catalyst for transforming traditional operations, products, and market strategies. It propels companies beyond the confines of conventional thinking into realms of untapped potential and new opportunities. Encouraging an innovation mindset within organizations and individuals alike is essential for navigating the complexities of today's fast-paced economy and for unlocking pathways to substantial growth.

Cultivating an Innovation Mindset

Embrace Curiosity and Continuous Learning: An innovation mindset starts with curiosity and the relentless pursuit of knowledge. Encourage continuous learning within your organization, foster a culture where questions are welcomed, and exploration is rewarded. By staying informed about the latest trends, technologies, and methodologies, you open the door to innovative ideas and approaches.

Encourage Experimentation and Risk-Taking: Innovation requires a willingness to experiment and take calculated risks. Create an environment where trial and error are part of the growth process, understanding that not all ideas will succeed but that each attempt provides valuable lessons. Celebrate both successes and failures as stepping stones to discovery and improvement.

Exploring New Ideas

Idea Generation: Promote brainstorming sessions, workshops, and think tanks within your team or organization to generate new ideas. Utilize techniques like design thinking to approach problems from different perspectives and develop creative solutions.

Cross-Industry Inspiration: Look beyond your industry for inspiration. Often, innovative solutions come from applying concepts or technologies from one field to another. This cross-pollination of ideas can lead to groundbreaking products, services, and business models.

Developing New Products

Focus on User Needs: Innovation should always be driven by user needs and preferences. Engage with your customers through surveys, interviews, and feedback channels to understand their challenges and desires. This customer-centric approach ensures that your innovations truly address market demands.

Leverage Technology: Utilize emerging technologies to enhance your product offerings. Whether it's incorporating AI for personalized experiences, blockchain for enhanced security, or IoT devices for better connectivity, technology can provide a competitive edge and open new avenues for product innovation.

Entering New Markets

Market Research and Analysis: Conduct thorough market research to identify emerging trends, underserved customer segments, or geographic regions ripe for expansion. Analyzing competitive landscapes and consumer behavior can uncover opportunities for innovation in new markets.

Strategic Partnerships: Forge partnerships with other companies, startups, or research institutions to explore new markets. Collaborations can provide access to new customer bases, technologies, and resources, facilitating smoother entry and faster growth in unfamiliar territories.

Conclusion: The Role of Innovation in Exponential Growth

Adopting an innovation mindset is not merely about creating new products or entering new markets; it's about fundamentally rethinking how value is delivered to customers. It involves challenging the status quo, continuously improving, and relentlessly pursuing growth opportunities. By fostering an environment that encourages innovation at every level, businesses can navigate the uncertainties of the digital age, adapt to changing market dynamics, and achieve exponential growth. Remember, in the landscape of modern business, innovation is not just an advantage; it's a necessity.

Marketing and Brand Building

- Strategic Marketing:

Strategic marketing is the compass that guides businesses through the competitive landscape, ensuring that they not only reach their target audience but also grow and scale effectively. As businesses evolve, their marketing strategies must adapt, leveraging digital marketing, personal branding, and network expansion to maintain momentum and foster growth. This outline provides a roadmap for crafting marketing strategies that can scale with your business.

Digital Marketing: Harnessing Online Platforms for Growth

Content Marketing: Develop a robust content marketing strategy that delivers valuable, relevant, and consistent content to attract and retain a clearly defined audience. As your business scales, diversify your content formats to include blogs, videos, podcasts, and infographics, ensuring broad appeal and engagement.

Search Engine Optimization (SEO): Implement an SEO strategy to improve your website's visibility in search engine results. Focus on keyword research, quality content creation, and website optimization. As you grow, continually refine your SEO tactics to adapt to algorithm changes and maintain high rankings.

Social Media Marketing: Utilize social media platforms to connect with your audience, build brand awareness, and promote your products or services. As your business expands, leverage social media advertising and influencer partnerships to reach broader audiences and drive conversions.

Email Marketing: Build and nurture an email list to engage directly with customers and prospects. Use segmentation and personalization to tailor messages to specific audience needs. Scaling involves automating email campaigns and analyzing performance data to refine your approach.

Personal Branding: Building a Connection with Your Audience

Develop a Strong Personal Brand: Entrepreneurs and business leaders should cultivate a personal brand that resonates with their target audience. Share your expertise, insights, and journey through speaking engagements, social media, and content creation to build trust and loyalty.

Leverage Thought Leadership: Position yourself as a thought leader in your industry by contributing to reputable publications, participating in panel discussions, and hosting webinars. This enhances your credibility and can attract new opportunities for business growth.

Network Expansion: Growing Through Strategic Relationships

Build Strategic Partnerships: Identify and cultivate partnerships with other businesses, influencers, and industry leaders that can offer mutual benefits. Collaborations can extend your reach, provide access to new markets, and contribute to your business's scalability.

Attend Industry Events: Participate in trade shows, conferences, and networking events relevant to your industry. These events offer opportunities to connect with potential customers, partners, and influencers who can play a role in your business's growth trajectory.

Engage with Online Communities: Actively participate in online forums, social media groups, and platforms related to your industry. Engagement can increase your visibility, establish your expertise, and open doors to new business opportunities.

Conclusion: Adapting Marketing Strategies for Scalability

Effective marketing strategies are dynamic, evolving with your business as it grows. By focusing on digital marketing, you can leverage the vast potential of online platforms to reach and engage your target audience. Personal branding allows you to build trust and connect on a deeper level, while network expansion ensures that you remain connected to the pulse of your industry and open to new growth avenues. As your business scales, continuously assess and refine your marketing strategies to ensure they align with your goals, market trends, and customer preferences. Remember, strategic marketing is not a set-it-and-forget-it endeavor but a continual process of adaptation and optimization.

- **Customer Engagement and Retention:**

Customer engagement and retention are pivotal to the sustainable growth of any business, serving as the bedrock upon which long-term success is built. In today's competitive marketplace, acquiring a new customer can be significantly more expensive than retaining an existing one, making the cultivation of strong customer relationships not just a strategic advantage but a necessity. This emphasis on customer loyalty is rooted in the understanding that satisfied customers are more likely to make repeat purchases, advocate for your brand, and provide valuable feedback.

The Importance of Customer Engagement

Building Emotional Connections: Engaging with customers on a regular basis helps to build emotional connections, fostering a sense of loyalty and belonging. This can be achieved through personalized communications, understanding customer needs and preferences, and responding to them in a meaningful way.

Leveraging Multi-Channel Communication: Utilize various channels — social media, email, blogs, and customer service platforms — to maintain a constant dialogue with your audience. This not only enhances visibility but also provides customers with multiple avenues to interact with your brand, increasing engagement.

Providing Value Beyond Transactions: Engagement should extend beyond mere transactions to include value-added interactions such as informative content, user communities, and loyalty programs. These initiatives keep customers connected and invested in your brand even when they are not making a purchase.

Strategies for Customer Retention

Exceptional Customer Service: Outstanding customer service is crucial for retention. This includes not only addressing complaints and issues promptly but also proactively reaching out to customers to ensure their satisfaction and gather feedback.

Personalization: Tailoring the customer experience to individual preferences and history with your brand can significantly enhance satisfaction. Personalized recommendations, communications, and rewards demonstrate that you value and understand your customers.

Feedback Loops: Implement mechanisms for regular customer feedback through surveys, reviews, and direct communication. This feedback is invaluable for making improvements and innovations that meet your customers' evolving needs.

Creating a Community: Foster a sense of community around your brand by encouraging customer interaction through social media, forums, and events. A strong community can enhance customer loyalty and provide a platform for advocacy and feedback.

The Impact on Sustainable Growth

Repeat Business and Upselling: Satisfied customers are more likely to return for future purchases and are more receptive to upselling and cross-selling efforts. This repeat business is a critical component of sustainable growth.

Word-of-Mouth and Referrals: Happy customers are the best advocates for your brand, providing word-of-mouth promotion that is both effective and cost-efficient. Encourage this by creating shareable content, referral programs, and incentives for customers who bring in new business.

Reduced Churn Rates: Effective engagement and retention strategies reduce customer churn, ensuring a stable revenue base and lowering the costs associated with acquiring new customers.

Enhanced Brand Reputation: A focus on customer satisfaction enhances your brand's reputation, making it easier to attract new customers and enter new markets.

Conclusion

Building strong relationships with customers through effective engagement and retention strategies is fundamental to the sustainable growth of any business. By prioritizing customer satisfaction, personalization, and community, companies can cultivate a loyal customer base that supports revenue growth, brand advocacy, and market expansion. In the long run, the effort and resources invested in retaining customers pay off manifold, solidifying the foundation for lasting success.

Financial Management and Investment

- Capital Allocation:

Efficient capital allocation is crucial for the sustained growth and health of any business. It involves strategically deploying financial resources to areas that generate the most significant returns, ensuring long-term profitability and stability. This guide explores the nuances of capital allocation, focusing on reinvestment strategies, fundraising, and operational cash flow management, to help businesses fuel their growth effectively.

Understanding Capital Allocation

Definition and Importance: Capital allocation refers to how a business distributes its financial resources among various departments, projects, or investments. Making informed decisions in this area ensures that every dollar spent contributes to the company's strategic objectives and overall growth.

Reinvestment Strategies

Reinvesting Profits: One of the most straightforward methods to fuel growth is reinvesting profits back into the business. This could mean expanding product lines, entering new markets, enhancing marketing efforts, or investing in research and development for innovation.

Prioritizing High-Return Investments: Focus on areas with the potential for high returns on investment (ROI). This requires a thorough analysis of past performance and future projections to identify opportunities that will likely yield the best outcomes.

Fundraising Strategies

Equity Financing: Selling shares of your company can provide the necessary capital for expansion while also sharing the risk with investors. However, it dilutes ownership and requires sharing future profits.

Debt Financing: Loans and lines of credit offer immediate capital with the flexibility of repayment over time. While debt must be repaid with interest, it doesn't dilute ownership.

Venture Capital and Angel Investors: For startups and high-growth companies, venture capital or angel investors can provide significant capital in exchange for equity. This route often comes with mentorship and strategic guidance but requires demonstrating high growth potential and a clear exit strategy.

Managing Operational Cash Flow

Efficient Cash Flow Management: Keeping a close eye on cash inflows and outflows ensures that your business can cover its operational costs and invest in growth opportunities. Tools like cash flow forecasts and budgets are essential for anticipating and managing liquidity needs.

Cost Control: Regularly review and optimize expenses to free up more capital for investment in growth. This might involve negotiating with suppliers, reducing overhead costs, or streamlining operations for efficiency.

Working Capital Optimization: Managing receivables, payables, and inventory efficiently can improve liquidity and provide more funds for reinvestment. Strategies include speeding up invoice payments, extending payables without incurring penalties, and reducing inventory without affecting sales.

Strategic Considerations

Balancing Short-Term and Long-Term Needs: Effective capital allocation requires balancing the immediate operational needs with long-term strategic investments. This balance ensures sustainability and competitiveness over time.

Risk Management: Diversify investments to manage risk effectively. Avoid over-concentration in any single area, product, or market to protect against unforeseen downturns.

Continuous Evaluation: The business environment and market conditions are always changing. Regularly evaluate your capital allocation decisions and adjust as necessary to ensure they align with your current strategic objectives and market realities.

Conclusion

Efficient capital allocation is an art that requires understanding your business's strategic goals, the landscape in which you operate, and the various financial tools at your disposal. By strategically reinvesting profits, wisely choosing fundraising options, and managing operational cash flow, businesses can fuel growth and build a strong foundation for future success. Remember, the goal is not just to grow but to do so sustainably and profitably, ensuring the long-term viability and resilience of your business.

- Investment for Expansion:

Investing for expansion is a critical strategic decision for any business aiming to scale, especially when targeting the milestone of achieving $1 million in monthly revenue. This process involves identifying and evaluating opportunities that not only align with the business's overarching goals but also possess the potential to significantly accelerate growth. The following outlines how businesses can strategically approach investment for expansion.

Identifying Investment Opportunities

Market Research: Conduct thorough market research to uncover trends, gaps, and emerging needs within your industry. This insight can reveal lucrative areas for expansion, such as new product lines, services, or markets.

Competitive Analysis: Assess your competitors' strengths and weaknesses. Identifying areas where your business can differentiate and excel may reveal unique investment opportunities for capturing market share.

Customer Feedback: Leverage direct feedback from your existing customer base to identify pain points, unmet needs, or desired improvements. Investments that address these areas can enhance customer satisfaction and loyalty, driving growth.

Technological Advancements: Stay abreast of technological trends and innovations within your industry. Investing in new technologies can streamline operations, improve product offerings, and open new channels for customer engagement.

Evaluating Investment Opportunities

Alignment with Business Goals: Ensure that any potential investment directly contributes to your business's strategic objectives. Whether the goal is market expansion, product innovation, or operational efficiency, the investment should have a clear role in driving these objectives forward.

Financial Analysis: Conduct a comprehensive financial analysis to assess the potential return on investment (ROI) of the opportunity. Consider using financial models like discounted cash flow (DCF) analysis to project future cash flows and determine the investment's value.

Risk Assessment: Evaluate the risks associated with the investment, including market risks, operational risks, and financial risks. Understanding these risks and developing mitigation strategies is crucial for making informed decisions.

Scalability Potential: Assess the scalability of the investment. Opportunities with high scalability can significantly impact revenue growth, moving your business closer to the million-dollar mark. Consider whether the investment can be scaled efficiently and what resources would be required.

Time to ROI: Estimate the time it will take to see a return on your investment. Investments with shorter ROI periods may be preferable for accelerating growth, but longer-term investments can also be valuable if they align with strategic goals and offer substantial growth potential.

Making the Decision

Consultation with Stakeholders: Engage with key stakeholders, including partners, investors, and advisors, to gain diverse perspectives on the investment opportunity. This can provide additional insights and aid in decision-making.

Pilot Projects: Where feasible, consider conducting pilot projects or limited rollouts of the investment. This approach can provide real-world data on the investment's potential impact and scalability before committing significant resources.

Preparation for Implementation: Develop a detailed plan for implementing the investment, including timelines, budgeting, resource allocation, and key performance indicators (KPIs) for monitoring progress.

Conclusion

Identifying and evaluating investment opportunities with the potential to accelerate growth requires a strategic approach that aligns with your business's goals and market dynamics. By carefully analyzing the financial viability, risks, and scalability of opportunities, and making informed decisions, businesses can effectively invest in their expansion. Achieving the million-dollar mark is not only about finding the right opportunities but also about executing on these investments effectively to realize their growth potential.

Mindset and Personal Development

- **Overcoming Psychological Barriers:**

Overcoming psychological barriers is essential for entrepreneurs and business leaders aiming for significant success. These barriers, often rooted in fear, doubt, and past experiences, can hinder progress, innovation, and the ability to scale. Recognizing and addressing these mental obstacles is crucial for fostering resilience, managing stress, and cultivating a growth mindset conducive to achieving and surpassing goals.

Identifying Psychological Barriers

Fear of Failure: Many individuals fear failure, viewing it as a reflection of their abilities or worth. This fear can prevent taking necessary risks or pursuing innovative ideas.

Impostor Syndrome: Feeling like a fraud, despite evident success, can undermine confidence and decision-making, leading to overcaution or inaction.

Resistance to Change: Comfort with the status quo can create resistance to change, stifling growth and adaptation to new market demands or opportunities.

Perfectionism: While striving for excellence is positive, perfectionism can lead to procrastination, indecision, and dissatisfaction with progress.

Strategies for Overcoming Psychological Barriers

Cultivating Resilience

Reframe Failure: View failures as learning opportunities. Analyze setbacks to extract lessons and strategies for future endeavors, reinforcing that failure is a step towards success.

Set Realistic Goals: Break larger objectives into manageable, realistic goals. Achieving these smaller milestones can build confidence and momentum.

Managing Stress

Mindfulness and Meditation: Incorporate mindfulness practices and meditation into your routine to reduce stress, enhance focus, and improve decision-making clarity.

Physical Activity: Regular exercise can alleviate stress, improve mental health, and boost cognitive function, aiding in overcoming psychological barriers.

Time Management: Prioritize tasks and delegate when possible to manage workload effectively and reduce stress. Use tools and techniques like the Eisenhower Box or Pomodoro Technique to enhance productivity.

Maintaining a Growth Mindset

Embrace Learning: Adopt a growth mindset by embracing learning in all aspects of your business. Encourage curiosity and continuous education among your team.

Seek Feedback: Actively seek and constructively use feedback from customers, mentors, and peers. This input can provide valuable insights and foster a culture of continuous improvement.

Celebrate Progress: Recognize and celebrate progress and achievements, both personally and within your team. Acknowledging accomplishments reinforces a positive outlook and motivates further effort.

Building Support Networks

Mentorship and Coaching: Engage with mentors or coaches who can provide guidance, support, and accountability, helping you navigate psychological barriers more effectively.

Peer Support: Build a network of peers who understand the entrepreneurial journey. Sharing experiences and strategies can provide mutual support and encouragement.

Conclusion

Overcoming psychological barriers is a critical component of personal and professional growth. By recognizing these barriers and implementing strategies for resilience, stress management, and cultivating a growth mindset, individuals can unlock their full potential. Embracing failure as a learning opportunity, managing stress through healthy practices, maintaining a focus on continuous improvement, and leveraging support networks are key steps in this journey. With these strategies, entrepreneurs and business leaders can navigate the mental challenges of scaling their ventures, paving the way for sustained success and fulfillment.

- Building a Support Network:

Building a robust support network is indispensable for navigating the complexities of scaling a business. This network, comprising mentors, professional connections, and a dedicated team, provides a foundation of knowledge, encouragement, and expertise that can significantly enhance your journey toward achieving ambitious goals. The importance of mentorship, networking, and assembling a visionary team cannot be overstated, as these elements collectively contribute to both personal growth and business success.

The Value of Mentorship

Guidance and Insight: Mentors bring a wealth of experience and knowledge, offering guidance that can help you navigate challenges, avoid common pitfalls, and make informed decisions. Their insights can be invaluable in refining your strategy and accelerating growth.

Accountability and Support: A mentor can serve as an accountability partner, helping you stay focused on your goals and progress. Their support can be particularly motivating during difficult periods, reminding you of your capabilities and vision.

Networking Opportunities: Mentors often have extensive networks and can introduce you to key contacts who can open doors to new opportunities, partnerships, and resources.

The Power of Networking

Expanding Your Professional Circle: Active networking allows you to meet individuals from various backgrounds and industries, expanding your perspective and opening up new avenues for collaboration and innovation.

Access to Resources and Opportunities: A diverse network can provide access to resources, advice, and opportunities that may not be available through your immediate circle. This can include potential clients, partners, investors, or talent to join your team.

Peer Support: Networking with peers offers mutual support, allowing for the exchange of experiences, strategies, and challenges. This camaraderie can be a significant source of encouragement and motivation.

Assembling a Visionary Team

Shared Vision and Values: Building a team that shares your vision and values is crucial for sustained growth. Team members who are aligned with the company's goals and culture are more likely to be engaged, committed, and productive.

Diverse Skills and Perspectives: A team with a diverse set of skills, backgrounds, and perspectives can foster creativity and innovation. This diversity can lead to more effective problem-solving and a stronger ability to adapt to changing market conditions.

Empowerment and Leadership: Empower your team by fostering a culture of leadership, where each member feels responsible for the company's success. Encouraging initiative, providing growth opportunities, and recognizing achievements can all contribute to a motivated and high-performing team.

Strategies for Building Your Support Network

Be Proactive: Actively seek out mentorship opportunities and networking events. Be clear about what you're looking for in a mentor or network and what you can offer in return.

Offer Value: Networking is a two-way street. Think about how you can provide value to others, whether through sharing knowledge, resources, or support.

Cultivate Relationships: Building a support network is not a one-time effort but an ongoing process. Invest time in cultivating and maintaining relationships, showing genuine interest in others' success as well as your own.

Conclusion

A strong support network is a cornerstone of entrepreneurial success, offering a blend of guidance, resources, and collaborative energy that propels businesses forward. Through mentorship, strategic networking, and building a cohesive team, entrepreneurs can navigate the path to scaling their businesses with confidence and clarity. This network not only accelerates growth but also enriches the entrepreneurial journey, making the ambitious goal of scaling a business not just achievable but also a shared and rewarding endeavor.

Action Plan: From Vision to Reality

- Goal Setting and Milestones:

Goal setting and establishing milestones are critical components of a strategic roadmap for any business aspiring to scale and achieve significant growth. This structured approach enables entrepreneurs to navigate the complexities of expansion with clarity, focus, and a sense of direction. By breaking down the journey into actionable goals and milestones, businesses can create a tangible framework for progress and accountability, ensuring that each step taken is aligned with their overarching objectives.

The Importance of Specific Goals

Clarity and Direction: Clear, specific goals provide a sense of direction and purpose, guiding daily operations and strategic decisions. They help to focus efforts on what is most important, ensuring that resources are allocated efficiently.

Measurability and Accountability: Specific goals are measurable, making it possible to track progress and evaluate performance. This measurability fosters accountability, both individually and across the team, as progress towards each goal can be objectively assessed.

Establishing Milestones

Breaking Down Large Goals: Milestones are key achievements or checkpoints along the path to reaching your larger goals. They serve to break down ambitious objectives into more manageable, achievable segments, making the process less daunting and more structured.

Motivation and Momentum: Reaching milestones provides a sense of achievement and progress, which can be incredibly motivating for you and your team. Celebrating these achievements can boost morale and maintain momentum towards the next goal.

Creating a Roadmap for Progress

Define Long-Term Objectives: Start by articulating your long-term objectives. What does success look like for your business? Be as specific as possible, whether it's reaching a certain revenue threshold, expanding to new markets, or launching new products.

Identify Short-Term Goals: Break down your long-term objectives into short-term goals. These should be actionable and achievable within a relatively short timeframe (e.g., quarterly or annually).

Set SMART Goals: Ensure that your goals are Specific, Measurable, Achievable, Relevant, and Time-bound. This framework increases the likelihood of success by making goals clear and trackable.

Determine Milestones: For each short-term goal, identify key milestones that mark progress. These could include launching a minimum viable product, reaching a sales target, securing a key partnership, or completing a round of funding.

Develop Action Plans: For each milestone, outline the specific actions, resources, and timelines required. This plan should include who is responsible for each task, how progress will be measured, and any dependencies or risks.

Monitor and Adjust: Regularly review your progress towards each goal and milestone. Be prepared to adjust your plans based on what is working and what isn't. Flexibility is key to navigating unexpected challenges and opportunities.

Leveraging Technology for Goal Management

Consider using project management software and tools to track progress towards your goals and milestones. Platforms like Asana, Trello, or Monday.com can help organize tasks, deadlines, and responsibilities, enhancing transparency and accountability across your team.

Conclusion

Setting specific goals and milestones is akin to charting a map for a journey. It not only outlines the destination but also marks the critical points along the way, providing a clear path forward and a mechanism for tracking progress. This structured approach to goal setting and milestone achievement is instrumental in scaling businesses, transforming ambitious visions into tangible realities through deliberate, measured steps. By regularly reviewing and adjusting this roadmap, businesses can navigate the path to growth with confidence, ensuring that every effort is aligned with their ultimate objectives.

- **Continuous Improvement and Scaling:**
Continuous improvement and scaling embody a commitment to perpetual evolution and growth in both business operations and personal development. This philosophy is founded on the principle that success is not a static achievement but a dynamic process of adapting, learning, and refining strategies to meet changing market demands, technological advancements, and personal goals. Encouraging an iterative approach to growth requires a mindset shift toward viewing challenges as opportunities for development and feedback as a valuable resource for learning.

Embracing Adaptability

Flexibility in Strategy: Businesses and individuals must remain flexible in their strategies, ready to pivot in response to new information, market trends, or unexpected challenges. This adaptability ensures resilience and relevance in a rapidly changing environment.

Learning from Failure: Viewing failures as learning opportunities is crucial. Each setback offers insights into what doesn't work, guiding future strategies and decisions. Encourage a culture where mistakes are openly discussed and analyzed for improvement.

Committing to Continuous Learning

Lifelong Learning: Foster a culture of lifelong learning within your organization and in your personal life. Encourage attendance at workshops, conferences, and courses. Stay abreast of industry trends and innovations by dedicating time to read, research, and engage with thought leaders.

Cross-Disciplinary Insights: Look beyond your immediate field or industry for learning opportunities. Insights from different disciplines can inspire innovative solutions and offer fresh perspectives on existing challenges.

Cultivating Openness to Feedback

Seeking Constructive Feedback: Actively seek feedback from customers, mentors, peers, and team members. Constructive criticism is invaluable for identifying areas of improvement and validating new ideas.

Implementing Feedback Loops: Establish mechanisms within your business processes to regularly gather and analyze feedback. This could involve customer satisfaction surveys, employee feedback sessions, or beta testing for new products or services.

Implementing Iterative Processes

Agile Methodologies: Incorporate agile methodologies into your project management and product development processes. Agile frameworks emphasize iterative development, where projects are divided into small, manageable increments with regular reassessments and adjustments.

Review and Refine: Schedule regular review sessions to assess progress towards goals, efficiency of processes, and overall satisfaction among stakeholders. Use these insights to refine your approach and make informed adjustments to your strategy.

Scaling with Purpose

Sustainable Growth: As you scale your business, ensure that growth is sustainable. This means balancing ambition with practicality, ensuring that your infrastructure, team, and resources can support expansion without compromising quality or values.

Personal Development: Scaling isn't just about business growth; it's also about personal development. As your business grows, continue to develop your leadership, communication, and strategic thinking skills. Personal growth enhances your capacity to lead your business through its scaling journey.

Conclusion

Continuous improvement and scaling are not merely strategies but philosophies that should permeate every aspect of your business and personal development endeavors. By embracing adaptability, committing to continuous learning, being open to feedback, and implementing iterative processes, businesses and individuals can navigate the complexities of growth with agility and resilience. This approach ensures that both business operations and personal competencies evolve in alignment with the overarching goal of sustained success and development.

Conclusion: The Journey Beyond a Million

- **Reflecting on Achievements:**

Reflecting on achievements is a vital practice for both personal growth and business development. It allows individuals and organizations to acknowledge progress, celebrate milestones, and recalibrate their focus towards larger visions. This process of reflection not only serves as a motivational tool but also as a strategic exercise in understanding what has been effective, what challenges were overcome, and how future endeavors can be optimized for success.

The Importance of Celebrating Milestones

Acknowledging Progress: Regularly taking stock of achievements, no matter their size, reinforces the progress made towards overarching goals. It provides tangible evidence of movement forward, which can be especially motivating during periods of slow growth or challenge.

Boosting Morale: Celebrating milestones boosts morale for you and your team. Recognition of hard work and success fosters a positive work environment and can significantly enhance team cohesion and individual satisfaction.

Learning from Success: Reflection allows you to analyze what led to your achievements. Understanding the strategies, decisions, and actions that contributed to success can inform future initiatives, making them more effective.

Staying Focused on the Larger Vision

Revisiting Goals: While celebrating milestones, it's crucial to revisit and reaffirm your larger vision. This ensures that short-term achievements are aligned with long-term objectives and that the direction of progress remains consistent with your ultimate goals.

Setting New Milestones: After reflecting on achievements, set new milestones that challenge you and your team to reach higher. These should be specific, measurable, achievable, relevant, and time-bound (SMART), guiding the next phase of your journey.

Maintaining Momentum: Use the energy and motivation derived from celebrating milestones to maintain momentum. Let the confidence gained from past successes propel you and your team towards tackling new challenges and achieving further goals.

Strategies for Effective Reflection

Scheduled Reflections: Incorporate regular reflection sessions into your routine or business cycle, such as quarterly or annually. This ensures that reflecting on achievements and planning for the future becomes an integral part of your process.

Documenting the Journey: Keep a record of milestones, challenges, and the strategies used to overcome them. This documentation can serve as a valuable resource for learning and can inspire resilience and creativity in future endeavors.

Sharing Stories: Share your journey and achievements with your team, stakeholders, and broader community. Storytelling can be a powerful tool for reinforcing your mission, values, and the impact of your work.

Conclusion

Reflecting on achievements is more than an exercise in self-congratulation; it is a strategic practice that fuels ongoing growth, learning, and development. By taking the time to celebrate milestones and analyze the journey thus far, businesses and individuals can strengthen their resolve, refine their strategies, and remain steadfastly focused on their larger visions. This practice not only enhances the sense of accomplishment but also solidifies the foundation for future successes, ensuring that every step taken is purposeful and aligned with broader goals.

- **Sustaining Success:**

Sustaining success in the business realm extends beyond maintaining financial growth and market share. It encompasses a broader vision of contributing to societal well-being, building a lasting legacy, and empowering the next generation of entrepreneurs. This holistic approach ensures that the impact of your success is far-reaching and enduring, creating a positive ripple effect that benefits not just your company but the community and industry at large.

Philanthropy as a Pillar of Success

Giving Back: Integrating philanthropy into your business model demonstrates a commitment to social responsibility. This can be achieved through donations, creating charitable foundations, or supporting social causes aligned with your business values. Philanthropy not only contributes to societal improvement but also enhances your brand's reputation and strengthens its relationship with customers and the community.

Strategic Partnerships: Collaborate with non-profits, NGOs, or community organizations. These partnerships can amplify the impact of your philanthropic efforts and provide opportunities for employee engagement through volunteerism, further embedding a culture of giving back within your organization.

Legacy Building for Long-term Impact

Defining Your Legacy: Consider what you want your legacy to be beyond the financial success of your business. This could relate to innovations, industry standards, community impact, or environmental sustainability. Clearly defining this legacy can guide your strategic decisions and actions, ensuring they are aligned with your long-term vision.

Sustainable Practices: Implementing sustainable business practices is a powerful way to build a positive legacy. This includes adopting green technologies, ensuring fair labor practices, and committing to ethical business operations. Such practices not only contribute to a healthier planet and society but also set a standard for others in your industry.

Mentoring the Next Generation

Sharing Knowledge and Experience: One of the most impactful ways to sustain success is by mentoring aspiring entrepreneurs. Sharing your knowledge, experiences, and lessons learned can help nurture the next generation, equipping them with the tools to navigate their entrepreneurial journeys successfully.

Creating Opportunities: Provide internships, apprenticeships, or funding for startups that show potential. These opportunities can be invaluable for young entrepreneurs, offering them a platform to develop their ideas, gain experience, and make meaningful connections.

Building a Culture of Continuous Improvement

Encourage Innovation: Foster a culture within your organization that values and encourages innovation at all levels. This ensures that your business continues to evolve and adapt, sustaining its success in the long term.

Invest in Professional Development: Investing in the ongoing professional development of your team can pay dividends. Skilled and motivated employees are more likely to contribute innovative ideas and drive the company's growth.

Engaging with the Wider Community

Community Involvement: Active engagement with your local community can strengthen your business's ties and support networks, creating a solid foundation for sustained success. This involvement can take many forms, from sponsoring local events to participating in community development projects.

Conclusion

Sustaining success is about more than just continuous growth; it's about creating a meaningful impact that transcends financial achievements. By engaging in philanthropy, striving to build a lasting legacy, mentoring the next generation, and fostering a culture of continuous improvement and community involvement, businesses can ensure their success is sustained and amplified. This multifaceted approach not only enriches the entrepreneur's journey but also contributes to a more prosperous, equitable, and sustainable world.

From Zero to Hero: A Step-by-Step Guide to Scaling Your Business to $1 Million in Monthly Revenue

Creating a business that generates $1 million in monthly revenue is a significant achievement that requires strategic planning, execution, and scaling. While the journey to this milestone varies by industry, product, and market conditions, a structured approach can guide businesses toward rapid growth. Below is a step-by-step guide designed to take a business from inception to achieving $1 million in monthly revenue.

Step 1: Market Research and Validation

Identify a Need

1. Desk Research: Foundation of Market Understanding

Desk research, or secondary research, involves the analysis of existing information to understand the market landscape thoroughly. This foundational step is critical for establishing a baseline understanding of the sector, identifying key players, and recognizing market dynamics.

Utilization of Varied Sources: Leverage a multitude of online resources, industry reports, academic papers, and market analysis studies. Databases such as Statista, IBISWorld, and company filings can provide invaluable insights.

Analysis of Industry Benchmarks: Understand industry standards, average financial ratios, and performance indicators. This information will aid in benchmarking your business against competitors and industry norms.

Market Segmentation: Identify distinct segments within the market to target your research and tailor your offerings more effectively.

2. Field Research: In-Depth Market Engagement

Field research offers a granular view of the market by interacting directly with the components that influence it, notably the consumers and the competitive environment.

Customer Interactions: Utilize surveys, interviews, and focus groups to gather direct feedback from current and potential customers. This interaction can reveal nuanced insights into customer needs, preferences, and dissatisfaction points.

Observational Studies: Conduct observational research to understand customer behaviors and interactions in real-world settings, which can be especially revealing in retail or service-oriented industries.

3. Competitor Analysis: Strategic Market Positioning

A thorough competitor analysis is imperative to identify market gaps and opportunities for differentiation.

Competitive Benchmarking: Assess the strengths and weaknesses of competitors by analyzing their product offerings, marketing strategies, and customer service practices.

Customer Feedback Review: Analyze customer reviews and feedback on competitor offerings to identify patterns that may indicate market gaps or areas for improvement.

4. Trend Analysis: Anticipating Market Evolution

Understanding and anticipating trends is crucial for maintaining relevance and competitive advantage in a rapidly evolving market landscape.

Industry Trends: Monitor industry reports, trade journals, and market research studies to stay informed about current and emerging trends.

Broader Market Trends: Look beyond your industry to identify societal, technological, economic, environmental, and political trends (STEEP analysis) that could impact your market or open new opportunities.

Data Analytics: Employ data analytics tools to analyze large datasets for trend identification and market forecasting, enabling data-driven decision-making.

Conclusion: Integrating Research Insights into Business Strategy

By systematically applying these market research strategies, businesses can acquire a comprehensive understanding of their market environment, enabling informed decision-making and strategic planning. It is crucial to integrate the insights gained from desk research, field research, competitor analysis, and trend analysis into a cohesive business strategy that is responsive to market dynamics and aligned with long-term objectives. This integrated approach ensures that the business remains competitive, customer-focused, and agile in adapting to market changes.

Validate Your Idea

The validation of a business idea is a critical step in the entrepreneurial journey, ensuring that the concept holds real market potential and addresses genuine customer needs. Below is a detailed framework outlining how to leverage various market research methods to validate your business idea effectively.

1. Customer Surveys: Precision in Feedback Collection

Customer surveys are instrumental in gauging market interest and validating the perceived value of your business proposition.

Designing Effective Surveys: Construct surveys with clear, concise questions that directly relate to your business idea's value proposition and customer pain points. Utilize a mix of open-ended and closed-ended questions to gain both quantitative and qualitative insights.

Sampling and Distribution: Ensure your survey reaches a representative sample of your target market. Utilize various distribution channels such as email, social media, and online platforms to maximize response rates.

Data Analysis: Employ statistical analysis to interpret the survey data, identifying trends, and extracting actionable insights that inform your business strategy.

2. In-depth Interviews: Uncovering Deeper Insights

In-depth interviews provide a nuanced understanding of your potential customers' preferences, experiences, and expectations.

Interview Guide Development: Craft a structured interview guide with open-ended questions that encourage detailed responses and uncover deeper insights into customer needs and behaviors.

Participant Selection: Carefully select interview participants who represent your target customer demographics and are likely to provide rich, informative feedback.

Analytical Approach: Analyze interview transcripts for recurring themes and insights, utilizing qualitative analysis methods to distill meaningful patterns and conclusions.

3. Prototype Testing: Tangible Product Feedback

Prototype testing allows potential customers to interact with your product or service concept, providing concrete feedback on its appeal and usability.

Prototype Development: Develop a functional, if basic, version of your product (an MVP) that embodies the core value proposition you wish to test.

User Interaction: Facilitate sessions where users engage with the prototype, observing their interactions and soliciting feedback on their experience and the product's perceived value.

Iterative Refinement: Use the feedback to refine your product iteratively, enhancing its relevance and appeal to the target market.

4. Pilot Programs: Real-World Validation

Pilot programs offer a controlled yet realistic platform to test your business concept comprehensively.

Program Design: Design a pilot that replicates the market conditions under which your business would operate, albeit on a smaller scale.

Monitoring and Evaluation: Collect data on customer engagement, satisfaction, and operational efficiency, using this information to identify strengths and areas for improvement.

Scalability Assessment: Analyze the pilot results to gauge your business concept's scalability and readiness for a broader market launch.

5. Feedback Analysis and Iteration: Continuous Improvement

Integrate feedback from all research activities to refine and enhance your business concept iteratively.

Pattern Identification: Look for common feedback themes across different research methods, prioritizing issues that are consistently highlighted.

Concept Refinement: Apply the insights gained to refine your business model, product features, and customer experience, ensuring alignment with market needs.

6. A/B Testing: Optimization and Validation

For digital or service-oriented offerings, A/B testing can provide empirical evidence of what variations in your product or marketing strategy resonate most with your audience.

Test Design: Develop controlled tests comparing two versions of a product feature, pricing strategy, or marketing message.

Performance Analysis: Measure and analyze the performance of each variant against predefined KPIs, using the results to inform your business development and marketing strategies.

By systematically applying these strategies, you can validate your business idea with a high degree of confidence, ensuring it is well-positioned to meet market needs and achieve sustainable success. This iterative, evidence-based approach not only minimizes the risk of market entry but also lays the foundation for ongoing adaptation and growth in response to evolving market dynamics.

Conclusion

Market research and validation are critical steps that set the foundation for a successful business. They enable entrepreneurs to make informed decisions based on empirical data and direct feedback, reducing the risk of market entry. By thoroughly understanding customer needs and validating your solution, you position your business to meet market demand effectively and resonate with your target audience. This process is iterative; as market conditions and customer preferences evolve, continually engaging in research and validation will keep your business aligned with its market and poised for growth.

Step 2: Business Model Development

Developing a robust business model is crucial for ensuring the sustainability and scalability of your venture. This step involves selecting a model that aligns with your market research and validation findings, and can accommodate growth as your business expands. Additionally, outlining your primary revenue streams is essential for financial planning and attracting investment. Here's how to approach this critical phase:

Choose a Scalable Model

1. **Assess Market Needs:** Reflect on your market research to identify how your target customers prefer to access and pay for services or products. This insight will guide your choice of a scalable business model that meets these preferences.

2. **Evaluate Scalability Potential:** Consider models known for their scalability. For example:

In the contemporary digital landscape, certain business models have demonstrated exceptional scalability, enabling rapid growth with relatively low incremental costs. Herein, we delve into three notable scalable business models: Software as a Service (SaaS), E-commerce, and Platform-based Models, elucidating their core characteristics, scalability mechanisms, and strategic considerations for implementation.

1. Software as a Service (SaaS): Leveraging Cloud Efficiency

The SaaS model epitomizes modern software delivery, offering applications via a subscription model that ensures predictable revenue streams and facilitates scalability.

Core Principle: SaaS eliminates the need for physical software distribution, providing access through the cloud. This model enables instantaneous updates and accessibility from any location, enhancing customer satisfaction and retention.

Scalability Features: Cloud infrastructure allows SaaS providers to scale resources dynamically based on user demand, ensuring cost-efficiency and performance optimization. The marginal cost of adding a new customer is relatively low, facilitating rapid scaling.

Strategic Considerations: To maximize scalability, focus on robust cloud architecture, continuous product enhancement, and data-driven customer acquisition strategies. Invest in customer success to ensure high retention rates, which are crucial for sustainable growth.

2. E-commerce: Expanding Market Reach Online

E-commerce platforms enable the selling of goods and services online, providing vast scalability through digital marketing and efficient logistics.

Core Principle: By operating online, e-commerce businesses can reach a global audience, unconstrained by geographical limitations. The integration of advanced analytics allows for targeted marketing and personalized customer experiences.

Scalability Features: E-commerce scalability can be achieved through various methods, including dropshipping, which eliminates the need for inventory management, and fulfillment services, which streamline logistics. Advanced e-commerce platforms can handle significant traffic increases and transaction volumes.

Strategic Considerations: Focus on optimizing the online customer journey, from discovery to delivery, ensuring high conversion rates and customer loyalty. Leverage data analytics to refine marketing strategies and inventory management, adapting to consumer trends and market demands.

3. Platform-based Models: Harnessing Network Effects

Platform-based businesses facilitate interactions between different user groups, gaining value and scalability from network effects.

Core Principle: These models create value by connecting two or more interdependent groups, such as buyers and sellers or service providers and consumers. As the platform grows, it becomes more valuable to each user group, creating a virtuous cycle that can fuel exponential growth.

Scalability Features: The scalability of platform-based models is inherently linked to network effects; as more users join the platform, the value for each user increases, attracting even more users. Scalability is further enhanced by digital infrastructure, which can support rapid user base expansion without proportional increases in costs.

Strategic Considerations: To build a successful platform, focus on creating a seamless, engaging user experience and cultivating a balanced ecosystem where all participants derive value. Implement robust feedback mechanisms to continuously improve the platform and address the evolving needs of its user base.

Each of these business models embodies the potential for rapid scaling in the digital era, provided they are underpinned by strategic planning, continuous innovation, and a deep understanding of customer needs. By focusing on these core principles and leveraging the unique advantages of each model, businesses can achieve substantial growth and long-term success in the digital marketplace.

3. **Analyze Operational Requirements:** Each model comes with its own set of operational demands. Assess whether your current or projected resources align with these requirements. For instance, a SaaS model requires continuous software development and customer support infrastructure.

4. **Future-proofing:** Ensure the model you choose can adapt to changing market conditions and technological advancements. Flexibility in your business model is key to scaling in response to future opportunities and challenges.

Plan Your Revenue Streams

1. **Diversify Revenue Sources:** Relying on a single revenue stream can be risky. Explore diversification, such as combining subscription fees with advertising revenue or offering premium services alongside a basic free offering.

2. **Subscription Models:** For businesses offering continuous value (like SaaS or content platforms), subscriptions can provide steady, predictable revenue. Determine pricing tiers based on feature access or usage levels.

3. Direct Sales: If you're selling physical or digital products, direct sales through an online storefront can be a primary revenue stream. Consider strategies for upselling, cross-selling, and repeat purchases.

4. Advertising and Sponsorship: If your business attracts a significant audience or user base, advertising can be a lucrative revenue stream. This is particularly relevant for content creators, media platforms, and social networks.

5. Ancillary Services: Offer related services or add-ons that complement your main offering. For example, an e-commerce platform might offer premium listing services to sellers, or a SaaS company could provide consulting or training.

6. Continuous Optimization: Regularly review and optimize your revenue streams based on customer feedback and market trends. Be prepared to pivot or introduce new revenue models as your business grows and evolves.

Conclusion

Developing a business model with high scalability potential is a foundational step in building a successful venture. By choosing a model that aligns with market needs and planning diversified revenue streams, you can create a robust framework for growth. It's important to remain adaptable, continuously refining your model and revenue strategies in response to market feedback, operational performance, and growth opportunities. This iterative approach to business model development ensures that your venture remains competitive, sustainable, and poised for scaling.

Step 3: Product Development

Developing a product, particularly one that effectively meets market needs and has the potential for growth, is a critical phase in the journey of any business. The concept of a Minimum Viable Product (MVP) plays a pivotal role in this process, allowing businesses to test, learn, and iterate with minimal upfront investment. Here's how to navigate the product development stage:

Build a Minimum Viable Product (MVP)

1. Identify Core Features: Focus on the essential features that solve the primary problem or meet the basic need of your target market. Avoid the temptation to add features that are nice to have but not necessary for the initial launch.

2. Rapid Development: Use agile development methodologies to quickly build your MVP. The goal is to bring a functional product to market as swiftly as possible to begin the learning process.

3. Cost-Effective Solutions: Utilize cost-effective tools and technologies that can speed up development without significantly impacting your budget. Open-source frameworks, no-code/low-code platforms, and cloud services can be particularly useful.

4. Prepare for Iteration: Design your MVP with the understanding that it will evolve. Ensure that your technology stack and design choices allow for easy updates and iterations based on feedback.

Gather Feedback

1. **Identify Early Adopters:** Target early adopters who are most likely to experience the problem your product solves. They're typically more willing to try new solutions and provide valuable insights.

2. **Feedback Channels:** Establish clear channels for gathering feedback, such as surveys, interviews, and usage data analytics. Make it easy for users to share their experiences and suggestions.

3. **Analyze Feedback:** Collect and analyze feedback systematically to identify patterns and common themes. Distinguish between one-off comments and feedback that indicates a widespread issue or opportunity.

4. **Prioritize Improvements:** Not all feedback will be immediately actionable or relevant. Prioritize changes based on their potential impact on user satisfaction and product-market fit.

5. **Communicate Changes:** Keep your early adopters informed about how their feedback is being used to improve the product. This transparency can build trust and encourage continued engagement.

Iteration and Improvement

1. **Continuous Iteration:** Product development doesn't stop with your MVP. Use ongoing feedback to iteratively improve and add features to your product, always focusing on enhancing value to your users.

2. **Scale Features Wisely:** As your product matures, carefully consider which new features to develop. Each addition should be based on solid evidence of user demand and aligned with your overall business strategy.

3. **Measure Success:** Establish key performance indicators (KPIs) to measure the success of your product. These could include user engagement metrics, customer satisfaction scores, and conversion rates.

Conclusion

Product development, centered around building and refining an MVP, is a dynamic and ongoing process. By focusing on core needs, gathering and acting on early adopter feedback, and continuously iterating, businesses can develop products that truly resonate with their target market. This approach not only enhances the chances of achieving product-market fit but also lays a solid foundation for future growth and innovation.

Step 4: Branding and Online Presence

In the digital age, a compelling brand identity and a strong online presence are indispensable for any business aiming to make a mark and attract customers. This step is about crafting a unique brand personality that resonates with your target audience and establishing a digital footprint that enhances visibility and engagement. Here's how to approach this crucial phase:

Create a Strong Brand Identity

1. **Define Your Brand Personality:** Start by defining the core characteristics of your brand. What values and emotions do you want your brand to convey? This personality should reflect your business's mission and appeal to your target audience.

2. **Choose a Memorable Brand Name:** Your brand name is often the first point of contact with potential customers, so it should be memorable, easy to pronounce, and reflective of your brand's essence. Conduct thorough checks to ensure it's unique and not trademarked by others.

3. **Design a Distinctive Logo and Visual Identity:** Your logo and visual identity (colors, typography, imagery style) are critical components of your brand. They should be distinctive and consistent across all your marketing materials and platforms. Hiring a professional designer or utilizing design platforms can ensure a polished and cohesive look.

4. **Develop a Brand Voice:** Your brand voice—how you communicate in text and speech—should align with your brand personality and resonate with your target audience. Whether it's professional, casual, playful, or inspiring, ensure consistency in all communications.

Establish an Online Presence

1. **Build a Professional Website:** Your website serves as the digital storefront for your business. It should be professional, user-friendly, and optimized for search engines (SEO). Ensure it clearly communicates your value proposition, showcases your products or services, and includes clear calls to action (CTAs).

2. **Choose Relevant Social Media Platforms:** Not all social media platforms will be relevant to your business. Select those where your target audience is most active. Focus on building a presence there through regular, engaging content that reflects your brand identity.

3. **Content Strategy:** Develop a content strategy that provides value to your audience while promoting your brand. This could include blog posts, videos, podcasts, infographics, or live sessions. Consistency and quality are key to building a loyal following.

4. **Engage with Your Audience:** Social media is not just a broadcasting platform; it's a two-way communication channel. Engage with your audience by responding to comments, messages, and reviews. This engagement builds community and enhances customer loyalty.

5. **Monitor and Adapt:** Use analytics tools to monitor the performance of your website and social media presence. Analyze traffic sources, engagement rates, and conversion metrics to understand what works and where improvements are needed. Be prepared to adapt your strategy based on these insights.

Conclusion

Building a strong brand identity and establishing an online presence are foundational steps for connecting with your audience and building trust. By carefully crafting your brand and strategically engaging with your audience online, you set the stage for meaningful relationships and business growth. Remember, your brand is more than just a logo or a website—it's the entire experience customers have with your business, so make it count.

Step 5: Marketing and Customer Acquisition

In today's competitive marketplace, a well-crafted marketing strategy and a focus on customer acquisition are crucial for business growth. This involves utilizing a combination of digital marketing techniques to attract, engage, and convert your target audience into loyal customers. Here's how to create and implement an effective marketing and customer acquisition strategy:

Develop a Marketing Strategy

1. **Define Your Target Audience:** Clearly identify who your target customers are, including their demographics, interests, and pain points. This information will guide all your marketing efforts and content creation.

2. **Content Marketing:** Develop and share valuable, relevant, and consistent content to attract and retain a clearly defined audience. Blog posts, videos, podcasts, and infographics can help establish your authority in your niche and solve your audience's problems.

3. **Search Engine Optimization (SEO):** Optimize your website and content for search engines to increase visibility in search results. Focus on keyword research, on-page SEO (like meta tags and content quality), and off-page SEO (such as backlinks) to drive organic traffic.

4. **Pay-Per-Click (PPC) Advertising:** Use PPC advertising on platforms like Google AdWords and social media to drive targeted traffic to your website. PPC allows for precise targeting based on demographics, interests, and behaviors, offering a quick way to increase visibility.

5. **Social Media Marketing:** Engage with your audience where they spend their time online. Choose platforms relevant to your target audience and post regularly, using a mix of promotional and value-driven content to foster community and brand loyalty.

Leverage Email Marketing

1. **Build an Email List:** Use your website, social media channels, and other touchpoints to encourage sign-ups for your email list. Offer incentives like free ebooks, discounts, or valuable content as a sign-up bonus.

2. **Segment Your Audience:** Segment your email list based on customer demographics, behaviors, or purchase history to send more personalized and relevant communications. This can significantly improve open rates and conversions.

3. Email Campaigns: Develop targeted email campaigns that nurture leads through the sales funnel. This can include welcome series, educational content, product recommendations, and special promotions.

4. Automation: Use email marketing tools to automate parts of your email strategy, such as sending triggered emails based on specific actions (e.g., cart abandonment emails) or scheduling regular newsletters.

5. Measure and Optimize: Track the performance of your email campaigns using metrics such as open rates, click-through rates, and conversion rates. Use these insights to continually refine your email marketing strategy for better results.

Conclusion

A comprehensive marketing and customer acquisition strategy is key to driving business growth. By combining content marketing, SEO, PPC, social media, and email marketing, you can create a multifaceted approach that attracts, engages, and converts your target audience. Remember, the goal is to provide value at every touchpoint, building trust and relationships that lead to long-term customer loyalty. Continuously analyze the performance of your marketing efforts and be prepared to adapt your strategies in response to changing market conditions and customer feedback.

Step 6: Sales Funnel Optimization

Optimizing your sales funnel is a critical step in maximizing the efficiency of your customer acquisition and retention strategies. A well-designed sales funnel not only guides prospects smoothly from initial awareness to the final purchase but also helps in identifying areas for improvement in your sales process. Here's how to approach sales funnel optimization:

Create a Sales Funnel

1. Define the Stages: Break down your customer journey into distinct stages: Awareness, Interest, Decision, and Action. Each stage represents a deeper level of engagement with your brand and product.

2. Identify Customer Actions: For each stage of the funnel, identify key actions that customers need to take to move to the next level. This could include visiting your website, signing up for a newsletter, or making a purchase.

3. Create Targeted Content: Develop content tailored to the needs and interests of prospects at each stage of the funnel. Educational content works well for the awareness stage, while detailed product comparisons are more suited for the decision stage.

4. Implement Lead Capture Mechanisms: Use lead magnets (e.g., free trials, ebooks, webinars) to capture contact information from interested prospects. This enables you to nurture these leads through email marketing or targeted advertising.

Optimize for Conversion

1. Landing Page Optimization: Ensure that your landing pages are clear, concise, and compelling. Each page should have a single focus and a clear call-to-action (CTA) that encourages the desired action.

2. A/B Testing: Conduct A/B testing on different elements of your landing pages, including headlines, CTAs, images, and copy. This helps in identifying the most effective versions that drive higher conversion rates.

3. Improve User Experience (UX): Analyze the user experience on your website. Navigation should be intuitive, and page load times should be fast. A positive UX can significantly increase the chances of conversion.

4. Personalization: Use data from website visits, previous purchases, and customer interactions to personalize the shopping experience. Personalization can increase relevance and drive conversions.

5. Nurture Leads: Not all prospects will convert on their first visit. Implement lead nurturing campaigns that provide value and gently guide leads towards making a purchase.

6. Monitor and Analyze Funnel Performance: Use analytics tools to track how prospects move through your sales funnel. Look for drop-off points or stages where conversions are lower than expected. These insights can guide your optimization efforts.

Conclusion

Sales funnel optimization is an ongoing process that requires continuous testing, analysis, and refinement. By understanding the customer journey, creating targeted content, and optimizing for conversions at every stage, you can increase the efficiency of your sales process. This not only leads to higher conversion rates but also enhances the overall customer experience, contributing to long-term business growth. Remember, the key to successful sales funnel optimization lies in understanding your audience deeply and providing them with value at every step of their journey.

Step 7: Customer Retention and Upselling

In the lifecycle of a business, acquiring customers is just the beginning. The real challenge—and opportunity—lies in retaining those customers and maximizing their lifetime value through strategic upselling. Exceptional customer service and thoughtful upselling strategies are pivotal in this regard, turning one-time buyers into loyal advocates and driving sustainable growth. Here's how to effectively approach customer retention and upselling:

Focus on Customer Service

1. Prioritize Responsiveness: Ensure that customer inquiries, complaints, and feedback are addressed promptly. Utilize various channels, including email, phone, social media, and live chat, to provide accessible and timely support.

2. **Train Your Team:** Equip your customer service team with the knowledge, tools, and empowerment they need to resolve issues efficiently and satisfactorily. Regular training and a clear understanding of your products/services are crucial.

3. **Personalize Interactions:** Tailor your customer service approach to the individual needs and history of each customer. Personalized interactions can make customers feel valued and foster loyalty.

4. **Solicit and Act on Feedback:** Regularly ask for customer feedback through surveys, follow-up emails, or direct conversations. More importantly, use this feedback to make tangible improvements to your products, services, and processes.

5. **Create a Customer Community:** Build a sense of community among your customers through forums, social media groups, or loyalty programs. This can enhance engagement, provide valuable insights, and encourage peer-to-peer support and referrals.

Implement Upselling Strategies

1. **Understand Customer Needs:** Effective upselling starts with a deep understanding of your customers' needs and how your products/services can meet them. Use purchase history, customer behavior data, and direct feedback to identify upselling opportunities.

2. **Offer Relevant Upgrades:** Present upselling options that are closely related to the customers' original purchase or interest. This could include premium versions, add-ons, or complementary products that enhance the value of their initial purchase.

3. **Time Your Offers:** The timing of your upsell offer can significantly impact its success. Consider upselling when customers are already engaged in the buying process or shortly after a purchase when their satisfaction is highest.

4. **Provide Value Propositions:** Clearly articulate the benefits of the upsell. Customers should understand how the additional purchase adds value to what they already have or are buying.

5. **Leverage Technology:** Use CRM and marketing automation tools to segment your audience and deliver personalized upsell offers at scale. Automated recommendations based on customer behavior and preferences can be particularly effective.

6. **Train Your Sales Team:** Ensure your sales and support staff are trained to recognize upselling opportunities and can communicate the value of additional products or services without being pushy.

Conclusion

Customer retention and upselling are integral to maximizing the revenue potential of your existing customer base. By delivering exceptional customer service, you not only foster loyalty but also create a conducive environment for presenting valuable upselling opportunities. Implementing thoughtful, customer-centric upselling strategies can significantly enhance customer lifetime value, contributing to the long-term success and sustainability of your business. Remember, the key is to focus on providing genuine value and enhancing the customer experience at every touchpoint.

Step 8: Scaling Operations

Scaling operations effectively is crucial for businesses aiming to grow sustainably while maintaining quality and customer satisfaction. This involves strategic automation, outsourcing, and the expansion of offerings in response to market demand and customer feedback. Here's a comprehensive approach to scaling your business operations:

Automate and Outsource

1. **Identify Repetitive Tasks:** Start by identifying tasks within your operations that are repetitive and time-consuming. These might include data entry, scheduling, email management, and social media posting.

2. **Implement Automation Tools:** Leverage technology to automate these tasks. Tools like CRM systems, email marketing software, scheduling tools, and social media management platforms can significantly reduce manual effort and free up time for strategic activities.

3. **Assess Non-Core Activities:** Identify activities that are necessary for your business but not part of your core competencies. These might include accounting, HR, IT support, and legal services.

4. **Choose Outsourcing Partners Wisely:** Outsource these non-core activities to reputable third-party providers or freelancers. Ensure that your outsourcing partners understand your business values and quality standards to maintain consistency in your operations and customer experience.

5. **Monitor and Optimize:** Regularly review the effectiveness of your automation tools and outsourcing arrangements. Be open to making adjustments to ensure they continue to meet your business needs as you scale.

Expand Your Offerings

1. **Gather and Analyze Customer Feedback:** Continuously collect feedback from your customers through surveys, interviews, and social media engagement. Analyze this feedback to identify patterns and insights that can guide your product development.

2. **Conduct Market Research:** Stay informed about trends and developments in your industry. Use market research to identify emerging opportunities and gaps that your business can address.

3. **Develop New Products or Services:** Based on customer feedback and market research, develop new products or services that meet the evolving needs of your market. Ensure that these new offerings align with your brand and core competencies.

4. **Test Before Full Launch:** Before rolling out new offerings broadly, conduct pilot tests or soft launches with a segment of your target market. This allows you to gather feedback and make necessary adjustments, reducing risk.

5. **Plan for Scalability:** As you expand your offerings, consider the scalability of production, delivery, and support. Ensure that you have the necessary systems, processes, and resources in place to support growth without compromising quality.

6. **Marketing and Promotion:** Develop a marketing plan to promote your new offerings. Use a mix of channels and strategies that resonate with your target audience to generate interest and drive sales.

Conclusion

Scaling operations is a delicate balancing act that requires strategic planning and execution. By automating repetitive tasks, outsourcing non-core activities, and thoughtfully expanding your product or service offerings, you can build a foundation for sustainable growth. Throughout this process, maintaining a focus on quality, customer satisfaction, and alignment with your business goals is paramount. Successfully scaled operations not only support growth but also enhance efficiency and the overall value proposition to your customers, positioning your business for long-term success in a competitive landscape.

Step 9: Financial Management

Effective financial management is the backbone of a successful business, especially during periods of growth and scaling. It involves diligent monitoring of cash flow, strategic management of expenses, and securing funding for expansion when necessary. This step is crucial for ensuring the business has the financial resources needed to grow without compromising its operational integrity or financial stability. Here's how to approach this critical phase:

Monitor Cash Flow

1. **Implement a Robust Accounting System:** Utilize accounting software to track income, expenses, and cash flow in real-time. This will provide a clear picture of your financial health and help in making informed decisions.

2. **Create a Cash Flow Forecast:** Develop a cash flow forecast to anticipate inflows and outflows over a specified period. This can help identify potential cash shortages and allow you to take preemptive action.

3. **Manage Receivables and Payables:** Actively manage your accounts receivable to ensure timely payments from customers. Similarly, manage your accounts payable to maintain good relationships with suppliers while optimizing your cash flow.

4. **Reserve Funds for Emergencies:** Maintain a cash reserve or emergency fund to cover unexpected expenses or downturns in revenue. This financial cushion can be critical for sustaining operations during challenging times.

Seek Funding if Necessary

1. **Assess Funding Needs:** Carefully assess your need for external funding. Consider whether funding is required for capital investments, entering new markets, or increasing production capacity, and how it will contribute to growth.

2. **Explore Funding Options:** Investigate various funding options, including:

Securing adequate funding is a cornerstone of business expansion and sustainability. Various financing avenues cater to different stages of business development, risk profiles, and growth trajectories. Here, we explore three critical funding sources: venture capital or angel investment, traditional loans, and crowdfunding, highlighting their implications, prerequisites, and strategic fit for diverse business models.

1. Equity Financing: Venture Capital and Angel Investors

Equity financing through venture capital or angel investors provides substantial capital infusion, often pivotal for businesses aiming for aggressive growth and market penetration.

Core Principle: This funding mechanism involves exchanging equity in your business for capital investment. It's well-suited for innovative startups with scalable business models and the potential to disrupt markets or achieve rapid growth.

Strategic Considerations: When pursuing equity financing, it is crucial to align with investors who bring not only capital but also strategic value through industry expertise, networks, and resources. Articulate a compelling vision, robust business model, and clear exit strategy to attract and engage these investors.

Operational Implications: Equity financing typically does not require immediate repayment, thereby reducing short-term financial pressure. However, it does dilute ownership and often brings investors into decision-making processes, necessitating a careful balance between growth objectives and investor relations.

2. Debt Financing: Business Loans

Traditional loans provide a structured funding path, emphasizing predictability and financial discipline, suitable for businesses with clear revenue models and stable cash flows.

Core Principle: Loans are borrowed funds that must be repaid with interest over a predetermined period. They are secured based on the business's financial health, creditworthiness, and sometimes collateral, without diluting equity.

Strategic Considerations: A robust business plan and solid financial projections are imperative to secure a loan. Businesses must demonstrate repayment capacity through consistent revenue streams and effective financial management.

Operational Implications: Loans introduce fixed repayment obligations, impacting cash flow management. While they preserve ownership and autonomy compared to equity financing, they also impose financial liabilities and necessitate disciplined budgeting and financial oversight.

3. Crowdfunding: Engaging the Community

Crowdfunding harnesses collective support from a broad audience, often leveraging small contributions from many backers, and can validate product demand while providing financing.

Core Principle: Crowdfunding platforms enable businesses to raise funds directly from the public, often in exchange for pre-orders, rewards, or even equity. This method can serve as a powerful tool for market validation and community engagement.

Strategic Considerations: Success in crowdfunding hinges on compelling storytelling, transparent communication, and effective marketing. It requires a captivating narrative that resonates with potential backers, showcasing the value and potential impact of the product or venture.

Operational Implications: Crowdfunding can provide early-stage funding without incurring debt or diluting equity. However, it demands significant marketing efforts and can entail obligations to deliver rewards or products, necessitating meticulous planning and execution.

In conclusion, selecting the appropriate funding avenue depends on the business's growth stage, industry, financial stability, and long-term objectives. Each option carries distinct strategic and operational implications, necessitating careful consideration to align funding choices with broader business goals and values. By understanding and leveraging the strengths of each funding source, businesses can secure the capital necessary for sustainable growth and innovation.

3. **Prepare a Compelling Pitch:** Whether you're seeking investors or crowdfunding, prepare a compelling pitch that clearly articulates your business value, growth potential, and how the funds will be used.

4. **Understand the Terms:** Carefully review the terms of any funding agreement, including interest rates, repayment schedules, equity stakes, and any other conditions. Ensure these terms align with your business goals and financial capacity.

Conclusion

Financial management during the scaling phase is not just about keeping the books balanced; it's about strategic planning and foresight to ensure the business's growth is sustainable and financially viable. Monitoring cash flow closely, managing financial operations prudently, and securing external funding when necessary are all critical components of this process. By staying vigilant and proactive in financial management, businesses can navigate the challenges of scaling, seize opportunities for growth, and build a strong foundation for long-term success.

Step 10: Analyze and Pivot

The ability to analyze performance and pivot when necessary is crucial for businesses in today's fast-paced and ever-changing market environment. This final step in the journey towards growth and scaling is about maintaining agility, continuously aligning your business strategies with market realities, and making informed decisions to steer your business towards success. Here's how to approach this critical phase:

Review Performance

1. **Set Clear KPIs:** Establish Key Performance Indicators (KPIs) that are aligned with your business goals. These could range from revenue targets and customer acquisition costs to website traffic and conversion rates, depending on your business model.

2. **Regular Performance Reviews:** Conduct regular reviews of your business performance against the set KPIs. Monthly, quarterly, and annual reviews can provide insights into trends, progress, and areas needing improvement.

3. **Utilize Analytics Tools:** Leverage analytics tools to gather data on various aspects of your business. From financial software for cash flow analysis to marketing platforms for tracking engagement and conversion, the right tools can provide a wealth of actionable insights.

4. **Involve Your Team:** Make performance review a collaborative process with your team. Different perspectives can offer valuable insights and foster a culture of continuous improvement.

Be Prepared to Pivot

1. **Listen to Your Market:** Stay attuned to market feedback, whether it comes from direct customer input, changes in consumer behavior, or shifts in the competitive landscape. This feedback is invaluable for identifying when a pivot might be necessary.

2. **Evaluate Pivot Options:** If performance data and market feedback indicate a need for change, evaluate your options thoroughly. This could involve adjusting your marketing strategy, redesigning your product, or even overhauling your business model.

3. **Plan and Test Your Pivot:** Before fully committing to a pivot, plan carefully and, if possible, conduct tests or pilot programs. This approach can help validate the direction of the pivot and minimize risk.

4. **Communicate Changes:** Clearly communicate any strategic pivots to your team and stakeholders. Transparency about the reasons for changes and the expected benefits can help ensure support and alignment.

5. **Monitor Impact:** After implementing a pivot, closely monitor its impact on your business performance. Be prepared for further iterations as you refine your approach based on ongoing feedback and results.

Conclusion

The journey of scaling a business is dynamic and requires not just a solid foundation in steps 1 through 9 but also the flexibility to adapt as you learn and grow. Regularly analyzing your business performance and being prepared to pivot based on this analysis and market feedback are essential practices for sustained success. They allow you to remain competitive, responsive to market needs, and on track towards achieving your business goals. Remember, the capacity to analyze, adapt, and pivot is not a sign of failure but a strategic advantage that can lead to greater innovation, customer satisfaction, and long-term growth.

Conclusion

Achieving $1 million in monthly revenue stands as a testament to unwavering dedication, adaptability, and strategic precision. This pinnacle of success, while challenging, is within reach for those who navigate their journey with a steadfast commitment to growth and resilience. Envision yourself embarking on this journey equipped with a dynamic blueprint—each step taken is a stride towards greatness, guided by an innate belief in your potential and the transformative power of perseverance.

As you traverse this path, let each moment of learning sculpt your journey, turning obstacles into stepping stones. Embrace the art of flexibility, allowing it to be the wind beneath your wings, propelling you towards your objectives with grace and agility. The essence of your ambition is fueled by a relentless pursuit of excellence, a journey not just of achieving goals but of continual self-discovery and evolution.

Patience and persistence become your trusted companions, reminding you that the road to success is a marathon, not a sprint. Each setback, a lesson; every failure, a fountain of insight, watering the seeds of future triumphs. Your journey is illuminated by a can-do attitude, a powerful force that transforms doubts into determination and challenges into opportunities for growth.

Let this journey redefine the essence of success, where surpassing the milestone of $1 million in monthly revenue becomes not just an achievement but a reflection of your unwavering spirit and dedication. Remember, the path to greatness is paved with the courage to persist, the strength to rise above setbacks, and an unyielding belief in your ability to conquer the seemingly insurmountable. With each step forward, you are not only closer to your goal but also to realizing the boundless potential that lies within.

Chapter 6: Architecting Your Wealth: Blueprint for Integrated Financial Success

- Define the concept of a wealth architect—a visionary who designs and constructs their financial future with intentionality and precision.

The concept of a Wealth Architect embodies the fusion of vision, strategy, and execution in the realm of financial empowerment. A Wealth Architect is not merely a passive participant in their financial journey but an active designer and builder of their future prosperity. This individual approaches wealth creation with the same intentionality and precision as an architect approaches the design and construction of a building. Just as an architect draws up blueprints based on specific goals, materials, and structural principles, a Wealth Architect crafts a detailed plan for their financial future, grounded in a deep understanding of financial principles, market dynamics, and personal aspirations.

Visionary Planning

At the heart of wealth architecture lies visionary planning. The Wealth Architect begins with a clear, vivid vision of their desired financial future. This vision encompasses more than mere numbers; it includes the lifestyle, impact, and legacy they aim to achieve through their wealth. With this vision in mind, they set about meticulously planning how to realize it, identifying the financial tools, investments, and strategies that will serve as the building blocks of their prosperity.

Strategic Design

Wealth Architects recognize that a robust financial structure requires a foundation of sound financial literacy. They invest time in educating themselves about various financial vehicles, from traditional stocks and bonds to alternative investments like real estate and private equity. This knowledge allows them to design a diversified investment portfolio tailored to their risk tolerance, time horizon, and growth objectives, much like an architect selects materials that balance aesthetics, functionality, and structural integrity.

Precision in Execution

With a plan in place, the Wealth Architect executes with precision. They monitor their financial health with the diligence of an architect overseeing a construction site, making adjustments as necessary to align with their evolving financial landscape and life goals. This might involve rebalancing their investment portfolio, exploring new income streams, or strategically managing debt to leverage growth opportunities.

Adaptive Innovation

Just as architectural designs evolve in response to new materials, technologies, and environmental considerations, Wealth Architects remain adaptive and innovative. They stay informed about economic trends, regulatory changes, and emerging opportunities, ready to pivot their strategies to optimize wealth growth. This adaptability ensures that their financial structures are not only resilient but also capable of expanding to encompass new possibilities.

Conclusion

The role of a Wealth Architect transcends traditional notions of personal finance and investment. It is a holistic approach to financial empowerment that integrates vision, strategy, and disciplined execution. Wealth Architects are defined by their proactive stance towards financial planning, their strategic mindset in wealth building, and their precision in navigating the financial markets. By embodying these qualities, they construct a financial future that is not only prosperous but also reflective of their deepest values and aspirations.

- Emphasize the integration of personal financial health and business prosperity as complementary facets of wealth architecture.

The integration of personal financial health and business prosperity represents a cornerstone principle within the realm of wealth architecture. This dual focus acknowledges that the pillars of individual wealth and entrepreneurial success are not isolated constructs but are deeply intertwined, each reinforcing the other in a symbiotic relationship. A Wealth Architect understands that a holistic approach to financial empowerment involves harmonizing personal financial strategies with business growth initiatives, creating a dynamic framework where both dimensions of wealth nourish and elevate one another.

Symbiotic Relationship

Imagine personal financial health and business prosperity as two currents within the same river, each contributing to the river's power and direction. Personal financial health provides the stability and security that allows for the calculated risks and investments necessary for business expansion. Conversely, the success and growth of a business inject vitality into personal finances, opening avenues for wealth accumulation and lifestyle enhancements that were previously unattainable.

Building a Foundation

The foundation of this integrated approach lies in robust financial literacy, encompassing both personal finance principles and business financial management. A Wealth Architect leverages this knowledge to make informed decisions, from budgeting and saving to investing and risk management, ensuring that personal finances are structured to support and amplify business objectives.

Designing a Blueprint

In designing their wealth architecture blueprint, individuals strategically plan how personal financial goals can align with and support their business visions. This may involve setting aside a portion of business profits for personal investment portfolios, or conversely, utilizing personal financial resources to seed business growth opportunities. The blueprint reflects a comprehensive strategy where personal and business finances are not competing interests but collaborative elements of a unified wealth-building plan.

Executing with Precision

Execution in this integrated framework requires a keen understanding of cash flow management, both personally and within the business. It involves meticulous tracking, analysis, and optimization of financial resources to ensure that every dollar is purposefully allocated towards achieving overarching wealth goals. This precision ensures that personal financial health and business prosperity are mutually enhancing, each element of wealth being carefully constructed to support and sustain the other.

Nurturing Growth

Just as an architect continuously assesses and adapts a building's design to environmental changes and new technologies, a Wealth Architect remains agile, ready to adjust their strategies in response to market shifts, economic trends, and personal life changes. This adaptability is crucial for nurturing long-term growth in both personal and business finances, enabling the Wealth Architect to capitalize on emerging opportunities and navigate challenges with resilience.

Conclusion

The integration of personal financial health and business prosperity within wealth architecture offers a more nuanced and effective approach to financial empowerment. By viewing these facets as complementary rather than separate, individuals can create a synergistic effect, where the growth and success of one domain fuel the expansion of the other. This holistic strategy not only accelerates the path to financial milestones but also ensures that wealth is built on a foundation of balance, sustainability, and harmony between personal aspirations and business ambitions.

Designing Your Financial Blueprint

- Vision Casting:

As students embarking on the journey of financial literacy and personal growth, the concept of Vision Casting invites you to look beyond the horizon of traditional success metrics and to envision a future defined by your deepest aspirations, values, and lifestyle goals. This process isn't merely about setting financial targets; it's an invitation to weave a comprehensive tapestry of your life's potential, where wealth serves not just as an end, but as a means to a richer, more fulfilling existence.

Embracing the Canvas of Imagination

Allow Yourself to Dream: Begin with the freedom to dream expansively. Imagine a life where financial constraints do not dictate your choices. What does this freedom enable you to pursue? How does it shape your day-to-day life? Engage in this imaginative exercise with the intent to uncover what truly resonates with you, painting your future with broad strokes of possibility.

Identifying Core Values: Your personal values are the compass that guides your vision. Whether it's fostering family connections, pursuing creative endeavors, seeking adventure, or contributing to societal welfare, these values anchor your financial and lifestyle goals, ensuring they reflect who you are at your core.

Envisioning Your Lifestyle Goals: Look beyond mere financial accumulation to define the essence of the life you wish to lead. This could encompass anything from global travel and lifelong learning to achieving a harmonious work-life balance. Such goals add depth and context to your financial ambitions, making them more compelling and personal.

Constructing Your Vision

Balancing the Horizon with Stepping Stones: While your vision sets the direction, establishing short-term milestones can provide clarity and motivation. These nearer-term objectives act as tangible steps towards your broader vision, offering a sense of progress and accomplishment.

Building in Flexibility: Life's only constant is change, and your vision should accommodate this reality. Allowing room for your goals and aspirations to evolve ensures that your vision remains relevant and resonant, even as you grow and navigate life's twists and turns.

The Power of Visualization

Engage in Regular Visualization: Make a habit of mentally projecting yourself into the future you wish to create. This practice not only keeps your motivation aflame but also aligns your subconscious mind with your goals, subtly steering your daily actions towards your envisioned future.

Craft a Vision Board: A tangible representation of your aspirations, a vision board can serve as a daily reminder of your goals. Collating images, quotes, and symbols that resonate with your vision can reinforce your commitment and focus.

Living Your Vision

Align Daily Actions with Your Vision: Each day presents opportunities to make choices that echo your long-term goals. Small, consistent actions aligned with your vision can have a profound cumulative effect, gradually sculpting the future you desire.

Surround Yourself with Support: The environment and company you keep can significantly influence your journey. Seek out mentors, join communities of like-minded individuals, and immerse yourself in inspiring content to nurture your vision and propel you towards its realization.

Conclusion

Vision Casting is not just an exercise in financial planning; it's a foundational step in crafting a life of intention, purpose, and fulfillment. As students standing on the threshold of your future, you are invited to dream with conviction, plan with purpose, and act with persistence. Through this visionary approach, you set the stage for a life where wealth transcends material success and becomes a catalyst for realizing your most cherished dreams and aspirations.

- **Strategic Planning:**

Strategic Planning is a critical step in transforming your vision of financial prosperity and personal fulfillment into tangible realities. As students navigating the complexities of both personal aspirations and potential future business endeavors, understanding how to meticulously craft actionable plans is essential. This process involves setting clear, achievable goals and outlining the steps necessary to realize them, ensuring that every action taken is a deliberate stride toward your envisioned future.

The Blueprint of Strategic Planning

Set SMART Goals: Begin by framing your objectives through the SMART criteria—Specific, Measurable, Achievable, Relevant, and Time-bound. This approach ensures that your goals are well-defined and actionable, providing a clear roadmap for progress.

In the quest for business success, setting clear and actionable goals is paramount. The SMART criteria—Specific, Measurable, Achievable, Relevant, and Time-bound—provide a robust framework for goal formulation, ensuring they are structured to foster accountability, clarity, and effectiveness. Here, we dissect each element of the SMART framework, elucidating its significance and application in the business context.

1. Specific: Precision in Goal Setting

The specificity of a goal lays the foundation for its achievability. Vague objectives are challenging to assess and pursue, whereas specific goals offer a clear direction and focal point for organizational efforts.

- **Application:** Define the goal with precision, identifying the who, what, where, when, and why. For instance, instead of aiming to "increase sales," a specific goal would be "increase sales of Product X by 20% in the North American market by Q4."

2. Measurable: Quantifying Success

Measurable goals enable performance tracking and facilitate progress assessment. By establishing quantitative or qualitative benchmarks, businesses can evaluate their achievements and adjust strategies as needed.

- **Application:** Incorporate metrics or indicators that reflect progress and completion. For a goal to "improve customer service," a measurable counterpart would be "achieve a customer satisfaction score of 90% within six months."

3. Achievable: Realism in Aspirations

Setting achievable goals ensures they are within the realm of possibility, considering the available resources, capabilities, and external factors. Unrealistic goals can demoralize teams and erode motivation.

- **Application:** Assess your organization's resources, capabilities, and external environment to confirm that the goal is attainable. If the objective is to "expand to three new international markets," ensure you have the requisite infrastructure, capital, and market understanding.

4. Relevant: Ensuring Alignment with Strategic Vision

Relevance ensures that each goal is in harmony with the broader organizational objectives and strategic vision. Goals that resonate with the company's core values and long-term aspirations are more likely to garner commitment and enthusiasm.

- **Application:** Align each goal with your business's overarching vision and strategy. If your strategic focus is on innovation, a relevant goal would be "launch two new product lines by the end of the year" rather than "cut costs by 10%."

5. Time-bound: Establishing Deadlines

Setting deadlines creates a sense of urgency and prioritizes goal-oriented activities. Time-bound goals help in resource allocation, monitoring progress, and maintaining momentum toward achievement.

- **Application:** Assign a specific timeframe to each goal, facilitating planning and urgency. For instance, transforming "increase market share" into "increase market share by 5% within one year" introduces a critical temporal dimension.

Conclusion

Employing the SMART framework imbues business goals with clarity, structure, and focus, vital for strategic planning and execution. These well-defined goals act as beacons, guiding decision-making, resource allocation, and operational initiatives. By meticulously crafting goals that are specific, measurable, achievable, relevant, and time-bound, businesses position themselves for measurable progress and sustained success in their endeavors.

Integrating Personal and Business Objectives

Harmonize Your Goals: Recognize the interplay between personal financial health and business success. Strive to integrate personal and business objectives, ensuring they support and amplify each other. For instance, personal goals related to savings and investment can fund business start-up costs, while business growth can contribute to personal wealth accumulation.

Balance Short-Term Actions with Long-Term Vision: Break down long-term goals into smaller, manageable tasks. Consider how daily decisions in both personal finance and business planning can incrementally lead to the achievement of your overarching vision.

Actionable Steps and Monitoring Progress

Action Plans: For each goal, develop an action plan detailing the specific steps needed to achieve it. Assign responsibilities (to yourself or team members if applicable), resources required, and deadlines for each task. This structured approach transforms abstract goals into a series of actionable steps.

Regular Reviews: Establish a routine for reviewing your progress toward both personal and business goals. Monthly check-ins allow you to assess whether you're on track, understand what adjustments may be needed, and celebrate milestones along the way.

Adaptation and Flexibility

Stay Agile: The path to realizing your vision may require adjustments. Stay open to pivoting your strategies in response to new information, unforeseen challenges, or evolving aspirations. This agility ensures that your strategic plan remains relevant and effective, even as circumstances change.

Leverage Resources and Tools: Utilize planning tools and resources to aid in your strategic planning process. From digital planners and budgeting apps to business model canvases, these tools can provide structure and clarity, simplifying the task of translating vision into action.

Conclusion

Strategic Planning is more than just a phase in the journey toward financial and personal achievement; it is an ongoing practice of intentionality and foresight. By setting SMART goals, integrating personal and business objectives, and committing to regular review and adaptation, you lay the groundwork for a future that aligns with your deepest values and aspirations. As students poised to embark on this exciting journey, embracing strategic planning empowers you to architect a life of prosperity, purpose, and fulfillment.

Foundations of Wealth Construction

- Financial Literacy as Your Toolkit:

Financial Literacy stands as the cornerstone of wealth architecture, equipping you with the knowledge and skills necessary to navigate the complex landscape of personal and business finance. For students and aspiring wealth architects, mastering financial literacy is akin to acquiring a comprehensive toolkit, one that enables informed decision-making, strategic planning, and the effective management of resources.

The Foundation of Your Financial Edifice

Understanding the Basics: Begin with a solid grasp of fundamental financial concepts—budgeting, saving, investing, and debt management. These are the bricks and mortar of your financial structure, the essential components that support more advanced wealth-building strategies.

Expanding Your Toolkit: Once the foundation is laid, expand your toolkit by delving into more sophisticated financial concepts tailored to wealth construction. This includes:

Tax Optimization Strategies: Learn how to navigate the tax landscape to minimize liabilities and maximize returns. Understanding tax implications for different investment vehicles, retirement accounts, and business operations can significantly influence your net wealth growth.

Investment Property Analysis: For those interested in real estate as a pathway to wealth, mastering investment property analysis is crucial. Learn to evaluate properties based on cash flow, capital appreciation potential, and risk factors. This knowledge allows you to make informed decisions that align with your wealth-building goals.

Business Financial Management: Acquiring skills in business finance—understanding balance sheets, income statements, cash flow analysis, and financial forecasting—is indispensable for aspiring entrepreneurs. This knowledge not only aids in the day-to-day management of business finances but also in strategic planning and investment decisions.

Tools for the Wealth Architect

Leveraging Technology: Embrace financial technology tools that facilitate more efficient management and analysis of your finances. From budgeting apps and investment platforms to accounting software for businesses, technology can streamline operations, provide valuable insights, and free up time for strategic thinking and growth activities.

Continual Learning: The financial world is dynamic, with new products, regulations, and opportunities emerging regularly. Commit to lifelong learning, staying abreast of financial news, trends, and innovations. This ongoing education ensures that your toolkit remains current and comprehensive.

Professional Guidance: Recognize when to seek advice from financial advisors, tax professionals, or business consultants. These experts can provide tailored advice, helping you navigate complex decisions and optimize your strategies for wealth construction.

Integrating Financial Literacy into Your Blueprint

Informed Decision-Making: Use your financial literacy to make decisions that are aligned with your long-term vision and goals. Whether assessing investment opportunities, planning for retirement, or managing business growth, an informed approach reduces risks and enhances outcomes.

Strategic Planning: Apply your financial knowledge to develop strategic plans that encompass both personal and business objectives. Financial literacy enables you to craft plans that are realistic, achievable, and aligned with your vision of wealth architecture.

Risk Management: Equip yourself with strategies to manage financial risk, ensuring that your journey toward wealth is marked by informed risk-taking rather than unnecessary exposure.

Conclusion

For students embarking on the path to becoming wealth architects, financial literacy is not just beneficial—it's essential. It empowers you to construct a future of financial prosperity and personal fulfillment with confidence and competence. By embracing financial literacy as your toolkit, you position yourself to build a legacy of wealth that transcends monetary value, enriching every facet of your life and the lives of those around you.

- **Risk Management:**

Risk Management is a critical component of the wealth-building process, acting as the safeguard that protects your financial edifice from potential downturns and uncertainties. For aspiring wealth architects, understanding and implementing innovative risk management strategies can significantly enhance the resilience of your financial portfolio. These strategies not only help in preserving capital but also ensure the continuity of your wealth growth trajectory.

Beyond Traditional Diversification

Exploring Alternative Asset Classes: While stocks and bonds are foundational to any diversified portfolio, exploring alternative asset classes can offer additional layers of protection and potential for higher returns. Real estate, commodities, private equity, and even collectibles such as art or vintage cars can serve as hedges against the volatility of traditional markets. Each of these asset classes behaves differently in various economic climates, thereby reducing overall risk through diversification.

Geographic Diversification: In a globally interconnected economy, geographic diversification is another layer of risk mitigation. Investing in markets across different countries and regions can protect your portfolio from being overly exposed to the economic downturns of any single country. This approach leverages global growth opportunities and mitigates country-specific risks, including political instability and currency fluctuations.

Leveraging Financial Derivatives

Options and Futures: Financial derivatives, such as options and futures, can be powerful tools for managing investment risk. Options provide the right, but not the obligation, to buy or sell an asset at a predetermined price, offering a way to hedge against price movements. Futures contracts, on the other hand, obligate the buyer to purchase, and the seller to sell, an asset at a future date and price, allowing investors to speculate on or hedge against future price changes.

Protective Puts: One specific strategy is the use of protective puts to insure your portfolio against significant losses. Purchasing a put option gives you the right to sell a specific amount of an underlying asset at a set price within a certain timeframe, acting as an insurance policy against a decline in the asset's price.

Strategic Use of Leverage

Caution with Borrowed Money: While leverage can amplify returns, it also increases risk. Educating oneself on the strategic use of borrowed money for investment purposes is crucial. Proper leverage involves assessing the cost of borrowing against the potential returns of an investment, ensuring that the use of leverage is judicious and aligns with your overall risk tolerance and investment strategy.

Continual Risk Assessment and Adjustment

Regular Portfolio Reviews: Conducting regular reviews of your investment portfolio is essential for ongoing risk management. This practice allows you to assess the performance of your investments, rebalance your portfolio to maintain your desired asset allocation, and adjust your strategies in response to changes in the market or your financial goals.

Stress Testing: Engage in stress testing your portfolio to understand how it might perform under various adverse conditions. This can help you identify potential vulnerabilities and make preemptive adjustments to mitigate those risks.

Conclusion

Innovative risk management is about more than just protecting assets; it's about ensuring the stability and longevity of your wealth-building journey. By embracing a broad spectrum of diversification strategies, leveraging financial derivatives wisely, and maintaining a disciplined approach to risk assessment and adjustment, you can navigate the financial markets with confidence. These strategies empower you to build a resilient financial portfolio, capable of withstanding the ebbs and flows of the economy while continuing to grow over time.

Building and Scaling Your Economic Structure

- Leveraging Business as a Wealth Engine:

Leveraging Business as a Wealth Engine transforms the concept of entrepreneurship from merely running a company to utilizing business ventures as dynamic vehicles for substantial wealth generation. This approach involves strategically selecting and managing business models that have the potential not only for steady income but also for significant capital appreciation. Here's how aspiring entrepreneurs and wealth architects can harness the power of business to fuel their journey towards financial prosperity.

Scalable Business Models

Identifying Scalable Opportunities: Focus on business models that offer scalability—those that can grow revenue with minimal incremental cost. Digital products, software as a service (SaaS), and online marketplaces are prime examples where the initial development and setup costs may be high, but the cost of serving additional customers is low.

Innovation and Market Needs: Scalability often hinges on innovation and the ability to meet or create market demands. Engaging in continuous market research and being attuned to emerging trends can reveal opportunities for scalable ventures that address unmet needs or introduce novel solutions.

Systems and Automation: Implementing efficient systems and automation is crucial in scaling operations. This includes leveraging technology for customer relationship management, inventory control, and marketing automation, allowing for expansion without proportional increases in workload or expenses.

Franchise Opportunities

Leveraging Established Models: Franchising offers a pathway to entrepreneurship with the support of an established brand and business model. It provides the structure and systems needed for success, reducing the uncertainty associated with starting a new venture from scratch.

Due Diligence: Careful selection of franchise opportunities is paramount. Prospective franchisees should conduct thorough due diligence, examining the franchisor's track record, the financial health of existing franchises, and the overall market potential of the business concept.

Community and Support: One of the benefits of franchising is the community and support network it offers. Engaging with other franchisees and leveraging the franchisor's resources can provide valuable insights and assistance in overcoming challenges and maximizing profitability.

Digital Entrepreneurship

Capitalizing on Digital Trends: The digital economy presents vast opportunities for entrepreneurship. E-commerce, content creation, online education, and technology services are areas with significant growth potential. Success in digital entrepreneurship requires staying abreast of technological advancements and consumer behavior trends online.

Building Online Platforms: Developing an online platform, whether for selling products, connecting service providers with clients, or hosting digital content, can serve as a foundation for multiple revenue streams. Effective digital platforms prioritize user experience, scalability, and adaptability to changes in technology and market demand.

Monetizing Digital Assets: Digital assets, including websites, apps, and intellectual property, can become continuous sources of income. Strategies for monetization include direct sales, subscription models, advertising, and affiliate marketing, each offering different pathways to revenue generation.

Conclusion

Business ventures, when strategically selected and managed, can serve as powerful engines for wealth generation. Whether through developing scalable businesses, investing in franchise opportunities, or diving into digital entrepreneurship, the key is to approach these ventures with a strategic mindset focused on growth, scalability, and innovation. By doing so, entrepreneurs can transform their businesses into significant assets that contribute to long-term wealth accumulation and financial independence.

- Investment Strategies for Compound Growth:

Investment strategies that harness the power of compound growth represent a sophisticated approach to wealth accumulation, enabling investors to significantly enhance their financial portfolios over time. Compound growth, the process by which earnings on an investment earn their own earnings, can turn prudent investments into substantial wealth. Here's how investors can engage with advanced investment strategies such as angel investing, venture capital participation, and strategic real estate development to achieve compound growth.

Angel Investing

Venturing into Startups: Angel investing involves providing capital to startups or young companies in exchange for equity ownership. This form of investing allows individuals to get in on the ground floor of potentially disruptive companies with high growth potential.

Due Diligence and Selection: The key to successful angel investing lies in rigorous due diligence and selection processes. Investors should look for companies with innovative solutions, scalable business models, strong management teams, and clear paths to profitability. Participation in angel networks or crowdfunding platforms can also offer access to curated investment opportunities.

Long-term Growth Potential: While angel investing carries higher risk due to the potential failure rate of startups, the long-term growth potential can be substantial. Successful exits through public offerings or acquisitions can result in significant returns, exemplifying the power of compound growth.

Venture Capital Participation

Joining Venture Funds: Venture capital participation allows investors to contribute to funds that invest in startups and early-stage companies with strong growth prospects. By pooling resources with other investors, individuals can access higher-caliber opportunities and leverage the expertise of professional fund managers.

Diversification within Venture Capital: Investing in a venture capital fund offers diversification within the high-growth startup space, spreading risk across multiple companies and sectors. Funds often focus on specific industries, such as technology, healthcare, or green energy, aligning with investors' interests and market trends.

Strategic Exits: The compounding effect in venture capital investing comes from strategic exits, where companies in the fund's portfolio go public or are acquired. These events can significantly increase the value of the initial investment, contributing to compound growth over the investment period.

Strategic Real Estate Development

Value-Add and Development Projects: Strategic real estate development focuses on value-add projects and ground-up developments. These projects involve purchasing underutilized properties or land and enhancing their value through renovations, rezoning, or complete redevelopment.

Leverage and Cash Flow: Real estate investments offer the opportunity to use leverage responsibly to amplify returns. Additionally, strategic developments can generate ongoing cash flow through rentals, which can be reinvested for compound growth.

Market Analysis and Timing: Success in real estate development hinges on thorough market analysis and timing. Understanding local market dynamics, zoning laws, and future urban planning can uncover opportunities where strategic developments have the potential for substantial appreciation.

Conclusion

Sophisticated investment strategies that focus on compound growth require a higher risk tolerance and a commitment to due diligence but offer the potential for significant returns. Whether through direct involvement in angel investing, participation in venture capital funds, or engaging in strategic real estate development, these strategies embody the essence of proactive wealth building. By carefully selecting opportunities, leveraging expertise, and focusing on long-term growth, investors can harness the power of compound growth to achieve transformative wealth accumulation.

Interior Design of Wealth: Lifestyle and Legacy

- Crafting a Wealth-Infused Lifestyle:

Crafting a Wealth-Infused Lifestyle is about much more than the accumulation of assets; it's about aligning your spending with your deepest values to create a life that not only reflects your achieved prosperity but also enhances your fulfillment and impact. This approach encourages a thoughtful consideration of how each financial decision—from daily expenditures to significant investments—can contribute to a lifestyle that is rich in meaning and joy, embodying the true essence of wealth.

Aligning Spending with Values

Conscious Consumption: Begin by embracing the principle of conscious consumption. This means making purchasing decisions that reflect your values and aspirations, whether that's sustainability, craftsmanship, innovation, or community support. It involves choosing quality over quantity, investing in items that bring lasting satisfaction rather than fleeting pleasure, and considering the broader impact of your consumption habits.

Budgeting for Joy: Allocate a portion of your budget for experiences and purchases that bring genuine joy and enrichment to your life. This could include travel, education, hobbies, or cultural experiences. By intentionally budgeting for these aspects, you ensure that your wealth serves not just your material needs but also your personal growth and happiness.

Luxury Asset Investing

Appreciating Assets: Consider investing in luxury assets that not only enhance your lifestyle but also have the potential to appreciate in value over time. This can include art, collectibles, vintage automobiles, or fine wines. Such investments allow you to derive enjoyment and aesthetic pleasure from your wealth while also contributing to your financial portfolio's growth.

Due Diligence: As with any investment, thorough research and due diligence are essential when investing in luxury assets. Understanding the market, the factors that drive value appreciation, and the potential risks involved can help ensure that your investments align with both your financial goals and your lifestyle aspirations.

Philanthropy and Giving Back

Impactful Giving: Philanthropy offers a powerful way to extend the impact of your wealth beyond your own life. By supporting causes and organizations that align with your values, you can contribute to meaningful change and leave a lasting legacy.

Strategic Philanthropy: Consider adopting a strategic approach to philanthropy, one that involves not just financial contributions but also leveraging your skills, network, and influence to amplify your impact. This might include establishing a charitable foundation, participating in impact investing, or engaging in philanthropic partnerships.

Cultivating a Community

Building Connections: Wealth can also be a tool for building and nurturing a community of like-minded individuals. Whether through hosting gatherings, supporting local artisans, or participating in community projects, your wealth can help foster connections and contribute to a vibrant, supportive community.

Sharing Knowledge: Consider sharing your journey and insights into wealth building and management with others. Mentoring, educational initiatives, or financial literacy programs can help empower others to achieve their financial goals, extending the benefits of your wealth to a broader audience.

Conclusion

Crafting a Wealth-Infused Lifestyle is about intentionally designing a life that reflects your achievements, values, and aspirations. It's a holistic approach that blends financial acumen with personal fulfillment, social impact, and community engagement. By aligning your spending with your values, investing in assets that bring both joy and growth, and using your wealth to contribute positively to the world, you create a lifestyle that truly embodies the richness of prosperity.

- Legacy Building:

Legacy Building is an integral aspect of wealth architecture that extends the impact of your financial achievements beyond your lifetime, ensuring that your wealth continues to benefit others and reflect your values for generations to come. This process involves strategic planning and thoughtful consideration of how to structure your assets, share your wealth, and impart your financial knowledge in ways that create lasting positive effects.

Estate Planning: Safeguarding Your Legacy

Foundations of Estate Planning: Begin with comprehensive estate planning to ensure that your assets are distributed according to your wishes upon your passing. This includes drafting a will, setting up trusts, and making clear designations for beneficiaries. Effective estate planning not only secures your financial legacy but also minimizes potential conflicts and legal complications for your heirs.

Tax Efficiency: Incorporate strategies to manage estate taxes and maximize the value of the inheritance you pass on. Utilizing trusts, gifting strategies, and other legal structures can help preserve your wealth for your beneficiaries by minimizing tax liabilities.

Charitable Foundations: Philanthropy as Legacy

Creating a Charitable Foundation: Establishing a charitable foundation can be a powerful way to perpetuate your values and impact causes you care about deeply. A foundation allows you to formalize your philanthropic efforts, providing ongoing support to charities and initiatives that align with your mission.

Engagement and Involvement: Encourage family members and heirs to become involved in the foundation's activities. This not only ensures the foundation's vitality but also instills a sense of purpose and philanthropic values in future generations.

Passing on Financial Wisdom: Educating Future Generations

Financial Education: Make a concerted effort to educate your children and grandchildren about financial management, investing, and the principles behind your wealth-building journey. This can include formal education, mentorship, and hands-on experience with financial decision-making.

Involvement in Wealth Management: Gradually involve heirs in the management of family assets or the charitable foundation. This hands-on experience is invaluable for teaching them about the complexities of wealth management and the responsibilities that come with it.

Ethical Wills: Sharing Your Values

Documenting Your Life Lessons: Consider creating an ethical will—a non-legal document where you share your life lessons, values, and hopes for your heirs. Unlike a traditional will, an ethical will is meant to pass on wisdom, values, and personal reflections.

Sustainable and Impactful Investing

Legacy through Impact Investing: Guide your heirs in continuing a legacy of impact by investing in causes and companies that align with your family's values. Impact investing focuses on generating social and environmental impact alongside financial returns, allowing your legacy to contribute to positive change in the world.

Conclusion

Legacy Building is about more than just the distribution of assets; it's a comprehensive approach that encompasses safeguarding your wealth, contributing to meaningful causes, and passing on your values and wisdom to future generations. Through careful planning and intentional actions, you can ensure that your legacy continues to make a positive impact, reflecting your life's work and values long into the future. This holistic view of legacy building enriches not only your immediate family but also the broader community and future generations, creating a lasting testament to your life and achievements.

Continuous Renovation and Innovation

- Adapting to Economic Shifts:

Adapting to Economic Shifts is crucial for maintaining and growing wealth in an ever-changing economic landscape. The ability to stay flexible, informed, and ahead of trends can differentiate between thriving and merely surviving. Here are strategic approaches to ensure resilience and capitalize on opportunities during economic fluctuations.

Continuous Education

Lifelong Learning: Commit to lifelong learning to keep your financial knowledge up-to-date. This involves regularly updating yourself on economic trends, financial markets, and new investment strategies. Resources such as online courses, financial news platforms, and industry reports can provide valuable insights.

Professional Development: Attend workshops, seminars, and conferences in your field or areas of interest. These opportunities not only expand your knowledge but also allow you to network with professionals who can offer diverse perspectives on navigating economic changes.

Market Research

Stay Informed: Regularly conduct market research to understand the current economic climate and forecast potential shifts. This includes analyzing market trends, consumer behavior, and regulatory changes that could impact your investments or business operations.

Sector Analysis: Pay special attention to the sectors or industries where you have significant investments or business interests. Understanding these sectors' specific trends and challenges can help you make more informed decisions and identify emerging opportunities.

Investment in Emerging Technologies

Embrace Innovation: Emerging technologies often lead the way in economic shifts, offering new opportunities for growth and efficiency. Stay abreast of developments in fields such as artificial intelligence, blockchain, renewable energy, and biotechnology.

Strategic Investments: Consider allocating a portion of your investment portfolio to emerging technologies or startups operating in these areas. While these investments may carry higher risk, they also offer the potential for substantial returns and can diversify your investment portfolio.

Diversification

Spread Your Risks: Diversification remains a key strategy in adapting to economic shifts. By spreading investments across different asset classes, sectors, and geographies, you can mitigate the impact of downturns in any single area on your overall portfolio.

Flexibility in Investment Strategy: Be prepared to adjust your investment strategy in response to economic changes. This might involve shifting your asset allocation, taking advantage of tax-efficient investment vehicles, or increasing your holdings in more stable, defensive assets during volatile periods.

Staying Agile

Quick Decision-Making: Develop the ability to make quick, informed decisions. This agility allows you to respond to economic shifts promptly, taking advantage of opportunities or mitigating risks as they arise.

Contingency Planning: Have contingency plans in place for your finances and business operations. This could include maintaining a liquidity reserve, having flexible business operations that can adapt to changing market demands, and regularly reviewing and updating your financial plans.

Networking and Collaboration

Build a Support Network: Cultivate a network of mentors, advisors, and peers who can offer advice, share insights, and provide support. A strong network can be invaluable in navigating economic uncertainties.

Collaborate for Innovation: Look for opportunities to collaborate with others in your industry or related fields. Partnerships can lead to innovative solutions that address the challenges posed by economic shifts, creating new avenues for growth.

Conclusion

Adapting to economic shifts requires a proactive, informed, and flexible approach to wealth management and business operations. By committing to continuous education, conducting thorough market research, investing in emerging technologies, and maintaining a diversified portfolio, you can navigate economic fluctuations successfully. Staying agile, planning for contingencies, and leveraging your network for support and collaboration further strengthen your ability to adapt to and thrive amidst economic changes.

- **Wealth Maintenance:**
Wealth Maintenance is an essential practice in the stewardship of your financial resources, ensuring that your wealth not only grows but also adapts and remains resilient in the face of life's inevitable changes. Regular review and adjustment of your financial plans are crucial for this process, allowing you to stay aligned with your evolving goals, market conditions, and personal circumstances. Here are key practices to ensure effective wealth maintenance.

Regular Financial Check-ups

Schedule Periodic Reviews: Just as regular health check-ups are vital for physical well-being, periodic financial reviews are essential for maintaining wealth health. Set a schedule for comprehensive reviews of your financial plan, such as quarterly or biannually, to assess progress and make necessary adjustments.

Assess Performance Against Goals: Evaluate the performance of your investments and other financial strategies in the context of your goals. Are you on track to meet your short-term and long-term objectives? Adjustments may be needed if certain investments are underperforming or if your goals have evolved.

Stay Responsive to Life Changes

Adapt to Life Events: Major life events—such as marriage, the birth of a child, a career change, or retirement—necessitate a reevaluation of your financial plan. These milestones can significantly impact your financial needs and goals, requiring adjustments to your saving, investment, and estate planning strategies.

Update Estate Plans: Regularly review and update your will and estate planning documents to reflect any changes in your family structure, financial status, or wishes. This ensures that your legacy intentions remain accurately represented and legally sound.

Market Conditions and Economic Trends

Monitor Market and Economic Trends: Stay informed about the broader economic environment and market trends, as these can influence the performance of your investments and the viability of your financial strategies. Being proactive in this regard can help you anticipate necessary adjustments to your portfolio.

Flexibility in Investment Strategy: Be prepared to adjust your investment strategy based on market conditions. This might involve rebalancing your portfolio to maintain your desired asset allocation or shifting towards more defensive investments during periods of market volatility.

Education and Collaboration

Continuous Financial Education: Commit to lifelong learning in financial matters. Keeping abreast of new financial products, investment strategies, and tax laws can help you make more informed decisions and identify new opportunities for growth.

Work with Financial Professionals: Consider engaging with financial advisors, tax professionals, or estate planners for expert guidance. These professionals can offer valuable insights, help you navigate complex financial decisions, and ensure that your plans are optimized for current laws and regulations.

Embrace Technological Tools

Utilize Financial Management Tools: Leverage technology to streamline the monitoring and management of your finances. Personal finance apps, investment tracking software, and budgeting tools can provide real-time insights into your financial health, making it easier to stay on top of your wealth maintenance.

Conclusion

Wealth Maintenance is not a set-it-and-forget-it endeavor but an ongoing process of engagement, review, and adjustment. By incorporating these practices into your financial routine, you ensure that your wealth management strategies evolve in tandem with your life, goals, and the financial landscape. This proactive approach to wealth maintenance not only safeguards your financial well-being but also enhances your capacity to achieve and surpass your financial aspirations.

Conclusion: Mastering the Art of Wealth Architecture

The journey of becoming a Wealth Architect is a transformative process that redefines the approach to personal and business financial management. It is a path marked by the deliberate and strategic orchestration of one's finances, aiming not just for wealth accumulation but for the creation of a harmonious and prosperous life that aligns with one's deepest values and aspirations. This journey underscores the power of proactive and intentional financial design in achieving a synthesis of personal fulfillment and business success.

Vision Casting and Strategic Planning

The foundation of wealth architecture begins with Vision Casting, where individuals dare to envision a future unbounded by current realities, defining success in terms of personal satisfaction, impact, and legacy. Following this vision, Strategic Planning serves as the blueprinting phase, translating dreams into actionable goals. Here, the Wealth Architect employs SMART criteria to outline a roadmap, integrating personal financial health and business prosperity with precision and care.

Financial Literacy: The Cornerstone

Central to the architect's toolkit is Financial Literacy, a comprehensive understanding of financial principles that guides every decision, from daily expenditures to significant investments. This knowledge base extends into sophisticated areas such as tax optimization, investment property analysis, and business financial management, enabling the Wealth Architect to navigate complex financial landscapes with confidence.

Innovating Through Risk Management

Innovation in Risk Management involves not just safeguarding against potential losses but strategically embracing risk for greater reward. Diversification, investment in emerging technologies, and the judicious use of financial derivatives exemplify the advanced strategies that protect and propel wealth growth, ensuring resilience amidst economic shifts.

The Dynamics of Wealth Generation

Leveraging Business as a dynamic vehicle for wealth generation highlights the entrepreneurial spirit of the Wealth Architect. Through scalable business models, franchise opportunities, and digital entrepreneurship, individuals harness the potential for exponential growth, turning business ventures into significant contributors to their wealth portfolio.

Investment Strategies for Compound Growth

The pursuit of Compound Growth through investments in areas like angel investing, venture capital, and strategic real estate development showcases the forward-thinking approach of the Wealth Architect. These avenues, chosen for their potential to generate substantial returns over time, illustrate the strategic allocation of capital towards assets that grow exponentially.

Crafting a Wealth-Infused Lifestyle

The creation of a Wealth-Infused Lifestyle is perhaps the most personalized aspect of wealth architecture. It's about aligning spending with values, investing in luxury assets that appreciate, and engaging in philanthropy. This approach ensures that wealth not only grows but enriches the life of the Wealth Architect and those around them, fostering a lifestyle that is both affluent and meaningful.

Legacy Building

Finally, Legacy Building encapsulates the ultimate goal of the Wealth Architect: to leave behind a lasting impact that transcends monetary value. Through estate planning, charitable foundations, and the transmission of financial wisdom to future generations, individuals ensure that their wealth serves a purpose beyond their lifetime, contributing to the well-being of others and the betterment of society.

Conclusion

Becoming a Wealth Architect is a journey of intentionality, where financial success is meticulously designed and skillfully constructed to achieve an integrated state of personal and business prosperity. It embodies a proactive approach to wealth management, where success is not measured by financial metrics alone but by the ability to live a life that is truly rich—in every sense of the word.

Embarking on the journey to become a Wealth Architect is both a privilege and a profound responsibility. You stand at the threshold of transforming not just your financial reality but your life's trajectory. The knowledge and strategies outlined in this chapter are more than just guidelines; they are the tools with which you can construct a future of prosperity, fulfillment, and legacy. Now, the time has come to take the first, decisive step towards constructing your wealth blueprint.

Embrace the Role of Architect

Understand that as a Wealth Architect, you are the master planner of your financial future. This role empowers you to design a life that reflects your deepest values, ambitions, and desires. Your journey begins with a vision—a clear, compelling picture of the life you aspire to create. Let this vision be your guiding star, illuminating the path forward even in moments of uncertainty.

Lay the Foundation with Financial Literacy

Your first step is to lay a strong foundation with financial literacy. Knowledge is power, particularly in the realm of finance. Commit to understanding the basics of budgeting, saving, investing, and debt management. Then, venture beyond into the realms of tax optimization, investment property analysis, and strategic business financial management. This education will serve as your bedrock, equipping you to make informed decisions that align with your vision.

Strategize and Plan with Precision

With your foundation in place, proceed to strategize and plan with precision. Utilize the principles of strategic planning to translate your vision into actionable goals. Remember, a goal without a plan is merely a wish. Break down your long-term objectives into manageable steps, setting milestones that mark your progress. This roadmap will guide your journey, helping you navigate through challenges and opportunities alike.

Embrace Innovation and Adaptability

The economic landscape is ever-evolving, and success as a Wealth Architect requires an embrace of innovation and adaptability. Stay attuned to economic shifts, emerging technologies, and new investment opportunities. Be prepared to adjust your strategies in response to new information and changing circumstances. This flexibility will ensure that your wealth blueprint remains relevant and dynamic, capable of weathering storms and capitalizing on winds of change.

Take Action Today

The most critical step in becoming a Wealth Architect is to take action. Begin today. Whether it's enhancing your financial literacy, setting your first SMART goal, or making your initial investment, the act of starting sets the wheels of progress in motion. Each action you take is a brick in the edifice of your future prosperity.

Cultivate a Community of Support

Remember, you are not alone on this journey. Cultivate a community of mentors, peers, and professionals who can offer guidance, support, and encouragement. Share your vision and plans with those you trust, and be open to receiving wisdom from those who have walked this path before you.

Conclusion

The journey of constructing your wealth blueprint is one of the most rewarding endeavors you can undertake. It is a path marked by growth, learning, and transformation. Armed with the knowledge and strategies outlined in this chapter, you possess everything you need to begin. Let today be the day you take that first, bold step towards becoming a Wealth Architect. Embrace the journey with enthusiasm and determination, for the blueprint you construct will not only shape your financial future but will also craft a legacy that endures.

Closing Thoughts

The journey towards financial mastery is akin to the process of architectural creation, where every decision, from the foundational plans to the intricate details of the interior, is made with intention and purpose. This reframed approach to Chapter 6 is designed to invigorate you, the reader, with a renewed perspective on wealth building, inviting you to step into the role of a Wealth Architect of your own destiny. Here, sophisticated financial strategies merge seamlessly with personal growth and entrepreneurial insight, enabling you to construct a future that is not only prosperous but deeply resonant with your most cherished aspirations and values.

The Blueprint of Prosperity

As a Wealth Architect, you are equipped to draft the blueprint of your financial future. This blueprint is unique, reflecting your personal aspirations, lifestyle goals, and the legacy you wish to build. It requires a clear vision, a comprehensive understanding of financial principles, and an unwavering commitment to your values. Just as an architect considers both the aesthetic and functional aspects of a building, you must balance the pursuit of financial growth with the enhancement of your life's quality and purpose.

Laying the Foundation with Financial Literacy

The foundation of your wealth architecture is financial literacy. Understanding the language of finance—how money works, how it can be grown, and how it can be protected—is essential. This knowledge empowers you to make informed decisions, from selecting the right investment vehicles to optimizing your tax strategy and managing risks effectively. Your financial literacy is both your shield and your tool, enabling you to navigate the complexities of the financial world with confidence.

Constructing with Strategic Investments

With your foundation in place, you then move to the construction phase, where strategic investments play a crucial role. This involves identifying opportunities that not only promise returns but also align with your vision and risk tolerance. Whether it's through angel investing, real estate ventures, or participation in the stock market, each investment choice is a deliberate addition to your wealth-building edifice, designed to bring you closer to your ultimate financial goals.

Personal Growth as an Integral Pillar

Personal growth is an integral pillar in your wealth architecture. It involves continuously evolving, learning, and adapting to new challenges and opportunities. This growth mindset enables you to stay resilient in the face of economic shifts, to innovate within your business ventures, and to seek out new avenues for wealth generation. It's about becoming a lifelong learner, always expanding your capabilities and understanding of what's possible.

Entrepreneurial Insight for Dynamic Expansion

Entrepreneurial insight adds dynamism to your wealth-building efforts. It's about seeing opportunities where others see obstacles, about leveraging your unique skills and resources to create value in the marketplace. Whether you're running a business, investing in startups, or developing side hustles, entrepreneurial insight allows you to explore new frontiers of wealth generation, contributing to both your personal prosperity and the broader economy.

Cultivating a Wealth-Infused Lifestyle

Beyond the accumulation of assets, cultivating a wealth-infused lifestyle is about ensuring your financial success translates into a meaningful and fulfilling life. It's about aligning your spending with your values, investing in experiences and assets that bring you joy, and using your wealth to make a positive impact in the world. This lifestyle is a testament to the fact that true wealth is not just about having resources but about living in accordance with your deepest values and aspirations.

Legacy Building: Your Architectural Masterpiece

Finally, legacy building is the culmination of your efforts as a Wealth Architect. It's about creating something that endures beyond your lifetime, whether through philanthropy, business enterprises, or the wisdom you pass on to future generations. Your legacy is your architectural masterpiece, a symbol of your life's work and values, crafted with intention and care.

Conclusion

This reframed approach to wealth building encourages you to embrace your role as a Wealth Architect, empowering you to design and construct a future that is not only financially prosperous but also rich in meaning and purpose. Armed with sophisticated financial strategies, personal growth, and entrepreneurial insight, you are well-equipped to build a legacy of prosperity that resonates with your deepest aspirations and values. The journey is yours to embark upon, with each decision and action shaping the masterpiece of your life's work.

Chapter 7: Manifesting a Million: The Subconscious Blueprint for Action

The Power of Visionary Thinking

The journey to unparalleled financial success commences not with the accumulation of wealth, but with the cultivation of a clear and vivid vision. Visionary thinking, the cornerstone of monumental achievements, is the practice of shaping one's future through the power of the mind's eye. It involves envisaging one's aspirations with such clarity and detail that they seem almost tangible. This practice is not merely fanciful or hypothetical; it is a deliberate strategy employed by many of the world's most successful individuals.

Consider the narratives of business magnates like Elon Musk and Oprah Winfrey, who have consistently emphasized the role of visualization and mindset in their paths to success. Musk, for instance, envisioned revolutionizing transportation and energy on a global scale, a vision that has propelled his ventures into unprecedented successes. Winfrey, through her unwavering belief in her purpose and potential, transformed her life from poverty to unparalleled media dominance. Their journeys underscore the power of a well-defined vision in converting abstract dreams into concrete realities.

Creating Your Financial Vision Board

To harness the transformative power of visionary thinking in your pursuit of earning $1,000,000 a month, begin by creating a financial vision board. This tool is not just an arrangement of images and words; it is a visual representation of your impending success, designed to stimulate and fortify your subconscious mind.

Select Images and Symbols: Choose images that resonate with the lifestyle and success you associate with earning $1,000,000 a month. These might include pictures of luxury homes, exotic destinations, influential meetings, or any visual representation of your aspirations and dreams.

Incorporate Sensory Elements: Enrich your vision board with elements that engage all your senses. For example, if a luxury home is part of your vision, include textures reminiscent of the home's interior or scents that represent its ambiance. The aim is to make the experience as real and immersive as possible.

Infuse Emotional Content: Every image or item on your board should evoke a strong emotional response. It should make you feel the joy, pride, satisfaction, or peace that you anticipate experiencing with your financial success. These emotions are powerful drivers that will motivate you to take consistent action towards your goal.

Place Your Vision Board Strategically: Position your vision board in a location where you will see it daily. Frequent exposure to these visual cues reinforces your financial goals and objectives, keeping them at the forefront of your mind and influencing your daily decisions and actions.

Update Regularly: Your vision board should evolve as you progress towards your goal and as your aspirations grow. Regular updates ensure that your board remains relevant and aligned with your objectives, providing ongoing inspiration and motivation.

In cultivating the power of visionary thinking through your financial vision board, you are not merely dreaming about the future; you are actively constructing it. This process sets the foundation for your subconscious mind to align with your financial aspirations, thereby transforming the dream of earning $1,000,000 a month from a mere possibility into an impending reality

Exercise: Crafting Your Financial Vision Board

Objective: To develop a financial vision board that vividly represents your goal of earning $1,000,000 a month, engaging both your subconscious and conscious mind in the journey toward financial success.

Materials Needed:

- A large poster board or digital platform (like Pinterest)
- Magazines, printouts, or digital images
- Scissors and glue (for a physical board) or image editing software (for a digital board)
- Markers, stickers, or any other decorative items
- Notepad or journal for reflection

Instructions:

Set the Scene:

- Find a quiet, comfortable space where you can think deeply and creatively.
- Set aside uninterrupted time to focus solely on this activity, ensuring you can delve into the process without distractions.

Visualization Meditation:

- Begin with a 5-minute meditation where you close your eyes and envision your life as a millionaire. Imagine your daily routine, the feelings associated with your success, and the freedom and opportunities your wealth provides.
- Take note of the sensory details in your visualization: the sights, sounds, textures, and emotions you experience.

Gather Inspirational Materials:

- Collect images, quotes, and symbols that resonate with your vision of earning $1,000,000 a month. These can be from magazines, online sources, or personal photos.
- Look for images that not only represent wealth but also the lifestyle, values, and achievements you associate with this financial success.

Create Your Vision Board:

- Begin placing your collected materials on the board, arranging them in a way that feels meaningful and inspiring to you.
- Include affirmations and motivational quotes that align with your financial goals and personal growth.
- Integrate sensory elements—textures, scents, or sounds—that can be associated with the images, enhancing the emotional and experiential aspect of your board.

Reflect and Write:

- After completing your vision board, spend some time reflecting on the process and the final product.
- In your notepad or journal, write about the feelings and thoughts that arose during this activity. Note any insights or revelations about your financial goals and the path to achieving them.

Strategic Placement and Regular Review:

- Place your vision board in a location where you will see it daily, ideally where you start your day or in your workspace.
- Dedicate time each week to review your board, reflect on your progress towards your financial goals, and make adjustments to your board as needed.

Outcome: This exercise will result in a personalized financial vision board that serves as a daily reminder and motivator of your goal to earn $1,000,000 a month. The process of creating and regularly engaging with your vision board will reinforce your commitment to your financial aspirations and align your subconscious and conscious efforts towards achieving them

Subconscious Conditioning for Success

Mindset Shifts

Dear students, the journey towards financial prosperity begins in the fertile grounds of your mind. The transformation from a scarcity mindset, which views wealth as finite and elusive, to an abundance mindset, which perceives limitless possibilities and opportunities for wealth, is pivotal. This shift is not merely an adjustment in thought patterns but a profound reprogramming of the subconscious mind to anticipate and embrace success and wealth.

Imagine the mind as a garden. A scarcity mindset plants seeds of doubt, fear, and limitation, which grow into weeds that choke potential and restrict growth. Conversely, an abundance mindset sows seeds of confidence, opportunity, and prosperity, cultivating a landscape where financial success can flourish.

To initiate this transformative journey, recognize and challenge the limiting beliefs that have taken root in your subconscious. Replace these with the conviction that success and wealth are not only possible but are natural and within reach. This mental shift is the first step in reprogramming your subconscious to align with the aspirations of financial achievement and fulfillment.

Affirmations and Positive Self-Talk

Affirmations are powerful tools for reinforcing this mindset shift. They are positive, present-tense statements that, when repeated regularly, can mold the subconscious mind's patterns and beliefs.

Crafting Effective Affirmations:

- Begin by writing affirmations that resonate with your personal financial goals and the abundance mindset you wish to cultivate.
- Use the first person and present tense to create immediacy and ownership, such as "I am confidently navigating my path to financial success" or "I effortlessly attract wealth and opportunities."

Daily Affirmation Practice:

- Dedicate time each day to repeat your affirmations, preferably in the morning to set a positive tone for the day and at night to reinforce them before sleep.
- Say your affirmations aloud, with conviction and feeling. Visualize the reality of these affirmations, immersing yourself in the sensory and emotional experiences they evoke.

Positive Self-Talk:

- Monitor your internal dialogue, ensuring that it supports your journey toward financial success. Replace negative or doubting thoughts with empowering affirmations.
- Encourage yourself as you would a dear friend, with kindness, understanding, and unwavering belief in your abilities.

By integrating these practices into your daily routine, you program your subconscious mind with a deep-seated belief in your capacity to achieve and exceed your financial goals. This internal shift is a critical component of your success, as it lays the psychological foundation upon which your financial strategies and actions are built.

Embrace this journey of subconscious conditioning with openness and dedication. As you align your inner world with the abundance and success you seek in the external world, you will discover that the path to financial prosperity is not only achievable but also immensely rewarding.

Strategic Action Planning

Transforming your abstract vision of earning $1,000,000 a month into a concrete, actionable plan is a pivotal step in your journey to financial success. This translation from vision to strategy involves breaking down your grand goal into manageable, measurable objectives that guide your daily actions and decisions.

Setting Clear Milestones:

- Begin by defining what $1,000,000 a month means in the context of your business or income sources. What will be the key revenue drivers?
- Set clear milestones that chart your progress towards this goal. For example, if your goal is to earn $1,000,000 a month within a year, break this down into quarterly, monthly, weekly, and daily revenue targets.

Action Planning:

- Develop a strategy for each revenue stream that contributes to your monthly goal. Detail the actions needed to achieve these targets, identifying what must be accomplished daily, weekly, and monthly.
- Prioritize tasks based on their impact on your revenue goal, focusing on activities that yield the highest return on investment of time and resources.

Monitoring and Adjustment:

- Implement a system for tracking your progress towards these milestones. Regular monitoring allows you to stay on course and make necessary adjustments to your strategy.
- Be flexible and ready to refine your plan as you gain insights and feedback from your efforts.

The Role of Habit Formation in Financial Success

The journey to achieving significant financial milestones, such as earning $1,000,000 a month, is greatly facilitated by the development of consistent, goal-oriented habits. These habits serve as the building blocks of your daily routine, propelling you towards your financial objectives with automatic action-taking.

Establishing Productive Habits:

- Identify key habits that directly contribute to your financial goals. For instance, daily market analysis, networking, and strategic planning might be critical habits for a business owner aiming for high monthly revenue.
- Start small, focusing on establishing one or two habits at a time until they become second nature. Gradual implementation ensures sustainability and reduces the risk of burnout.

Consistency Over Intensity:

- Consistency in performing these habits is more important than the intensity of the effort. Regular, small actions accumulate to produce significant results over time.
- Schedule your critical financial activities during your peak productivity hours to ensure consistency and effectiveness.

Habit Tracking and Accountability:

- Use habit-tracking tools or methods to monitor your adherence to these critical routines. Tracking provides visual proof of your consistency and progress.
- Establish accountability mechanisms, such as regular check-ins with a mentor or business coach, to maintain your commitment to these habits.

By methodically breaking down your vision into strategic actions and cultivating the necessary habits to execute these strategies, you set a robust framework for achieving your financial aspirations. This approach not only makes the goal of earning $1,000,000 a month more attainable but also integrates this objective into the fabric of your daily life, ensuring sustainable progress and long-term success.

Leveraging Intuition and Decision-Making

In the realm of business and finance, intuition plays a crucial role in facilitating swift and effective decisions that can catalyze financial growth. Intuition, often referred to as the 'gut feeling,' is the subconscious synthesis of one's experiences, knowledge, and insights, enabling rapid decision-making without overt analytical reasoning.

Intuitive Business Decisions

Intuitive decision-making in business involves trusting these internal cues to make judgments that may not always be immediately justifiable through logic or data but are nonetheless sound. It's the process of making decisions that feel right, even when they defy conventional analysis. This intuitive process can be especially valuable in situations where time is of the essence or when available information is incomplete or too complex.

Successful entrepreneurs and business leaders often recount moments where their intuition guided them to make pivotal decisions that led to substantial financial growth. For instance, a decision to invest in a startup, launch a new product, or enter a market may be driven more by intuition than by rigorous analysis.

To enhance intuitive decision-making:

- **Cultivate Self-Awareness:** Understanding your intuition's signals requires a deep awareness of your thoughts and feelings. Regular reflection and mindfulness practices can heighten this awareness.
- **Gather Experience:** The more experience you have in your field, the more data your subconscious has to draw upon, refining your intuitive insights.
- **Trust Your Gut:** Develop confidence in your gut feelings by recalling past instances where your intuition led to successful outcomes.

Risk Assessment and Management

While intuition is a powerful tool, balancing it with logical risk assessment is essential to ensure sound business decisions that maximize wealth creation opportunities. Risk assessment involves systematically analyzing potential risks and their impacts, enabling informed decision-making.

To effectively balance intuition and risk assessment:

- **Define the Risks:** Identify and categorize potential risks associated with a decision. This could include financial, operational, market, or strategic risks.
- **Evaluate Probability and Impact:** Assess the likelihood of each risk occurring and its potential impact on your business. This helps prioritize which risks need more attention and which can be accepted.
- **Develop Mitigation Strategies:** For risks with high probability and impact, develop strategies to mitigate them. This might involve diversifying investments, enhancing security measures, or improving operational efficiency.
- **Combine Intuition and Analysis:** Use your intuition to guide you towards which areas need detailed analysis and let logical risk assessment provide a safety net to your intuitive decisions.

Balancing intuitive insights with a structured approach to risk assessment and management allows business leaders to make decisions that are both swift and informed. This balanced approach ensures that opportunities for wealth creation are maximized while potential downsides are mitigated, leading to sustainable financial growth and success.

Embracing Continuous Improvement as a Way of Life

To truly internalize the essence of sustained growth, view continuous learning and self-improvement as integral parts of your identity. Just as a tree naturally grows and adapts to its environment, let your journey towards financial mastery evolve instinctively, driven by a deep-rooted desire for progress and excellence.

- **Visualize Your Growth Journey**: Regularly imagine yourself mastering new skills and adapting to changes with ease and confidence. Picture your knowledge expanding, and your financial success growing as a direct result of your commitment to learning and adaptation.

- **Affirm Your Evolution**: Use affirmations such as "I am constantly evolving and growing financially" or "Learning and improvement are naturally integrated into my life, leading me to greater success."

Internalizing the Cycle of Success

Achieving your goal of earning $1,000,000 a month is a monumental milestone, but in the landscape of your subconscious, it represents the planting of a seed from which endless opportunities grow. To deeply embed the cycle of success into your subconscious:

- **Reflect on Past Successes**: Regularly take time to reflect on your achievements and how they have set the stage for future success. This reflection reinforces the belief in your ability to achieve and surpass your goals.
- **Create a Success Ritual**: Establish a daily or weekly ritual where you visualize your continued success journey, imagining each new goal as a natural extension of the last, seamlessly leading to greater achievements and expanding wealth.
- **Cultivate Gratitude and Optimism**: Foster a deep sense of gratitude for your successes and a confident expectation of future triumphs. This mindset embeds the cycle of success into your subconscious, making it a core part of your worldview and self-identity.

By integrating these practices into your daily life, the principles of sustained growth and the cycle of success become deeply ingrained in your subconscious. This not only motivates you to take consistent action towards your goals but also transforms these aspirations into a self-fulfilling prophecy of ongoing achievement and financial prosperity.

Inspirational Closure
Success Stories and Testimonials

Imagine the tales of those who have traversed the path you now stand upon, reaching the pinnacle of financial achievement and beyond. These are individuals from varied backgrounds and industries, who once dreamed, as you do, of surpassing the $1,000,000 a month milestone. Their stories are not just narratives of success but beacons of potential that lies within you.

Visualize a young entrepreneur, who, against all odds, turned a simple idea into a thriving enterprise, breaking the million-dollar ceiling with relentless passion and determination. Picture a seasoned executive who transformed a struggling company into a market leader, generating millions in revenue, fueled by innovative strategies and a visionary approach.

These stories resonate in the depths of your mind, not as distant, unattainable achievements, but as reflections of your own journey waiting to unfold. Each narrative seeds your subconscious with the conviction that your goals are not only achievable but are already in progress, propelling you towards action, often without conscious realization.

Call to Action

Now, as you stand at the threshold of your own success story, feel the surge of inspiration and certainty that your financial aspirations are not just dreams but impending realities. The path to earning $1,000,000 a month is already laid out before you, paved by the footsteps of those who have walked it.

Let this moment be the catalyst, the point of no return where you step into the realm of action, driven by an unstoppable force from within. With every story of success etched in your mind, let a voice, clear and resolute, awaken your inner powerhouse, urging you to move, to act, to manifest the destiny that is rightfully yours.

Embrace this journey with the knowledge that the seeds of greatness are already sown within you, nurtured by tales of triumph and the unyielding belief in your imminent success. Start now, driven by the invisible yet palpable force of your subconscious, guiding you towards actions that culminate in achieving and surpassing your goal of $1,000,000 a month.

Remember, in this journey, success is not a possibility but an inevitability. Your actions, fueled by the silent whispers of your subconscious, are the final pieces completing the puzzle of your financial legacy.

Conclusion

In this journey through the realms of financial mastery, we have traversed the landscapes of the mind and the strategic pathways of wealth creation. This chapter has been a confluence of motivational psychology and practical financial strategies, designed to engage and harmonize your subconscious and conscious faculties in the pursuit of extraordinary financial success.

The power of visionary thinking has opened the doors to a world where your financial goals are not just imagined but vividly experienced, creating a mental blueprint for success. Through subconscious conditioning, we have sowed the seeds of an abundance mindset, cultivating a fertile ground for wealth to proliferate. Strategic planning has translated these mental constructs into actionable steps, charting a clear path toward the coveted goal of earning $1,000,000 a month.

Intuitive decision-making has emerged as a crucial ally, enabling swift and effective choices that align with your deeper wisdom and experience. The journey does not end with the achievement of this financial milestone; rather, it marks the beginning of a continuous growth process, where learning and adaptation become perpetual drivers of success.

By integrating these elements, you are not merely acquiring knowledge; you are constructing a robust psychological framework that supports and sustains your financial ambitions. This holistic approach ensures that your quest for a monthly income of $1,000,000 is underpinned by both the clarity of strategic thinking and the dynamic power of your subconscious mind.

As you close this chapter and reflect on the journey, remember that the essence of financial success is not encapsulated in numbers or strategies alone but is deeply rooted in the synergy between your internal beliefs and external actions. Armed with this integrated perspective, you are not just prepared but powerfully poised to achieve and sustain a monthly income of $1,000,000, turning the vision of your financial ascent into a living, breathing reality..

www.ingramcontent.com/pod-product-compliance
Lightning Source LLC
LaVergne TN
LVHW031616060526
838201LV00008B/190